History

D0927716

Jo Thomas
Keely Rogers

DYNAMIC
LEARNING

HODDER
EDUCATION
AN HACHETTE UK COMPANY

How to use this book

Welcome to Hodder Education's *MYP by Concept* series! Each chapter is designed to lead you through an *inquiry* into the concepts of history, and how they interact in real-life global contexts.

KEY WORDS

Key words are included to give you access to vocabulary for the topic. **Glossary** terms are highlighted and, where applicable, **search terms** are given to encourage independent learning and research skills.

As you explore, activities suggest ways to learn through *action*.

■ **ATL**

■ Activities are designed to develop your *Approaches to Learning* (ATL) skills.

◆ Assessment opportunities in this chapter:

Some activities are *formative* as they allow you to practise certain parts of the MYP History *Assessment Objectives*. Other activities can be used by you or your teachers to assess your achievement against all parts of an assessment objective.

Each chapter is framed with a *Key concept* and a *Related concept* and is set in a *Global context*.

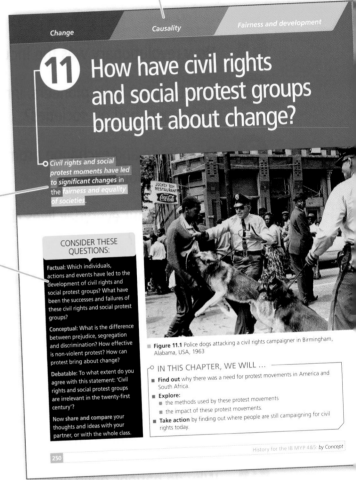

| Change | Causality | Fairness and development |

11 How have civil rights and social protest groups brought about change?

Civil rights and social protest moments have led to significant changes in the fairness and equality of societies.

CONSIDER THESE QUESTIONS:

Factual: Which individuals, actions and events have led to the development of civil rights and social protest groups? What have been the successes and failures of these civil rights and social protest groups?

Conceptual: What is the difference between prejudice, segregation and discrimination? How effective is non-violent protest? How can protest bring about change?

Debatable: To what extent do you agree with this statement: 'Civil rights and social protest groups are irrelevant in the twenty-first century'?

Now share and compare your thoughts and ideas with your partner, or with the whole class.

■ **Figure 11.1** Police dogs attacking a civil rights campaigner in Birmingham, Alabama, USA, 1963

○ IN THIS CHAPTER, WE WILL ...
- ■ **Find out** why there was a need for protest movements in America and South Africa.
- ■ **Explore:**
  - ■ the methods used by these protest movements
  - ■ the impact of these protest movements.
- ■ **Take action** by finding out where people are still campaigning for civil rights today.

The *Statement of Inquiry* provides the framework for this inquiry, and the *Inquiry questions* then lead us through the exploration as they are developed through each chapter.

Key *Approaches to Learning* skills for MYP History are highlighted whenever we encounter them.

Hint

In some of the activities, we provide hints to help you work on the assignment. This also introduces you to the new Hint feature in the on-screen assessment.

ℹ Information boxes are included to give background information, more detail and explanation.

EXTENSION

Extension activities allow you to explore a topic further.

Finally, at the end of each chapter, you are asked to reflect back on what you have learnt with our *Reflection table*, maybe to think of new questions brought to light by your learning.

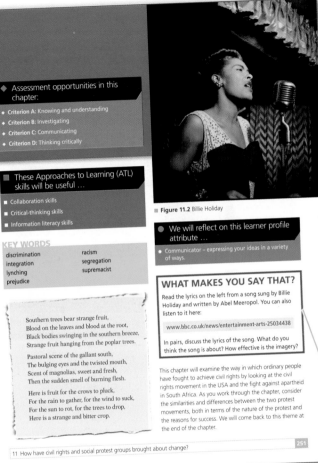

◆ Assessment opportunities in this chapter:

◆ **Criterion A:** Knowing and understanding
◆ **Criterion B:** Investigating
◆ **Criterion C:** Communicating
◆ **Criterion D:** Thinking critically

■ These Approaches to Learning (ATL) skills will be useful …

■ Collaboration skills
■ Critical-thinking skills
■ Information literacy skills

KEY WORDS

discrimination	racism
integration	segregation
lynching	supremacist
prejudice	

Southern trees bear strange fruit,
Blood on the leaves and blood at the root,
Black bodies swinging in the southern breeze,
Strange fruit hanging from the poplar trees.

Pastoral scene of the gallant south,
The bulging eyes and the twisted mouth,
Scent of magnolias, sweet and fresh,
Then the sudden smell of burning flesh.

Here is fruit for the crows to pluck,
For the rain to gather, for the wind to suck,
For the sun to rot, for the trees to drop,
Here is a strange and bitter crop.

11 How have civil rights and social protest groups brought about change? **251**

● We will reflect on this learner profile attribute …

● Communicator – expressing your ideas in a variety of ways.

WHAT MAKES YOU SAY THAT?

Read the lyrics on the left from a song sung by Billie Holiday and written by Abel Meeropol. You can also listen to it here:

www.bbc.co.uk/news/entertainment-arts-25034438

In pairs, discuss the lyrics of the song. What do you think the song is about? How effective is the imagery?

This chapter will examine the way in which ordinary people have fought to achieve civil rights by looking at the civil rights movement in the USA and the fight against apartheid in South Africa. As you work through the chapter, consider the similarities and differences between the two protest movements, both in terms of the nature of the protest and the reasons for success. We will come back to this theme at the end of the chapter.

Reflecting on our learning …
Use this table to reflect on your own learning in this chapter.

Questions we asked	Answers we found	Any further questions now?			
Factual					
Conceptual					
Debatable					
Approaches to learning you used in this chapter:	Description – what new skills did you learn?	How well did you master the skills?			
		Novice	Learner	Practitioner	Expert
Communication skills					
Critical-thinking skills					
Transfer skills					
Learner profile attribute	*Reflect on the importance of the attribute, for our learning in this chapter.*				
Knowledgeable					

We have incorporated Visible Thinking – ideas, framework, protocol and thinking routines – from Project Zero at the Harvard Graduate School of Education into many of our activities.

▼ Links to:

Like any other subject, History is just one part of our bigger picture of the world. Links to other subjects are discussed.

● **We will reflect on this learner profile attribute …**

Each chapter has an *IB learner profile* attribute as its theme, and you are encouraged to reflect on these too.

! Take action

! While the book provides opportunities for action and plenty of content to enrich the conceptual relationships, you must be an active part of this process. Guidance is given to help you with your own research, including how to engage in historical research, guidance on forming a research question, as well as linking and developing your study of the past to events happening today. This should give you a better understanding of global issues in our twenty-first century world.

You are prompted to consider your conceptual understanding in a variety of activities throughout each chapter.

1 How revolutionary was the Industrial Revolution?

○ *Innovations* in *science and technology* can lead to *revolutionary changes* in the ways we live and work.

■ **Figure 1.1** The city of Sheffield, in Britain, in the 1800s

CONSIDER THESE QUESTIONS:

Factual: What factors are necessary for industrial revolutions to occur? What factors were necessary for the Industrial Revolution to start in Britain? What key inventions drove the Industrial Revolution? Why did an Industrial Revolution start in Japan? What reforms were implemented in Meiji Japan?

Conceptual: How are causal factors linked? Can innovations lead to revolutionary change?

Debatable: To what extent can innovation and revolutionary change bring benefits to society? Did industrialization create more winners than losers?

Now **share and compare** your thoughts and ideas with your partner, or with the whole class.

○ IN THIS CHAPTER, WE WILL …

■ **Find out** how environmental, political, social and economic factors led to revolutionary changes in industry and working conditions in Britain and Japan.

■ **Explore:**
  ■ the key events and changes that led to the Industrial Revolution
  ■ the relationship and links between causal factors and the impact of revolutionary change on societies
  ■ the relationship between innovation and revolution.

■ **Take action** by exploring where child labour still exists today.

■ These Approaches to Learning (ATL) skills will be useful …

■ Collaboration skills
■ Communication skills
■ Creative-thinking skills
■ Critical-thinking skills
■ Organization skills
■ Transfer skills

KEY WORDS

colony
manufactured goods
raw materials
revolution
textiles
urbanization

History

● We will reflect on this learner profile attribute …

● Knowledgeable – exploring knowledge across a range of disciplines, engaging with issues and ideas that have local and global significance.

◆ Assessment opportunities in this chapter:

◆ **Criterion A:** Knowing and understanding
◆ **Criterion B:** Investigating
◆ **Criterion C:** Communicating
◆ **Criterion D:** Thinking critically

SEE–THINK–WONDER

The two pictures in Sources A and B are both of Leeds, a city in Britain, but at different times.

In pairs, **identify** the changes that have taken place in the city over the 100-year period.

THE INDUSTRIAL REVOLUTION

SOURCE A

■ **Figure 1.2** Leeds in 1750

SOURCE B

■ **Figure 1.3** Leeds in 1850

Why did the Industrial Revolution start in Britain?

Between 1750 and 1850 Britain became an industrialized country. The lives of people changed dramatically during this period, which is known as the 'Industrial Revolution'.

Until 1750, the population in Britain was about 11 million; the majority of people lived in villages or small towns and depended on agriculture for their living. However, by 1850, the population had grown to about 21 million; 50 per cent lived in cities and over 40 per cent of the workforce was employed in factories.

This massive 'revolution' in turn had an impact on living conditions, travel, types of work and social and political change.

Britain was the first country in the world to have an industrial revolution and this was due to many factors.

The population was increasing

Around 1740, the population of Britain began to increase. This meant there was more demand for goods. It also meant that there were plenty of workers for the factories.

Britain's overseas trade was growing

In 1750, British **merchants** had many opportunities to trade overseas due to the fact that Britain had many **colonies**. This meant that many merchants became wealthy enough to have capital to invest in new businesses. The British **Empire** also provided a source of both raw materials and markets for British goods. For instance, raw cotton could be obtained from India and then the manufactured cotton goods could be sold back to India.

Britain's agriculture had improved

An agricultural revolution in Britain had already increased the amount of food that farmers could produce. This was important as it meant that there was enough food for the growing population, particularly the people in towns, who could not grow their own food. Farm workers were also paid more, so they had money to spend on goods produced by the new industries.

Transport was improving

Between 1660 and 1750, it became much easier to transport goods around Britain. This was due to the improvement of roads and rivers and the building of canals. This allowed raw materials such as coal and iron to be moved more easily around the country, which also kept costs down. It also allowed the finished goods to be transported to a wider range of markets. Letters, orders for goods and even new ideas could all travel much more quickly.

Britain had entrepreneurs and inventors

Britain had individuals who were prepared to risk their money in new ventures. There was also a great interest in science and technology, which meant that many new inventions were made in the textile and iron industries. These inventions enabled manufacturers to improve industry.

Britain had plenty of raw materials

Britain had the raw materials that were necessary for the Industrial Revolution. It possessed large quantities of iron, which was needed for making the machines and railways. It had coal to drive the steam engines in the factories.

Britain was at peace

The relatively stable political situation and absence of war allowed the British to pursue economic activities, and for trade to flourish between Britain and its colonies.

ACTIVITY: Causes of the Industrial Revolution

In pairs, add details, examples and short explanations from pages 4–7 to a copy of the mind map below. Show what you have learnt about the importance of each factor in the Industrial Revolution.

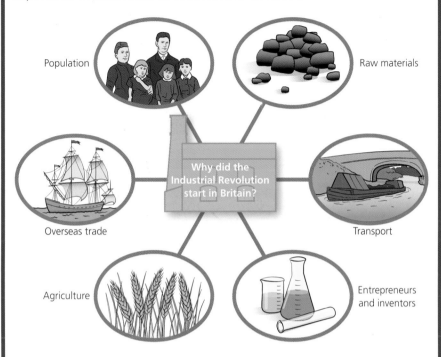

Population

Raw materials

Overseas trade

Why did the Industrial Revolution start in Britain?

Transport

Agriculture

Entrepreneurs and inventors

■ **Figure 1.4** Why did the Industrial Revolution start in Britain?

Which of these factors do you consider to be the most important in causing industrialization to start in Britain?

Could the Industrial Revolution have taken place if any one of these factors had not been present in Britain?

WHAT WERE THE KEY INVENTIONS THAT ALLOWED THE INDUSTRIAL REVOLUTION TO TAKE PLACE?

The textile industry

The first industry to move into factories was the textile industry. The rapidly growing population after 1750 meant that there was a need for industry to produce goods in large amounts. In particular, there was a demand for cloth, and the domestic system by which spinning and weaving was done in people's homes could not meet the demand. Thus it was the textile industry that first moved to powered machinery and to factories.

ⓘ The domestic system

■ **Figure 1.5** Spinning

Before factories, spinning and weaving took place in people's homes. Spinning was usually done by the women on a simple spinning wheel. Mothers, daughters and sometimes grandmothers would work together. The hours could be long, but were decided on by the workers themselves. The thread was woven into cloth by spinners, who could be in another part of the house. Alternatively, the thread would be collected and taken to a weaver's cottage by the wool or cotton merchant – who ultimately would take the finished cloth to be sold in town.

ⓘ Making cloth

Cotton and wool had to go through several stages in the process of making cloth:

- **Washing and carding:** the cotton was cleaned and washed and then combed out into straight lines.
- **Spinning:** the cotton or wool fibres were spun together to make a thread or yarn.
- **Weaving:** the yarn was woven into cloth.

John Kay invented a weaving machine called the flying shuttle. This was hand-powered but it did speed up the weaving process – one weaver could weave as much cloth as two weavers did before. However, this led to a shortage yarn as the hand-weavers were unable to keep up with the weavers.

1733

1764

John Hargreaves invented the spinning jenny, which had 16 spindles but was still small enough to be used in the home. By 1788, there were 20 000 spinning jennies in use.

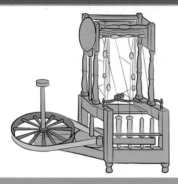

Richard Arkwright, who was a wig-maker from Preston, invented the water-frame. This was another spinning machine but was powered by water. It was too big for a house and so he built a mill at Cromford in Derbyshire; this was the first factory.

1769

Samuel Crompton invented another spinning machine (the mule), which improved on Arkwright's by making the thread much finer – but also strong. This too had to be put in factories. The water-frame and mule meant that now the weavers were kept busy and were paid well for their work, which was in demand.

1779

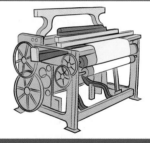

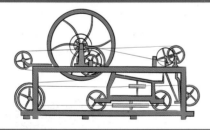

Edmund Cartwright invented a power loom which could speed up the work of weaving. However, it was not until the 1820s that this was able to work efficiently and produce good cloth. As a result of this invention, the hand-loom weavers were gradually put out of work. The weekly earnings of weavers in the town of Bolton fell from 25 shillings in 1800 to 5 shillings in the 1830s. Thousands lost their jobs and had to join the ranks of the unskilled poor looking for jobs in the new factories.

1785

■ **Figure 1.6** Timeline for key inventions in the textile industry

Some of the key inventions are shown in Figure 1.6. It is interesting to note that because there are so many processes in the textile industry, the speeding up of one process could cause a problem in another area. For instance, if a spinning machine was invented to produce more yarn, then the weavers would be unable to keep up, until a machine was found for them. Thus one invention tended to lead to another.

THINK–PAIR–SHARE

Consider the following questions on your own first, and then **discuss** them with a partner.

Both Kay and Hargreaves faced hostility to their inventions from workers. Kay had to flee to France and Hargreaves had his home set on fire. Why do you think this was? What can be the disadvantages of introducing new technology into the workplace? What examples can you think of today where there is hostility or concern regarding new technologies?

The iron industry

Vital inventions also took place in the iron industry, allowing it to produce the iron necessary to make the machines that were being invented in other areas.

By 1700, Britain faced a shortage of timber for making charcoal, which was necessary for smelting iron ore. However, in 1709, Abraham Darby I discovered that if coal was first turned into coke, it could successfully be used for smelting. Although kept a secret at first, by the 1750s this method was being widely used.

Darby's method produced iron that was suitable for casting, i.e. pouring into moulds to make items such as pots and cannons. It was very hard but also brittle. Wrought iron, which is more flexible and so can be used for a wider range of goods, was also needed. In 1793, Henry Cort devised a method called 'puddling', which enabled wrought iron to be produced.

The steam engine

The invention of steam engines to drive machines was one of the most important factors in the development of the Industrial Revolution.

In the early eighteenth century, only the traditional forms of power were used for working the new machinery: horse power, wind power and water power. However, as the factory system started to develop, it became clear that a more reliable source of power was needed; this need led eventually to the steam engine being perfected by James Watt.

The first steam engines were found in the coal-mining industry. As the demand for coal grew to make iron, mines become deeper and thus faced more problems with flooding. In 1712, Thomas Newcomen managed to build an 'atmospheric engine', which used steam to work a pump that could be used to drain mines. By 1775, there were over 100 of these machines at work in the tin and coal mines. However, they could only be used for pumping water and were very expensive to run because they needed so much coal.

In 1763, James Watt, an instrument maker at Glasgow University, was asked to repair a demonstration model of a

■ **Figure 1.7** Old Bess is the oldest surviving Watt engine, and the third-oldest surviving beam engine. It is now housed and preserved in the Power Gallery of the Science Museum, London

Newcomen engine. He noticed that the engine had several design faults and worked out how to improve the engine so that it did not waste so much energy; this involved including a separate condenser.

In 1781, Watt, helped by William Murdoch, devised a rotary motion steam engine which used sun and planet gears. Watt was also helped by John Wilkinson, the iron-master, who invented a lathe which could produce accurately bored cylinders.

The rotary steam engine could be used to drive machinery in textile mills and other factories, which no longer had to be built near rivers for their power. It could be used in iron foundries and in canal building. It also led to the development of the first railway.

▼ Links to: Physics; Sciences

Look at these websites to see how the Watt and Newcomen engines worked:

www.animatedengines.com/newcomen.html

http://science.howstuffworks.com/steam-technology3.htm

Explore the science behind the innovations in the steam engine. What was the impact of the improvements to the steam engine invented by Watt and Newcomen? What was the relationship between the development of the Industrial Revolution and developments in physics and the world of science?

ACTIVITY: Inventions of the Industrial Revolution

■ ATL

- Communication skills – Use a variety of speaking techniques to communicate with a variety of audiences; Negotiate ideas and knowledge with peers and teachers
- Collaboration skills – Listen actively to other perspectives and ideas; Negotiate effectively; Encourage others to contribute; Give and receive meaningful feedback
- Organization skills – Use appropriate strategies for organizing complex information

Work in groups. Each group should take one of the inventions of the Industrial Revolution and prepare a pitch to the rest of the class, who will take on the role of potential investors. Your group needs to sell the benefits of your invention – how will it improve industry or people's lives? The rest of the class will then vote as to whether you have been convincing, and thus whether they are prepared to invest in your invention.

You could use Figure 1.8 to guide you through the assignment.

◆ Assessment opportunities

- ◆ This activity can be assessed using Criterion B: Investigating and Criterion D: Thinking critically.

Formulate your research question (you could discuss this in pairs or with the whole group). Briefly explain your choice of research question.

Plan your investigation. Write a brief plan of how you will research your question, and what initial themes/lines of argument you will investigate.

Gather, record and document the sources of relevant information.
- Use one standard method to collect and record your sources – for example, the Modern Language Association (MLA) citation style. MLA is a recognized method for acknowledging sources used in a research paper. Citations are put in the text of a paper and these link to the 'works cited' list, collated alphabetically at the end of the paper. For more information on MLA, visit this website: www.library.cornell.edu/research/citation/mla
- Collect diagrams and images to show how your invention works. Note down all the benefits and strengths of the invention, any quotes from users, etc.
- Set down how you reflect on the research process.
- Allocate tasks within your group – make sure that everyone knows what he or she is doing to contribute to the task.

Communicate your information with structure and style. You could design a poster or create a video as an advert to sell your invention. Alternatively, you could create a PowerPoint presentation to accompany your pitch.
Give your presentation!

Reflect on your investigation and the response it received.
- The amount of investment that you get from the rest of the class will give you an idea as to how convincing you were. Discuss how you could have improved on your presentation.
- Reflect on how effective your research process was: Did you find a range of good sources? Did you answer your research question effectively? Did you document your sources appropriately? What would you have done differently? Are there areas that you did not address in your research?

■ **Figure 1.8** Planning and communicating research

How did factories change life in Britain?

WHAT WERE CONDITIONS LIKE?

The first cotton factory was built by Richard Arkwright to house his water frame. This was the start to the cotton industry leading the way in industrialization. Mill owners became nationally important figures, and the mills (factories) themselves were revolutionary in the way they changed not only the landscape of the country, but also the working conditions and lifestyles of the population.

Because the machines were automatic, the work in the mills was done mainly by unskilled labour, and two-thirds of the workforce in 1833 was made up of women and children. Some of the children were pauper apprentices: orphans sent to work in the factories by the town authorities or the workhouses that looked after them. In other cases, whole families (both children and parents) worked together in the mills. For mill owners, the advantages of employing children were that they did not have to pay them as much as adults and they could crawl under the machines to repair broken threads (fixers) or to clean up loose cotton (scavengers). The workers were watched by the overseers – who were always men.

ACTIVITY: Origin and purpose

> **Hint**
> To find the purpose of a source, think about why the source was written, spoken or drawn, and who it was for – who was the audience?

■ ATL

- Critical-thinking skills – Gather and organize relevant information to formulate an argument; Recognize unstated assumptions and bias; Evaluate evidence and arguments; Consider ideas from multiple perspectives

1 Read Sources C to H on the following pages, and **identify** *four* conditions of work in the factories and *two* effects of the working conditions on workers. Complete a table like the one below.

Conditions
1
2
3
4

Effects
1
2

2 Outline the purpose, values and limitations for Sources E and F with reference to the origin stated in the table below.

Source	Origin	Purpose	Values	Limitations
E	*An illustration from a book called* The Adventures of Michael Armstrong, Factory Boy, *published in 1840. It was written by Francis Trollope, who campaigned to stop children working in the factories*			
F	*Mr John Moss, who was in charge of apprentice children at Backbarrow Mill, was questioned by a Parliamentary Committee at the House of Commons in 1816*			

3 **Identify** the message of the cartoonist in Source G.
4 Compare Sources D and E regarding the impact of the factory conditions on children.
5 Both Frances Trollope (Source E) and Cruikshank (Source G) were against children working in factories. Does this mean that these sources are worthless to the historian? **Explain** your answer.

◆ Assessment opportunities

- ◆ In this activity you have practised skills that are assessed using Criterion D: Thinking critically.

Sources

Sources are key for historians for finding out about the past. A key skill is being able to extract information from sources and also to compare them. By comparing and contrasting the content of sources and checking their value and limitation by looking at their origin and purpose, we can start to draw conclusions about the past.

SOURCE C

A list of fines published in a strike pamphlet by spinners of Tyldesley, 1823

Any spinner found with his window open .... 1 shilling

Any spinner found dirty at his work.................................. 1 shilling

Any spinner found washing himself................................. 1 shilling

Any spinner found whistling .... 1 shilling

Any spinner being five minutes after last bell rings.......... 1 shilling

Any spinner having a little waste on his spindles .... 1 shilling

Any spinner being sick and cannot find another spinner
to give satisfaction must pay for steam for the day.......... 1 shilling

SOURCE D

An extract from the memoir of Robert Blincoe, an orphan working in the factories. He started at the age of seven and became so deformed that he left and worked for himself at home. He published his memoir, under the name of John Brown, in 1928

'They reached the mill about half-past five [in the morning]. The moment he entered the doors, the noise appalled him, and the stench seemed intolerable.

'The task first given him was to pick up the loose cotton that fell upon the floor. Apparently nothing could be easier and he set to eagerly, although much terrified by the whirling motion and noise of the machinery, and not a little affected by the dust and flue [fluff] which he was half suffocated.

'Unused to the stench he soon felt sick and, by constantly stooping, his back ached. He therefore sat down, but this he soon found was strictly forbidden. His taskmaster gave him to understand he must keep in his legs. He did so, till twelve o'clock. Blincoe suffered greatly with thirst and hunger.'

SOURCE E

■ **Figure 1.9** An illustration from a book called *The Adventures of Michael Armstrong: Factory Boy*, published in 1840. It was written by Francis Trollope, who campaigned to stop children working in the factories

ACTIVITY: Comparing domestic and factory systems

Refer back to the description of the domestic system on page 5. **Describe** the ways in which the lives of textile workers in the domestic system were different from the lives of workers in the factory system.

SOURCE F

Mr John Moss, who was in charge of apprentice children at Backbarrow Mill, was questioned by a Parliamentary Committee at the House of Commons in 1816

Q. Were there any children employed at the mill?

A. There were 111. All parish apprentices, mostly from London, between the ages of seven and eleven.

Q. What were the hours of work?

A. From five o'clock in the morning till eight at night.

Q. What time was allowed for meals?

A. About half an hour for breakfast and half an hour for dinner.

Q. Would the children sit or stand at work?

A. Stand.

Q. Were they usually tired at night?

A. Yes, some of them were very tired. I have frequently found some asleep on the mill floor.

Q. Were any children injured by machines?

A. Very frequently. Very often their fingers were crushed and one had his arm broken.

SOURCE G

■ **Figure 1.10** 'English factory slaves', a cartoon by Cruikshank from the early nineteenth century

SOURCE H

Joseph Hebergam, aged 17, was also questioned about his work in a mill in Huddersfield

'After I had worked for half a year I could scarcely walk. In the morning my brother and sister used to take me under each arm and run with me, a good mile, to the mill. If we were five minutes late, the overlooker would take a strap and beat us till we were black and blue. I have seen my mother weep at me sometimes, but she would not tell me why she was weeping.'

How and why were the factories reformed?

By the 1830s, it was realized that there was an urgent need for reform. The factory system had grown so that there were now 30000 children under 13 and 75000 children aged 13–18 working in the factories. Adult workers also faced low wages and long hours.

Because of this situation there was more pressure for reform and a demand for a restriction on working hours. In the textile areas of Yorkshire and Lancashire the **trade unions** campaigned for working hours to be a maximum of ten hours for children. They were supported by one or two factory owners, some writers and **campaigners** and some Members of Parliament. However, the idea of reform was strongly opposed by many factory owners, who believed that it was not the role of governments to interfere in private business; they believed in '**laissez-faire**' – allowing industry to do what it thought was best for making money.

However, due to pressure from campaigners, and a growing awareness that the Industrial Revolution was creating new conditions which needed government intervention to protect workers, a committee was set up by Parliament to interview children and adults about factory conditions.

ACTIVITY: Debate on child labour

ATL

- Communication skills – Paraphrase accurately and concisely; Negotiate ideas and knowledge with peers and teachers

Visit this website:

http://spartacus-educational.com/IndustrialRevolution.htm

On this website, you will find details of children, campaigners, factory workers and doctors who gave evidence to the parliamentary committee on whether Parliament should pass a law to restrict the working hours of children to ten hours. Each student should take on the role of one of the people listed under 'Factory Workers' and the 'Debate on Child Labour'.

Your goal is to convince the committee of the British Parliament of your point of view – either to change the law on child labour or keep it the same.

Role

Your character is explained on the website; you may find examples of what your person actually said at the real Parliamentary Commission, which you can include in your speech.

Audience

The other students in the class will be your audience as they are also part of the committee, but they will also be in their character role and they may decide to challenge you!

Performance

You need to write a speech from the point of view of your character. You should indicate whether or not you are in favour of the government passing a law to restrict the hours of children working in factories. Give evidence for your arguments and try to be convincing!

Standards and criteria for success

Your speech must be about two minutes long. At the end, your class should vote on whether or not Parliament should intervene.

> Hint
>
> This website gives some good hints on how to make an effective speech:
>
> www.bbc.co.uk/bitesize/ks3/english/speaking_listening/speaking/revision/3/

◆ Assessment opportunities

- ◆ This activity can be assessed using Criterion C: Communicating and Criterion D: Thinking critically.

EXTENSION

Investigate child labour in the world today and then **summarize** your findings in a report. You could focus on one specific region or choose to research one case study from two or more regions.

Your report should be between 700 and 1500 words. You can use the following to help you:
- State your research question clearly.
- **Explain** the scope of your research. Think about the timeframe and case studies you will focus on. Think about what themes and ideas you will focus on in your research – for example: How widespread is it? In what areas do children work and why do they work? What are the conditions that children face today? Why do families allow their children to work? How is this different from or similar to the situation in nineteenth-century Britain?
- **Explain** the methods you will use to research your question. What types of sources will you look for? Why would you look at different viewpoints?
- Remember to state the convention you will use to collate and cite your sources of information.

Once you have completed your research and report, you will need to **evaluate** your investigation process and your results. Consider the following questions when writing up your evaluation:
- How did the initial planning process aid in the development of your final report?
- What type of sources did you find most useful and least useful in the development of your report?
- What other sources could you have used to improve your final report?
- Were you accurate and consistent in citing your sources?
- How could you have organized your information to develop your arguments more effectively?
- To what extent did you answer your research question?
- What would you do differently in your next research project?
- Did you use your research time effectively?

◆ Assessment opportunities

- ◆ In this activity you have practised skills that are assessed using Criterion B: Investigating and Criterion C: Communicating.

1833 FACTORY REFORM ACT

The interviews by the Parliamentary committee gave evidence of accidents, ill health, beatings and poor treatment of children. Eventually, after pressure from campaigners such as Lord Shaftsbury and Edwin Chadwick, the Factory Reform Act of 1833 was passed. This **Act** had the following provisions:
- No children under the age of 9 could work in the mills.
- Children between 9 and 13 were to work no more than 12 hours a day.
- No one under 18 was to work the night shift.
- Four factory inspectors were appointed to oversee the Act.

However, it was difficult to ensure that these provisions were carried out. Four inspectors could not possibly visit all of the factories, and it was often difficult to establish the true ages of children. Parents and factory owners would often lie about the ages of workers. Schooling was often avoided or carried out in an unsatisfactory way and even if a factory owner went to court, the fine was minimal.

Nevertheless, the idea of inspection was now established and the situation continued to improve so that the Factory Act of 1853 laid down a working day of 6a.m. to 6p.m. or 7a.m. to 7p.m. with an hour and a half in breaks. This gave a normal working day of ten-and-a-half hours.

Laws after 1850 also extended such protection to workers other than those in the textile mills. Indeed, as more and more official reports revealed poor working conditions, and Parliament continued to pass **legislation**, people got used to the idea that the government needed to intervene in the lives of people. In later years, governments also passed laws providing free education, old age pensions, free health care and unemployment benefits.

└ Socialist?!

Why did the Industrial Revolution cause social and political change?

Once factories could use steam engines for power, they were not dependent on being situated near to fast-flowing water. Many factories moved to the cities where they could more easily get labour and be near to the roads and railways for carrying goods. Towns thus grew fast. By 1851, more than half the people of England and Wales lived in towns which had over 50 000 people.

This rapid growth caused terrible living conditions as parts of the city became overcrowded with inadequately built housing. An 'Inquiry into the State and Condition of the Town of Leeds' in 1842 reported that:

> 'In one road in Leeds there are 34 houses, and in ordinary times, there dwell in these houses 340 persons, or ten to every house. The name of this place is Boot and Shoe yard from whence the Commissioners removed, in the days of cholera, 75 cartloads of manure, which had been untouched for years.

> 'To build the largest number of cottages on the smallest space seems to have been the original view of the speculators. Thus neighbourhoods have arisen in which there is neither water, nor offices [toilets].'

Diseases flourished in these conditions. Typhoid, typhus fever and tuberculosis all spread quickly, causing many deaths. In 1831, cholera first appeared. Further outbreaks occurred in 1838, 1848 and 1854, killing hundreds of thousands of people. *Industry illness!*

SOCIAL CHANGE

Wealth was now available to new groups of people; a **middle class** developed that made its money from the factories or investing in new businesses such as the railways. These people had a whole new range of products to buy – in

small business benefits

cotton, pottery and iron. However, people who owned small businesses, professional people and shopkeepers also made more money and benefited from the lower prices of manufactured goods, and the wider range of food now available because of the railways bringing in fresh goods.

Skilled workers could also earn good money. While some, such as wool combers and weavers, were put out of business by the machines (see page 6), at the same time there was a demand for new skilled trades such as engine drivers, engineers and fitters. Unskilled workers could also earn up to three times the amount of agricultural workers in the north of England. However, unskilled workers could lose jobs overnight whenever there was a fall in demand. They also had to cope with the appalling working and living conditions.

POLITICAL CHANGE

As well as changing people's home and working lives, the Industrial Revolution caused changes in people's attitudes towards the political system. Many people came to believe that the existing political system no longer represented the needs of the middle and **working classes**:

- The new towns, which produced most of the wealth of the country, were not represented in Parliament (see Figure 1.11).
- There was now a large middle class which, by 1830, was paying as much tax as the landowners but could not vote in elections. Their business interests were not being represented in Parliament, where voting and eligibility to stand as a Member of Parliament (MP) was dependent on ownership of land.
- The working classes had many grievances regarding working and living conditions but could not vote and were not represented in Parliament. As the Declaration of the Birmingham Political Union, 1829, explained:

> 'That honourable House [of Commons], in its present state, is … too far removed in habits, wealth and station [position], from the needs and interests of the lower and middle classes of people, to have … any close identity of feeling with them. The great aristocratic interests of all kinds are well represented there … But the interests of Industry and Trade have scarcely any representatives at all!'

The beginning of the nineteenth century saw violent clashes between working-class people and the government. In 1819, as a result of the 'Peterloo' massacre in Manchester, 11 people were killed when the military forcibly broke up a peaceful, mainly working-class meeting which was demanding political reform. However, the government realized that there was a need for reform and in 1832 a Reform Act was passed, which increased the number of people who could vote. In 1830, there were 435 000 voters; after the 1832 Act there were 652 000. In addition, the Act gave more representation to the industrial towns.

However, the Reform Act did not address the political demands of the workers – the great majority of the men and all women in Britain still had no right to vote. Working people started a new movement, drawing up petitions and charters to present to Parliament, asking for more reform.

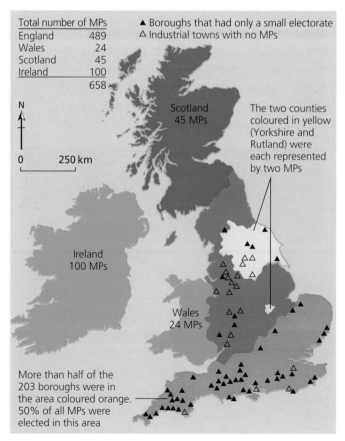

Total number of MPs	
England	489
Wales	24
Scotland	45
Ireland	100
	658

▲ Boroughs that had only a small electorate
△ Industrial towns with no MPs

N

0   250 km

Scotland
45 MPs

The two counties coloured in yellow (Yorkshire and Rutland) were each represented by two MPs

Ireland
100 MPs

Wales
24 MPs

More than half of the 203 boroughs were in the area coloured orange. 50% of all MPs were elected in this area

■ **Figure 1.11** Map showing the boroughs or constituencies that elected Members of Parliament (MPs) in the early nineteenth century

ACTIVITY: The demands of the Chartists

In pairs, **analyse** the People's Charter, looking at each of the demands made by the Chartists. What was their aim in asking for these reforms? To what extent do these reforms exist in your own country?

One of the first charters was handed in to Parliament in 1837. It reads:

> 'It was the fond hope of the people that a remedy for their grievances would be found in the Reform Act of 1832. They have been bitterly let-down. The Reform Act has meant simply a transfer of power from one wealthy group to another.'

Workers came up with six points that they wanted the government to agree to. These 'Six Points' made up the People's Charter and people who supported these points were known as the **Chartists**.

Some Chartists wanted to use force to get their demands accepted. In 1839, for instance, there was a Chartist uprising in Newport, Wales. Other Chartists wanted to persuade Parliament. In 1839, 1842 and 1848, huge petitions were presented to Parliament. In 1848 there was a big rally in London to take the final petition, which had 5 million signatures. However, many of these signatures turned out to be forgeries. Included among the signatures were 'Her Majesty', 'Queen Victoria, 'The Duke of Wellington' (several times) – but also 'Pug nose', 'Flat nose' and 'No cheese'. The Charter was rejected and was never adopted by Parliament.

However, political reform did continue in Great Britain and eventually most of the demands of the Chartists were achieved.

🛈 The People's Charter

- A vote for every man of at least 21 years of age
- A secret **ballot**
- No property qualification for Members of Parliament
- Payment of Members of Parliament
- Equally sized constituencies
- General Elections to be held each year

EXTENSION

Women had their own pressure groups, the Suffragists and the Suffragettes, to try and get the vote. Research the activities of each of these groups up to 1914. How did they differ in the way that they tried to put pressure on the government? Which group was more successful in your opinion?

The new working classes of Britain also looked to protect themselves by joining other movements. Research the actions and the success of the Luddites and those who attempted to establish trade unions.

SOURCE I

Electoral reform 1800–85

First 'Great' Reform Act 1832

New constituencies: 56 boroughs were **abolished** (they had elected 112 MPs) and 30 boroughs with a population under 4000 elected one, rather than two, MPs. 142 MPs were now elected by voters in industrial towns.

Qualification for vote: reduced and made more uniform.

Number of voters: rose by 200 000.

This Reform Act was followed by two more, in 1867 and 1884. Thus, by 1885, all male householders could vote, only one MP was allowed for each constituency and boroughs with a population under 15 000 were abolished so that the industrial cities could now be fairly represented.

Secret Ballot Act 1872

No more 'open' elections – people to vote in secret.

Corrupt Practices Act 1883

Election expenses for candidates standardized and bribery and corruption punished.

ACTIVITY: Review

■ ATL

■ Critical-thinking skills – Analyse complex concepts and projects into their constituent parts and synthesize them to create new understanding

Use the information and sources in this chapter to draw a diagram to show the impact of the Industrial Revolution in Britain. This could be a mind map or a flow diagram, or another type of infographic.

Assessment: '**Analyse** the relationship between innovation and revolution.'

To answer this question you will need to review the content, ideas and concepts covered in this chapter thus far. You will need to write a response that is around 700 words and includes two paragraphs, one suggesting how innovation and revolution may be linked and the other about the differences between the two.

Discuss this question as a class and make notes of the discussion. You will need to consider how these two factors work together, how innovation may foster revolution and how revolutions can lead to innovations. You should also consider the idea that innovations may not lead to revolution.

◆ Assessment opportunities

◆ This activity can be assessed using Criterion A: Knowing and understanding and Criterion C: Communicating.

SOURCE J

Percentage of adults (over age 21) allowed to vote, 1831–1928

Date	% of voters
1831	5
1833	7
1867	16
1884	28.5
1918	74
1928	97

What was the impact of the Industrial Revolution in Japan?

By 1850 Britain, as you have seen, was an industrialized country. Japan, by contrast, was a closed country in 1850, cut off from the rest of the world; it was very much a feudal society with an economy based mainly on agriculture.

The reasons for Japan's move to industrialization are different from those of Britain. The impetus for change for Britain came mainly from internal factors such as population growth, whereas the impetus and the timing of change for Japan came from a combination of internal and external factors.

WHAT INTERNAL FACTORS CAUSED AN INDUSTRIAL REVOLUTION IN JAPAN?

The outdated feudal system

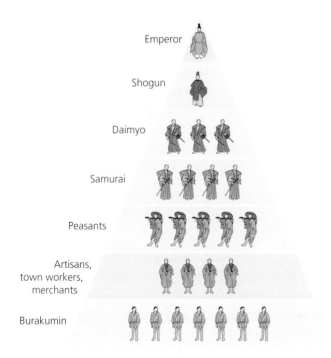

Emperor

Shogun

Daimyo

Samurai

Peasants

Artisans, town workers, merchants

Burakumin

■ **Figure 1.12** The feudal system by the middle of the nineteenth century; although there were fewer artisans than peasants, they come below the peasants on the diagram as they were considered lower in status

In theory, Japan was ruled by an emperor, but in practice power lay in the hands of the Shogun, the most senior soldier in Japan; this was also a hereditary position.

From 1603, the Shogun belonged to the rich and powerful Tokugawa family. The Shogun governed from his palace in Edo (Tokyo) and the Emperor was a virtual prisoner in the old imperial capital Kyoto. It was the Shogun who appointed all senior officials and it was to him, not the Emperor, that they swore an oath of loyalty. However, by 1850 the Shogun faced revolutionary pressure from below.

Japan was divided into provinces (called *han*) and each of these was ruled by a feudal lord or daimyo, who owed his position to the Shogun. The Shogun controlled the daimyo by making sure that they spent every other year living in his headquarters in Edo. When a daimyo returned home he had to leave his family behind as 'hostage'.

The Shogun kept Japan isolated from the West partly to make sure that no daimyo ever made **alliances** with other countries or got weapons from other countries. By 1850, the daimyo were frustrated with the shogunate system, and some were already starting to modernize their armies.

Below the daimyo in the feudal 'pyramid of power' came the samurai or warrior class. They had certain privileges, for example the right to wear swords, and they had to live by a certain code of behaviour called *bushido* (the way of the warrior) which stressed loyalty, bravery and honour. A samurai who behaved dishonourably was expected to commit suicide publicly by the ritual of *seppuku* (belly-cutting). They were awarded a wage or stipend, and some samurai played an important part in the government of the daimyo, but others were very poor. By 1850 the samurai were struggling with changes from a rice-based economy to a cash-based one. They were also increasingly urbanized and desirous of consumer products; they did not like the fact that the merchants were becoming wealthier than them.

The majority of the population were peasants. They mainly cultivated rice. However, they were kept in poverty by the high feudal taxes, which meant that the daimyo took between 40 and 60 per cent of a peasant's household rice production every year. By the middle of the nineteenth century, the peasants were discontented with their heavy tax burden. Their livelihoods were also vulnerable to natural disasters and there were many peasant uprisings.

The artisans and merchants were at the bottom of the pyramid of power, but their wealth meant that they were often more influential than those higher in the social order. They were growing in numbers and power and they wanted this power reflected by the position they held in society.

At the very bottom of the feudal system were the 'untouchables' or 'burakumin'. These people did the dirty jobs in society – digging and filling cesspits and burying the dead.

In 1637, the Shogun ordered that no Japanese person should ever leave the country. Also, foreigners had been banned from entering the country. From this time until the middle of the nineteenth century, Japan was almost entirely successful in pursuing its policy of *sakoku* or 'closed country'. Nonetheless, some contacts had been made and, by 1850, there were iron works in Choshu and Satsuma, factories making guns in Mito and Satsuma, textile mills, and other works. Many of these innovations came from Japanese contacts with the Dutch, who had a small trading station in Nagasaki harbour.

WHAT EXTERNAL FACTORS CAUSED AN INDUSTRIAL REVOLUTION?

The Americans were interested in Japan for two reasons:

1 As the Americans expanded their territories westwards, and Oregon and California became part of the USA in 1848, the Pacific Ocean became a sphere of interest.
2 It would be very useful if American ships trading between China and San Francisco could take on fresh provisions in Japan before crossing the vast expanse of the Pacific Ocean. Yokohama was nearly 2000 km closer to San Francisco than Shanghai.

In 1853, the Americans therefore sent an armed naval mission to negotiate with the Japanese. The mission was led by Commodore Matthew Perry. The Americans impressed the Shogun with their show of force – steam-powered, iron-clad warships with heavy guns.

In 1854, Perry returned to Edo Bay with twice as many ships as before. The Japanese believed that he would attack if the American demands were not granted, and they agreed to negotiate. As a result, the Treaty of Kanagawa was signed.

Terms of the 1854 Treaty of Kanagawa

In the treaty, the Japanese agreed to:

■ open up the isolated ports of Hakodate and Shimoda to ships from the USA
■ allow the Americans to station a consul in Shimoda
■ treat shipwrecked sailors well
■ give the USA 'most favoured nation' status.

This treaty was quickly followed by other treaties – with Britain in October 1854, with Russia in February 1855 and with the Netherlands in 1855.

By 1858, the Japanese had been persuaded via the Treaty of Edo with America, and similar treaties with other countries, to open up fully to commercial trade. However, these treaties were unequal. First, they allowed 'extraterritoriality', which meant that foreigners could be tried according to the laws of their own countries if they committed a crime (see page 55 for more discussion on this).

Second, the Japanese could not control their own **tariffs** levied on goods coming into Japan; and finally the USA got the benefit of any extra terms negotiated with other countries as it had 'most favoured nation' status.

What were the effects of the 'unequal treaties' on the Japanese?

The unequal treaties had a momentous impact on Japan. First, they led to a change in the political system. The weakness of the Shogun in allowing the treaties helped to bring about the restoration of the Emperor as the source of power in Japan. This was the demand of many influential Japanese. They took as their slogan *Sonno, Joi*, meaning 'Revere the Emperor, Expel the Barbarians'.

There followed 14 years of disturbance in Japan, which ended in 1868 when the Emperor Meiji decided that he would take over all the powers of the Shogun. He left Kyoto and moved to Yedo, which he renamed Tokyo. He also announced that from that time onwards Japan would take its place among the nations of the world, with the slogan *Fukoku Kyohei:* 'Enrich the country, strengthen the military'.

A delegation was sent to the West in 1871 to 'renegotiate' the unequal treaties. Although this was an unsuccessful mission, the delegation's leader now better understood that Britain had become strong through industrialization and that this had happened relatively quickly. This convinced the delegation that the Japanese *could* catch up.

Japan undertook a rapid programme of modernization that meant that in just 30 years the country was transformed from a semi-feudal state into one capable of winning a war against a European country.

> Wораed Eurocenticism

ACTIVITY: Comparing Japan and Britain

Refer back to the mind map that you completed on the reasons for Britain's Industrial Revolution. Annotate a mind map to show the causes of Japan's industrialization. Compare and contrast your two mind maps and the reasons for Britain's and Japan's industrialization.

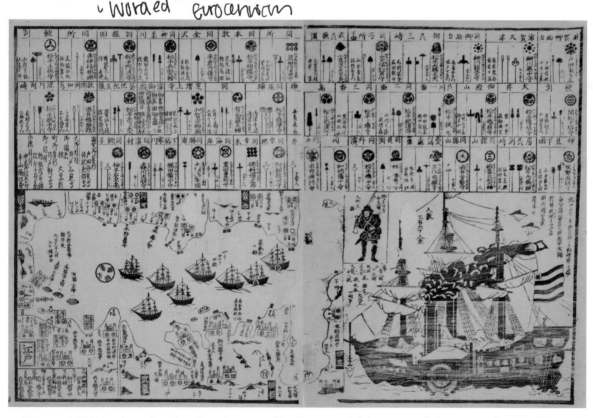

■ **Figure 1.13** Woodcut showing Perry's steamship (*bottom right*), a map of the coast of Soshu (*bottom left*) and various Japanese coats of arms (*top*), published between 1850 and 1900

What were the Meiji reforms?

THE MEIJI RESTORATION

Figure 1.14 The Meiji Emperor. *Meiji* means 'enlightened'

The Emperor was too young to rule on his own, but he had some brilliant young samurai advisers. In April 1868, the young Emperor signed the Charter Oath. This was an important demonstration of the new government's intention to reform and modernize Japan.

The Charter Oath was important because it declared that from now on promotion to the highest positions in society was open to all – not just those in the privileged classes. It also told the Japanese people to *learn from the rest of the world*.

THE MEIJI REFORMS

Abolition of the feudal system

Japan's new rulers understood that to modernize they would have to get rid of Japan's medieval feudal system. They needed to break up the power of the daimyo and samurai and strengthen the power of the central government. This would mean creating *one* army and not a number of powerful private armies, and having *one* strong government rather than a number of regional leaders.

First, they abolished the domains and privileges of the daimyo. This could have been very difficult – but the government had the support of some powerful daimyo that had been part of the force that overthrew the Shogun. The daimyo were also compensated, and many became local governors over their former territories. As the daimyo no longer had to pay the samurai, and as they had had their debts written off, many of them became wealthier after the reform.

Second, the government abolished the privileges of the samurai. Their stipends were initially halved, and then replaced with government bonds. In 1876 their proudly held privilege of wearing swords was forbidden. There was a lot of hardship among the samurai, who struggled to find a new role in Meiji society.

Political reforms

Even though the Meiji Emperor had announced the Charter Oath, Japan was not a **democracy**. It was ruled by the elites (the most powerful, wealthy sections of society). However, under pressure at the end of the nineteenth century, the government prepared for a new constitution. It sent Ito Hirobumi to Europe in 1882 to study the different systems of government there. When he returned, Japan set to achieve its goal of a constitutional monarchy through a number of stages.

In 1889 the Constitution was announced as a 'gift' from the Emperor to the Japanese people.

Key points set down in Meiji Japan's constitution

- The legislature was called the Diet.
- The Diet consisted of the House of Peers and the House of Representatives.
- Voters had to be male, over 25, and 15 yen per year taxpayers. This meant between 98 and 99 people in 100 could *not* vote.
- Supreme power rested in the hands of the Emperor.
- The Emperor was the supreme commander of Japan's armed forces.
- Everyone in Japan had the right to free speech and free worship, and had the freedom to join political parties.

Nevertheless, Japan continued to be governed by a small elite group of leaders called the *genro*.

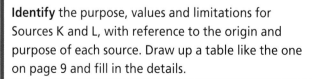

ACTIVITY: Source evaluation

Identify the purpose, values and limitations for Sources K and L, with reference to the origin and purpose of each source. Draw up a table like the one on page 9 and fill in the details.

Economic reforms

As we have seen, the Japanese government decided to learn about the West. Delegations were sent to Europe and the USA. The Japanese hoped that these foreign governments would understand that the government of Japan had changed, and that they would then be willing to renegotiate the unequal treaties. They were not successful in this aim – but did make careful note of the societies and technologies they saw and adopted key models, as can be seen in the sources below.

SOURCE K

Okubo Toshimichi, a Japanese official on the Iwakura Mission of 1871–73

'In every city there are many factories. The shipyard in Liverpool, the spinning mill in Manchester and the cotton mills in Glasgow, in particular, are equipped with powerful machines which are in constant operation. Besides these, there are countless large and small plants. When I saw them I realized how Britain had become such a powerful and wealthy nation. In remote places there are roads and bridges. Railways are in use, not to mention horse-drawn carriages for transportation. I was impressed by the convenience of it all.'

SOURCE L

'Japan's general progress, during the short space of half a century, has been so sudden and fast that it [is] … rare in the history of the world. This leap forward is the result of the stimulus which the country received on coming into contact with the civilisation of Europe and America … We possess today a powerful army and navy, but it was after Western models that we laid their foundations … We reorganised the systems of central and local administration and effected reforms in the educational systems of the empire. All this is nothing but the result of adopting the superior features of Western institutions.'

Okuma Shigenobu. 1908. Fifty Years of New Japan.

When Japan opened up to the West it was primarily an agricultural economy but by 1920 less than half the population were peasants or fishermen. This was partly due to the implementation of new farming methods, stronger crops and effective use of fertilizers. However, these improvements did not bring about a corresponding improvement in the standard of living for most peasants, who continued to live in poverty.

The decline in people working in agriculture was also due to the increase in those employed in industry, trade and finance, which grew from 1.6 million in 1870 to 5 million in 1900. Indeed, many new factories opened due to investment from the government – the new Ministry of Industry developed and ran coal mines, cement works, shipbuilding yards and textile mills.

The silk industry was particularly successful. The first silk mill using machinery was opened in 1870 and the government gave money to develop the industry. The production of silk multiplied five times in 25 years and the **export** of silk helped to pay for the imports of raw materials needed for other industries.

Industrialization led to the expansion of domestic and foreign trade. The building of merchant ships and the establishment of banks helped to encourage commercial growth.

As Japan industrialized, transport and communications were modernized. In 1869, the first telegraph line was built. Work on Japan's first railway began in 1870 and, in 1871, a government postal system was established. Gas lighting was introduced into Japanese cities in 1872, and electricity became available in Tokyo by 1887.

However, the government could not afford to keep investing in industry as it had to foot the bill to compensate the samurai in 1876 and to pay to put down the Satsuma **Rebellion** in 1877. Prices rose sharply, and the cost of rice doubled between 1877 and 1880. The government had to sell off many of its factories to private investors to raise money. Many were bought by very rich families called *zaibatsu*.

■ **Figure 1.15** Japan's first railway leaving Yokohama in 1872

Social reforms

As well as copying the West in terms of industrialization, the Japanese also adopted many Western customs. Many wealthy Japanese began to wear Western clothes. Men wore moustaches, top hats, bow ties and Western-style suits, and carried umbrellas.

The Japanese began to use a Western calendar in 1872, and adopted a metric system 50 years before it was introduced into Britain!

The key social reforms were in education. The new government understood that to modernize it *had* to have a modern education system. It made education compulsory for four years in 1872, and it built primary and secondary schools. Western knowledge was taught as well as traditional Japanese beliefs and skills. Children were brought up with a strong sense of patriotism and reverence for the Emperor. In 1890, the Emperor Rescript on Education, which set down the aims for education, was issued to schools. It was memorized by children, who promised to obey their parents and to 'guard and maintain the prosperity of our Imperial Throne'. Tokyo University was founded in 1877 and Kyoto University in 1897. Initially, thousands of Japanese students were sent to foreign universities but this declined as Japan developed its own colleges.

Military reforms

Modernization of the military had already begun before the fall of the shogunate as some powerful daimyo were impressed by Western forces. The Meiji decided that they would copy the best from the West. The navy was modelled on that of the British, which was the strongest navy in the world at that time. The army was initially modelled on the French, but later adopted methods from the Germans. The Choshu and Satsuma armies were combined to form the new Imperial Army in 1872.

Conscription was introduced in 1873 and these peasant conscripts proved themselves when they were able to defeat the samurai in the rebellion of 1877. The new Imperial Army was well trained, equipped with modern weapons and effectively led – and went on to defeat the European power of Russia in the Russo-Japanese war of 1894–95.

■ **Figure 1.16** Japanese people began to adopt Western customs and dress

Revision of the unequal treaties

A key reason why the reformers had embarked on a **radical** programme of modernization was to enable Japan to revise the unequal treaties and take back control of their own country. Two key elements which emphasized foreign superiority *had* to be undone – first the extraterritorial rights and, second, foreign control of customs duties.

Japan reformed its legal code in 1889 and so there was little reason for foreign nationals to want to live under another justice system. Britain, and then the other Western powers, gave up its extraterritorial rights in 1894. Foreign control over tariffs was also removed in 1911.

To what extent were the Meiji reforms beneficial to Japan?

Japan's change from a closed feudal society to a modern industrial state took place very quickly – and the impact of this change was not always positive. Indeed, for many people in Japan at this time the reforms did not improve their standard of living and made life more unpredictable. The Japanese who were able to adapt to the 'new' Japan and take advantage of modernization, such as the factory owners and traders, did well, but many were left behind.

WHAT WAS THE IMPACT OF ENDING THE FEUDAL SYSTEM?

As you have read, the samurai saw the end of their privileged lifestyles, they could no longer wear their swords and their salaries were stopped. All in all, their traditional respected status in Japanese society no longer existed. This led to much discontent and this resentment finally exploded in the Satsuma Rebellion in 1877. Other samurai attempted to form political parties to legally pressure the government for improvement – and greater democracy. This was more successful than the violent uprisings and in 1889 a written constitution gave Japan an elected parliament, albeit a limited democracy with only four per cent of Japanese men allowed to vote (see page 21).

WHAT WAS THE IMPACT OF INDUSTRIALIZATION?

The peasants were also unhappy with the Meiji reforms and this led to problems in the countryside with violent uprisings occurring at a rate of 30 a year between 1869 and 1874. The peasant revolts continued through to the end of the nineteenth century – with a peasant army of 10 000 burning down government buildings east of Osaka in 1876, and widespread rioting in Fukushima in 1882 and Chichibu in 1884. The peasants revolted against the changes made by the Meiji government in the way taxes were paid. Instead of being able to pay in rice, taxes now had to be paid in cash.

The peasants believed that the 'assessments' made of their plots of land were too high. Even if there had been a bad season and the crop yield was low, the peasants still had to pay their cash tax and were often forced into debt. Many peasant farmers were forced to borrow money, and this in turn forced them to sell their land when they could not pay the debt. Between 1883 and 1890, 300 000 farmers had to sell their land and either move to the cities to find work or take on jobs as labourers.

The peasants also were impoverished by the impact of foreign trade. Many peasant farmers survived not only on their crop but made ends meet with home industries that were supported by their wives and children. Homemade cloth, candles and other products were no longer needed; imported paraffin oil lamps replaced these candles and the industrialized machine-made, mass-produced cotton goods were better than the homemade peasant cloths. There was some attempt to **boycott** these goods, but with little effect. The Japanese could not do anything about the situation until it was strong enough to revise the unequal treaties.

The urban workers also suffered with the changes. Workers in the new factories lived in squalid conditions in unsanitary slum housing; sometimes they were housed in wooden dormitories above the factory they worked in. As in Britain, the majority of the workforce was made up of women and children; conditions were grim and the hours long. Discipline was harsh, with heavy fines for arriving a few minutes late or opening a window. Diseases were common – and spread through the cramped factories and overcrowded dwellings easily.

Industrial accidents were common and workers had no protection. The sources on this page give an indication of what conditions were like.

SOURCE M

From a 1904 report

'Take the case of the condition of the factory girls of Osaka. Many of them are children of ten, a few of eight, even of six. One account tells us, 'The employees are usually pale and sickly-looking, more especially the younger girls. The atmosphere in the mills is oppressive and impregnated with dust and small particles of cotton. There are small pivot windows in the buildings. The manager informed me that these windows are usually opened three or four times per day for a few minutes.''

SOURCE N

Song sung by girls working in the silk and cotton factories

'Factory work is prison work

All it lacks are iron chains.

More than a caged bird, more than a prison,

Dormitory life is hateful …

How I wish the dormitory would be washed away,

The factory burn down,

And the gatekeeper die of cholera!

In this troubled world

I am just a silk-reeling lass,

But this lass wants to see

The parents who gave her birth.

Their letter says they are waiting for the year's end.

Are they waiting more for the money than for me?'

Quoted in Tsurumi, P. 1992. Factory Girls: Women in Thread Mills of Meiji Japan.

ACTIVITY: Comparing the Industrial Revolution in Japan and Britain

What similarities can you see in Sources M and N to conditions in the first British factories? Look at the date of Source M. Why would this situation not be happening in Britain by 1904?

ACTIVITY: Reforms

Work in groups of three. Each group should choose one area of reform from the table below. **Identify** key points from the text on your area of reform and write them down as bullet points. You should include dates, details and examples. Make sure it is clear when and what changed in Japan. You should also note the benefits and disadvantages of the Meiji reforms for Japan.

Economic reforms	Social reforms	Military reforms
e.g. Opening of Japanese silk factory	e.g. The Iwakura Mission was sent abroad to learn from the West in 1871	e.g. Conscription introduced in 1873

Assessment task

Your task is to **explain** the extent of change in Japan in the nineteenth century.

Role

You need to choose one of the products (right) in which to **explain** the impact of the reforms.

Audience

If you choose the children's picture book, you need to consider the audience carefully.

Situation

The focus of your task should be on **describing** what Japan was like before the reforms and how radically the country changed as a result of industrialization and political reform.

Product

You will create one of the following:
- **Poem** (150 words minimum). Choose an appropriate poetic form – for example, haikus are perhaps not appropriate as they are too short and acrostics are too simplistic. Your poem does not necessarily have to rhyme.
- **Diary** (500–1000 words). As the focus of the task is to **describe** and **explain** the impact of the reforms, one diary entry is not enough. A number of entries spanning a particular period of time is more appropriate.
- **Painting** (A3 size minimum). Any design or style of painting is acceptable. You may have words in addition to pictures in your painting. There should be dates and details.
- **Short story** (700–1500 words). Use the narrative techniques and structure you have learnt in English to help you plan this task.
- **Children's picture book** (700–1000 words). Read several picture books before you begin to give you an idea of the layout, level of language and type of illustration used. It is important to aim your picture book at a particular age group. 'Children' is not specific enough – you should focus on an age group from 6-year-olds or older.

◆ Assessment opportunities

- ◆ This activity can be assessed using Criterion A: Knowing and understanding and Criterion C: Communicating.

ACTIVITY: Assessing the impact of industrialization

Write an essay. There is no word limit for this assessment. You will have 1 hour to complete the task.

Essay: 'Industrialization brings benefits to society.' To what extent do you agree with this claim?

Answer with reference to Sources O to S (see pages 28–29) and also with reference to your own knowledge of the impact of industrialization. You do not need to focus only on Japan and Britain if you have evidence from other countries (Source S is about industrialization in America).

You could make use of this essay frame.

Essay frame

Plan

Organize the sources into those that suggest that society *did* benefit from industrialization and those that suggest it did not. Then add details and examples from your own knowledge to both sides of the argument.

Introduction

You need to set down your line of argument. This could be that the Industrial Revolution did indeed bring substantial benefits to certain sections of society and certainly changed the lives of most people. However, there were groups of people who did not benefit, or who suffered as a result of the changes. You could briefly state which sources agree and which do not.

First section

Here **explain** the groups of people who did benefit. You could consider factory owners, the middle classes, certain groups of workers. Do not forget to have a clear opening sentence that links to the question, for example *There were several groups of people who*

benefited from the Industrial Revolution. First … (Refer to the sources that claim it did benefit – Q, R and some of S.)

Second section

Now **explain** groups who did not benefit. You could consider children, poor workers in cities, etc. Do not forget to use linking words: *However, there were groups who did not benefit such as …* (Refer to the sources that claim it did benefit – O, P and some of S.)

Third section

Here you may want to consider groups who gained or lost or whose fortunes changed over time, such as factory workers (good wages but no job security) and weavers in Britain (who made lots of money to start with but were put out of business once the power loom was invented). You may also want to consider changes that affected everyone, such as the railways.

Conclusion

You should write a sentence or two that answers the question. This should fit with the weight of evidence you have provided.

> **Hint**
> Useful linking words for joining together your arguments in an essay include: However, Moreover, In contrast, In addition, furthermore.

◆ Assessment opportunities

- ◆ This activity can be assessed using Criterion A: Knowing and understanding, Criterion C: Communicating and Criterion D: Thinking critically.

SOURCE O

'As in the rest of the world, the factory system in Japan meant much misery. Since machines could be worked by women, and even children, there was no need to employ men. This majority of factory workers were women, working up to fourteen hours a day in some cases, without regular lunch or rest periods. Child labour was used, discipline was harsh and diseases like tuberculosis and beri beri were common, and there were some appalling industrial accidents. This was especially so in the coal mines, of course, where 2,000 miners were killed in one explosion in 1878. But it was also true of the factories, for safety precautions were few, and workers were often housed in dormitories above the flimsy wooden sheds in which they worked.'

Bolitho, H. 1977. Meiji Japan. *Cambridge University Press, p. 46.*

SOURCE Q

'Communications expanded rapidly. The first railway line was built between Tokyo and Yokohama in 1872, and within a short time was carrying almost two million passengers a year. Four years later Osaka was linked with Kyoto, and soon the whole country was covered with a complex network of rails. By 1911 there were nearly 9,000 kilometres of track, and rail was firmly established as a major means of communication.'

Koutsoukis, A.J. 1992. From Samurai to Sanyo: A History of Modern Japan. *Perth, W.A. Batavia Press – Bookland, p. 20.*

SOURCE P

■ **Figure 1.17** Ring spinners in a cotton factory in the north of England, c.1890

SOURCE R

'In the grey mists of the morning, in the atmosphere of a hundred conflicting smells and by the light of a faintly burning gas, we see supplies for the great London markets rapidly unloaded from the night trains: fish, fresh food, butter and diary-fed pork, apples, cabbages and cucumbers, cart-loads of watercress. No sooner do these disappear then other trains appear, with Manchester packs and bales, Liverpool cotton, carpets and hardware. At a later hour of the morning these are followed by other trains, carrying stones, bricks, iron girders, iron pipes, ale, coal, hay, straw, grain, flour and salt.'

From the Railway News *magazine, United Kingdom, 1850s.*

SOURCE S

'By the 1890s it was clear that industrialisation had created many problems as well as bringing wealth to some. The depression of 1893–97, with an estimated twenty per cent of the workforce unemployed, 16,000 businesses closed and over 600 banks failing, accelerated the demands for a positive government response. However, there was confusion about the role of government. It was clearly responsible for supporting business and industry for the good of the nation, but could the government, at the same time, protect those used and abused by the realities of rapid industrial growth?'

de Pennington, J. 2007. Modern America: The USA, 1865 to the present.
London. Hodder Murray.

! Take action

! Refer back to your report on child labour in the world today. Make a display of your findings to raise awareness of this issue in your school.

Reflection

In this chapter we have studied the reasons for the Industrial Revolution. We have found out about the different inventions that made this revolution possible, and the impact that it had on the working and living conditions of people in Britain and Japan. We have compared the causes and effects of industrialization in Britain to the causes and effects of industrialization in Japan.

Reflecting on our learning … Use this table to reflect on your own learning in this chapter.					
Questions we asked	Answers we found	Any further questions now?			
Factual					
Conceptual					
Debatable					
Approaches to learning you used in this chapter:	Description – what new skills did you learn?	How well did you master the skills?			
		Novice	Learner	Practitioner	Expert
Collaboration skills					
Communication skills					
Creative-thinking skills					
Critical-thinking skills					
Organization skills					
Transfer skills					
Learner profile attribute	*Reflect on the importance of being knowledgeable for our learning in this chapter.*				
Knowledgeable					

2 What impact have pioneers, innovators and developers had on societies?

○ The **significance** of pioneers, **innovators** and developers is dependent on their **time and place**.

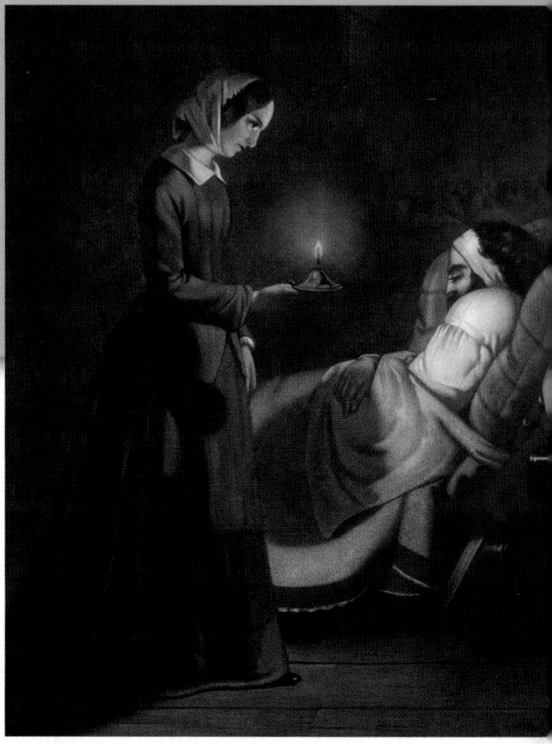

■ **Figure 2.1** Florence Nightingale, a pioneer in nursing, and Alexander Graham Bell with his long-distance telepnone line

CONSIDER THESE QUESTIONS:

Factual: Who were the significant pioneers, innovators and developers of the nineteenth century? Who were the first pioneers in America? Why did nineteenth-century America encourage innovation?

Conceptual: Is the success of pioneers and innovators dependent on the place in which they live? Or is it dependent on the time in which they live?

Debatable: To what extent are pioneers and innovators products of their time? Who have been more significant in affecting your life: pioneers or innovators?

Now **share and compare** your thoughts and ideas with your partner, or with the whole class.

○ IN THIS CHAPTER, WE WILL ...

■ **Find out** what it means to be a pioneer, innovator or developer and why nineteenth-century America was a time of innovation.

■ **Explore:**
  ■ the achievements of different pioneers in nineteenth-century America
  ■ the factors that encourage and hold back innovation and the ways in which pioneers and innovators have been products of their time.

■ **Take action** by reviewing the work of the pioneers and innovators of today.

■ These Approaches to Learning (ATL) skills will be useful ...

■ Communication skills
■ Critical-thinking skills
■ Information literacy skills
■ Media literacy skills
■ Transfer skills

● We will reflect on this learner profile attribute ...

● Inquirer – developing skills for inquiry and research.

Assessment opportunities in this chapter:

◆ **Criterion A:** Knowing and understanding
◆ **Criterion B:** Investigating
◆ **Criterion C:** Communicating
◆ **Criterion D:** Thinking critically

KEY WORDS

innovation
mass production
patent

In this chapter we will be finding out about some of the key pioneers, innovators and developers of the nineteenth century. As well as those you have already come across in Chapter 1, we will examine some case studies of people from the USA and think about the factors that enabled them to have such an impact on the modern world.

ACTIVITY: Pioneer, innovator or developer?

■ ATL

- Critical-thinking skills – Evaluate evidence and arguments
- Transfer skills – Inquire in different contexts to gain a different perspective

Read the following definitions.

Pioneer: The original definition of pioneer is 'one who ventures into unknown or unclaimed territory to settle'. It has since also come to mean 'one who opens up new areas of thought, research or development'.

Innovator: 'one who creates or introduces something new'.

Developer: 'a person who develops something – takes it further'.

1 In pairs, reflect on these definitions. What are the differences between these terms? Can you think of examples of people that you know from history or from today who might fit these different definitions?
2 Refer back to Chapter 1. You read about several different individuals and groups: Richard Arkwright, Samuel Crompton, Abraham Darby I, James Watt, the leaders of the Chartist movement, the Suffragettes and the Meiji rulers of Japan. Do you think these individuals are pioneers, innovators or developers?
3 **Identify** the factors that helped or hindered them in becoming pioneers, innovators or developers.

◆ Assessment opportunities

◆ In this activity you have practised skills that are assessed using Criterion A: Knowing and understanding.

Who were the first pioneers in America?

The original pioneers in the USA were those men and women who trekked westwards to open up the interior of America and settle in the west. Their actions, ultimately, led to the development of America into the country that we see today.

The first pioneers of this westward exploration were Captain Meriwether Lewis and Captain William Clark; they were the first US officials to venture into US territory west of St Louis. When America bought the whole of the Mississippi Valley from France in what was known as the Louisiana Purchase, the way west was opened for pioneers to explore, and so in May 1804, Lewis and Clark led a group of 50 Americans north-west along the Missouri River from St Louis.

The object of your mission is to explore the Missouri river, & such principal stream of it, as, by its course & communication with the waters of the Pacific Ocean, offer the most direct & practicable water communication across the continent for the purposes of commerce. Beginning at the mouth of the Missouri, you will take observations of latitude and longitude at all remarkable points on the river, and especially at the mouths of rivers, at rapids, at islands, and other places. . . .

The interesting points of portage between the heads of the Missouri and the water offering the best communication with the Pacific Ocean should be fixed by observation and the course of that water, to the ocean. . . . Your observations are to be taken with great pains and accuracy. . . . The commerce which may be carried on with the people inhabiting the line you will pursue renders a knowledge of these people important.

You will therefore endeavor to make yourself acquainted . . . with the names of the nations and their numbers; the extent and limits of their possessions; their relations with other tribes or nations; their language, traditions . . . ; their food, clothing . . . ; the diseases prevalent among them, and the remedies they use . . . ; and articles of commerce they may need or furnish and to what extent.

Other objects worthy of notice will be: the soil and face of the country, its growth and vegetable productions, especially those not of the U.S.; the animals of the country . . . ; the mineral productions of every kind . . . ; volcanic appearances; climate as characterized by the thermometer, by the proportion of rainy, cloudy, and clear days, by lightning, hail, snow, ice . . . , by the winds, . . . the dates at which particular plants put forth or lose their flowers, or leaf, times of appearance of particular birds, reptiles, or insects.

President Jefferson's instructions to Lewis and Clark

ACTIVITY: What was the aim of the expedition?

■ ATL

- Critical-thinking skills – Evaluate evidence and arguments

Read through President Jefferson's instructions to Clark and Lewis. **Identify** the objectives of the expedition. As you read, make a note of the relevant points and then work in pairs to put them into a list.

ACTIVITY: Lewis and Clark's expedition

■ ATL

- Critical-thinking skills – Gather and organize relevant information to formulate an argument; Evaluate evidence and arguments

Study Sources A–D on the following pages.

1 **Identify** the main points made in the sources regarding:
   - **Lewis and Clark's relationship with Indians**
   - **the extent to which they followed Jefferson's instructions.**
2 **Evaluate** the value and limitations of Sources A, B, C and D in terms of the origin and purpose of each source.

◆ Assessment opportunities

- ◆ This activity can be assessed using Criterion D: Thinking critically.

■ **Figure 2.2** The first pioneers of America, Captain Meriwether Lewis and Captain William Clark

The round trip was nearly 6400 kilometres and took almost two-and-a-half years. The expedition left the Mississippi at St Louis on 14 May 1804, and travelled up the Missouri River to its headwaters. Here they hired Indian guides and horses and travelled 480 kilometres over mountains to the headwaters of the Clearwater River where they built canoes. They then travelled by canoe down the Clearwater and the Colombia to the Pacific Ocean.

During the first winter, Lewis and Clark hired a French-Canadian fur trader and his Indian wife, Sacagawea, who served as guides and interpreters for them. Sacagawea's knowledge of the west and her language skills played an important role in the success of the expedition.

Follow their journey on this interactive map:
www.nationalgeographic.com/ lewisandclark/journey_intro.html

SOURCE A

Extracts from Lewis and Clark's diaries

December 17, 1804

'A very cold morning. The thermometer stood at 45 degrees below zero. . . . About 8 o'clock P.M., the thermometer fell to 74 degrees below freezing point. The Indian chiefs sent word that buffalo were in the neighborhood, and if we would join them in the morning they would go and kill them.

January 13, 1805

'A cold, clear day. Great numbers of Indians move down the river to hunt. Those people kill a number of buffalo near the villages and save a great proportion of the meat. . . . Their corn and beans, etc., they keep for the summer, and as a reserve in case of an attack from the Sioux, of which they are always in dread, and seldom go far to hunt except in large parties. . . .

April 22, 1805

'. . . The broken hills of the Missouri, about this place, exhibit large irregular and broken masses of rock and stone; some of which, though 200 feet above the level of the water, seem at some former period to have felt its influence, for they appear smooth as if worn by the agitation of the water. This collection consists of white and gray granite, a brittle black rock, flint, limestone, freestone, some small specimens of an excellent pebble and occasionally broken . . . stone which appears to be petrified wood. . . . Coal or carbonated wood, pumice stone, lava, and other mineral appearances still continue. The coal appears to be of better quality. I exposed a specimen of it to the fire, and found that it burned tolerably well; it afforded but little flame or smoke, but produced a hot and lasting fire. . . .

November 20, 1805

'Found many of the Chinooks with Captain Lewis, of whom there were 2 chiefs, Comcommoly and Chillarlawil, to whom we gave medals, and to one a flag. One of the Indians had on a robe made of two sea-otter skins. The fur of them was more beautiful than any fur I had ever seen. Both Captain Lewis and myself endeavored to purchase the robe with different articles. At length, we procured it for a belt of blue beads which the squaw wife of our interpreter Charbonneau [Sacagawea] wore around her waist.

January 3, 1806

'Our part, from necessity having been obliged to subsist some length of time on dogs, have now become extremely fond of their flesh. It is worth of remark that while we lived principally on the flesh of this animal, we were much more healthy, strong, and more fleshy than we have been since we left the buffalo country. For my own part, I have become so perfectly reconciled to the dog that I think it an agreeable food and would prefer it vastly to lean venison or elk.

February 14, 1806

'I completed a map of the country through which we have been passing from the Mississippi, at the mouth of the Missouri, to this place. On the map, the Missouri, Jefferson's River, the S.E. branch of the Columbia or Lewis's River, Kooskooskee, and Columbia from the entrance of the S.E. fork to the Pacific Ocean, as well as a part of Clark's River and our trek across the Rocky Mountains, are laid down by celestial observations and survey. The rivers are also connected at their sources with other rivers.'

Figure 2.3 Clark's drawing and description of a sage grouse

SOURCE C

Captains Lewis & Clark holding a Council with the Indians   Page 17

Figure 2.4 'Captains Lewis and Clark holding a Council with the Indians' – an engraving added to the first eyewitness accounts of the expedition to appear in print

SOURCE D

Figure 2.5 A twentieth-century painting by Olaf Seltzer, called 'Lewis' First Glimpse of the Rockies', illustrates a remarkable moment in the famous journey to the Pacific

SOURCE E

'It [the expedition] strengthened the United States' position in the struggle for control of North America, particularly in the Pacific Northwest. Lewis and Clark's trek also inspired explorers, trappers, traders, hunters, adventurers, prospectors, homesteaders, ranchers, soldiers, businessman and missionaries to move westward – spurring a century of rapid settlement which peopled the West with European-Americans and disrupted the cultures and lifestyles of countless American Indians.

'Lewis and Clark contributed to geographical knowledge by determining the true course of the Upper Missouri River and its major tributaries while William Clark produced maps of tremendous value to later explorers. They forever destroyed the dream of a Northwest Passage (a water route across the continent), but proved the success of overland travel to the Pacific.

'They made the first attempt at a systematic record of the meteorology of the West, and less successfully attempted to determine the latitude and longitude of significant geographical points. Through the Expedition's peaceful cooperation with the American Indian tribes they met, they compiled the first general survey of life and material culture of the tribes of the Missouri, Rocky Mountains and the Northwest coast. Lewis and Clark also made significant additions to the zoological and botanical knowledge of the continent, describing at least 120 mammals, birds, reptiles and fish, as well as almost 200 plant specimens. By any measure of scientific exploration, the Lewis and Clark Expedition was phenomenally successful in terms of accomplishing its stated goals, expanding human knowledge and spurring further curiosity and wonder about the vast American West.'

www.nps.gov/nr/travel/lewisandclark/intro.htm

Why did nineteenth-century America encourage innovation?

THINK–PAIR–SHARE

Thomas Edison said: 'To invent, you need a good imagination and a pile of junk.'

Do you agree? **Evaluate** the extent to which other factors help innovation.

Here is a list of possible factors identified by researchers as contributing to creativity:

- **Liberty/freedom to discuss ideas**
- **Availability of resources**
- **A person's character, for example a questioning mind, being prepared to experiment**
- **Living in a place where there are lots of other people to discuss ideas with, for example in a city or Silicon Valley**

What role do you think each can play in helping an individual to be innovative?

Eric Schmidt, Google's CEO, has said:

> 'The characteristic of great innovators … is they see a space that others do not. They don't just listen to what people tell them; they actually invent something new, something that you didn't know you needed, but the moment you see it, you say, "I must have it."'

Do you think that it is easier or harder to be an inventor today than in the nineteenth century? Share your thoughts with your partner, and then find out what the rest of the class thinks.

ACTIVITY: What other examples are there of pioneers?

■ ATL

- Information literacy skills – Identify primary and secondary sources; Collect, record and verify data; Create references and citations, use footnotes/endnotes and construct a bibliography according to recognized conventions
- Media literacy skills – Locate, organize, analyse, evaluate, synthesize and ethically use information from a variety of sources and media

The term 'pioneer' continues to be used to describe someone who pushes the boundaries and explores new areas, such as in medicine, technology, the space race and human rights. Here are some examples of nineteenth-century US pioneers: Booker T. Washington, Charlotte Perkins Gilman, Susan B. Anthony and Edward Alexander Bouchet.

In pairs, research each of these individuals. Decide why each individual has also been considered a 'pioneer'.

- You do not need to **formulate** your own research question as you are answering the given question about each individual: Why have they been considered a 'pioneer'?
- With your partner, you need to draft an action plan to follow when investigating your pioneers.
- **Use** and record appropriate and varied information from both primary and secondary sources (where possible).
- Structure your information and ideas clearly as short reports of maximum 400 words per pioneer.
- Consistently **document** your sources of information using a recognized convention.

◆ Assessment opportunities

- ◆ This activity can be assessed using Criterion B: Investigating and Criterion C: Communicating.

THOMAS EDISON

The nineteenth century also saw important innovators in the USA. Probably the most famous inventor of the nineteenth century in America was Thomas Edison, who was responsible for hundreds of inventions – many of which have influenced life around the world. He obtained a total of 1093 patents within the USA – the first was at the age of 21 and the last one was granted two years after his death, in 1933. He also got more than 1200 patents in other countries.

He used mass production and large-scale teamwork in the process of invention. His laboratory in Menlo Park, New Jersey was so productive that at one point he promised to turn out 'a minor invention every ten days and a big thing every six months or so'.

One of Edison's inventions was the phonograph (a machine to play music). While working on improvements to the telegraph and the telephone, Edison worked out a way to record sound on tinfoil-coated cylinders. In 1877, he created a machine with two needles: one for recording and one for playback. When Edison spoke into the mouthpiece, the sound vibrations of his voice were indented onto the cylinder by the recording needle. The phonograph was the first machine that could record the sound of someone's voice and play it back. In 1877, Edison recorded the first words on a piece of tinfoil. He recited the nursery rhyme 'Mary had a little lamb'. In 1878, Edison established the Edison Speaking Phonograph Company to sell the new machine.

However, Edison is best known for his invention of the light bulb. Although the light bulb had been around for a number of years, it was unreliable, expensive and short-lived. Many other inventors were already trying to make an efficient and practical light bulb, but it was Edison who, after much experimentation, succeeded. By creating a vacuum inside the bulb, finding the right filament to use, and running lower voltage through the bulb, Edison was able to create a light bulb that lasted for many hours. Edison also patented a system for electricity distribution in 1880; by 1887, there were 121 Edison power stations in the USA delivering direct current (DC) electricity to customers.

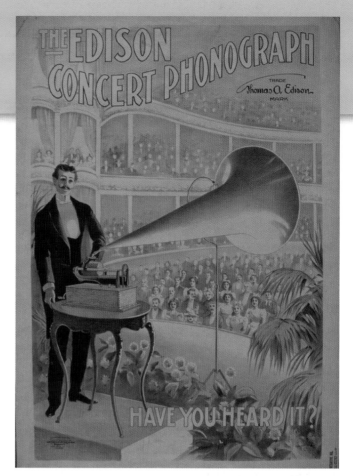

■ **Figure 2.6** Advert for Edison's phonograph

■ **Figure 2.7** Thomas Edison with his light bulb

Edison's other inventions included a motion picture camera, the electrographic vote recorder, the universal stock printer, ore separator, alkaline battery and cement.

ACTIVITY: Edison – pioneer, innovator or developer?

ATL

■ Communication skills – Negotiate ideas and knowledge with peers

Read Sources F and G. In pairs, **discuss** the following questions:

1 **To what extent would living in the USA have contributed to Edison's success as an inventor?**

2 **To what extent was the time in which he was living important to his success?**

> Hint
>
> When you have the terms in a question like 'To what extent', you need to think of ideas to agree with the point made in the question, for example how living in the USA contributed to Edison's success. Then think of points that might challenge this assumption.

3 **Do you think that Edison could also be considered a 'pioneer'? Could he be considered a 'developer' rather than an 'innovator' in some cases?**

SOURCE F

'Thomas Edison, the American inventor, once said that genius is 1% inspiration and 99% perspiration. America had a gift for both of these. "Yankee ingenuity" had resulted in the invention of the electric light bulb, the sewing machine, the phonograph and telephone. Coupled with this was the "work ethic" of the USA – "rugged individualism" which encouraged hard work and thrift.

'… the USA had developed a strong business class and powerful industrial infrastructure. Self-made millionaires such as Andrew Carnegie and John D. Rockefeller epitomised the "American Dream". If you worked hard enough, you could be prosperous. The immigrant population provided hard-working and cheap labour which made industrialisation such a success.'

Murphy, D., Cooper, K. and Waldron, M. 2001. United States 1776–1992. *Collins, p. 165.*

SOURCE G

'Edison brought to the problem of invention a system which has its parallels in mass-production. His research laboratory was not a boffin's retreat but a factory with the methods and aims of a factory: to produce new goods cheaply for a market.

'His factory was a place of invention. Not discovery. He made a clear distinction between the two: "Discovery is not invention. A discovery is more or less in the nature of an accident."

'Edison discovered the phonograph, he invented everything else, taking other people's ideas and developing them for profit. From 1876, first at Menlo Park and later at Orange, New Jersey, he "invented to order". There was no room for "accidents". Accidental discoveries couldn't be programmed and time-tabled; inventions could.'

Norman, B. 1976. The Inventing of America. *BBC, p. 126.*

THINK–PAIR–SHARE

Think about the following questions on your own, and then share your thoughts with a partner.

Why did Josephine Cochrane become an innovator? **Describe** the factors that helped her to be successful as an inventor. What factors hindered her work as an inventor?

JOSEPHINE COCHRANE

■ **Figure 2.8** Josephine Cochrane

Josephine Garis Cochrane invented the first workable dishwasher.

Cochrane did a lot of entertaining, giving dinner parties for which she used valuable heirloom china. She had servants to wash the dishes, but was fed up with the china getting chipped while being washed. This led her, so the story goes, eventually to invent a machine that could wash the dishes for her. When her husband died leaving her with large debts, she realized that inventing a new machine could also be a way to earn the money she needed. Thus she came up with a design that involved putting dishes into wire compartments and then putting the compartments into a wheeled cage that was lowered into a copper tub. A motor then pumped jets of hot soapy water and then hot clean water over the dishes, which were then left to dry.

The first men that she got to design the dishwasher did not follow her instructions:

> 'I couldn't get men to do the things I wanted in my way until they had tried and failed on their own. And that was costly for me. They knew I knew nothing, academically, about mechanics, and they insisted on having their own way with my invention until they convinced themselves my way was the better, no matter how I had arrived at it.'

http://blogs.oregonstate.edu/tinagrissom/culture-site/the-first-dishwashing-machine-and-how-it-came-to-be/

Finally, a man named George Butters helped to construct her original idea and she received her patent in December 1886.

Cochrane had intended her invention to help housewives, but they did not want to spend money on an invention that they did not need. Thus it was hotels that first bought her dishwasher. As a woman in the nineteenth century, she also faced challenges when selling her inventions. She once told a reporter:

> 'You asked me what was the hardest part of getting into business. I think crossing the great lobby of the Sherman House [hotel] alone. You cannot imagine what it was like in those days … for a woman to cross a hotel lobby alone. I had never been anywhere without my husband or father – the lobby seemed a mile wide. I thought I should faint at every step, but I didn't – and I got an $800 order as my reward.'

http://superforty.com/women-in-history-josephine-cochrane-invented-the-dishwasher/

After exhibiting her invention at the World's Columbian Exposition in Chicago, where she won the highest prize for 'best mechanical construction, durability and adaption to its line of work', she was able to convince restaurants to use her invention. As a result she opened a factory in an abandoned schoolhouse. Other customers included hospitals and colleges; eventually home owners started using it too. She started the Garis-Cochrane Manufacturing Company, which was later bought out by KitchenAid, which became part of Whirlpool Corporation.

ACTIVITY: Finding out about other pioneers and innovators

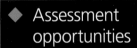

ATL

- Information literacy skills – Collect and analyse data to identify solutions and make informed decisions; Identify primary and secondary sources
- Critical-thinking skills – Interpret data; Evaluate evidence and arguments

Your goal in this activity is to find out more about a pioneer or innovator from your own country.

You need to research your chosen individual and write a report on him or her.

- **Your report should be about 700–1500 words long.**
- **It should be clearly structured.**
- **You must consistently and accurately cite your sources and you must include a bibliography.**

Assessment opportunities

- This activity can be assessed using Criterion A: Knowing and understanding, Criterion B: Investigating and Criterion C: Communicating.

1 Formulate your own overarching research question.

To get you thinking about your chosen pioneer or inventor, consider the following specific questions:

- What did your individual achieve in their lifetime?
- What was the motivation of your individual?
- Is he or she an innovator or a pioneer or a developer? Explain your reasoning.
- In what ways did the country that they were living and working in help them to achieve their goals?
- In what ways did the time that they were working in help them to achieve their goals?
- Did their place of work, and/or the time in which they were living, hold them back in any way?
- What other factors influenced their innovations or pioneering work?

2 Plan your investigation.

3 Gather, record and document the source of relevant information

- State the research question clearly.
- Outline the scope of your research – the timeframe and dates you will focus on and the different lines of argument or themes you will research.
- Outline the methods you will use to research your question.
  ◊ What types of sources will you look for?
  ◊ Why would you attempt to find primary and secondary sources?
  ◊ Why would you look at different historians' viewpoints?
- State which method you will use to record and reference/cite your sources.

4 Communicate your information with structure and style.

5 Reflect on your investigation.

You will have to **evaluate** your process and your results. Think about the following questions to guide your reflection:

- How did the initial planning process aid in the development of the final report?
- What type of sources did you find most useful and least useful in the development of your report? What other sources could you have used to improve your final report?
- How could you have organized your information to develop your arguments more effectively?

■ **Figure 2.9** Planning and communicating research

▼ Interdisciplinary links

Think about the other subjects you are studying. Who would you describe as a pioneer, innovator or developer in those fields? For example, you could consider Berthold Brecht in Theatre arts; Alan Turing in Mathematics and Computer science; and Stephen Hawking in Physics.

Explore the idea of innovators and pioneers in your Science classes. Who are the significant innovators and pioneers of modern science?

! Take action

! As a class, review your findings on different pioneers, innovators and developers in your own countries.

! Are there any pioneers, developers or innovators from today who you think will help change the lives of individuals, or the world as a whole, for the better?

! Conduct brief interviews with teachers in different subject areas (for example, Mathematics, Languages, Arts and Science) and find out who they consider to be a pioneer or innovator in their subject in the twenty-first century. Are there any individuals or groups that are identified in more than one subject area?

! You could create a display of twenty-first century pioneers, innovators and developers.

Reflection

In this chapter we have looked at examples of men and women who have been considered inventors and pioneers. We have also analysed the reasons for their success.

Reflecting on our learning …
Use this table to reflect on your own learning in this chapter.

Questions we asked	Answers we found	Any further questions now?			
Factual					
Conceptual					
Debatable					
Approaches to learning you used in this chapter:	Description – what new skills did you learn?	How well did you master the skills?			
		Novice	Learner	Practitioner	Expert
Communication skills					
Critical-thinking skills					
Information literacy skills					
Media literacy skills					
Transfer skills					
Learner profile attribute	*Reflect on the importance of being an inquirer for our learning in this chapter.*				
Inquirer					

3 Does trade and exchange promote cooperation or lead to exploitation?

○ **Cooperation** in trade can foster positive **global relations**; however, **global trade** based on exploitation is not **sustainable** and can cause **conflict**.

CONSIDER THESE QUESTIONS:

Factual: What trading routes had developed by the end of the nineteenth century? What aid and exchanges developed from trade?

Conceptual: How can interactions between states lead to cooperation and cultural exchange? How can interactions lead to exploitation and hostility?

Debatable: Does globalization harm more people than it helps?

Now **share and compare** your thoughts and ideas with your partner, or with the whole class.

■ **Figure 3.1** Different 'goods' being traded: silk, slaves and opium

○ IN THIS CHAPTER, WE WILL ...

■ **Find out** about some of the international trade routes and commodities.
■ **Explore:**
   ■ the factors that led trade to encourage aid and exchange as well as bring exploitation and tension
   ■ the ways in which trade can foster both international cooperation and international tension.
■ **Take action** by investigating human trafficking today.

KEY WORDS

commerce
famine
globalization
monopolies
privilege

■ These Approaches to Learning (ATL) skills will be useful ...

■ Communication skills
■ Critical-thinking skills
■ Information literacy skills
■ Transfer skills

ACTIVITY: Aspects of nineteenth-century trade

Look at the three images in Figure 3.1 and read Sources A and B. **Describe** the content of the images and the sources in pairs. **Identify** what is being traded and what the results of the trade might be for a) the traders and b) the purchasers. What factors in these sources do you find particularly surprising or shocking?

SOURCE A

'Slaves were an economic asset and their owners sought to use them in the most profitable fashion. Their importance to their owners – slave traders and planters – was reflected in the monetary value those owners noted in their ship's logs and plantation ledgers, often entering the commercial value of the individual slave alongside his own names, age, occupation and physical condition. Here were people, counted in their millions, whose lives were measured out by their monetary value to someone else. Africans carried an initial price on their heads when they first entered the slave ship and a new price when they were sold on landing in the Americas. Then, year after year, their value to their current owner in the Americas would rise and fall with fluctuations in their age, sickness or skills. In 1756 Thomas Thistlewood in Jamaica paid £43 for a 16 year old slave named Lincoln. Thirty years later the same man was valued at £50.'

Walvin, J. 2011. The Slave Trade. *London, UK. Thames & Hudson, p. 80.*

SOURCE B

'As Britain entered the [opium] trade at the end of the eighteenth century, they insisted that they were simply providing a service: satisfying, not creating demand. Those Britons involved were at pains to present it to audiences back home as quite the most honourable line of business in the East … It was also a hands-off and sure source of revenue for East India Company employees in India, who only had to look after the opium as far as Government House in Calcutta, letting private British and Indian, and then Chinese sellers handle the dirty business of getting it to the Chinese coast, and inland.'

Lovell, J. 2011. The Opium War. *Oxford, UK. Picador Macmillan.*

What were some of the key trades and trading routes?

In this chapter, we will be finding out about some of the key trades and trading routes that had developed by the end of the nineteenth century. We will examine the ancient spice and silk routes and how these had fostered cultural exchange and cooperation between different regions and societies. We will also consider the negative impact on international relations and societies caused by the exploitative trade in opium and slaves.

THE SPICE TRADE

The trade in spices dates back to the classical period of history. Civilizations in Asia, north-east Africa and Europe would trade spices such as cinnamon, ginger, pepper and turmeric as well as opium. The trade was conducted via sea routes and overland. Muslim traders dominated the maritime spice routes until the Europeans began to take over with a particular interest in the trade of pepper in the 1400s. The Portuguese explorer Vasco da Gama navigated a new route around the African coast to Asia in 1498.

Cultural exchanges due to trade

In Southeast Asia much of the economic activity created by the spice trade was managed by Buddhist and Hindu groups. These associations were trusted with the huge profits generated, and the funds were often used to benefit the local community. Religion spread through the spice routes, with Buddhism promoting art and **literacy**. Both Muslim and Christian traders were important to the trade, and at times competed to spread their religion and practices. The 'Spice Islands' in current-day Indonesia accommodated both religions.

The spice trade led to a sharing of languages and cultural customs between Europe, Africa and Asia. A common trading language was needed to facilitate commerce and after da Gama's successful opening of the maritime route, Portuguese was used for a time.

A shared language meant that different societies could more readily share their ideas with each other. In addition, food and cuisine travelled along the spice routes with the traders. Indonesian, Indian and Malaysian recipes mixed spices and ideas from each other's countries and the Portuguese introduced vinegar to India. By the nineteenth century, Britain had restaurants that offered a range of Indian dishes on the menu.

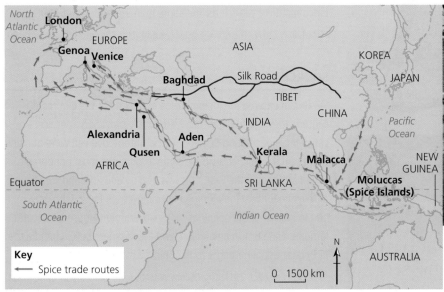

Figure 3.2 The spice trade routes

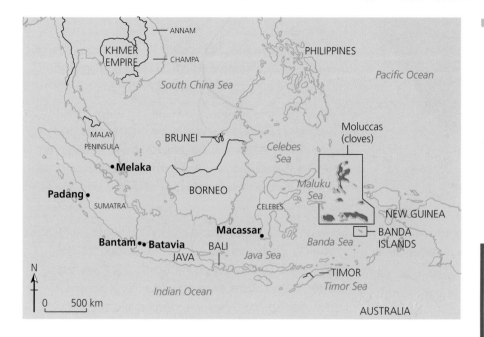

■ **Figure 3.3** The Spice Islands

Some explorers developed new spice trade routes by accident, for example Christopher Columbus attempted to find a new route to India and discovered America. Columbus, and other explorers, brought chillies back to Europe.

The USA engaged in the world spice trade from the early eighteenth century and traded directly with the Asian growers rather than through merchants in Europe. From the beginning of the nineteenth century, Massachusetts became a centre of the North American spice trade after one voyage from Salem to Indonesia earned a 700 per cent profit on its return with a cargo of pepper.

As more and more companies became involved in the trade, spices became more common. Their value began to fall and spices were no longer seen as a luxury but as an everyday item.

Asia remains the largest producer of spices today; however, other regions now compete for market share, for example Brazil is now a leading producer of pepper. The spice trade has historically been dominated by the leading economic powers of the time. Currently, the USA is the main purchaser of spices.

Although the spice trade led to cultural exchanges and the benefits to society of shared knowledge about medicines, etc. there was a negative side to the trade. Indeed, due to the lucrative nature of spices, countries were drawn into violent competition to dominate the market.

The competition between the Spanish and the Portuguese over the cloves trade in the sixteenth century was a key factor in fuelling the expansion of the European empires in the eighteenth and nineteenth centuries. The global spice trade led to international conflicts.

ACTIVITY: Source analysis

In pairs, consider Source C and **identify** the key points it makes about the spice trade.

SOURCE C

'It was evident that, in just two centuries, Europeans had changed the spice trade forever. The spices that were once limited to tiny islands in hidden archipelagos were being grown around the world and in large quantities. Trade routes that spanned oceans were becoming commonplace and, as such, competitive.

'The Dutch did their best to buck the trend [stop this development], destroying their stocks so blatantly that, according to one observer, the streets of Amsterdam were "flooded with nutmeg butter". But it was all in vain. Spices were no longer that hard to come by. Monopolies gave way to markets.'

'A taste of adventure: The history of spices is the history of trade'. The Economist. *17 December 1998.*

THE SILK TRADE

The Silk Route or Silk Road was a series of trading and cultural towns and passageways connecting Asia to Europe from China through India to the Mediterranean Sea. The route was over 6400 kilometres long and was named after its profitable trade and transport of silk.

It was not only goods and merchants that travelled the Silk Road, it also carried along its path pilgrims, holy men, soldiers and adventurers. The towns and villages along its route became wealthy, and many thrived as centres for cultural exchange. The Chinese wanted to protect their trade and extended the Great Wall to protect the Silk Route.

To trade and move goods along the Silk Road was extremely difficult due to the climate and geography, which included deserts and mountains (see map below). Goods were transported on pack animals – a camel caravan could be on the road for six months. There was also the constant danger of attack from bands of thieves.

The Silk Road had a major impact on the development of the civilizations in Asia and Europe. Its main traders changed over time, with Chinese, Persians, Greeks, Romans and Indians in the early modern era and Arab traders in the Middle Ages.

A wide variety of goods were traded on the route, and new technologies, medicine, ideas, philosophies and religions were also shared. Judaism, Buddhism, Christianity and Islam all spread through Asia and Europe at least in part due to the Silk Road.

Silk was used as a common currency and became a religious symbol. Its symbolism can be seen influencing the arts of different cultures involved in the trade. The Silk Road fostered many cultural exchanges and this promoted a better understanding between peoples and encouraged cooperation.

Initially, Buddhism was the religion that dominated the route and its monasteries provided places of sanctuary. Later, with its rise in Central Asia, Islam replaced Buddhism as the faith of influence on the Silk Road.

However, the paths along this route were also a means of spreading diseases from region to region. In fact some historians believe that the Silk Road was the route the Black Death followed to infect Europe from Asia in the mid-fouteenth century.

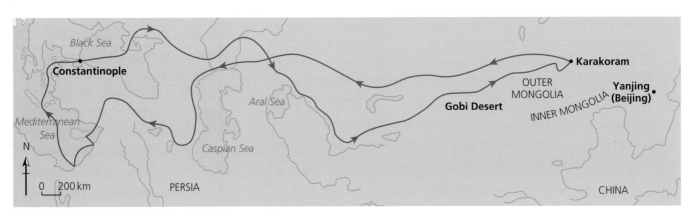

■ **Figure 3.4** The routes that together form the Silk Road

ACTIVITY: Exploring the Silk Road

■ ATL

- Transfer skills – Inquire in different contexts to gain a different perspective

1   Using Google Earth (or a similar mapping program), **describe** the length of the Silk Road and the types of territory covered.
    This website is also useful:

    http://web.stanford.edu/group/spice/SilkRoad/SilkRoad.html

2   Try to find the following cities on a map:
    - Chang'an (Xi'an)
    - Delhi
    - Kashgar
    - Ferghana Valley
    - Baghdad
    - Damascus
    - Rome

    Discuss the diversity of the geography of these locations. How might these locations influence the development and exchange of goods?

3   In small groups look at the list of goods traded along the Silk Road:
    - Chang'an (Xi'an): Silk, rhubarb, paper, gunpowder, mirrors
    - Delhi: Cotton, herbal medicine, jade
    - Kashgar: Pack animals, tea, dried fruit
    - Ferghana Valley: Horses, rugs, nuts, copper
    - Baghdad: Dates, dyes, lapis lazuli
    - Damascus: Almonds, purple dye, swords, glass, cloth
    - Rome: Gold coins, glass and glazes, grapevines, alfalfa

    Discuss these questions:
    - Why did traders take on such difficult, and dangerous, expeditions?
    - How does the region you live in help determine the way you do business?
    - What types of cultural exchange might result from this trade?
    - How might the Silk Route encourage cooperation between different societies and communities?

◆ Assessment opportunities

◆ In this activity you have practised skills that are assessed using Criterion D: Thinking critically.

THINK–PAIR–SHARE

In groups, choose a product that could be sold along the Silk Route today. It could be something that is modern and technology based or perhaps music from your region.

Consider:

a   what would be a product that would promote cooperation and understanding between different cultures
b   what barriers there might be to trade (e.g. language, local conflicts).

Now join with another group. What product did they choose? Which product, your group's or another group's, would be better for promoting cooperation and international understanding?

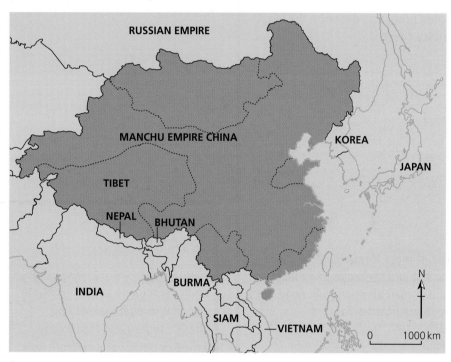

■ **Figure 3.5** China as the 'Middle Kingdom', at the start of the nineteenth century

THE OPIUM TRADE

Opium was also a significant part of international trade in the nineteenth century. It was used for both medicinal and recreational purposes and could offer merchants rich profits. However, opium is extremely addictive and the recreational use of opium was highly damaging to people's health. By the end of the eighteenth century, there were bans across Europe and in parts of Asia, including China, on the 'opium dens' or bars that sold the product to smoke. It was the attempt by British traders to breach Chinese law and continue to sell opium to the vast Chinese market that led to war between China and Britain in 1839. (See more on this on page 52.)

At the beginning of the nineteenth century China believed it was culturally superior to the rest of the world. Surrounded by tributary states or deserts or mountains, it saw itself as the Middle Kingdom.

▼ Links to: Languages

Writing Chinese names

The Chinese language does not use the system of letters familiar to speakers of European languages. It is therefore impossible to read (unless you have learnt Mandarin) and very difficult to use in a book written in a European language.

Chinese names (of people and places) have therefore been transliterated into a form that can be recognized and used. Until the 1980s the Wade–Giles system was used but more recently the Pinyin system has become the accepted version.

What this means is that there are often two versions of the same name. Older books will use one, and more modern books use the other. In this book, names are usually written in the Pinyin version, but in contemporary sources the Wade–Giles form may be used – with the Pinyin in brackets afterwards.

Here are both versions of some of the key names used in the text:

Wade–Giles (old)	Pinyin (new)
Canton	Guangzhou
Kuang Hsu	Guangxu
Kwantung	Guangdong
Liaotung	Liaodong
Nanking	Nanjing
Peking	Beijing
Tientsin	Tianjin
Tsingtao	Qingdao
Tzu Hsi	Cixi

The smaller states surrounding China had accepted 'tributary status' or, in other words, had accepted that they were inferior to China and paid 'tribute' to the greater power. These countries included Korea, Tibet and Vietnam.

The Chinese can claim many great achievements – including being the first to invent: paper, gunpowder, waterproof lacquer, money, drought-resistant rice, asbestos suits, credit cards, acupuncture, the compass, the rudder, seismographs for measuring earthquakes, and printing. They also had crossbows and cast iron more than a thousand years before the Europeans. They had mechanical clocks six hundred years before Europeans, too.

At the beginning of the nineteenth century, China had been ruled by a succession of royal dynasties for 3500 years. The head of the family was the Emperor, who was considered the Son of Heaven. All his subjects had to be unquestioningly loyal and obedient. The Emperor was said to have the 'Mandate of Heaven', which meant his authority was given by the gods. It was believed that when China had good harvests, and there was peace and prosperity, that mandate was secure. However, if the dynasty was successfully challenged by an army from within or a foreign invasion from outside – then the belief was that the Mandate of Heaven had shifted. Therefore, a ruling dynasty could lose the Mandate of Heaven.

From the 1640s the new ruling dynasty in China was the Manchu or the Qing dynasty. The Manchus came from the north-east and took over from the failing Ming Dynasty. However, they kept the capital in Beijing and retained the existing **civil service** to ensure the smooth running of the vast empire. They continued to use the old system of examinations to recruit new members to the bureaucracy. Manchu rule brought peace and stability to China. China was relatively wealthy and new intensive farming techniques were developed. This helped to foster a population explosion – the population grew from 150 million in 1700 to 400 million in 1850. The vast majority of these people were peasants.

ACTIVITY: A guide to nineteenth-century China

■ ATL

- Information literacy skills – Collect, record and verify data; Make connections between various sources of information; Process data and report results

Produce a tourist guide to China in the early nineteenth century. Your guide should include 700–1500 words, but you can choose the most appropriate format.

You need to research China between the dates of 1730 and 1830. You could use the following questions to guide your research:

- **How was China governed at the beginning of the nineteenth century?**
- **What were the key religions and beliefs in China at this time?**
- **What was life like for women in China at this time?**
- **How did people spend their leisure time?**
- **What types of art would you find in China at this time?**
- **What types of technology were there?**

Remind yourself how to develop an action plan and how to **evaluate** your results by looking back to Chapter 2, page 40.

> Hint
>
> Make sure you record the sources you use as you research nineteenth-century China and use one standard method of referencing.

◆ Assessment opportunities

- ◆ This activity can be assessed using Criterion B: Investigating and Criterion C: Communicating.

ⓘ Confucianism

As part of your research for your tourist guide, you will need to look at the impact of Confucianism on Chinese life and culture. This was a set of beliefs, founded on the teachings of Confucius, who had lived in the sixth–fifth century BCE.

What was Manchu China's attitude to trade with the West?

The Manchu did not want to develop contacts with the West. They resisted contact with European culture and attempted to prevent European merchants, who were increasingly interested in China, from entering the country. Britain was particularly interested in finding new markets for its manufactured goods. Britain also wanted to be able to access key Chinese goods as cheaply as possible – in particular, tea and silk. Other Europeans were interested in China for similar reasons. The Portuguese not only wanted the luxury goods that could be obtained from China, but also wanted to 'save Chinese souls' by sending missionaries there.

The Europeans did not have a good reputation in China: where the Chinese came into contact with them in the port cities, the Europeans behaved very badly. Often sailors would get drunk and get into fights and they were rude to the local Chinese. They were also ignorant of Chinese culture and customs, and unaware of local laws. The Chinese regarded the Europeans as barbarians who were rough, unshaven and uncivilized.

Finally, the Europeans were expelled from China. The Chinese authorities attempted a 'closed door' policy, which allowed only a limited amount of trade with the Europeans, and this could only take place in a restricted number of ports and under strict regulations. The Europeans hated these restrictions, but they also disadvantaged Chinese merchants – for example, two of the main commodities, silk and tea, often had to be transported hundreds of kilometres from villages and towns across China. The Westerners were allowed only to trade with 13 Hongs, which were business organizations set up to deal with the 'foreign devils'.

Figure 3.6 The Imperial Palace of the ruling Manchu dynasty

The Europeans were only permitted to enter small areas in these designated ports. They could not go outside of these areas. They were not allowed to bring their wives to the trading ports, and they were not allowed to settle in these areas. Ordinary Chinese people could not meet the European traders, and if any Chinese national was caught teaching the Chinese language to foreigners, death was the penalty.

The foreign merchants were not at all pleased with all these restrictions. They also did not want to be subject to Chinese laws, which they believed were inhumane and barbaric. A key issue for the merchants was that trade was made very expensive for them as the Chinese insisted on being paid in silver for their goods. This meant trade was 'one way' as the Chinese would not accept any Western goods in exchange for their tea and silk. The British were particularly hostile to this arrangement as they wanted to use China as a mass market for their manufactured goods.

The exchange of silver was also expensive for European merchants as they had to buy silver rather than using their readily available manufactured goods. Silver was also dangerous to carry in ships across the world from Europe to Asia because it was a target for pirates. This in turn made it expensive to insure.

Why did the opium trade lead to war between China and Britain in 1839?

LONG-TERM CAUSES OF WAR

Cultural and diplomatic differences

As we have seen, the Chinese saw themselves as the 'centre' of the world – the Middle Kingdom. However, by the early nineteenth century the British too believed themselves to be the number one power in the world, and the most civilized and cultured nation. Thus, the two countries viewed each other as 'inferior' and 'barbaric'.

Britain and China also clashed over how they engaged in international relations. The Chinese tribute system established China as the dominant nation in the region with 'inferior' states expected to offer gifts to China. The British also had a long-established system of 'diplomacy' by which to conduct international relations. This system assumed a degree of equality with foreign nations, but often Britain adopted a superior position. Britain's diplomats expected respect and privileged status.

Economic differences/attitude towards trade

The British were frustrated by China's 'closed door' trading system – known as the Canton system. They wanted an 'open door' or **'free trade'** policy – where their merchants and businesses could trade freely without restriction in China.

■ **Figure 3.7** Chinese Emperor Qianlong, who ruled from 1735 to 1796

The British sent two diplomatic missions to China tasked with improving trade relations between the two countries.

In 1793 an important British mission, led by Lord Macartney, went to China with instructions from King George III to set up diplomatic relations and trade agreements. The mission brought with it gifts for the Emperor and was royally entertained but it failed to secure trade agreements. To the Chinese, the idea of trading with Britain as an equal was abhorrent, and they viewed the mission not as an equal diplomatically but as one from a 'tribute' state paying homage to the Emperor.

An imperial response to the mission was sent to George III:

> 'Our celestial Empire possesses all things in prolific abundance and lacks no product within its own borders – there is therefore no need to import the manufactures of outside barbarians for our own produce. The Throne's principle is to treat strangers from afar with indulgence and exercise a pacifying influence over the barbarian tribes the world over. Your barbarian merchants will assuredly never be permitted to land there [Tientsin and Chekiang], but will be subject to instant expulsion. Tremblingly obey and show no negligence. A special Mandate.'
>
> *Quoted in Roper, M. 1981.* Emperor's China: People's China.

A second mission in 1816 was also unsuccessful. The leader of the mission, Lord Amherst, outraged the Chinese court when he refused to 'kowtow' to the Emperor. The kowtow was a ceremonial gesture made when meeting a person of higher social rank. To perform a kowtow you made three deep bows, prostrating yourself three times after each one with your nose touching the floor. The kowtow operated on all social levels in China – children to their parents, courtiers to the Emperor and the Emperor to Heaven. Lord Amherst refused to demean himself by lying face down on the floor! The Chinese saw his refusal as extremely bad manners and it confirmed their view of Europeans as barbarians.

The two British missions failed to set up full diplomatic relations or to relax trade restrictions for Britain's merchants. They also showed up the key cultural differences and misunderstandings between Britain and China.

ACTIVITY: Source analysis

In pairs, consider the extent to which Source D's description is supported by the image in Source E.

SHORT-TERM CAUSES OF WAR

The dispute over the opium trade

The British merchants wanted to end the massive flow of silver from Britain to China. They wanted to find something they could trade that would interest the Chinese market. They came up with the idea of selling opium to China. Opium is a narcotic drug that for centuries had been used medicinally in China to relieve pain. But the British introduced the drug as a recreational habit, and, being highly addictive, smoking opium quickly took hold in China.

A key motive for the British traders was that the demand for Chinese tea had grown at home, which offered vast profits for companies. The main company trading with China was the British East India Company. This company had sponsored the growing of opium poppies in India. Originally opium had been popular in European cities – where the bars known as 'opium dens' were set up. Due to the horrific impact of opium addiction on the general public, European governments banned the drug. This meant that the growing companies needed a new market.

SOURCE D

A British observer in China wrote of those addicted to opium:

'The evils which arise from opium-smoking are many. It injures the health and physical powers, especially of the working and poorer classes, whose wages are only sufficient to meet their necessities, and who curtail the amount spent on food and clothing to gratify their craving for the vice … Those who have yielded to it for years, and who are slaves to the pipe, are miserable if circumstances should arise to debar them from their accustomed whiffs: it is extraordinary to see how perfectly wretched they are; every attitude, every feature of the face, every sentence, is a living witness that they are in agony till the craving is satisfied. The opium sots or 'opium devils', as the natives term them, are pitiable objects, emaciated almost to a skeleton, until they finally succumb to their vice …'

Quoted in Ball, J. D. 1903. Things Chinese. *Hong Kong. Kelly & Walsh.*

SOURCE E

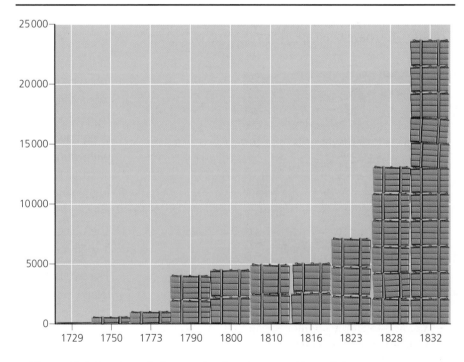

■ **Figure 3.8** Number of chests of opium imported into China

The East India Company exchanged vast amounts of opium for tea in China. The social and economic impact of the drug soon had an effect on the Chinese authorities. Opium addiction destroyed families, with some poor families selling their own children to fund their habit.

Instead of silver flowing into China, silver now poured out into the hands of the British opium traders. Indeed, the demand for opium far outweighed the demand for tea. It became far more profitable than selling tea and silk to the home markets. For the Chinese government, opium was not only a social problem but an economic one too, as the Chinese population became less productive. In response the Chinese passed two laws banning the importation of the drug in 1729 and 1796. To get around this ban, and continue making huge profits, the East India Company began to sell opium to Chinese merchants who were able to smuggle it into China. Despite the bans the opium trade grew and grew.

The trade was so lucrative that merchants from other countries, including Portugal, France and America, also got involved.

ACTIVITY: Action plan for the Imperial Government of China, 1838

ATL

- Critical-thinking skills – Gather and organize relevant information to formulate an argument; Consider ideas from multiple perspectives

Task

You and a partner are Chinese officials in the nineteenth century. You have been asked by the Emperor to solve the key problems facing China at this time:

- **More and more Chinese people are becoming addicted to opium.**
- **Many officials are becoming corrupted and are taking part in the opium trade themselves.**
- **China is losing a lot of wealth to Western countries because of the opium trade.**

Requirements

You need to fill in a copy of the proposal to the Emperor, set out on the right. It is up to you to decide what action your government should take.

Some options are:

- **Arrest, try and execute all Westerners found guilty of dealing in the opium trade.**
- **Confiscate all the opium you can find and destroy it; refuse to give compensation to the Westerners who were selling it.**
- **Execute or imprison all Chinese who are opium addicts.**
- **Threaten the Western powers with war unless they stop selling opium.**
- **Offer to make a lot of concessions to the West – open up ports to trade, give them the right to live in China, allow them to be tried in their own courts *if* they stop selling opium.**

Action Plan for the Imperial Government of China, 1838

Your Majesty, I your humble slave recommend the following:

With regard to the opium situation and the foreign devils we should ...

I predict that, as a result of this action, the English barbarians will react as follows ...

◆ Assessment opportunities

- ◆ This activity can be assessed using Criterion A: Knowing and understanding.

Figure 3.9 Chinese official, Lin Zexu, overseeing the destruction of opium in Guangzhou

Lin Zexu attempts to stop the opium trade

In 1838, Emperor Dao Guang, who ruled from 1820 to 1850, sent Commissioner Lin Zexu to Guangzhou to finally end the opium trade. Lin ordered the confiscation of all the British merchants' opium supplies. In all, 20 283 chests of the drug were seized and destroyed. The merchants were furious. The new Superintendent of Trade in China, Captain Charles Elliott, then promised the merchants compensation from the British government.

Lin did not only attempt to end the trade by force, he also appealed to the British monarch, Queen Victoria, to assist the Chinese government.

ACTIVITY: Response to Lin Zexu

■ ATL

■ Critical-thinking skills – Evaluate evidence and arguments

With reference to Lin Zexu's letter (right), answer the following questions:

1 In pairs, **identify** the key points made by Lin in his letter and write these out in a bullet point **list**.
2 Underline where Lin seems to be trying not to offend the British.
3 In pairs, reflect on how you think the British responded to Lin's letter. Write down your ideas.

The Way of Heaven is fairness to all; it does not suffer us to harm others in order to benefit ourselves. Men are alike in this the world over: that they cherish life and hate what endangers life …

But there is a class of evil foreigner that makes opium and brings it for sale, tempting fools to destroy themselves, merely in order to reap profit … it appears that this poisonous article is manufactured by certain devilish persons in places subject to your rule. It is not, of course, either made or sold at your bidding, nor do all the countries you rule produce it, but only certain of them. I am told that in your own country opium smoking is forbidden under severe penalties. This means that you are aware of how harmful it is. But better than forbid the smoking of it would be to forbid the sale of it and, better still, to forbid the production of it, which is the only way of cleansing the contamination at its source. So long as you do not take it yourselves, but continue to make it and tempt the people of China to buy it, you will be showing yourselves careful of your own lives, but careless of the lives of other people, indifferent in your greed for gain to the harm you do to others …

Letter from Lin Zexu to Queen Victoria. Quoted in Waley, A. 1968. The Opium War Through Chinese Eyes.

IMMEDIATE CAUSE OF WAR

Britain claims extraterritoriality

Tension between Britain and China intensified. The trigger for the outbreak of war came not from an incident specifically to do with the opium trade – but as the result of the murder of a Chinese national by drunken British sailors in a fight in the city of Kowloon. Charles Elliott paid compensation to the Chinese man's family, but the Chinese authorities wanted the culprits handed over to stand trial. The British refused, arguing that the men would not get a fair trial under Chinese law as confessions were extracted under torture. They also objected to the public execution the men faced if they were found guilty.

Therefore, the trigger for war was the British attempt to claim **extraterritoriality**.

The British conducted their own trial of the men and did not hand them over to the Chinese authorities. In retaliation, Lin ordered the ports to be **blockaded** and stopped food supplies to foreigners. The British response was to send warships to Guangzhou to 'protect their interests'. These warships then destroyed a large number of inferior Chinese war junks, leading to a huge loss of life.

The British were then expelled from Guangzhou – which led to 20 warships being sent to China with 4000 troops on board. These bombarded Guangzhou and then sailed up and down the coast, causing many deaths and widespread destruction.

🛈 Extraterritoriality

Extraterritoriality is where people are exempted from local law. In the nineteenth century, the British claimed extraterritoriality for their nationals working in China. This meant that if a foreign national committed a crime in Chinese law they could not be prosecuted in China's courts but would be judged under the jurisdiction of their own government.

■ **Figure 3.10** The destruction of Chinese war junks, 1841

THE END OF THE FIRST OPIUM WAR

The First Opium War lasted from 1839 until 1842. The British forces were better trained and better armed – the Chinese were no match for them. The Chinese were fighting to stop the import of opium into their country – and the British fought to protect this lucrative trade. Many historians have suggested that this war was one of the most shameful in British history.

The war ended with the signing of the Treaty of Nanjing. The treaty did not mention the opium trade, which had been the key cause of the conflict.

🛈 Treaty of Nanjing

The terms of the treaty included:
- Four additional ports were to be opened up to trade with the West.
- The British were no longer to be subject to Chinese law – but were to be subject to the laws of their own country (extraterritoriality).
- The British were to have special rights in areas where they lived, called 'Concession Areas'.
- The Chinese had to pay 21 million silver dollars in compensation for the war. They also had to pay for all the opium they had destroyed.
- In all future dealings, China had to treat Britain as an 'equal'.
- Britain was to be given the port city of Hong Kong.
- Britain was given 'most favoured nation' status, which meant that it could demand the same rights granted by China to any other country.

The Manchu rulers were not consulted on the terms of the treaty, nor did they have any choice but to sign it. British ships threatened to again bombard Chinese coastal towns until the treaty was signed. This was the first 'unequal treaty'. It was unequal because Chinese interests were completely ignored.

After the war, opium flowed into China in ever increasing quantities. The Chinese authorities could only impose harsher and harsher punishments on users to try to cut down on the drug use. For example, possession of the drug was punishable by beheading, and the drug user's family could not sit the civil service exams for three generations. France, the Netherlands and the USA increased their involvement in selling opium in China too.

WHY WAS THERE A SECOND OPIUM WAR?

Another war broke out between China and Britain in 1856. This time the war was triggered by an incident involving a ship called the *Arrow*. The ship was flying a British flag – although it was owned by a Hong Kong Chinese – and it was boarded by Chinese officials who believed that there were some well-known pirates on board. The Chinese police arrested the crew but in the struggle that followed the British flag was torn down. The British were furious and ordered the release of the crew and an official apology for the treatment of the flag. The Chinese returned the crew but did not apologize. Chinese gangs attacked and set fire to British homes and warehouses and the British warships bombarded Guangzhou. War broke out again, and again the Chinese were humiliated. The war ended in 1858 with another unequal treaty, the Treaty of Tientsin.

ⓘ Treaty of Tientsin

- Six more ports were opened to foreign trade.
- Opium importation to China was made legal with a small import duty.
- Christian missionaries were to be given complete freedom to convert people.
- Europeans were allowed to travel anywhere in China without restriction.
- Ambassadors of European countries were allowed to set up residence in Beijing – the Imperial capital.

Tension remained high between the British and the Chinese – the latter attempted to resist fully implementing the unequal treaties. In 1860 British and French troops were sent to Beijing to enforce the terms of the treaties. While they were there, allegedly in response to the death of 21 members of a negotiating team, the troops looted and burnt the Imperial Summer Palace and forced the Emperor to flee into exile. The violence was widespread and the Chinese were again forced to sue for 'peace' and grant even more concessions (see information box below).

China had been utterly defeated and demoralized. By the end of the nineteenth century, Britain, France and Germany had seized huge territories in China, which were known as their 'spheres of influence'. Russia had also taken territory in the north, and had gained influence in Manchuria and Mongolia. The final humiliation came in 1894–95, when China was beaten by a much smaller Asian nation – Japan. Japan had formerly been a tributary state. Japan took control of Korea, Taiwan and the Ryukyu islands.

ⓘ Concession of Beijing

- Reaffirmed the rights of diplomats to live in Beijing
- Increased the cash compensation China had to pay
- Gave the Kowloon Peninsular to the British

What were the effects of the opium wars on China?

The unequal treaties gave foreign powers certain advantages:

- They had control and/or influence in some Chinese cities.
- The import of opium was now legal.
- The Chinese had to agree low tariffs on imported manufactured goods from Europe, which damaged China's own industries.
- Extraterritoriality meant that the Chinese government had no effective control over foreigners in their own country.
- The tribute system was ended.
- Missionaries were now able to live and work in China (this led to a lot of discontent).
- Britain had 'most favoured nation' status.

China had been thoroughly humiliated by the West, but the social and political structure of China remained intact. The Emperor still controlled the country; however, he needed to deal with the situation that the unequal treaties had created. Some Chinese began to believe that the Mandate of Heaven may have shifted away from the ruling dynasty.

HOW DID WESTERN INFLUENCE AND EXPLOITATION AFFECT CHINA DOMESTICALLY?

While China was facing external threats from the Western powers, it was also having to deal with several internal rebellions. The largest of these was the Taiping Rebellion, which lasted from 1850 to 1864. The rebellion was led by a Christian convert who claimed to be the younger brother of Jesus. He said that God had instructed him to drive the Manchu rulers out of China. This was a serious rebellion and at one time the Taipings controlled one-third of China and had their capital in Nanjing. The rebellion was finally put down by Imperial forces but with the help of European troops. The Europeans wanted to crush the rebellion to prevent the Taipings damaging their trading interests.

The rebellion caused devastation over parts of China. The damage to agriculture and trade meant that fewer people could pay taxes and so government income was reduced. Millions of people died in the fighting which took place between the Taipings and Imperial troops – some historians have estimated there were as many as 20 million casualties.

However, the fact that the Imperial troops had to have assistance from the foreigners to put down this internal rebellion was a further sign of the ruling dynasty's weakness. It demonstrated how dependent the Qing rulers had become on foreign forces to maintain control. It also again showed the significance of the superiority of Western technology.

HOW SHOULD CHINA'S GOVERNMENT RESPOND TO EXCHANGE WITH THE WEST?

In the late 1850s and 1860s contact between Westerners and Chinese increased. This led some Chinese officials to realize that the country would remain weak unless an effort was made to learn Western technology. The leading reformers believed that modernization should be introduced, but without abandoning the Confucian way of life. In other words, their aim was not to Westernize China but to build a strong defence against the foreign powers. The modernizing movement was known as the 'self-strengthening' movement.

SOURCE F

Feng Kuei-Fen

'We should set up translation offices at Canton and Shanghai to translate Western books. Brilliant students up to 15 years of age should be selected to live in these schools. Westerners should be invited to teach them Western languages and Chinese teachers should teach them traditional subjects. These students should learn Mathematics. (Note: all Western knowledge is based on Mathematics. Every Westerner of ten years of age or more studies Mathematics. If we wish to adopt Western knowledge we must learn Mathematics.)

'After three years, all students who have memorized the various Western books should become graduates and if there are some very clever ones who are able to suggest changes and improvements, they should be given a higher degree. There are many brilliant people in China – there must be some who can learn from the barbarians and do better than them.

'If we let Chinese customs remain the basis of our society and add Western methods of becoming rich and strong, this would be the best policy.'

▼ Links to: Mathematics

Is there a relationship between Mathematics and the modernization and advancement of Western societies?

Find out more about Mathematics and culture by using the search term ethnomathematics in classrooms.

Consider this in relation to your own culture and daily life.

SOURCE G

Wo-Jen

'I agree that scholars should learn Mathematics. But I think that Mathematics are of very little use. If these subjects are going to be taught by Westerners it will do great damage.

'The way to make a country great is for it to behave correctly – according to its customs. If we let the barbarians be teachers the cunning barbarians may not teach us the real secrets of their strength.

'Even if the teachers do genuinely teach, all we will achieve is the training of mathematicians. I have never heard of anyone who could use Mathematics to increase a nation's power. And, our Empire is so big that we have the people with the necessary ability. If Mathematics has to be taught we should find Chinese who have mastered it. Why is it necessary to learn from the barbarians?'

The self-strengthening movement had very limited success in modernizing China. This was, in part, due to the divisions within the movement itself. The movement lasted from 1860 until the outbreak of the Sino-Japanese war in 1894. The movement initially just borrowed Western technology. In the later years, it included the development of Western-style industries, schools and improving the transport and communication systems in China.

The fact that China was defeated by Japan in 1895 demonstrated the failure of the self-strengthening movement.

WHY DID SELF-STRENGTHENING FAIL?

- Many of the reforms were carried out at a local level by provincial governors but lacked support from the Imperial court. Many Chinese officials believed that Western learning might weaken their power. This meant there could be no overall coherent plan for modernization.
- The Empress Dowager Cixi, who effectively ruled China from 1861 until her death in 1908, did not believe in reform. She spent the money intended to build a new Imperial navy on a new Summer Palace!
- There was no attempt to introduce a full programme of industrial and social change. The reformers wanted to maintain a society that was based on Confucian ideas, but with Western technology. However, industrialization was impossible without social change.
- There was a lack of money to invest in the new projects.

■ **Figure 3.11** The opening of the first railway in China in 1876; it was built by the British but dismantled by the Chinese government a year later

DISCUSS

Refer back to Chapter 1, which investigated Japan's reaction to Western ideas and influence. **Explore** the differences between the approaches of China and Japan to the West.

ACTIVITY: The new railways come to China

■ **ATL**

- Communication skills – Read critically and for comprehension; Make effective summary notes

Read the following extract from C. Hibbert's *The Dragon Wakes* in Source H. It discusses the Chinese attitude towards the new railways and telegraph systems that began to be built across China between 1864 and 1891.

Briefly **summarize** – in bullet-point notes – the reasons why self-strengthening may have failed according to this extract.

SOURCE H

'Railways carried "fire-carts" and rattling, iron-wheeled wagons all over the country, desecrating burial places, disturbing the spirits of the earth, putting honest carters and porters, trackers and boatmen, muleteers and camel men out of work. Equally obnoxious were the foreign operators of the chugging steamships on the inland waterways, the foreign mining engineers whose deep shafts upset the feng-shui even more than the railway tracks did, the foreign mechanics who put up the wires and the poles for the telegraph companies.

[A member of the Boxer movement who wanted to rid China of the 'foreign devils' commented:]

'The iron roads and iron carriages are disturbing the terrestrial dragon and are destroying the earth's beneficial influences … the red liquid which keeps dripping from the iron snake [the rust coloured rain water that dripped from the telegraph wires] is nothing but the blood of the out-raged spirits of the air.'

Quoted in Hibbert, C. 1970. The Dragon Wakes: China and the West, 1793–1911.

Did the West bring aid to China in the nineteenth century?

CHRISTIAN MISSIONARIES

Christian missionaries aimed to bring aid to China. They set up orphanages, schools and hospitals. They also provided famine relief and medicines for the poor. However, their mission was to convert the Chinese people to Christianity. Some Christian activities were viewed with suspicion by locals, and hostility towards the 'hairy barbarians' grew. Christian churches were seen as being weighed down by their high steeples and were a threat to the spirits of the earth. The Chinese did not understand why missionaries opened orphanages for unwanted children who were bound to die anyway. They readily believed rumours that the **missionaries** were using the children's bodies for magical potions. The missionary practice of offering money for unwanted children led to criminals kidnapping children for the cash. Sometimes the missionaries attempted to look more Chinese – but dressing like the locals offended them too.

The religious ceremonies of the missionaries were alleged to include cannibalism, as encouraged by the practice of eating the body and drinking the blood of their god. Their converts, 'secondary devils', were said only to pretend to believe in order to get rice.

Indeed, the Chinese were warned that:

- missionaries extracted the eyes, marrow and heart of the dead to make medicines
- drinks offered by missionaries were poison
- those who attended their religious services would become 'bewitched'
- children in orphanages were killed.

Suspicion and fear of the missionaries at times led to attacks on them. There was a massacre of nuns and priests at Tientsin in 1870.

■ **Figure 3.12** Boxers heading for the city of Tientsin

ⓘ

The Boxer Rebellion

Tensions between the Chinese and foreigners exploded in The Boxer Rebellion, which started in 1900. An anti-foreign movement known as The Boxers aimed to remove all 'foreign devils' from China. They attacked foreigners' businesses and Chinese businesses that sold foreign goods. The rebellion ended in a siege of Europeans in a European compound in Beijing. However, the Boxers, who believed that they were invincible to foreign weapons and were armed with only basic weaponry, were defeated by a force of 2000 troops from Britain, France, Russia, Japan and America.

How can interactions lead to exploitation and hostility?

THE SLAVE TRADE

During the late 1400s a trade in human beings began to develop between Europe and Africa. This trade in slaves was to last until the end of the nineteenth century. It led to depopulation and economic underdevelopment in Africa and great wealth for many Europeans. The slave trade increased when the Europeans discovered the Americas in the 1500s and there was a corresponding increase in the demand for labour. Indeed, by the late 1700s, sugar and cotton **plantations** were established in the Americas and these were labour intensive. Most slaves destined for the Americas were exported from the west coast of Africa. Historians do not agree on the total number of men, women and children taken as slaves from Africa during this period – but a recent estimate put the figure at 11 million people. Over one-tenth of those shipped across the Atlantic died due to the appalling conditions on board slave ships.

■ **Figure 3.13** Slaves being boarded onto a slave ship on the west coast of Africa

■ **Figure 3.14** An engraving of a slave auction in the USA

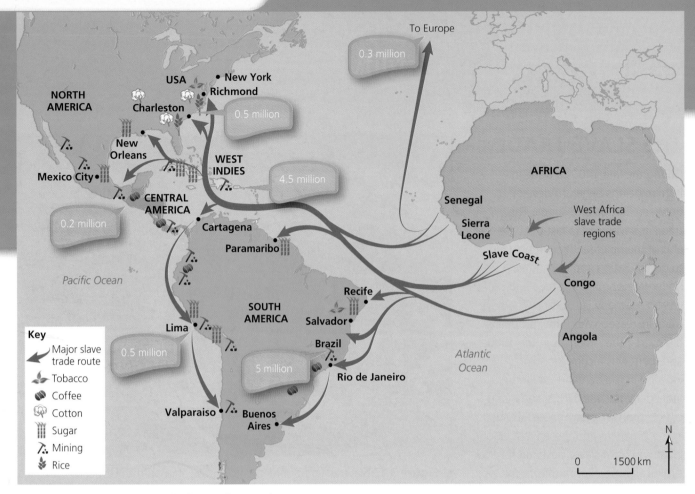

Figure 3.15 The slave trade from Africa to the Americas

In addition, people captured in the interior of Africa often died en route to the slave ports on the west coast. Any attempts to fight back and resist were brutally supressed. Despite this, historians have suggested that there were rebellions on as many as one in five slave ships.

There were also slave ports on the east coast of Africa, from where Africans were enslaved in the Arab world through this period. Some estimates have put the total enslaved from the east coast at 14 million people. The total number of Africans enslaved was staggering.

It was not only the trade in human beings that exploited the African continent – its raw materials were traded too.

The following sources relate to the slave trade in the eighteenth and nineteenth centuries.

SOURCE I

Testimony of James Perry, the captain of a slave ship, to a British Parliamentary Committee, 1789

- 'The slave ships at Liverpool are built on purpose for this trade and are accommodated with air ports and gratings for the purpose of keeping the slaves cool.
- The slaves are comfortably lodged in rooms fitted for them, which are washed and fumigated every day.
- The whole of the slaves are brought upon deck every day, when the weather permits.
- The surgeon also generally attends to wash their mouths with vinegar or lime juice in order to prevent scurvy.
- A warm meal is provided for them.
- They are amused with instruments of music of their own country.
- The women are supplied with beads which they make into ornaments.
- The reputation of the Captain, the officers, the surgeons and their future employment depend on the care they take of the slaves.'

SOURCE J

From the autobiography of Olaudah Equiano, a former slave

'One day, two of my wearied countrymen who were chained together jumped into the sea: immediately another quite dejected fellow, who on account of his illness was allowed to be out of irons, also followed their example … Two of the wretches were drowned but they got the other, and afterwards flogged him unmercifully for preferring death to slavery. In this manner we continued to undergo more hardships than I can now tell, hardships which are inseparable from this accursed trade.'

Equiano, O. 1789. The Interesting Narrative of the Life of Olaudah Equiano.

SOURCE K

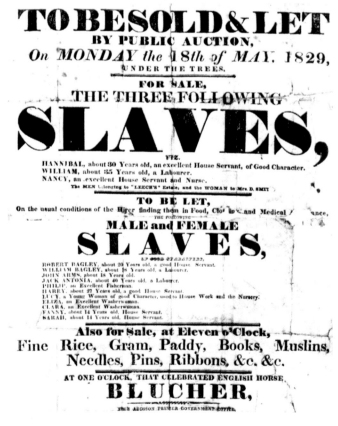

■ **Figure 3.16** Poster for a slave auction, published in 1829

SOURCE L

'We know of numerous local merchants in Europe's major slave ports, Liverpool and Bordeaux for example, established family fortunes and trading dynasties through investing in slave ships and plantations … In truth, the wealth created by slavery was shared out in ways that are not always obvious. Financial institutions in 18th century Britain and 19th century USA – banks and insurance companies – invested in slave ships, plantations and slaving ventures. Indeed, many other institutions benefitted from the slaving business. Major American universities, Yale and Brown for example, profited from slavery. The Bank of England was active in slaving investments … many of those working in senior positions on the slave ships and plantations enjoyed rewards gained from slavery … The economics of slavery permeated American and European life … The ownership of slaves had, by the 1830s, become widely dispersed, especially through metropolitan British life. The same was true in the United States where, on the eve of the Civil War, 400,000 people owned slaves. Clearly, slavery made some people very rich.'

Walvin, J. 2011. The Slave Trade. *London. UK. Thames & Hudson*, pp. 122–26.

SOURCE M

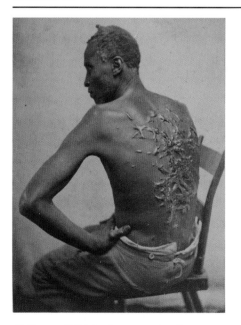

■ **Figure 3.17** A photograph of an escaped slave called Peter or Gordon, showing his scars, 1863

THE EFFECTS OF THE SLAVE TRADE

As the market for slaves grew, it led to internal conflict in Africa as merchants and traders attempted to meet the demand. The only beneficiaries in Africa were the rulers and wealthy merchants who engaged in the slave trade. A factor facilitating the trade was the lack of a national or regional identity in Africa and this could be used in the slave trader's favour. With growing demand, raids and local wars were ignited in order to seize captives and prisoners of war to sell on. European traders also exchanged guns and ammunition for slaves and this led to more internal conflict.

The slave trade led to population stagnation and in some places population decline. It arrested the economic development of African nations and laid the way for the colonial conquest of Africa in the nineteenth century. Slavery was justified by racist ideologies that developed throughout this period. You will examine these ideologies in more depth in Chapter 7.

It was not until 1833 that Britain abolished slavery throughout its empire. The trade had enriched Britain, providing work for shipbuilders and sailors, had led to an increase in the demand for metals and cloth to exchange for slaves in Africa and, of course, provided huge profits from the sale of slaves. The trade helped to fuel the Industrial Revolution in Britain. It also improved the standard of living for many British people and made goods such as sugar, tobacco and rum freely available. Whole cities flourished due to the slave trade, particularly Liverpool and Bristol. However, the trade had a wholly negative impact on African nations where the main export became human beings. Not only did it reduce the population, but it also meant that Africa did not have its own industrial revolution. Industry in fact declined because there was no need to manufacture cloth, or mine for metals and ores, as these items were imported by the Europeans in exchange for slaves. The racial inequality at the heart of the slave trade undermined African rulers and destroyed tribal customs and traditions. It also damaged African society by causing tribal conflicts, which in turn led to periodic famine.

EXTENSION

Explore further … Look into the famous slave revolt on the island of Haiti.

In April 1791, a rebellion of African slaves against their French slave masters began on the Caribbean island of Haiti. The revolt spread and became highly organized with inspirational and brilliant military leaders, such as Jean-Jacques Dessalines. The French were ultimately defeated in 1803 and Haiti became the first independent country run by a former Africa slave.

What was the international response to this new state?

■ ATL

■ Information literacy skills – Collect, record and verify data; Make connections between various sources of information

Think

First, brainstorm what you already know about slaves and how they lived and worked on plantations.

Puzzle

Then, in pairs, brainstorm and write down a **list** of questions you would like to ask to find out more about the lives of slaves on plantations. Sort these questions into factual questions, conceptual questions and debatable questions.

Explore

In pairs, research the answers to your questions.

Share your results with the rest of the class. What are your conclusions about slave life?

WHY DID SLAVERY CONTINUE IN THE USA UNTIL 1865?

Initially, the transatlantic slave trade supplied the sugar plantations of the Caribbean and Spanish America with only a small fraction of the slaves being sent to North America. However, throughout the seventeenth century slavery was legalized in the British colonial states. By the time of the American Revolution, and the American Declaration of Independence in 1776, there were vast cotton and tobacco plantations in the southern states that depended on slave labour. Slavery was key to the economy of the southern states in the USA.

There were several slave rebellions and by the turn of the nineteenth century an anti-slavery or 'abolitionist' movement had developed across North America. In 1808 the USA banned the import or export of slaves but did not ban the internal slave trade. The northern states in the USA began to pass legislation banning slavery despite the southern states' determination to retain it. The actions of the abolitionist movement provoked outrage with some plantation owners in the south. A network of 'safe houses' was developed, in which runaway slaves could hide before making their way to Canada and freedom. In 1854 armed conflict broke out in Kansas when it had to vote on whether to join the union as a 'free' or 'slave' state. The issue of slavery divided the nation and was a key cause of the American Civil War between the northern and southern states that broke out in 1861.

During the American Civil War, President Lincoln declared the Proclamation of Emancipation in 1863, which gave slaves their freedom. At the end of the civil war the USA went through a period of reconstruction and slavery was ended throughout the southern states. However racism continued, and in the South laws were implemented that led to the **segregation** of Blacks from Whites until the 1960s. You will study the movement to end racial prejudice and give all Americans civil rights in Chapter 11.

The UN Declaration of Human Rights in 1948 prohibited slavery in any form. Article 4 states:

> 'No one shall be held in slavery or servitude; slavery and the slave trade shall be prohibited in all their forms.'

DISCUSS

Using Sources I–L, and your own knowledge, assess the impact of the globalization of trade.

! Take action

! The UN Declaration of Human Rights outlawed slavery in any form in 1948. However, human trafficking remains an international problem. Indeed, some estimates suggest that almost 30 million people are living in slavery today. Particularly vulnerable to human trafficking are children.

! In groups, investigate modern-day slavery. You can look for newspaper articles from your own country and compare these with evidence from other countries and regions.

! Prepare a presentation for your year group or school on the issue of human trafficking and the organizations that attempt to stop the twenty-first-century slave trade.

What is the importance of aid?

During the period of trade you have studied in this unit there was little associated 'aid' from the companies and governments that benefited from the interactions with countries that were less developed and potentially prone to famine and disease. The European and American missionaries who went to Africa and Asia through to the twentieth century attempted to offer support and 'aid' to communities

> ### ⓘ International aid
>
> Aid refers to the transfer of goods or services from one country to another with the aim of helping the recipient country. Bilateral aid is where money or assistance is provided by one country to another. Multilateral aid is provided through an organisation such as Oxfam.

such as famine relief, the provision of orphanages, basic education and some labour and medical expertise. However, their main goal was to spread the Christian doctrine and to 'save souls' by converting people to Christianity. (See page 60 for the results of such 'aid' in China.)

However, the twentieth century has seen a growth in 'aid' from developed to developing countries. As you will study in Chapter 8, the First World War led to the establishment of the League of Nations. This international organization had several committees that were dedicated to aiding communities globally. This foundation for aid was developed further after the Second World War with the formation of the United Nations. The UN has many dedicated bodies that focus on crisis response, health care, welfare, and social and economic development.

ACTIVITY: International trade and globalization

■ ATL

■ Communication skills – Collaborate with peers using a variety of digital environments and media

In small groups, review the material in this chapter.

1 **Identify the positives of international trade and globalization and the negatives of international trade and globalization.**
2 **Consider what principles may make international trade more positive for all societies. Using the IB Learner Profile attributes, select attributes that would be useful as guidelines for the global markets.**
3 **How can the international community ensure that trade is fair?**

Present your findings to the class. You could use a poster, or PowerPoint or other visual aids.

◆ Assessment opportunities

◆ This activity can be assessed using Criterion A: Knowing and understanding, Criterion C: Communicating and Criterion D: Thinking critically.

ACTIVITY: The impact of aid?

■ ATL

■ Criticial-thinking skills – Analyse and evaluate issues and ideas

In groups inquire into one aid initiative or programme in the twentieth century. Explore the following:

a **aims of the initiative or programme**
b **which country or countries were to benefit**
c **evidence of success**
d **evidence of failure.**

Now, take a copy of a map of the world. As each group feeds back in a short 10-minute presentation, plot on the map which countries received aid.

In your groups now discuss the following:

1 **Which initiatives or programmes were the most successful?**
2 **Which were more successful: bilateral or multilateral programmes?**

As a class, what conclusions can be drawn about what makes aid effective?

ACTIVITY: Aid or trade?

■ ATL

- Communication skills – Use a variety of speaking techniques to communicate with a variety of audiences
- Critical-thinking skills – Gather and organize relevant information to formulate an argument

■ **Figure 3.18** Food aid being distributed in Somalia, 2013

Looking at your maps from the previous activity, identify which countries or regions seem to have been the recipients of most aid programmes in the twentieth century. Do you think this has changed in the twenty-first century?

There is a debate among academics, leaders and policy-makers regarding the impact of aid, and whether developing states would fare better if wealthier countries encouraged economic growth through trade.

Divide the class into two teams in preparation for a debate on the following resolution:

'Developing countries need trade not aid.'

You will need two teams of three speakers to carry out the debate. The rest of the team should help with research for the speeches and be prepared to ask questions of the opposing team.

Reflection

This chapter has investigated different types of global trade that have existed at different times, and looked at where trade can bring about benefits and how it can also cause conflict when it is based on exploitation. We have also considered different types of aid and the positive and negative consequences of aid.

Reflecting on our learning …					
Use this table to reflect on your own learning in this chapter.					
Questions we asked	Answers we found	Any further questions now?			
Factual					
Conceptual					
Debatable					
Approaches to learning you used in this chapter:	Description – what new skills did you learn?	How well did you master the skills?			
		Novice	Learner	Practitioner	Expert
Communication skills					
Critical-thinking skills					
Information literacy skills					
Transfer skills					
Learner profile attribute	*Reflect on the importance of being an inquirer for our learning in this chapter.*				
Inquirer					

4 Why have our everyday lives changed over the past century?

○ *Scientific and technical innovations change individual, household and daily life.*

CONSIDER THESE QUESTIONS:

Factual: What key changes were brought by industrialization to daily life in the nineteenth and twentieth centuries? How did mass production change daily life? What key changes were brought by war to daily life in the twentieth century? What impact have governments had on daily life in the twentieth century?

Conceptual: How has technical innovation changed our daily lives?

Debatable: To what extent has new technology improved the lives of individuals? To what extent does conflict bring lasting change to daily life? Has technology or government action been more important for changing daily lives in the twentieth century?

Now **share and compare** your thoughts and ideas with your partner, or with the whole class.

■ **Figure 4.1** Advertising the latest forms of travel in the 1920s

○ IN THIS CHAPTER, WE WILL ...

■ **Find out:**
  ■ about the impact of technology on daily life
  ■ about the impact of war on daily life.
■ **Explore** the ways in which government can impact on daily life.
■ **Take action** by raising awareness of the fact that daily lives in developing countries are very different to daily lives in developed countries.

■ These Approaches to Learning (ATL) skills will be useful ...

■ Creative-thinking skills
■ Critical-thinking skills
■ Information literacy skills
■ Media literacy skills

● We will reflect on this learner profile attribute ...
  ● Inquirer – researching either independently or in groups.

e Luxe Modes of Travel ,
LOON & WHITE STAR LINE R.M.S OLYMPIC.

DISCUSS

Refer back to Chapter 2, where we looked at several inventions: the phonograph, the electric light bulb and the dishwasher.

What impact did these inventions have on a) individuals and b) households?

What other inventions have had an impact in these areas? In pairs, draw up a list of key inventions that have changed daily life. You may want to include inventions from the list below:

- **Steam engine**
- **Flush toilet**
- **Telegraph**
- **Antibiotic medicines**
- **Vaccinations**
- **Electricity**
- **Computer**
- **Washing machine**

Which invention from your list has had the greatest impact on daily life? Which invention has done the most to improve people's lives?

ACTIVITY:
The washing machine

Now watch Hans Rosling explain his view on the invention that he believes has had the biggest impact on daily life:

www.gapminder.org/videos/hans-rosling-and-the-magic-washing-machine

Discuss: What reasons does Hans Rosling give for his choice of the washing machine? What other points does he make about the impact of industrialization on the daily life of people in developing countries?

In 2013 *TIME* magazine carried out a poll, surveying 10 197 people, to find out what they thought the most useful inventions were. Can you guess what they identified as the top three most useful inventions?

http://techland.time.com/2013/11/14/the-time-invention-poll/

◆ Assessment opportunities in this chapter

- ◆ **Criteron A:** Knowledge and understanding
- ◆ **Criterion B:** Investigating
- ◆ **Criterion C:** Communicating
- ◆ **Criterion D:** Thinking critically

KEY WORDS

assembly line
consumers
totalitarian

How did the Industrial Revolution change everyday life?

ACTIVITY: The impact of the Industrial Revolution on daily life

■ ATL

- Creative-thinking skills – Apply existing knowledge to generate new ideas, products or processes

Draw up a spider diagram or mind map to show the impact of the Industrial Revolution in the nineteenth century on the lives of individuals and households. You may want to do separate diagrams for Britain and for Japan; if you do this, look for similarities and differences in the impact of industrialization on the two countries.

Headings that you could consider for your spider diagram:
- **Employment opportunities**
- **Wages (buying power)**
- **Goods available to purchase**
- **Fashion**
- **Education**
- **Travel**
- **Food**
- **Housing**

Remember to focus on how these factors affected everyday life.

Hint

For a spider diagram or mind map, you need to try to show the links between the themes as you show your understanding of the impact of industrialization on daily life.

◆ Assessment opportunities

- In this activity you have practised skills that are assessed using Criterion A: Knowing and understanding.

■ **Figure 4.2** A Ford motor assembly line, c.1910

The daily lives of individuals and of households have changed profoundly in the last 200 years. This is linked very much to technology. Today, with the rapid changes taking place, you will probably have found that your own lifestyles have changed even from a few years ago because of the impact of, for example, the smartphone.

However, other factors are also important in influencing individual and household lifestyles. In this chapter, we will look first at the impact of the Industrial Revolution, and then at the impacts of war and of government legislation.

The Industrial Revolution, which started in Britain and then spread to the rest of Europe, America, Asia and ultimately to much of the world, was a major turning point in terms of everyday life. Almost every aspect of daily life – which had remained largely unchanged up until this time – was impacted in some way.

You have already looked at the impact of industrialization on everyday life in Britain and Japan in the nineteenth century. Refer back to Chapter 1 and in particular your essay on the benefits of industrialization.

What was the impact of mass production?

HENRY FORD

A key aspect of the Industrial Revolution in the twentieth century was mass production. This took off in the USA after Henry Ford pioneered mass production to manufacture cars just before the First World War. The impact of mass production had a huge impact on people's lives as the cheaper production meant that people could now afford a wide range of goods.

Henry Ford built his first motorcar in 1896. He founded the Ford Motor Company in 1903, and in 1909 he started producing the Model T in one colour – black. Rather than build each car by hand, as had been done in the past, Ford devised a new method to mass produce the cars. This involved the following:

- Identical cars: the parts could then be a standard size and shape.
- Division of labour: instead of one or two workers constructing a car and using a range of skills, each worker had only one job to do over and over again.
- A moving assembly line: each worker stayed in the same place and the job came to them on a conveyer belt.

ACTIVITY: The impact of mass production

■ ATL

- Critical-thinking skills – Evaluate evidence and arguments; Draw reasonable conclusions and generalizations

1 **What benefits would each of the aspects of mass production bring to Henry Ford, consumers and workers? Can you see any disadvantages of this new process for consumers or workers?**
2 **Now read the Sources A and B and add any extra points to your original answers for question 1.**
3 **Think back to Chapter 2. In what ways can Henry Ford be considered a) an innovator and b) a pioneer?**

◆ Assessment opportunities

- ◆ This activity can be assessed using Criterion D: Thinking critically.

SOURCE A

From Henry Ford's autobiography

'In April 1913, we experimented with an assembly line, just on the magneto (the ignition system). We try everything in a little way first – we'll rip out anything once we find a better way, but we must be certain the new way will be better before doing anything drastic.

'One workman could make one magneto in 20 minutes. Dividing his job into 29 steps cut the assembly time to 13 minutes, 10 seconds. Then we raised the height of the line 8 inches. This cut the time to 7 minutes. Changing the speed of the line cut the time down to 5 minutes.'

Ford, H. 1952. My Life and Work.

SOURCE B

'Henry Ford's new "moving assembly line" meant that cars could be made in greater numbers, and therefore more cheaply than before. This boosted sales enormously. A Ford Model T cost $1, 200 in 1909 but only $290 in 1925 (less than three months' wages for the average worker), and Ford was turning out 9,000 cars a day.

'The motor industry created a huge demand for steel, rubber, glass and oil, and all these industries boomed as a result. Roads had to be built for the cars to travel on, and this created yet more jobs. The cars needed petrol to run on, boosting the oil industry too.'

DeMarco, N. 2001. The USA: Divided Union?. Longman, p. 14.

WHAT WAS THE IMPACT OF MASS PRODUCTION ON OTHER INDUSTRIES?

Following the great success of Ford's mass production system, other industries began to use the same methods. Soon, new products such as fridges, radios, vacuum cleaners and washing machines were also being mass produced. This of course led to a drop in the prices of these goods, which in turn increased sales. Real wages were also increasing, allowing consumers to buy more goods; even if people lacked the money, it was easy to get credit in the USA in the 1920s. Thus many people bought goods on 'hire purchase' (HP), paying off their debt in instalments. Many of the products bought relied on electricity and the percentage of homes supplied with electricity increased from 33 per cent in 1920 to nearly 70 per cent by 1929.

To help fuel the buying frenzy, advertising companies started using more sophisticated techniques to encourage people to spend.

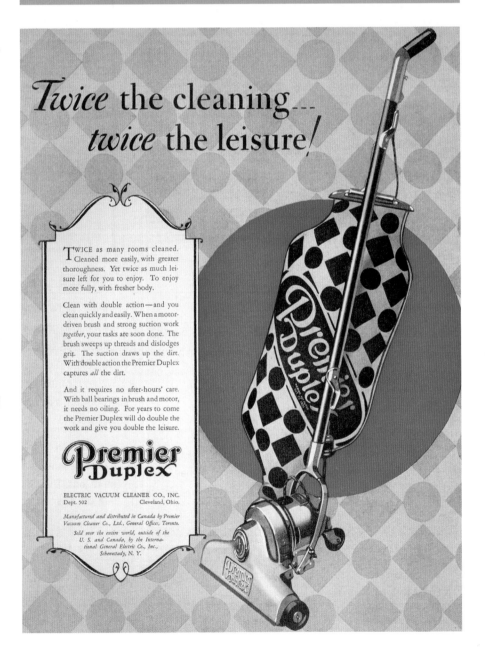

■ **Figure 4.3** An example of an advert in the 1920s

THINK–PAIR–SHARE

Read Sources C–F. Using the information in this chapter, along with the information in these sources, **list**:

- **all the ways in which the lives of many Americans changed in the 1920s**
- **the causes of these changes.**

Then share your findings with a partner. Show the results of your discussion as a diagram. Share your ideas and diagrams with the rest of the class.

SOURCE C

'During the 1920s the average pay of industrial workers doubled. Much of the extra income was spent on consumer goods. This also helped business to boom.

'There were many new "gadgets" which people wanted to buy … In 1920 America's first radio station, Station KDKA, went on the air. Within a year radio became a craze, and by 1929 ten million homes had radio sets. Over 900,000 people bought refrigerators. Sales of vacuum cleaners, irons, ovens and telephones rocketed.'

Brooman, J. 1986. The Age of Excess: America, 1920–32. *Longman, p. 19.*

SOURCE D

'Visualise a typical 1920s scene; eating your Kellogg's cornflakes for breakfast and enjoying your toast from your General Electric toaster, dressed in ready-made clothes, you drive to work in your black Model T Ford, watch Charlie Chaplain or Rudolph Valentino at the local movie house and return to your suburban home to read the *Saturday Evening Post* or the *Readers' Digest* by electric light, or listen to music and commercials on the radio.

'What were you doing? Exactly the same thing as thousands of other Americans across the continent, because mass production, transportation and advertising encouraged you to spend.'

de Pennington, J. 2005. Modern America: 1865 to the Present. *Hodder Education, p. 91.*

SOURCE E

Cars on the roads in the USA

1910	468 000
1920	9 239 000
1930	26 750 000

SOURCE F

'Beginning in the early 1920s, people who had never taken a holiday beyond the nearest lake or mountain could explore the whole United States. Most of all the Model T gave to the farmer and rancher, miles from anywhere, a new pair of legs.'

Cooke, A. Alistair Cooke's America. *BBC. 2009.*

▼ Links to: Sciences; Physics; Design technology; Economics; Geography

Think about what you have studied in the subjects mentioned above. How does your understanding in these subject areas support your understanding of the impact of the Model T on individual, household and daily life?

What was the impact of the Second World War on daily life in Britain?

■ **Figure 4.4** London during the Blitz

Wherever they took place, industrialization and mass production had, in most cases, not just a dramatic but also a permanent impact on the lives of individuals and households. During the twentieth century, the First and Second World Wars also led to significant changes in the lives of individuals and on households in all countries involved in fighting – though not all of these changes were permanent.

The Second World War had a dramatic impact on the lives of individuals and households. Between May and August 1940, Britain faced the threat of invasion, and then, between 7 September 1940 and mid-May 1941, civilians in many cities faced nightly bombing raids, which became known as the Blitz. In addition to the impact that these attacks had on daily life, the Emergency Powers Act, which was passed in May 1940, gave the British government extensive powers over people and property. British people were also encouraged to volunteer for war work, to change their lifestyles to save food, and to look after evacuees sent out of the cities.

THE BLITZ

During the period known as the Blitz, towns and cities throughout Britain were bombed. Two months of nightly bombing of London were followed by bombing of other cities such as Coventry, Liverpool and Glasgow. By the time the Blitz ended in May 1941, as many as 1 400 000 Londoners had been made homeless and, across the country, 43 000 people had been killed.

Nightly bombing clearly had a disruptive impact on everyday life. People had to spend nights in air-raid shelters – either in their own home or garden or in the Underground stations in London. Many volunteered as Civil Defence workers – in the fire service, as Air Raid Precaution Wardens or at the First Aid Post, which meant working at night as well as doing a normal job by day.

The Blitz meant that civilians had to maintain a 'blackout' at night so that German bombers could not see cities from the air. Thus streetlights were not lit and cars had to drive without lights. As a result there were many accidents. In December 1939 over 1500 people were killed on British roads, compared with the pre-war average of 600 deaths per month.

EVACUATION

In order to try to reduce the number of casualties, the government evacuated children and young mothers from the big cities to safer parts of the country. This meant a new way of life for many people. Many of the evacuees were working-class children who were visiting the countryside for the first time. On the other side, many of the host families were richer, middle- or upper-class people, so different groups of people were put together for the first time.

RATIONING

Food rationing was introduced in January 1940, which caused a major change in people's lives. Britain was facing shortages because much of its food and other goods came from overseas, and German U-boats (submarines) were sinking supply ships crossing the Atlantic. The rationing system made access to the limited supplies fairer; families were given books of ration stamps, which they used to buy a fixed amount of certain products. There was also an extra allowance for luxury items such as tinned fruit. The Board of Trade issued recipes showing people how to make healthy meals using the food that was available.

Clothes were rationed from 1941. The government also encouraged people to save by mending their own clothes and using cheaper, more basic clothes and furniture.

People were encouraged to grow as much of their own food as possible and to keep their own animals.

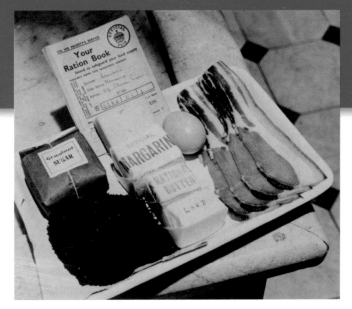

■ **Figure 4.5** One week's worth of rations; one benefit of rationing was that some people ate more healthily

The hardships which scarcity of food and resources brought about during the war did not end in 1945 at the end of the fighting. Rationing continued for the next few years.

THE LIVES OF WOMEN

Conscription was introduced in 1939. Most men aged between 18 and 40 had to do military service, which meant that work at home – in farms and factories – had to be done by women. At first women volunteered but by 1941 industry was so short of workers that unmarried women were conscripted. They could choose between the Woman's Land Army, women's sections of the armed forces and work in factories. By 1943, nine out of ten single women, as well as many married women, were doing war work.

Women were now given the opportunity to do a wide range of jobs from which they had hitherto been barred simply because they were women. This gave them new freedoms and the chance to learn new skills. However, at the end of the war, women were expected to return home and give their jobs back to the returning men.

SOURCE G

Clement Attlee, the deputy prime minister, writing about the work women did in the war

'The work the women are performing in **munitions** factories has to be seen to be believed. Precision engineering jobs which a few years ago would have made a skilled turner's hair stand on end are performed with deadly accuracy by girls who had no industrial experience.'

■ **Figure 4.6** Government poster encouraging British people to grow their own food

WOMEN OF BRITAIN
COME INTO THE FACTORIES
ASK AT ANY EMPLOYMENT EXCHANGE FOR ADVICE AND FULL DETAILS

■ **Figure 4.7** Poster encouraging women to work for the war effort

THE GOVERNMENT AND PROPAGANDA AND CENSORSHIP?

The Ministry of Information was responsible for propaganda and **censorship**. You have seen some examples of propaganda posters earlier in this chapter; propaganda was used to encourage people to join the voluntary war effort, to warn people of the dangers of 'careless talk' and to encourage people to save for the war effort and live more carefully without wasting food or materials. Propaganda and censorship were also used to keep up the morale of the population; the resilience and good humour of the British in the face of the Blitz was stressed in news reports. Conversely, negative stories were not reported.

SOURCE H

Mona Marshall, a nursemaid before the war and a steelworker during it

'To be honest, the war was the best thing that ever happened to us. I was as green as grass [inexperienced] and terrified if anyone spoke to me. I had been brought up not to argue. My generation of women had been taught to do as we were told. At work you did exactly as your boss told you and you went home to do exactly as your husband told you. The war changed all that. The war made me stand on my own two feet.'

ACTIVITY: London's Blitz (1941)

■ ATL

- Critical-thinking skills – Recognize unstated assumptions and bias

Watch the following Pathé News report:

http://youtu.be/clKxrDza1d8

In what ways was this news report designed to maintain morale? Give specific examples from the report to support your answer; consider both the language and the images.

Evaluate the Pathé News report as a source for historians studying the impact of the Blitz on Britain. **Analyse** the origin and purpose to find the value and limitations of the source.

Hint

Remember to consider the following when looking for the value and limitations of a source: who wrote or made it, when it was created, where and why it was made, and who its intended audience was.

◆ Assessment opportunities

- ◆ In this activity you have practised skills that are assessed using Criterion D: Thinking critically.

THE GOVERNMENT AND WELFARE

The government also intervened more in the welfare of the nation. Health care was improved and nurseries were set up to look after the children of working mothers. Special food rations and vitamins were made available to young children and mothers.

In addition, the transport system became a public service rather than a private business. These changes were to provide the foundations for legislation that was introduced after the war, in particular with regard to the National Health Service and the welfare state (see page 78).

ACTIVITY: Life in Britain during the Second World War

■ ATL

- Critical-thinking skills – Evaluate evidence and arguments

1 **List** the ways in which the lives of individuals changed during the Second World War in Britain.
2 **Identify** changes that:
   - had the most negative impact on people's lives
   - were more positive
   - lasted only for the duration of the war
   - affected the lives of individuals beyond the war.

◆ Assessment opportunities

- This activity can be assessed using Criterion A: Knowing and understanding.

ACTIVITY: The impact of the Second World War on daily life in other countries

■ ATL

- Information literacy skills – Access information to be informed and inform others; Present information in a variety of formats and platforms

Work in groups of four or five.

Aim

Choose another country that was affected by the Second World War and research the impact of the war on civilians and their daily lives in this country.

How will you achieve this?

Find a range of sources, including first-hand accounts from civilians, photographs and posters.

How will you present your findings?

You should aim to create a display to show:
- the ways in which people's lives changed during the war
- the changes that had the most negative impact
- the changes that might have been welcomed
- the changes that were only for the duration of the war
- any changes to daily life that remained after the end of the war.

Your word count should be between 700 and 1500 words.

◆ Assessment opportunities

- This activity can be assessed using Criterion B: Investigating, Criterion C: Communicating and Criterion D: Thinking critically.

How has the role of government impacted on everyday life in the twentieth century?

As you have read, the rapid changes brought about by the Industrial Revolution forced governments to pass legislation that affected the workplace, education and public health.

The First and Second World Wars further increased the role of government in people's lives and in some countries this continued to be the case after the war. In Britain, for example, the new Labour government that was elected into power in 1945 at the end of the Second World War was committed to improving the population's health and education. The aim was to tackle the five 'Giant Evils' of Want, Ignorance, Squalor, Idleness and Disease that were identified by a government report, known as the Beveridge Report, published in 1942.

Laws passed by the British government after the Second World War

Education Act 1944: Provided compulsory and free school education up to the age of 15.

Family Allowances Act 1945: Gave every family five shillings per child per week.

Slum clearances: Slums were demolished and new housing was built with running water and sanitation.

National Insurance Act 1946: The government and the employer made contributions to allow workers to receive benefits when they were ill or unemployed. It also meant that people could get a pension when they reached 65 years of age. It also provided for maternity payments to women.

National Health Service 1948: Provided free health care for all, meaning that people could get services that they had not been able to afford previously.

ACTIVITY: The impact of government on the daily lives of individuals

■ ATL

- Information literacy skills – Collect and analyse data to identify solutions and make informed decisions
- Media literacy skills – Seek a range of perspectives from multiple and varied sources

The impact of government intervention in the lives of citizens has always varied from country to country. In totalitarian regimes, the laws passed by the governments have a profound and intrusive impact on the lives of individuals. This can be both positive and negative. In democracies, the role of government can be less obvious but still has a significant impact on daily life. The ideology of a government can also have an impact as will be discussed further in Chapter 7.

Aim

Find out about the impact of government on the daily lives of individuals at different times and in different countries.

How will you do this?

Choose one of the following countries/time periods and research the role of government in impacting on the daily life of individuals (or decide on a country and time period of your own choice).

DISCUSS

How did each of the laws passed by the British government tackle the five 'Giant Evils' which had been identified in the Beveridge Report?

To what extent can these laws be seen as 'revolutionary' in the way they changed the lives of individuals and households?

Here are some questions that you might consider, though you may also want to develop your own questions:

- **What are the key laws that affected people's lives?**
- **Identify both the positive and negative impact on the daily lives of individuals.**
- **Did some groups of people benefit more or suffer more than others as a result of government intervention?**

Time periods you could consider:
- **Nazi Germany, 1933–45**
- **The Soviet Union under Stalin, 1929–53**
- **The USA under Roosevelt, 1933–45**
- **East Germany, 1945–89**
- **China, 1949–76**
- **Cuba under Castro, 1959–2008**

How will you present your findings?

Prepare a brief presentation to the rest of the class on your country. Your presentation should be between 700 and 1500 words long.

Class discussion

Which factor has had most impact on the daily life of individuals in your own country over the past 50 years – technology or government intervention?

◆ **Assessment opportunities**

◆ In this activity you have practised skills that are assessed using Criterion B: Investigating, Criterion C: Communicating and Criterion D: Thinking critically.

Reflection

In this chapter we have examined the impact of technology, war and government on daily life.

Reflecting on our learning ... Use this table to reflect on your own learning in this chapter.				
Questions we asked	Answers we found	Any further questions now?		
Factual				
Conceptual				
Debatable				

Approaches to learning you used in this chapter:	Description – what new skills did you learn?	How well did you master the skills?			
		Novice	Learner	Practitioner	Expert
Creative-thinking skills					
Critical-thinking skills					
Information literacy skills					
Media literacy skills					
Learner profile attribute	*Reflect on the importance of being an inquirer for our learning in this chapter.*				
Inquirer					

! **Take action**

! Daily life also varies considerably from one part of the world to another. In 2000, the UN identified eight goals that the world needed to address to improve the quality of daily life for people in developing countries. These became known as the Millennium Development Goals; the deadline for achieving these goals was 2015.

Research using the search term Millennium Development Goals and investigate how far the world has been successful in implementing these goals.

! Prepare a report or display to show your findings. What do you think still needs to be done to improve daily life in developing countries? (You will have the chance to look in more depth at problems in health, in particular, in Chapter 5.)

5 How have health and medicine improved over time?

The **health of communities** requires effective **governance** and the development of welfare **systems**.

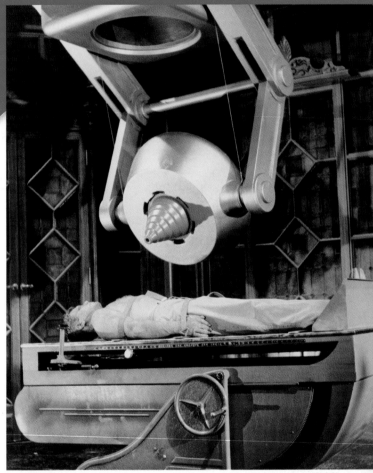

■ **Figure 5.1** Examples of medicine, health and technology; the patient on the right has smallpox

CONSIDER THESE QUESTIONS:

Factual: What were the important developments in medicine in the nineteenth century? How did war lead to improvements in medicine in the twentieth century?

Conceptual: How do developments in medicine impact on societies? How dependent is health on wealth?

Debatable: How far do you agree that governments should provide free health care to all its citizens?

Now **share and compare** your thoughts and ideas with your partner, or with the whole class.

○ IN THIS CHAPTER, WE WILL ...

■ **Find out:**
  ■ about some of the key changes in medicine and health in the nineteenth and twentieth centuries
  ■ about the factors that led to the improvement of health and medical practice.
■ **Explore:**
  ■ the roles of significant individuals in improving medical knowledge
  ■ the role of war in medical progress.
■ **Take action** by raising awareness of global and local health initiatives.

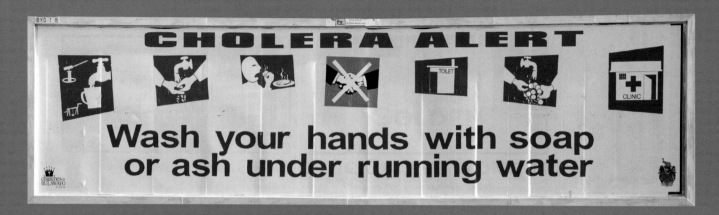

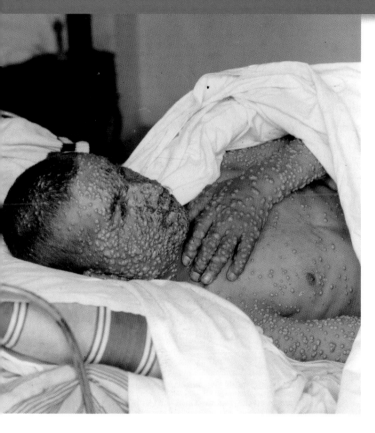

We will reflect on this learner profile attribute ...

- Open minded – looking at the values and traditions of different societies and time periods and how these have impacted on medical developments.

Assessment opportunities in this chapter:

- **Criterion A:** Knowing and understanding
- **Criterion B:** Investigating
- **Criterion C:** Communicating
- **Criterion D:** Thinking critically

These Approaches to Learning (ATL) skills will be useful ...

- Collaboration skills
- Communication skills
- Critical-thinking skills
- Information literacy skills
- Organization skills

In Chapter 4, you read about factors that have influenced daily life. The focus of this chapter is on changes in health and medicine. These changes have also had a profound impact on daily life through the ages.

KEY WORDS

cauterize	prognosis
gangrene	sterilize
ligature	

How have medicine and health developed over time?

SOURCE A

From Hippocrates' teaching and practice in the fifth century BCE

'Diseases have natural causes. The body's humours become unbalanced and this causes illnesses. We can see this when a patient sweats or vomits when ill. This is the body trying to get rid of the excess humours in a natural way. There is no need to look for magical cures because illness is not caused by magic. We must use natural treatments, for example, rest and change in your diet and then perhaps when you are feeling stronger some more regular exercise. If this does not work then we can bleed or purge to remove the excess humours.'

SOURCE B

This source, from an account written by a French doctor in 1349, relates to the Black Death or plague epidemic that crossed Europe from Asia in the mid-thirteenth century

'This epidemic … kills almost instantly, as soon as the airy spirit leaving the eyes of the sick man has struck the eye of a healthy bystander looking at him, for then the poisonous nature passes from one eye to the other.'

SOURCE C

This source, from a letter to Christchurch Abbey in Canterbury, Britain in 1348, relates to the Black Death or plague epidemic that crossed Europe from Asia in the mid-thirteenth century

'Terrible is God towards the sons of men … He often allows plagues, miserable famines, conflicts, wars and other forms of suffering to arise, and uses them to terrify and torment men and so drive out their sins. And thus, indeed, the realm of England, because of the growing pride and corruption of its subjects, and their numberless sins … is to be oppressed by the pestilences …'

ACTIVITY: Change over time

1   In pairs, consider Sources A–C. **Identify** the similarities and differences between the ideas expressed in the Ancient Greek work of Hippocrates and the beliefs in Europe during the Middle Ages. Do you find anything surprising?

> **Hint**
> Take two highlighter pens and highlight where Sources A, B and C agree in one colour, and use the second colour to highlight where they disagree.

2   Look at the origin of the sources and when they were written (their **provenance**). Does this suggest anything about change over time in history?
3   Is there evidence that medicine and health improved over the period of more than a thousand years between the fifth century BCE and the fourteenth century?

DEVELOPMENTS IN MEDICINE BEFORE 1750

Over time, medicine and health have substantially improved. The most dramatic improvements in medicine have come in the last 200 years; however, there were key developments before the modern era.

In the prehistoric period serious illnesses were treated by 'medicine men'. Often midwifery and basic care for the sick were left to women. It was believed that illnesses had either supernatural causes, such as vengeful gods or evil spirits, or natural causes as in the case of an injury from hunting or an insect bite. The treatment was to use a combination of ritual, prayer, herbs and basic surgery such as trephining, as shown in Figure 5.2. Trephining is the drilling of a hole through the scalp and the skull to relieve pressure on the brain. There is evidence that people survived this operation in prehistoric times.

Similarly, in ancient Egypt, for more than a thousand years BCE, high priests and women had the role of healers and key caregivers respectively.

Spirits and gods were still seen as the cause of illnesses; however, it was also believed that if 'channels' in the body became blocked then a person would get sick. Treatments varied little from prehistoric times, though there was an emphasis on hygiene to prevent disease.

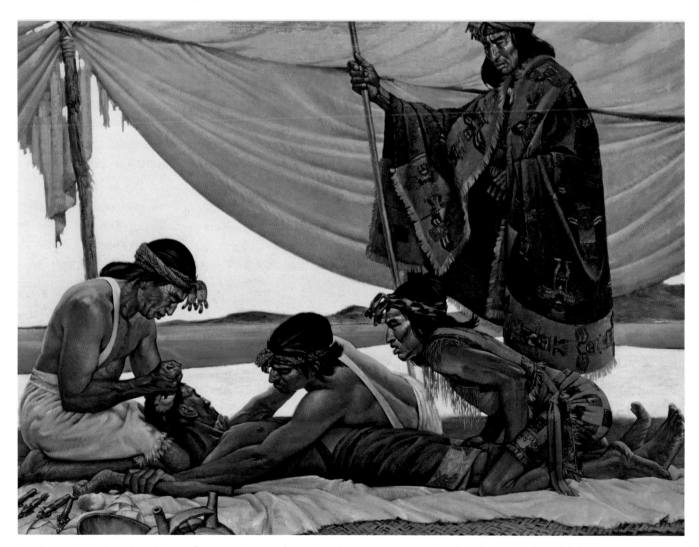

■ **Figure 5.2** There is evidence from skull records that early peoples understood and practised trephining

THE ANCIENT GREEKS

As you have seen in Source A, the Ancient Greeks were reflective inquirers. They saw the gods as important to health and had temples to the god of healing – Asclepius. The sick would go the temple of healing and sleep there and during the night they believed that Asclepius and his daughters would come to heal them.

However, they also had some new ideas about what caused sickness and how it could be treated. Greek thinkers and doctors attempted to understand what caused illness through careful observation of the sick. From observations they saw that during an illness body fluids were usually expelled – phlegm, blood, black bile and yellow bile.

From this developed the theory that illness was caused by having an imbalance of the four humours in your body. The theory was further linked to the four elements: fire, air, earth and water, and the four seasons: spring, summer, autumn and winter. Water was cold and moist, as was winter; in winter many people suffered with sneezing and had too much phlegm. Phlegm was therefore linked to the season winter and the element water. Greek doctors believed they could see the humours causing the illness and thus understand why people got sick. The Greek theory of the four humours was to be followed for over one thousand years.

Greek doctors were trained to observe patients' symptoms and then diagnose. Some kept very detailed notes of their observations and this enabled them to make a prognosis based on their observations of others with similar symptoms. To treat the sick, Greek doctors used their theory of the four humours. Following this theory, doctors would try to help restore the 'balance' by inducing vomiting or purging in a patient, or bleeding them. If all treatment failed, the patient would be sent to the Asclepius temple. Simple surgery and the use of herbal medicines continued.

The key theorist of the four humours and most significant individual in Greek medicine from the classical period was Hippocrates. He set down the professional standards for doctors in his oath (see Source D). This oath is still sworn by new doctors today.

SOURCE D

From the Hippocratic Oath, written by the Ancient Greek doctor in the fifth century BCE

'I will swear by Apollo, Asclepius and by all the gods that I will carry out this oath. I will use treatment to help the sick according to my ability and judgement but never with a view to injury or wrongdoing. I will not give poison to anybody … whatever I see or hear professionally or in my private list which ought not to be told I will keep secret.'

Hippocrates also left behind a collection of medical books and treatises, not all written personally, that provided a vast amount of detail on symptoms and treatments. For hundreds of years doctors used these as the foundation for their practice. Hippocrates had demonstrated how important it was to observe patients and record their symptoms and the progress of their illness in order to better understand and treat diseases. Hippocrates wanted people to look for natural causes of illness, rather than seeking supernatural causes and turning to the gods for help.

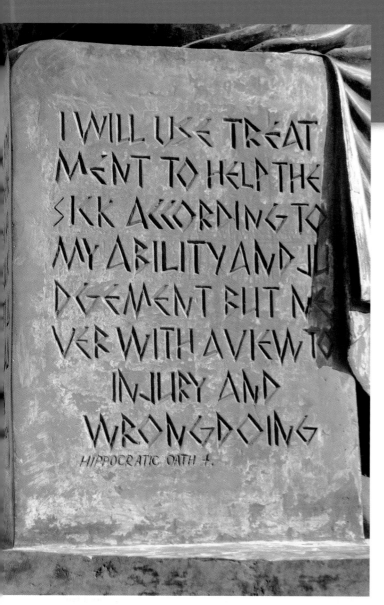

I WILL USE TREAT
MENT TO HELP THE
SICK ACCORDING TO
MY ABILITY AND JU
DGEMENT BUT N
VER WITH A VIEW TO
INJURY AND
WRONGDOING

HIPPOCRATIC OATH 4.

■ **Figure 5.3** Part of the Hippocratic Oath on a monument in Greece

THINK–PUZZLE–EXPLORE

From the time of the ancient Egyptians there were widespread trade links to other societies in Africa and across regions to China and India. Traders would bring new herbs and plants for treating illnesses. Herbal medicine followed the trade routes. Diseases were also carried along with the merchants and their goods.

Review Chapter 3 for information on the Silk Road and spice routes. Research and **explore** what types of medicines would be passed down the trading routes, and **discuss** what diseases may have been spread at the same time.

THE ROMANS

During the Roman era, Hippocrates' ideas continued. However, professional medical treatment was expensive, so many ordinary people used family herbal medicines and resorted to asking the gods for help.

The Romans borrowed so many ideas from the Greeks that they even built a temple to Asclepius. The most famous Roman doctor was Galen, who lived in the second century CE. He followed Hippocrates' methods of observation and believed in the theory of the four humours. However, he had a new idea; he thought that the humours could be rebalanced using 'opposites', for example taking pepper or something hot when you had a cold.

Galen was also interested in anatomy and carried out dissections to find out more about the human body. Galen learnt from his dissections about how each body part fitted together and taught his students about how well the human body was designed. This idea about design was later taken up by the Christian Church, which saw it as evidence of God's creation of mankind.

Galen wrote 60 books that combined Greek ideas with Roman theories, and his arguments were so persuasive that his writings laid the foundation for medicine for the next one-and-a-half thousand years. The key idea which flourished throughout the Roman Empire was that of **public health**. The Romans attempted to keep their cities and people clean by constructing sewers, aqueducts that brought in clean water and public bath-houses.

THE MIDDLES AGES

During the early Middle Ages in Europe, after a long period of civil and regional war during which central governments had collapsed, the Christian Church's power had grown. By the 1300s the Church had set up universities where doctors could be trained, and Galen's ideas were rediscovered.

In the mid-1340s a catastrophic **epidemic** called the Black Death spread from Asia to Europe. It is estimated that the Black Death, or bubonic plague, killed over 40 per cent of the population. The causes of the disease were not understood and therefore people desperately sought explanations in the work of Galen, in the movement of the stars and planets, in factors that might be making God angry and in natural causes such as dirty smells from poor sanitation and poisons in the air. Some believed that the disease was spread from looking into the eyes of a sick person. Some blamed minorities in their own communities such as the Jews.

Groups called the 'flagellants' tried to atone for their sins and the sins of others and to appease a vengeful God. They would roam from town to town and village to village, whipping themselves and asking people to repent (see Figure 5.5).

Doctors used a number of different treatments for illnesses in the Middle Ages. They attempted to balance the humours, as they had done in ancient times, and one of the most common remedies was bleeding a patient. They also used astrology and herbal medicines.

Women were not permitted to go to university and could not train to be professional doctors. Nevertheless, they continued to be the key care providers for the sick in most towns and villages and were also midwives, taking care of childbirth.

■ **Figure 5.4** A contemporary drawing showing the effects of the Black Death

■ **Figure 5.5** A group of flagellants in the Netherlands, 1349

Within the image:
Der Doctor Schna-bel von Rom

Figure 5.6 A plague doctor from the seventeenth century

ACTIVITY: The plague doctor

■ **ATL**

■ Critical-thinking skills – Recognize unstated assumptions and bias

● In pairs, look at the drawing of a plague doctor from the seventeenth century in Figure 5.6.
● **Discuss** the reasons for his strange mask.
   ○ What might it be for?
   ○ What does this suggest about what people believed caused the plague more than three centuries after the 1340s outbreak?
● Sketch the picture in rough and add labels to your drawing in answer to these questions.

◆ **Assessment opportunities**

◆ In this activity you have practised skills that are assessed using Criterion D: Thinking critically.

THINK–PAIR–SHARE

Some historians believe that Christianity and Islam may have hindered medical progress. Why do you think they suggest this? Share your thoughts with a partner.

When most of Europe had descended into chaos and conflict after the fall of the Roman Empire, a new civilization developed in the Middle East founded on Islam. The central religious text of Islam, the Qur'an tells Muslims that it is important to care for the sick.

Islamic scholars took on the work of Galen, and many sources suggest that their understanding and medical practices were far more advanced than those in Western Europe at the time. Large hospitals were built across the Islamic world in the Middle Ages. A famous Arab doctor was Ibn Sina who worked in the early eleventh century and wrote a significant, one-million word book on medicine. However, many Arab doctors, including Sina, believed that theory was more important than practice and did not engage with surgery.

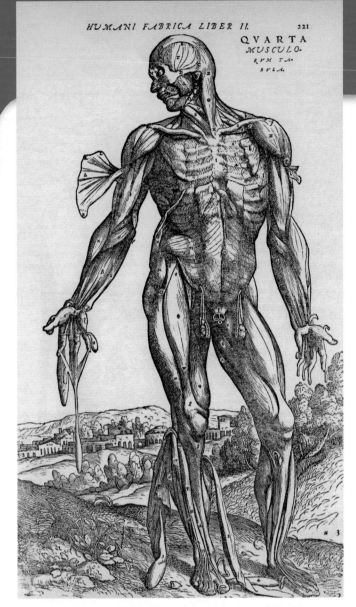

THE RENAISSANCE

From 1500 to 1650 there were a number of medical breakthroughs, and this period is often called the 'Medical Renaissance'. A significant individual in this period was Andreas Vesalius, a Belgian who studied medicine in France and Italy. His major achievement was to show that Galen had been wrong about elements of human anatomy.

Vesalius believed that it was important for knowledge and understanding for doctors to perform human dissections. He argued that ideas had to be tested and not just followed blindly. He wrote *On the Fabric of the Human Body* (*De Humani Corporis Fabrica*) and the *Epitome* in 1543, which included detailed illustrations. His work led to a much better understanding of human anatomy.

Another significant individual working in the 1530s and 1540s was the Frenchman Ambroise Paré. His major achievement was in surgery. After becoming an army surgeon in 1536, he spent 20 years with the army treating battle wounds.

For deep wounds and amputations, doctors in the past had stopped the bleeding by cauterizing the wound. They did this by sealing it with a red-hot iron. They would also pour boiling oil onto wounds as they thought it would help them to heal. Paré stopped using the boiling oil as he did not think this worked, and instead would use bandages. He also stopped cauterizing wounds and instead would tie the ends of arteries using silk thread to stop the bleeding. Paré became influential, and many doctors began to follow his methods. His ideas on surgery were spread beyond France by his book, *Works on Surgery*, which was published in 1575.

■ **Figure 5.7** An illustration by Andreas Vesalius from the sixteenth century

A British doctor, William Harvey, who had studied medicine at Cambridge University, was influential in the 1600s and made breakthroughs in understanding the circulation of blood in the human body. He also published an important book, *An Anatomical Account of the Motion of the Heart and Blood in Animals* in 1628.

Up until Harvey, many doctors still believed Galen's theory that new blood was constantly being made in the liver to replace blood that was burnt up in the body. Harvey proved that the heart acted as a pump, and that blood is carried away from the heart by the arteries and is returned to it by the veins. Harvey showed that new blood was not constantly created as it does not get burnt up – it is re-circulated around the body by the heart.

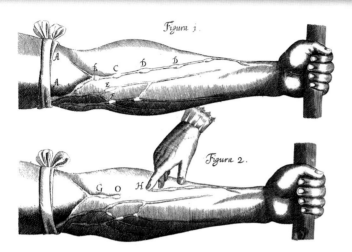

Figure 5.8 William Harvey's experiments on the valves of the veins

Despite the significant discoveries made by these individuals, the work of Vesalius and Harvey had little impact on people's everyday health and life expectancy. Paré's work had more immediate impact, as wounds were more routinely bandaged than covered in oil and this did help patients survive.

THINK-PAIR-SHARE

To what extent do we still face dangers today from epidemics or even pandemics? How do we cope with such dangers today?

However, Paré's idea of silk ligatures was less widely copied as doctors found that patients still died after having this treatment. The problem was that Paré did not have **antiseptics** and disinfectants, and therefore the threads took infections deep into the wound. Many doctors continued to cauterize as this did help to stop infections.

The Black Death continued to infect Europe periodically throughout the 1400s and 1500s. Then, in 1665 a catastrophic plague epidemic hit London. It was a stark demonstration of how limited medical progress had been in the 300 years since the mass plague epidemics of the fourteenth century that many of the treatments recommended and sold at the time were very similar to those of the 1340s:

- days of fasting and praying set by the government
- charms and amulets to ward off the plague
- brimstone burnt to 'cure' the bad air
- various potions, for example 'plague water'.

ACTIVITY: Factors that brought about change in medicine

■ ATL

- Collaboration skills – Listen actively to other perspectives and ideas

- In small groups, review the material in this chapter thus far.
- **Identify** which of the factors shown in Figure 5.9 was most important to a medical discovery being made.
- Does this change over time?
- Which factor seems to be consistently the most significant?

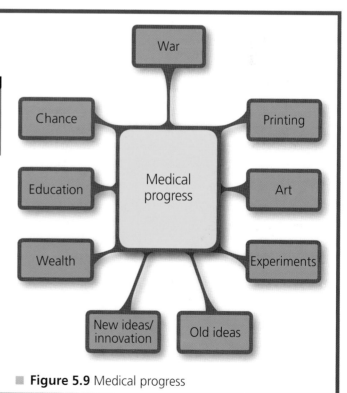

Figure 5.9 Medical progress

What were the significant breakthroughs in medicine in the nineteenth century?

ENLIGHTENMENT – THE SCIENTIFIC REVOLUTION

By the 1700s, during a period known as the Enlightenment, there was a move towards new thinking and a focus on scientific explanations. During this scientific revolution, modern science evolved into what we understand it to be today.

Instead of learning from ancient texts such as those of Galen, scientists started to use their own observations and experiments to gain knowledge. The work of the significant individuals you have read about in this chapter was, however, important for shaping new ideas in medicine. Scientists were proving old ideas wrong – for example, the Ancient Greek idea of the four humours was disproved when it was discovered that air itself was made up of different gases. Old explanations for diseases did not fit with what was observed in the natural world.

From the 1600s scientists had been able to use a new invention for observation – the microscope. Doctors' training had become more sophisticated and they undertook dissections, used microscopes and could challenge old thinking. The Catholic Church no longer dominated education and this was important as it had strongly supported the ideas of Galen.

THE IMPACT OF THE INDUSTRIAL REVOLUTION

As you have read in Chapter 1, profound economic, technological and social changes took place during the Industrial Revolution and these changes had an impact on medicine.

There was a growth in the population and rapid urbanization in many countries. As towns grew, so health problems grew with them. There was poor housing, overcrowding, dirty water and poor sanitation. This meant that there were frequent epidemics that could spread quickly through the cramped conditions in the cities. However, there were key positive factors for medical progress in the nineteenth century. For example, in Britain in 1800 the government did not believe that it should intervene to improve the health of its citizens but this changed throughout the course of the century and by 1900 there were laws passed to improve public health (see page 99 for further discussion of this).

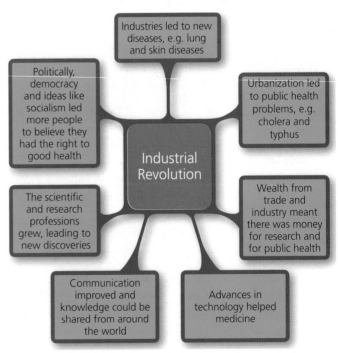

Figure 5.10 The impact of the Industrial Revolution on medicine and health

The Industrial Revolution fostered scientific research. In Britain, Joseph Jackson Lister invented the multi-lens microscope in 1826; in Germany, Carl Ludwig invented the kymograph in 1847 to accurately measure a person's pulse, and another German, Wilhelm Röntgen, discovered X-rays; in 1900 Willem Einthoven in Holland discovered electrocardiographs to measure heart activity.

Consider the relationship between health and medical progress and scientific discovery and new technology.

Charles Darwin and his ideas on evolution were increasingly accepted and they challenged further the control of the Church over medicine. Technology also made warfare more deadly and this led to the development of new techniques and practices.

Scientists made key breakthroughs in the nineteenth century with regard to the link between micro-organisms and disease. They discovered a dye that could be used to kill **bacteria**. They also discovered a gas that could be used as an anaesthetic. New technology also improved treatments, such as in metals, where stronger needles made of hollowed steel led to safer injections, and new types of glass led to better microscopes and to the invention of the first thermometer.

The developments in transport and communications during the Industrial Revolution also played a role. The new railways meant that doctors could travel more quickly around the country to conventions and conferences. The wide distribution of newspapers meant that new theories and ideas could spread throughout the population and across borders and continents.

■ **Figure 5.11** An early microscope

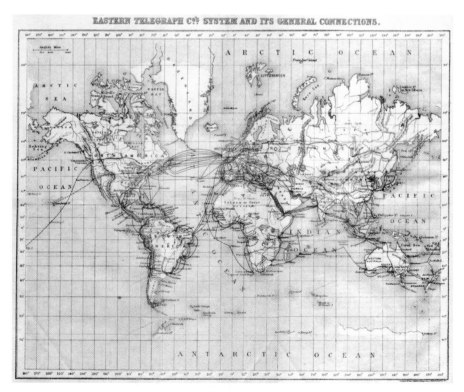

■ **Figure 5.12** Telegraph communications across the globe by the end of the nineteenth century

Medicine became a highly profitable business and money was invested in scientific research. War was a factor again in this period and it meant doctors could practise using new equipment: they could experiment using new techniques on a range of serious wounds and injuries and improvements were also made in hygiene and nursing.

Nationalism was also a factor. For example, there was nationalist rivalry between Pasteur and Koch (see page 94) and the Japanese doctor Shibasaburo Kitasato and the French doctor Alexandre Yersin, who competed to discover the bacterium that caused the plague in 1894.

Knowledge about the body improved in the nineteenth century. The American William Beaumont studied the digestive system in detail (he used a patient who had an open hole into his stomach) in 1822; the German doctor Theodor Schwann found that animals were made up of cells and not humours, and a Scottish surgeon, Henry Gray, published *Gray's Anatomy* in 1858, which included thousands of detailed illustrations of human anatomy. This book was then studied by students in universities.

VACCINATIONS – SMALLPOX

Smallpox was a terrible disease and there were outbreaks across the world periodically for centuries. Figure 5.1 on page 81 includes a picture of a smallpox sufferer. The disease not only killed people but those who survived it were left permanently scarred.

In the seventeenth century a method for preventing the disease was brought by merchants from China, where it had been used for centuries. The method was inoculation. The Chinese had observed that some people who had survived a mild form of smallpox did not die when there was a new epidemic. Chinese doctors would take a scraping from a smallpox scab and spread it onto a small open wound,

Figure 5.13 Jenner vaccinating Edward Phipps

giving the patient a mild dose of the disease. Doctors could make huge profits from giving inoculations. However, this method carried risks; some patients would die even from the mild dose they were given and others would go on to carry the disease and spread the infection. In any case, the majority of people were too poor to afford the treatment.

The British doctor Edward Jenner had a new idea after hearing that local farmers did not take inoculations, as they believed that they would not catch smallpox after having had the relatively mild disease of cowpox.

Jenner published his findings in 1798. He observed 23 different cases in which cowpox sufferers had not gone on to develop smallpox when in contact with the disease. He took matter from a cowpox sore and inserted it into two small cuts on a healthy eight-year-old boy (Edward Phipps). The boy was a little unwell for a couple of days and then fully recovered. To test that his idea had worked, Jenner then inoculated the boy with smallpox on two different occasions and the boy was unaffected. Jenner called his new preventative treatment 'vaccination' (*vacca* is Latin for cow). Vaccinations against smallpox quickly spread to the USA and by 1812 there were Arabic translations of Jenner's work.

WOMEN IN MEDICINE

By the nineteenth century, women still held the traditional roles in medicine they had played throughout history, as midwives and primary caregivers to the poor.

However, there were changes during this period. Some women began to make a significant impact – for example, Elizabeth Blackwell was the first woman to qualify as a doctor in the USA in 1849, and the work of Florence Nightingale (see page 97) and Mary Seacole during the Crimean War (1853–56) had an important impact on nursing and the cleanliness of hospitals.

Figure 5.14 Mary Seacole

ACTIVITY: Women in medicine

■ ATL

■ Critical-thinking skills – Gather and organize relevant information to formulate an argument

- In pairs, research and **identify** the impact of one woman in medicine in the nineteenth century. You should present a written report with citations and a 'works cited' list. Your report should be between 700 and 1500 words long.
- Look back to Chapters 1 and 2 to remind yourself how you **formulate** your research question and your action plan.

◆ Assessment opportunities

◆ In this activity you have practised skills that are assessed using Criterion B: Investigating and Criterion C: Communicating.

GERM THEORY

The nineteenth century saw many breakthroughs in the understanding of diseases and how to prevent and treat them.

Louis Pasteur was a French scientist who was asked by a brewing company to investigate why their vats of alcohol were going bad. Pasteur had an interest in micro-organisms. He observed that one type of micro-organism was multiplying fast and may have been the cause of the problem. Pasteur developed 'germ theory' and published a book on this in 1861. He argued against the old theory of 'spontaneous generation' as the cause of decay and said that it occurred because tiny living organisms fall from the air and cause decay. But Pasteur was a scientist and not a doctor, so his ideas were taken forward into medicine by a German doctor called Robert Koch.

Koch studied the bacteria in infected organs and developed a method of isolating and growing bacteria to observe. Koch inspired other scientists to study the causes of diseases – including Pasteur himself. Koch's team identified the causes of tuberculosis in 1880 and cholera in 1883. Other scientists using his methods discovered the causes of typhus in 1880, tetanus in 1884, pneumonia in 1886, meningitis in 1887, plague in 1894 and dysentery in 1898. Pasteur developed vaccines to prevent chicken pox, cholera, anthrax and rabies. Pasteur's discovery led to the pasteurization process of milk (germs in the milk were killed and then it was sealed off from the air, which prevented milk from going sour).

▼ Links to: Biology

Think about the scientists you have come across in your Biology lessons and the contributions they have made to medical technology and innovation.

Emil von Behring, a German scientist, won the Nobel Prize in Medicine in 1901, after pursuing the work of Pasteur and Koch and finding that some animals produce anti-toxins to fight harmful bacteria. He then injected them into humans to prevent diseases such as diphtheria.

A British doctor, Patrick Manson, discovered in 1884 that mosquitos were 'carriers' of a worm that caused elephantiasis. This was significant as scientists soon found that other diseases, such as malaria, were spread by carriers. Charles Chamberland from France discovered viruses – organisms smaller than bacteria that carried diseases.

SURGERY

Surgery was still limited by three key obstacles: pain, infection and blood loss. Indeed, before the nineteenth century, all operations were appalling and traumatic experiences, and many patients died of shock. In London some hospitals had an 80 per cent death rate post-operation.

Despite the lack of anaesthetics and antiseptics, many surgeons attempted new experimental surgeries, with some pioneering operations in the USA in the early nineteenth century. Some historians suggest that surgeons in America were more ready to try out new techniques on black slaves. But to improve patient outcomes, surgeons had to find a way of removing pain, of preventing infections and of compensating for the loss of blood.

THINK–PAIR–SHARE

In pairs, **describe** what is happening in the cartoon in Source E on page 95. What conclusions can be drawn about how surgery was performed at the turn of the nineteenth century? Share your ideas with others in the class.

Explore the history of chemicals used for anaesthetics over the years.

SOURCE E

■ **Figure 5.15** British cartoon from 1793 of an operation to **amputate** a leg

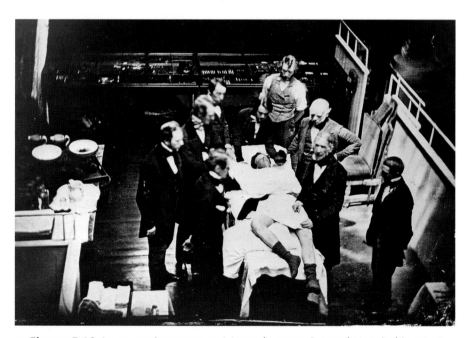

■ **Figure 5.16** An operating room at Massachusetts General Hospital in 1847

Pain had always been a part of surgery and therefore doctors attempted to perform operations as quickly as possible. Chemists began to discover different chemicals that could have anaesthetic results on patients. In the USA in 1842 a patient had a tumour removed from their neck using ether as an anaesthetic; ether was also used in London during the amputation of a leg. In 1845 the American doctor J.C. Warren attempted to use laughing gas to remove a tooth without pain, but it was unsuccessful. Although effective at knocking a patient out, ether was a gas that irritated the lungs and made patients cough throughout a procedure.

Chemists and doctors soon found alternatives – including chloroform in 1847, discovered by the Briton James Simpson, which became widely used. Chloroform induced a rapid sleeping state and was difficult to manage. Some patients died of the effects, others died as surgeons attempted more complex and longer surgeries now that their patients were not screaming and writhing in agony. The impact of the new anaesthetics was often more fatal infections and loss of blood. In 1884 the German doctor Carl Koller used cocaine as a local anaesthetic, which was less dangerous as the patient remained awake. Cocaine was only useful for minor operations.

SOURCE F

On the use of chloroform in childbirth

'It is a most unnatural practice. The pain and sorrow of labour exert a most powerful and useful influence upon the religious and moral character of women and upon all their future relations in life.'

Letter to the British medical journal, The Lancet. *1853.*

SOURCE G

British Army Chief of Medical Staff, 1854

'. . . the smart use of the knife is a powerful tool and it is much better to hear a man bawl lustily than to see him sink silently into the grave.'

DISCUSS

You might think that everyone would be happy to accept the relief from pain brought by the new anaesthetics. However, many individuals and groups objected to their use.

Look at Sources F–H. Consider in pairs or small groups what objections there might be to using anaesthetics in the nineteenth century.

SOURCE H

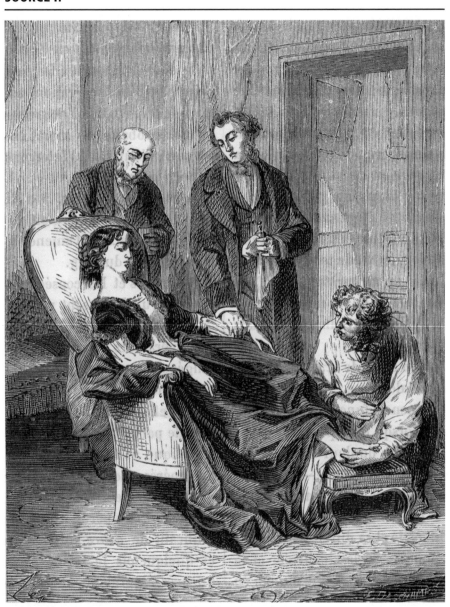

■ **Figure 5.17** Etching from 1848 of Hannah Greener, who died after being given chloroform for an operation to remove a toenail

INFECTION

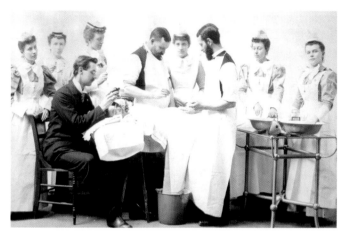

■ **Figure 5.18** A surgeon pictured c.1880, wearing an apron, but without surgical gloves or face-mask

Doctors in the nineteenth century did not wash their equipment after operating, reused bandages and did not clean their clothes or wash their hands. This inevitably spread diseases and infections.

In the 1840s, a Hungarian doctor called Ignaz Semmelweis was concerned by the mortality of babies, specifically those delivered by medical students. He concluded that the higher death rate of babies delivered by students who had come from dissecting corpses was due to their not washing their hands. Semmelweis petitioned for this simple hygiene measure but was not taken seriously by many.

During the Crimean War a British nurse, Florence Nightingale, came to prominence for asserting that cleanliness was critical to the recovery of injured soldiers. She produced diagrams that graphically showed the mortality of soldiers from infections and disease in field hospitals. This led to improvements in the cleanliness of hospitals.

A British surgeon, Joseph Lister, studied gangrene and infections in wounds. He was interested in Pasteur's germ theory. He experimented with carbolic acid and found that if this was sprayed over a wound during surgery it would heal better and gangrene would be prevented. As with all other innovations in medicine, there were objections. Some argued that Lister's methods slowed down surgery and

meant more blood loss. Other surgeons often did not get the same positive results and Lister kept experimenting and changing his methods. Many doctors simply had not read or understood germ theory.

When Koch discovered the bacteria that caused septicaemia in 1878, his evidence supported the methods of Lister. This then led to some revolutionary changes in medical practice as hospitals, instruments and clothing were sterilized regularly and thoroughly.

In the 1890s aseptic surgery began, which meant that all equipment and clothing was steam cleaned; an American surgeon, W.S. Halstead, used rubber gloves when operating, and German surgeons began wearing face-masks. Significant progress in preventing infections had been made.

SOURCE I

'When it had been shown by the researches of Pasteur that the septic property of the atmosphere depended on minute organisms suspended in it, it occurred to me that decomposition in the injured part (following an operation) might be avoided by applying some material capable of destroying the life of the floating particles.'

Lister, J. 1869. An article in the British medical journal, The Lancet.

SOURCE J

'When Lister moved from Glasgow to become Professor of Surgery at King's College Hospital in London in 1877, many surgeons complained that it took too long to keep washing everything. In any case, they refused to believe that infection was spread by dirty operating theatres and tools. People who have new ideas are often regarded as odd. A famous London surgeon at the time could often get a laugh by saying to his students, "Shut the door quickly or one of Mr Lister's microbes may come in".'

Hartley, L. 1984. History of Medicine. *Blackwell.*

DISCUSS

Read Sources I and J. Why was there resistance to Lister's ideas and methods for preventing infection?

BLOOD LOSS

The discoveries made by Lister helped to make Paré's ligatures safer and more effective as the threads used were now sterilized before use. However, blood loss remained a key problem in surgery during the nineteenth century. Experiments were attempted with blood transfusions but blood could not be stored as it would clot and become unusable, and even when blood was usable and directly pumped from a donor the patient would often die after the transfusion was given.

ACTIVITY: Reviewing changes in medicine

■ ATL

- ■ Critical-thinking skills – Gather and organize relevant information to formulate an argument; Consider ideas from multiple perspectives

Aim

Write a news report on the changes to medical practice and understanding between 1800 and 1900.

Who are you?

You are a journalist writing at the end of the nineteenth century.

Who is your audience?

As a journalist, you are writing for a newspaper which will be read by the middle and upper classes in your country. You need to remember to keep your language and tone formal – but use language and expressions that your class will understand.

What should you include?

Include quotes from interviews you have conducted with different people, including the very rich, the middle classes and the poor, those who have benefited from the changes and those who have not, those who supported the new ideas and those who did not accept them, and from doctors and scientists.

How long should your report be?

Aim to make your report approximately 700 words long.

> Hint
>
> Remember to include specific dates, details and examples as, although you are writing as a journalist, for Criterion A you must demonstrate your knowledge and understanding of the changes in medicine between 1800 and 1900.

◆ Assessment opportunities

- ◆ This activity can be assessed using Criterion A: Knowing and understanding and Criterion C: Communicating.

PUBLIC HEALTH

Industrialization, urbanization and population growth, together with the new ideas and medical theories of the nineteenth century, had an impact on the role played by governments in public health. For example, in Britain, sewers were built in cities to remove sewage and to improve water supplies. The government had followed a 'laissez-faire' policy with regard to public health but this approach was challenged by the growth of huge industrial cities with poor housing, no sanitation and no clean water. The lack of proper sewers and clean water had led to severe cholera epidemics, and a London doctor called John Snow had proven the link between the spread of cholera and polluted water supplies.

By the end of the nineteenth century, governments were not only providing sewers and cleaner water supplies but also legislation was passed to prevent the pollution of rivers, to improve the quality of food and even to make some vaccinations compulsory.

DISCUSS

In pairs or small groups, **discuss** why, despite better trained doctors, new scientific discoveries and government interventions in some countries to improve public health, life expectancy and the general health of the poor had not improved significantly by the end of the nineteenth century.

SOURCE K

'These houses of three or four rooms and a kitchen form, throughout England, the general dwellings of the working-class. The streets are generally unpaved, rough, dirty, filled with vegetable and animal refuse, without sewers or gutters, but supplied with foul, stagnant pools instead. Moreover, ventilation is impeded by the bad, confused method of building of the whole quarter, and since many human beings here live crowded into a small space, the atmosphere that prevails in these working-men's quarters may readily be imagined.'

Engels, F. 1845. The Condition of the Working Class in England.

ACTIVITY: Significant individuals and their work

■ ATL

- ■ Organization skills – Use appropriate strategies for organizing complex information

Create a diagram that shows the links between the significant individuals and their work and discoveries in the nineteenth century. This could be a mind map or a flow diagram. Make sure you show how individual discoveries are linked to discoveries, and new ideas and techniques, that came before and after.

What were the significant breakthroughs in medicine in the twentieth century?

In the twentieth century the changes and improvements in medicine continued and gained pace. There were many new scientific discoveries and inventions, and scientific knowledge and understanding made rapid progress. New technology was developed as industrialized societies became richer and there was continued population growth and urbanization. Communications improved further and this meant information and ideas could be shared and tested quickly. Many societies became less religious and looked to scientists for answers to their medical problems.

Many societies were also democratic in the twentieth century and this led voters to pressure their governments to provide better health care for their citizens. The USA became the economic and militarily dominant power and it could afford to invest in research and spread its ideas and products around the world.

In 1901 an Austrian called Karl Landsteiner discovered blood groups and in 1913 the German Richard Lewisohn found that sodium citrate stopped blood from clotting. Knowledge of the human body increased at the beginning of the century when Ernest Starling and William Bayliss discovered the first hormone in 1902, and the Polish chemist Casimir Funk discovered the first vitamins in 1912, which for the first time proved that some diseases were caused by poor diet.

However, the twentieth century also was the century in which more people died of disease, famine and war than in any other.

THE FIRST WORLD WAR

As you will study in Chapter 8, the First World War was a war on a vast and industrialized scale. Huge armies of millions of men could be rapidly mobilized on the railways to the **front lines** and they were armed with deadly weapons that could be mass produced.

War on this scale led to millions of casualties. For example, in the Battle of the Somme in 1916 millions of men were injured on both sides of the conflict. However, this situation led to substantial improvements in surgery because:

- surgeons were dealing with thousands of horrific injuries on a daily basis
- surgeons were sharing ideas to deal with this situation much more than in peace time
- doctors and researchers were united in working for the war effort
- governments devoted more resources to new medical materials and equipment.

Blood loss

The weapons used in the First World War caused severe injuries, not only gunshot and machine-gun wounds but injuries caused by the impact of the big guns in the bombardments.

In 1901 the mystery of why blood transfusions only worked for some patients was solved as different blood groups were identified. However, transfusions were performed on the spot from the donor to the patient. This was not practical or possible on a mass scale and the urgent need to transfuse blood to thousands of casualties led to breakthroughs in understanding how to store blood.

Doctors found that they could separate the liquid part of the blood, the plasma, from the corpuscles. This meant blood could be stored without clotting and then be made usable by adding a saline solution.

French doctors developed the 'triage' system to treat mass casualties, whereby injured men were divided into categories – those who would benefit most from the treatment available, those who would most likely survive and those who were likely to die regardless of what treatment was given. Those most likely to benefit were treated first.

Although X-rays had been invented before the war, in 1895 by a German scientist, Wilhelm Röntgen, they were for the first time used routinely to find bullets and shrapnel in patients. During the war, Marie Curie, a Polish-born French

■ **Figure 5.19** A mobile X-ray vehicle in the First World War

national who had been awarded the Nobel Prize for her research into radiation in 1903, established a front-line X-ray service on the battlefields in France and Belgium. She worked hard fundraising and training staff for mobile X-ray vans.

Infections

Bullets and shrapnel took infection deep into the body, and attempts were made to find new ways of fighting infections. Soldiers' wounds were often infected by fragments of their clothing that carried bacteria and caused deadly gas gangrene. Through experimenting on the vast numbers of injured men, doctors found that cutting away infected tissue and soaking the wound in saline had the best results.

Surgery

Broken bones were common, and new techniques were tried to repair them. Surgeons used skin grafts; indeed, their work was the foundation for plastic surgery.

Many soldiers suffered injuries to their head or face, and surgery to eyes, ears, throat and even the brain, improved. Harold Gillies, through his efforts to help them, became known as the father of modern plastic surgery. One of Gillies's biggest successes was William M. Spreckley (see Figure 5.20), who lost his entire nose in the Battle of Ypres. The surgeon implanted a section of cartilage from one of Spreckley's ribs under his forehead. Then he 'swung' the cartilage and a flap of skin into the nasal cavity to create a new nose. Over time, the new tissue fused with the old and filled the hole.

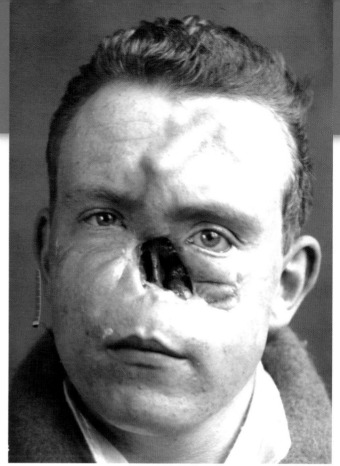

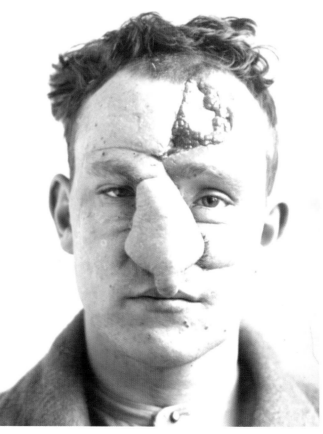

■ **Figure 5.20** One of Harold Gillies's success stories: William M. Spreckley (*top*: before the surgery; *bottom*: after the surgery)

ACTIVITY: Was the First World War good for medicine?

Watch the first 15 minutes of this documentary about medicine in the First World War:

www.nato.int/docu/review/2014/war-medicine/WWI-WW1-Health-care-medicine/EN/index.htm

List the points made in the clip.

Innovations developed in the First World War had a massive impact on survival rates – such as the Thomas splint, named after pioneering Welsh surgeon Hugh Owen Thomas, which secured a broken leg. At the beginning of the war, 80 per cent of all soldiers with a broken femur died. By 1916, 80 per cent of soldiers with this injury survived.

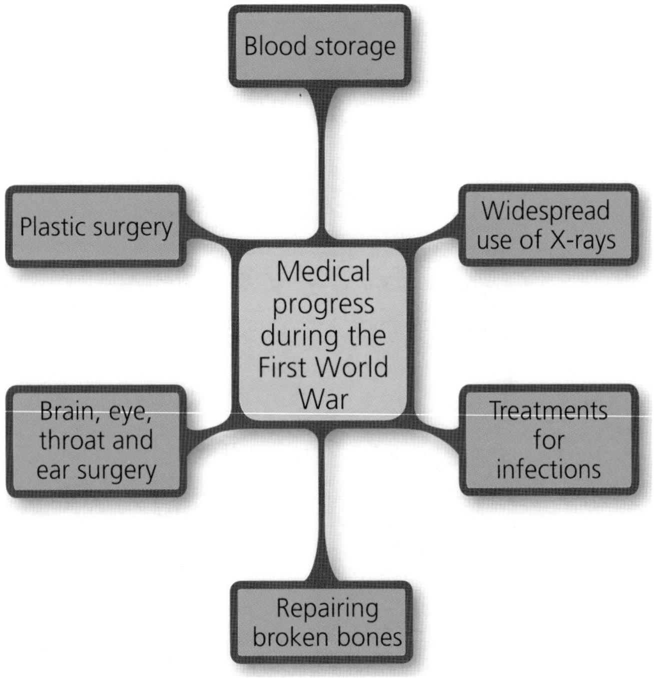

■ **Figure 5.21** Medical progress during the First World War

Did the First World War benefit medicine?

Even though there seem to have been key breakthroughs made during the war, thousands of doctors and medical researchers were drafted away from home to work on the frontlines and in military hospitals which meant that their research work and other practical work was held back. For example, the research that had followed on from Koch's, such as Paul Ehrlich's work on chemical compounds that would kill bacteria, stopped during the war.

The nature of trench warfare led to many illnesses such as trench foot and typhus and it spread diseases among the men living in close proximity in filthy conditions. There was also the negative and often debilitating psychological impact of the war which led to conditions such as shell shock.

However, on the positive side, the First World War led to an increased commitment by governments to intervene in public health. During the war governments had introduced conscription which meant that all men of certain ages had to join up to fight. However, the recruiting officers found that many of the men had physical problems and diseases and were malnourished.

After the war the victorious countries promised better conditions for the working people. In Britain the Prime Minister Lloyd George said that he would build half a million new homes offering better housing that would be 'fit for heroes'. A Ministry of Health was set up to investigate and improve sanitation and health and it trained doctors, nurses, dentists and midwives. This involvement by the government in attempting to improve public health even continued when a deep global economic depression developed in the 1930s, with the introduction of free milk for all school children in 1934.

THE SECOND WORLD WAR

'If any good can be said to come of war, then the Second War must go on record as assisting and accelerating one of the greatest blessings that the twentieth century has conferred on Man – the huge advances in medical knowledge and surgical techniques.

'War, by producing so many and such appalling casualties, and by creating such widespread conditions in which disease can flourish, confronted the medical profession with an enormous challenge – and the doctors of the world rose to the challenge of the last war magnificently.'

Brian J. Ford, American research biologist, 1970

As you will study in Chapter 8, the Second World War was a war on an even greater scale than the First World War. Millions were mobilized around the world and fought in a conflict that brought war to the **home front** as never seen before.

In the years between the wars, 1918–39, research had continued on both the prevention and the cures of diseases, aided by new inventions. In 1931 the electron microscope was invented, and in the USA Edgar Allen discovered the female hormone oestrogen in 1923; a decade later, the male hormone testosterone was found.

In 1909 Paul Ehrlich found a chemical compound to treat syphilis bacteria. The search to find more so-called 'magic bullets' that would attack microbes in the body to cure illnesses led to a breakthrough by a German doctor, Gerhard Domagk, in 1932. He found that Prontosil had a positive impact on mice with blood poisoning and tested it on his own daughter when she became desperately ill with blood poisoning. Due to the invention of a powerful new type of microscope, the active ingredient in Prontosil was soon identified by French scientists. These sulphonamides led to the development of a range of new drugs to treat diseases such as pneumonia.

Penicillin

In addition, in the interwar period, penicillin was developed. The mould from which it is made was first discovered in the nineteenth century and Lister had used it to treat an infected wound.

However, Lister did not document his work and it was not until 1928 that penicillin was rediscovered and experimented with by Alexander Fleming in London. It seems that he found the mould growing by accident in a dish and realized its potential to fight infections. However, he did not have financial support to develop his ideas.

■ **Figure 5.22** Alexander Fleming

When the Second World War broke out in Europe in 1939, an Oxford scientist, Howard Florey, asked the British government for funding to develop penicillin. By 1941 the team had tested it with good results on mice and needed to produce more penicillin to test on humans. The production of penicillin was very slow and costly. Even though there were huge numbers of casualties who could benefit from the production of penicillin, the British government lacked funds and was also vulnerable to aerial bombing, which could destroy expensive production sites.

The USA joined the Second World War at the end of 1941. In 1942, US companies received $80 million of government money to start the mass production of penicillin. This led to quick results and by 1943 penicillin was being mass-produced. It was used by the British Army in North Africa with astonishing effects. Lieutenant Colonel Pulvertaft, of the British Army in North Africa, wrote in 1943:

'We had enormous numbers of infected wounded, terrible burn cases … Sulphonamides had absolutely no effect on these cases. The last thing I tried was penicillin … The first man I tried it on was a young New Zealand officer … He had been in bed with compound fractures of both legs. His sheets were soaked with pus and the heat of Cairo made it smell intolerable. Normally he would die in a short time. I gave three injections a day of penicillin … the thing seemed like a miracle. In ten days' time the leg was cured and in a month's time the young fellow was back on his feet. I had enough penicillin for ten cases. Nine out of ten of them were complete cures.'

■ **Figure 5.23** A war poster about penicillin

By 1944 there was enough penicillin for every injured soldier during the D-Day landings in Normandy. In the aftermath of D-Day, penicillin was found to be very good at preventing gangrene.

The US army was using approximately 2 million doses of penicillin a month by 1945, and some suggest that allied deaths would have risen by almost 15 per cent without it. The period of time from when a soldier was injured to when they could be operated on had not improved since the First World War; in the British army it was estimated to take 14 hours. This delay in treatment would allow wounds to become dangerously infected and penicillin reduced the infection and increased survival rates. The penicillin developed in 1945 was 20 times more powerful than that used in 1939.

Surgical techniques

The Second World War also led to developments in the treatment of severe burns. In Britain, Archibald McIndoe pioneered new techniques, and in Russia Vladmir Filatov pioneered reconstructive plastic surgery with a new form of skin graft. The Russians also researched 'biogenic agents' that would aid healing.

The war also led to the growth of a far more sophisticated blood transfusion system, where blood could be stored in bulk and transported quickly to where it was needed.

Combating diseases

The Second World War was fought across the globe, with the main theatres of fighting in Europe, North Africa and Asia. The war in the Pacific brought hundreds of thousands of troops into contact with mosquitoes and the threat of malaria. For the first time there was a coherent scientific investigation into mosquito bites. The Australian doctor Neil Hamilton Fairley experimented on volunteers and found that one tablet of Mepacrine a day could limit the spread of malaria, and German scientists made similar findings using Atebrin against malaria. Soldiers were also immunized against tetanus before being sent into battle and this proved to be very effective.

Improvements to public health

As had happened after the First World War, governments intervened to improve public health after the Second World War. In Britain, a government commission was set up during the war, in 1942, to offer benefits for all people after the war. The resulting Beveridge Report recommended that a welfare state should be set up which would provide free health care, education, housing and employment after the war (see also page 78).

The British National Health Service (NHS) began in July 1948. Hundreds of thousands of new homes were built. However, much of the 'slum' housing in Britain's cities had been destroyed by bombing and there was an acute housing shortage, food and fuel shortages and a lack of clean water across post-war Europe. Many countries on both sides of the conflict were economically devastated and could not afford urgent medical treatment for injured and disabled servicemen, and public health was not the priority.

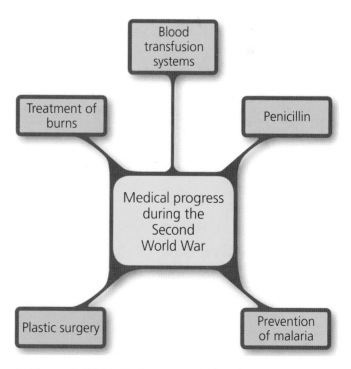

■ **Figure 5.24** Medical progress during the Second World War

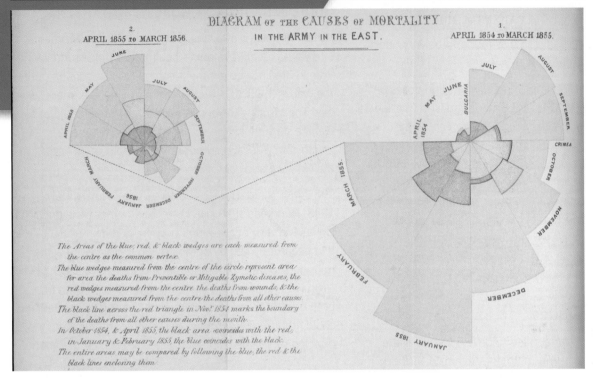

■ **Figure 5.25** Diagrams by Florence Nightingale recording the causes of death in field hospitals during the Crimean War, 1854–56

SOURCE M

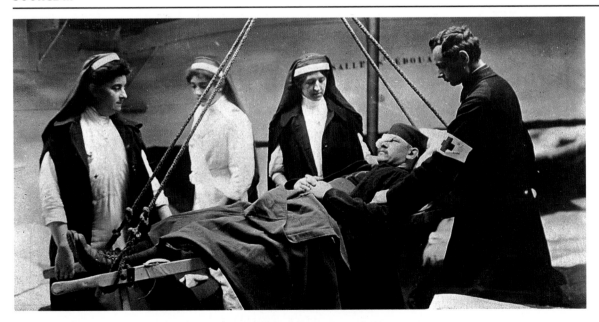

■ **Figure 5.26** Nurses tending to wounded soldiers in France, 1915

SOURCE N

The role of Major Jonathan Letterman in the US Civil War, 1861–65

'Before Letterman's innovations, wounded men were often left to fend for themselves. Unless carried off the field by a comrade, or one of the regimental musicians doubling as a stretcher bearer, a wounded soldier could lie for days suffering from exposure and thirst. Letterman started the very first Ambulance Corps, training men to act as stretcher-bearers and operate wagons to pick up the wounded and bring them to field dressing stations. He also instituted the concept of triage for treatment of casualties.'

'Jonathan Letterman, Major, December 11, 1824 – March 15, 1872'. The Civil War Trust. Web. 2014.

SOURCE O

■ **Figure 5.27** US poster from 1942

ACTIVITY: The impact of war on medical progress

■ ATL

- Critical-thinking skills – Gather and organize relevant information to formulate an argument; Recognize unstated assumptions and bias

1 In pairs, **discuss** what each of these sources (L to Q) suggests about the impact of war on medical progress in the nineteenth and twentieth centuries.
2 With reference to the origin and purpose, **analyse** the values and limitations of using Sources N and O to assess the impact of war on medical progress.
3 **Using** Sources L to Q and your own knowledge from this chapter, draft a detailed essay plan to answer the following question: 'War has been the key factor in improving medical knowledge and practice.' To what extent do you agree with this statement?

◆ Assessment opportunities

- ◆ This activity can be assessed using Criterion A: Knowing and understanding and Criterion D: Thinking critically.

SOURCE P

'Fleming's discovery of penicillin in 1928 was initially over-looked and was only made into an effective drug in World War Two, when medical researchers were seeking a method of infection control in troops.'

Selve, H. 1975. From Dream to Discovery: On Being a Scientist. USA. Arno Press.

SOURCE Q

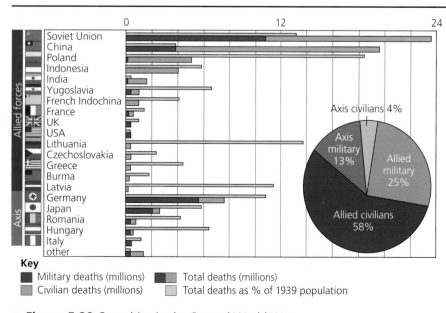

■ **Figure 5.28** Casualties in the Second World War

ACTIVITY: Bringing medical change up to date

What is your goal?

Your goal is to research the key discoveries and developments that have taken place in medicine since the 1950s.

- Work in groups and research medical breakthroughs. You could include: contraceptive pills, DNA, stem cells, CAT scanners, MRI scans, the Human Genome Project, open-heart surgery, organ transplants, joint replacements and keyhole surgery.
- Examine the role of key causal factors, for example, significant individuals, war, new inventions and technology and wealth in these medical advances.

How will you achieve this?

- Use the topic as a foundation for you to **formulate** and refine your own research question.
- As a theme, you could include the role of causal factors in medical progress, for example war or significant individuals or wealth.
- See earlier chapters and research activities for help with **evaluating** your investigation process and results.
- Communicate your information clearly and make sure you have structured your report coherently.
- Remember to use one standard or recognized method to **document** your sources of information.
- You must keep within the word count: 700–1500 words.

◆ **Assessment opportunities**

- ◆ This activity can be assessed using Criterion B: Investigating and Criterion C: Communicating.

DISCUSS

You have inquired into medicine through time in this chapter. Now **discuss** in class the role of governments in the progress of medicine. To what extent should governments be responsible for public health? Should governments increase taxes to pay for free health care for all in society?

! Take action

! Medicine in the twenty-first century still faces many challenges. Although life expectancy has consistently risen in the developed world since the nineteenth century, doctors are still unable to cure certain diseases, viruses and cancer. Illnesses related to old age, such as dementia, are also more common.

! Another challenge is health inequality. In most societies, the poor have lower life expectancy than the wealthy and the poor have limited access to medical treatment.

! Investigate the actions of the World Health Organization (WHO) and promote its initiatives in your school. Inquire into local organizations in your community that fundraise for medical research and find out how your class can support them.

Reflection

In this chapter we have examined the key developments in medicine and health in the nineteenth and twentieth centuries by investigating the impact of the Industrial Revolution, war and individuals in bringing about change.

Reflecting on our learning …
Use this table to reflect on your own learning in this chapter.

Questions we asked	Answers we found	Any further questions now?			
Factual					
Conceptual					
Debatable					
Approaches to learning you used in this chapter:	Description – what new skills did you learn?	How well did you master the skills?			
		Novice	Learner	Practitioner	Expert
Collaboration skills					
Communication skills					
Critical-thinking skills					
Information literacy skills					
Organization skills					
Learner profile attribute	*Reflect on the importance of being open minded for our learning in this chapter.*				
Open minded					

 Do social, cultural and artistic movements reflect the era in which they take place?

○ *Social, cultural and artistic movements* reflect the *time, place and space* of their *civilization*.

■ **Figure 6.1** Poster by Alexander Rodchenko encouraging workers to attend education classes following the Bolshevik Revolution in Russia

CONSIDER THESE QUESTIONS:

Factual: What are some of the social, cultural and artistic movements of the nineteenth and twentieth centuries? What factors caused these movements?

Conceptual: How are artists influenced by the time period in which they live?

Debatable: To what extent can social, cultural or artistic movements bring about change in society?

Now **share and compare** your thoughts and ideas with your partner, or with the whole class.

○ IN THIS CHAPTER, WE WILL ...

■ **Find out** about different art and cultural movements.
■ **Explore:**
  ■ the reasons why these movements developed
  ■ the impact of these movements.
■ **Take action** by considering current cultural movements and looking at how far they reflect today's society.

DISCUSS: What can paintings tell us?

What can paintings tell us about the time period in which they were painted?

Study the paintings in Figure 6.2 and reflect on what you can learn about the societies from which they come.

Now consider and **discuss** these questions:
- **How useful do you think such artwork is to a historian?**
- **What other art forms can be helpful to a historian in finding out about the past?**

■ **Figure 6.2** (*top*) *Madonna and Child* by Berlinghiero, thirteenth-century Italy (the Middle Ages) and (*bottom*) *Madonna of the Meadow* by the Italian artist Giovanni Bellini in the fifteenth century, the period known as the Renaissance

Often, as historians, we focus primarily on the political and economic developments of any given time period. However, these same political and economic developments often impact also on the art, and cultural and social developments, of the day.

Thus, by looking at art, for instance, we can learn much about the attitudes of the time as well as the technological developments which are reflected in the styles and the forms of artwork.

This chapter will look at two historical events: the Industrial Revolution and the First World War, both of which are covered elsewhere in this book from a political angle. Here, we look at how these historical developments influenced art and culture. In addition, we examine the impact of the Russian Revolution on Soviet art and culture, and the significance of the youth movement of the 1960s in causing social and cultural change in the USA and Europe.

How did the Industrial Revolution affect developments in art?

ROMANTICISM

At the start of the Industrial Revolution, the main painting style was Romantic. Romanticism referred back to a pre-industrial life; the artists used past lifestyles for their inspiration, for example, rural scenes and landscapes or scenes from classical mythology. They showed an appreciation for life before industrialization and offered an escape into a 'better', more romanticized life that had existed in the past.

REALISM

Realist artists, such as Luke Fildes and George Bellows, whose paintings are shown here, reacted against Romanticism and attempted to portray the world as it really was. The urban worker and the common labourer were now the subjects – along with real scenes from rural and urban landscapes, with artists trying to accurately portray some of the harsh conditions of the poor. Thus, while the artists of Romanticism tried to show an idealized, optimistic picture of mankind, Realism often showed a more realistic view that did not avoid unpleasant or uncomfortable aspects of how people lived at the time.

■ **Figure 6.3** *The Widower* by Luke Fildes

■ **Figure 6.4** *New York* by George Bellows

A leading Realist was the French painter Gustave Courbet (1819–77), who said that his goal was 'to change the public's taste and way of seeing'. Courbet claimed to never use imagination but just to paint what he saw. This shocked contemporary opinion; however, his revolutionary ideas of focusing on truth and accuracy in art spread to other countries.

In Russia, a group called the Peredvizhniki or Wanderers formed in the 1860s and included Realists such as Ilya Repin. They wanted to use their paintings to focus on inequalities and injustices in everyday life. In America, the Ashcan School included artists such as George Bellows and Robert Henri, and in England, Luke Fildes and L.S. Lowry were both Realist painters who depicted the everyday lives of the poorer sections of society.

Such paintings were bought by the new wealthy middle classes, who could afford the time and money to buy art. These people were more interested in buying paintings that reflected their own activities and real life. Their middle-class homes did not have space for vast canvases, so paintings became smaller.

The Industrial Revolution also encouraged the growth of the Realist movement by making it easier for painters to travel outside their studios to paint. The invention of metal tubes for storing oil paint was particularly important.

DISCUSS

What can you learn from these paintings about life and work in the nineteenth century? Why do you think that Courbet's aim to paint only what he could see shocked public opinion? Why would many people still prefer Romanticism in art?

■ **Figure 6.5** *Barge Haulers on the Volga* by Ilya Repin

■ **Figure 6.6** *The Stone Breakers* by Gustave Courbet

PHOTOGRAPHY

Technological developments in the Industrial Revolution, particularly the access to chemicals, led to the invention of the camera and a new art form – photography. This helped 'Realism' to become more popular. The new wealthy middle class also encouraged photography; these people wanted to be photographed in the same way that the nobility had wanted their portraits painted in earlier times. However, it was both easier and cheaper to get portraits done by photography rather than by oil painting.

Photography also played a role in revealing – in even more detail than the Realist paintings – the conditions in factories. The American photographer Lewis Hine, for example, used photos to document child labour in the USA, thus helping to raise awareness and change child labour laws.

■ **Figure 6.7** Photo by Lewis Hine, glassworks at midnight, 1908

ACTIVITY: The impact of the Industrial Revolution on art

■ ATL

- ■ Information literacy skills – Access information to be informed

The Industrial Revolution affected artists in many different ways. Some embraced the opportunities offered by the new conditions and new technologies, while others rejected them or tried to return to an earlier age of craftsmanship.

Write the following essay: '**Evaluate** the impact of the Industrial Revolution on artistic developments.' Your word count should be between 700 and 1500 words.

Consider the impact of the following in your answer:
- **Changes in living and working conditions and how this affected the *motives* of artists**
- **The growth of an affluent middle class**
- **Technological developments**

Before starting to write your essay, research the impact of the Industrial Revolution on the artists below. Make brief notes on each artist:
- **William Morrison**
- **Josiah Wedgewood**
- **An Art Nouveau artist of your choice**

◆ Assessment opportunities

◆ In this activity you have practised skills that are assessed using Criterion A: Knowing and understanding and Criterion C: Communicating.

DISCUSS

In what ways could Realist art and photography help bring about social change in the nineteenth century?

What impact did the First World War have on culture?

'One can say that all the fundamentals of our world have been affected by the war, or more exactly, by the circumstances of the war; something deeper has been worn away than the renewable parts of a machine … The Mind has been cruelly wounded; its complaint is heard in the hearts of intellectual men; it passes a mournful judgement on its self. It doubts itself profoundly.'

Paul Valery, a French thinker and poet, speaking in 1922

The First World War was the first war to bring about a wealth of artistic output from soldiers who fought on the battlefields; writers and artists who took part all produced works that tried to deal with the horrors of this war and to help future generations understand what had gone on in the trenches. Paul Nash, who was sent out by the British government as an official artist, wrote:

'It is unspeakable, godless, hopeless. I am no longer an artist interested and curious, I am a messenger who will bring back word from the men who are fighting to those who want the war to go on for ever. Feeble, inarticulate, will be my message, but it will have a bitter truth, and may it burn their lousy souls.'

Nash, P. 1949. Outline: An Autobiography and other Writings. London. Faber and Faber.

ACTIVITY: The First World War in art and literature

■ ATL

- ■ Transfer skills – Inquire in different contexts to gain a different perspective

Task 1

Visit this website:

> **www.memorial-caen.fr/10EVENT/EXPO1418/gb/ visite.html**

You will find many different First World War artworks by artists of different nationalities. Choose the four paintings that you find the most powerful or interesting. Copy each one into a Word document and write your own **explanation** of the painting and why you have chosen it. Print off your document and use it to create a display of First World War artwork where you have the opportunity to read each other's comments.

Task 2

Research literature inspired by the war. Choose either a poem, a play or a novel written in the 1920s and write a review of what it reveals about the First World War. This should be no more than 700 words long.

◆ Assessment opportunities

- ◆ In this activity you have practised skills that are assessed using Criterion B: Investigating, Criterion C: Communicating and Criterion D: Thinking critically.

▼ Links to: Literature

Why do you think the First World War captured the literary imagination? Think about the poets, novelists and writers you have studied in your Literature lessons.

DISCUSS

In pairs, and using Criterion D – analysing and evaluating sources in terms of their origin and purpose – **discuss** the value and limitations to historians of the poems, novels or plays you have researched while studying the First World War.

DADA MOVEMENT

'The painter once believed in something, but now he paints only a hole without meaning, without anything – nothing but nothingness, the nothingness of our time.'

George Grosz

■ **Figure 6.8** *Deutschland, ein Wintermärchen* (Germany, A Winter's Tale) by George Grosz, 1918

The First World War also helped to foster new artistic and cultural movements. One of these was Dada. This movement began at the start of the First World War and was a protest against bourgeois, nationalist and colonialist interests, which many believed had been responsible for the war.

It was a movement that rejected reason and logic and put value on nonsense and irrationality. In fact, it was called 'anti-art' as it was contrary to everything that art stood for. It was against beauty and attempting to please the eye; it was intended to offend people – particularly traditionalists. Indeed, given the horrors of the First World War, these artists believed that 'nice' art had no place left in the world.

Dada had only one rule, which was 'Never follow any known rules.' It developed in different ways in different countries. In Germany, which was suffering from political turbulence and economic crisis after the First World War, Dada was used by artists such as Hannah Hoch and George Grosz to express support for communist ideas. Grosz's works attack conservatism, **militarism** and ultra-nationalism.

In 1920, Grosz, along with other Dada artists, organized the First International Dada Fair in Berlin. Among the paintings was Grosz's *Gott mit uns* (God is with us), which included a sketch of a crucified Jesus wearing a gasmask and combat boots. Another exhibit which was designed to shock was the effigy of a German soldier with the head of a pig. Many Germans were outraged and Grosz and several others were put on trial for 'grossly insulting the German army'.

ℹ

Dada

The origin of the term Dada is unclear. It could be just a nonsense word, thus supporting the aims of Dada. Another theory is that the name 'Dada' came when a paper knife was stuck into a French–German dictionary during a meeting of the artists and that it happened to point to *dada*, a French word for hobbyhorse.

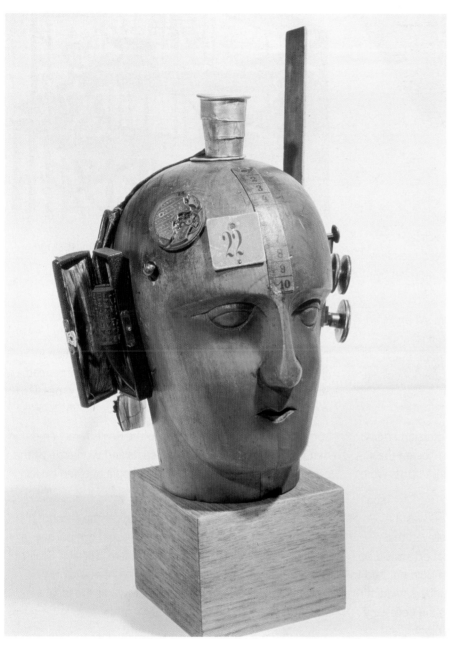

■ **Figure 6.9** *Mechanical Head – Spirit of Our Age* by Raoul Hausmann, 1919, made from a mannequin head, parts of a camera and watch, a tape measure and other objects

How did the Bolshevik Revolution in Russia affect culture and society?

Figure 6.10 1920s design for a Constructivist stage setting in a theatre by Alexandra Exter

Revolution in Russia

In 1917, there was a revolution in Russia, which overthrew the Tsar. However, the Provisional Government, which then ruled Russia, was itself overthrown by the Bolsheviks, who followed the ideas of Karl Marx, and were aiming for a revolution led by the proletariat or workers.

The Bolsheviks were led by Vladimir Lenin. When Lenin died in 1924, after surviving a civil war against anti-Bolshevik forces, he was succeeded by Joseph Stalin. Russia became a one-party totalitarian state during this period.

Following the Bolshevik Revolution in 1917, Russian artists also experimented with new art forms that rejected the bourgeois way of life and bourgeois art. These artists were known as 'avant-garde'.

One movement which emerged in this period was the Constructivist movement. Constructivists believed that there should not be 'art for art's sake' or that art should be separate from society – but rather that art should be used to change society. One of the movement's founders, Vladimir Tatlin, wrote, 'Not the old, not the new, but the necessary'. Constructivists supported the Bolshevik Revolution and wanted to create a new proletarian culture based on the worker and on industrial technology. Art was to help alter everything – from the way people dressed to how they lived and how they travelled.

Everything was constructed in 'industrial style', which used geometrical shapes and straight lines.

WHAT WAS SOCIALIST REALISM?

In the 1930s Stalin put an end to all experimentation in art. Avant-garde artists were looked down upon. Instead, Socialist Realism became the officially approved type of art in the Soviet Union for nearly 60 years.

Socialist Realism had similarities to the Realism movement in that it put ordinary people – peasants and workers – at the centre of art and showed ordinary people in common life situations.

However, unlike the Realism movement of the second half of the nineteenth century, artists could not portray ordinary people exactly as they saw them. Socialist Realism had a political aim, which was to highlight and glorify the proletariat's (workers') struggle towards the ideal socialist state.

Andrei Zhdanov, in a speech 1934 at the first All-Union Congress of Soviet Writers, first used the term 'Socialist Realism'. He explained that art should 'depict life faithfully', while showing 'reality in its revolutionary development', and that 'Soviet literature must be able to show our heroes, must be able to glimpse our tomorrow'. Although he was talking about literature, the same ideas were to apply to all arts.

Thus, in paintings, workers were always portrayed in a heroic way; they were always shown as being happy, fit and healthy – enjoying their work, which was helping to develop the Socialist state. Bold colours were used and the message was easily understood; such art was designed to appeal to the masses and the intention was that, by viewing it, the workers and peasants would see the importance of their work, which would help to educate them in the goals of communism.

Stalin described the artists of Socialist Realism as 'engineers of the soul'. Posters were the most common form of this type of art in the Soviet Union. Sculpture, literature and cinema also followed Socialist Realism.

Case study: Vsevolod Meyerhold (1874–1940)

Meyerhold was a well-known theatre director. He was also a founder of the avant-garde theatre which had flourished in the 1920s when the Bolsheviks took over.

In 1937 Meyerhold decided to produce a play based on a novel by Nikolai Ostrovsky, called *How the Steel was Tempered*. However, the play was not allowed as it did not follow the rules for Socialist Realism; it was realistic about the horrors of the Russian Civil War that had occurred in the 1920s, but this was not the kind of realism that was now expected.

In 1937, Meyerhold was attacked in *Pravda* (the government newspaper) and then his theatre was closed. His views on Socialist Realism can be seen in Source B. He was arrested, tortured and shot in January 1940.

ACTIVITY: Critics of Socialist Realism

■ ATL

- Critical-thinking skills – Evaluate evidence and arguments

1 In Source A, what points does Peter Kenez make about Socialist Realism as an art form in the Soviet Union?

2 In Source B, in which ways does the theatre director Meyerhold agree with Peter Kenez?

3 What do these sources, and the information box on Meyerhold, reveal about the link between state and culture in the Soviet Union?

◆ Assessment opportunities

- In this activity you have practised skills that are assessed using Criterion D: Thinking critically.

SOURCE A

'Stalinist art was counterfeit [false]; its great power resided in its ability to exchange an artificial world surreptitiously for the real one. The victims of this sleight of hand were shown an entirely imaginary and yet seemingly realistic and self-consistent universe over and over again. The make-believe universe was full of references to itself. For example, there was a series of films about a mythical revolutionary character called Maxim. He was more real to audiences than a historical character. At the time of World War Two it was Maxim who turned to the Soviet people, encouraging them to fight … For socialist realist art to [do what it was meant to], it had to enjoy complete monopoly … it had to completely dominate the artistic world.'

Kenez, P. Cinema and Soviet Society: From the Revolution to the Death of Stalin, I.B. Tauris, p. 145.

SOURCE B

'I, for one, find the work of our theatres at present pitiful and terrifying. This pitiful and sterile something that aspires to the title of socialist realism has nothing in common with art … go to the Moscow theatres and look at the colourless, boring productions which are all so alike and differ only in their degree of worthlessness … In your efforts to eradicate formalism, you have destroyed art!'

Meyerhold, V. quoted in Tucker, R.C. 1992. Stalin in Power: The Revolution from above, 1928–1941. Norton, p. 563.

WHAT WAS THE IMPACT OF SOCIALIST REALISM IN THE SOVIET UNION?

As only Socialist Realism was allowed, artists and writers who wanted to pursue other types of art were forced to keep silent. The historian Robert Service concludes that in the USSR 'No great work of literature was published in the 1930s and all artistic figures went in fear of their lives.'

The case study on Meyerhold (page 119) gives you an idea of what happened to artists who refused to conform.

SOURCE C

■ **Figure 6.11** *The Worker and the Kolkhoz Woman*, Vera Mukhina, 1937

SOURCE D

■ **Figure 6.12** *A Kolkhoz Celebration*, 1937, by Sergei Gerasimov (1885–1964) (a *kolkhoz* was a communal farm)

■ **Figure 6.13** *Unforgettable Meeting* by Vasili Yefanov, 1930s

DISCUSS

1 Consider Sources C–E, examples of Socialist Realism. What message is being given to the viewer in each case?
2 Why do you think that Socialist Realism rarely showed scenes of family or domestic life?

THINK–PAIR–SHARE

Using the examples that we have looked at in this chapter, plus any others that you are familiar with, consider the following questions. When you have come up with your own ideas, **discuss** them with a partner. Then have a class discussion.

1 To what extent are art movements influenced by the environment of the time?
2 'Art helps to change views/ideas.' How far do you agree with this statement? **Explain** the reasons for your conclusions and include examples.
3 **Identify** other examples where governments have used art to change people's ideas.

Why were the 1960s a period of cultural and social change?

In the 1960s, a youth movement developed which led to radical cultural and social developments. It started in the USA and in the UK and then spread throughout much of the Western world. It is often called a 'counter-culture' movement as it was anti-establishment, which means it went against the existing ideas and norms of society and politics. It also gained momentum from the fight for civil rights (see Chapter 11) for both black Americans and for women, and the protest against the Vietnam War.

WHY DID THIS MOVEMENT DEVELOP?

The 1950s was a period of affluence in the USA so it might seem strange that a rebellious movement should develop at this time. However, there are several factors that contributed to this youth movement and helped to further the protest that became a part of it:

- The 1950s had seen a 'baby boom' and so by the 1960s there were many teenagers, an increasing number of whom were attending university. This helped ideas to spread.
- These children had grown up in the Cold War with the continual threat of nuclear annihilation; there was frustration and anger about this.
- Young people also rebelled against the consumerism which had obsessed the 1950s post-war and post-depression generation.
- Films of the 1950s such as *Rebel Without a Cause* and the emergence of rock 'n' roll helped to fuel this rebellion, especially as adults hated the new type of music.

The Vietnam War

In 1965, President Johnson started sending US troops to South Vietnam to prevent the government there falling to communism. Americans believed that if Vietnam became communist, then there would be a 'domino effect' on other countries in the region causing them to become communist too.

The American soldiers fought the guerilla forces of the Vietnamese communists and casualties were high; over 68 000 Americans died in this war.

By 1968, many Americans were protesting against US involvement in the war, which seemed to be achieving nothing and resulting in so much death. The brutal actions of the US troops against the Vietnamese, which Americans watched on television, also turned many against the war. Students led the protest against President Johnson. In the first half of 1968, there were over 100 demonstrations against Vietnam, involving 40 000 students.

- Although there was increasing wealth in the USA, there were large minority groups that were not part of this wealth – many poor white Americans as well as black Americans, who had low-paid jobs and lived in slum areas of cities.
- There was growing frustration at the lack of civil rights for black Americans.
- Women who had gained freedom and work experience during the Second World War (see page 75) were frustrated at the expectations that they should remain at home. This frustration was exacerbated by the fact that increased wealth meant more household devices, which lessened the need for domestic work. The growth of suburbs, meanwhile, encouraged families to move into bigger houses and this increased the isolation of women who were at home all day. In addition, many women now had university degrees.
- In 1961 the new president of the USA, John F. Kennedy, was the youngest president ever and with his youth and glamour raised expectations that it was possible to provide solutions to America's problems. However, the **assassination** of Kennedy in 1963 disillusioned many young Americans and drove them into protest movements.

SOURCE F

Jim Morrison, lead singer of the group The Doors, 1969

'I like ideas about the breaking away or overthrowing of the established order. I am interested in anything about revolt, disorder, chaos, especially activity that seems to have no meaning. It seems to me to be the road towards freedom – eternal freedom is a way to bring about internal freedom.'

SOURCE G

A statement issued by Students for a Democratic Society (SDS) in 1962

'Universal controlled disarmament must replace deterrence and arms control as the [American] national defense goal … It is necessary that America make disarmament, not nuclear deterrence, "credible" to the Soviets and to the world.'

SOURCE H

From the song 'The Times they are A-changin'' by Bob Dylan, written in 1963

'Come mothers and fathers throughout the land
And don't criticize what you can't understand
Your sons and your daughters are beyond your command
Your old road is rapidly ageing
Please get out of the new one if you can't lend a hand
For the times they are a-changin''

SOURCE I

Mario Savio, a student from Berkeley University, California, which was one of the centres of student radicalism

'There is a time when the operation of the machine becomes so odious, makes you sick at heart, that you can't take part; you can't even passively take part and you've got to put your bodies upon the gears and upon the wheels, upon the levers, upon all the apparatus and you've got to make it stop.'

SOURCE J

Country Joe McDonald singing at the Woodstock Festival in the 1960s. This rock festival attracted half a million young Americans and was a celebration of the hippy lifestyle

'And it's one, two, three, what are we fighting for?
Don't ask me I don't give a damn. Next stop is Vietnam
And it's five, six, seven, open up those pearly gates
Well I ain't got time to wonder why. We all gonna die.'

ACTIVITY: Source evaluation

■ ATL

- Critical thinking skills – Recognize unstated assumptions and bias

Read Sources F–J. **Analyse** and **evaluate** these sources in terms of origin and purpose and **identify** the concerns and the aims of young people in the 1960s.

> Hint
>
> Make sure you make a note of the concerns and aims expressed in each source before you write your response. Some sources may express similar ideas. Do not leave any of the sources out of your write up.

◆ Assessment opportunities

- ◆ This activity can be assessed using Criterion D: Thinking critically.

DISCUSS

Two of these sources (H and J) are from songs of the time. What effect do you think such songs would have had on young people? How useful are song lyrics as historical evidence of society at this time?

■ **Figure 6.15** Hippies in the 1960s

WHAT WERE THE RESULTS OF THE 1960S YOUTH MOVEMENT?

Social developments

By the end of the 1960s, lifestyles of the young had changed radically. This is when the term 'teenager' came into use and young people started having their own culture – magazines, television programmes, music and fashion.

The new culture brought more freedom – in relationships, which was influenced further by the introduction of the contraception pill, in fashion, for example the miniskirt, and in music, where songs were often about peace, free love and drugs.

■ **Figure 6.14** New fashions for women in the 1960s

The hippie movement

Some young people decided to drop out of society altogether and become hippies. They developed an alternative lifestyle, often travelling around the country in buses or vans or living in communes and promoting 'peace not war'. They wore distinctive clothes, had long hair and wore flowers as a symbol of peace. They experimented with drugs such as marijuana and LSD and refused to work. Many were middle-class white college students, which was a particular source of alarm to parents and politicians.

Student protest

Students were involved in protest movements in the 1960s. They organized rallies and marches to support the civil rights campaign and took part in direct action such as sit-ins (see page 259).

In addition, they led the protest against the war in Vietnam – not just in the USA but in other countries as well. In the USA, a group called Students for a Democratic Society (SDS) was established, which denounced the Cold War and demanded controlled disarmament to prevent the possibility of a nuclear war.

SDS, and students in universities across Europe, demanded a greater say in how courses and universities were run, leading to demonstrations and strikes. 1968 was a key year for students; in Paris, student protests against the establishment brought France to a standstill in this year.

ACTIVITY: Investigating the social and cultural developments of the 1960s

■ ATL

- Information literacy skills – Access information to be informed and inform others

Watch the following video: *People's Century: New Release 1968* and answer questions 1–3:

http://youtu.be/tBjZRh4KOOl?list=PLuL26fXZ8eTNLLn ugg2BTyOZQ7HT-QZk4

1 **What reasons do people in the programme give for youth rebellion?**
2 **What examples does the video give of the social and cultural impact of this rebellion?**
3 **What impact did this rebellion have on politics in the USA and in Europe?**

Now, **investigate** the culture of the 1960s further.

How will you achieve this?

Get into groups. Each group should **investigate** one of the following areas of youth culture that developed in the 1960s:

- **Fashion (for both males and females)**
- **Television**
- **Film**
- **Dance**
- **Magazines**
- **Protest songs**

How will you present your findings?

Your group will prepare a presentation, which can be via PowerPoint, video or posters. You could also present this as a formal report with a clear introduction, main body and conclusion. Your report should be 700–1500 words long.

◆ Assessment opportunities

- This activity can be assessed using Criterion A: Knowing and understanding, Criterion B: Investigating and Criterion C: Communicating.

! Take action

! **Investigate** artistic developments in one country today. Find out if, and how, artists in this country are influenced by society and/or by government. Make a display of your findings.

Reflection

In this chapter we have examined the impact of the Industrial Revolution, the First World War and the Bolshevik Revolution on artistic and cultural movements. We have also investigated the momentous social and cultural developments of the 1960s.

Reflecting on our learning ... Use this table to reflect on your own learning in this chapter.					
Questions we asked	Answers we found	Any further questions now?			
Factual					
Conceptual					
Debatable					
Approaches to learning you used in this chapter:	Description – what new skills did you learn?	How well did you master the skills?			
		Novice	Learner	Practitioner	Expert
Critical-thinking skills					
Information literacy skills					
Transfer skills					
Learner profile attribute	*Reflect on the importance of being knowledgeable for our learning in this chapter.*				
Knowledgeable					

7 How have ideas reflected change in the last 200 years?

○ *Intellectual and ideological movements* have *changed* our *identities* and have *impacted relationships* within communities and between nations.

■ **Figure 7.1** Rallies promoting different idealogical movements

CONSIDER THESE QUESTIONS:

Factual: What were some of the key intellectual and ideological movements of the nineteenth and twentieth centuries?

Conceptual: How do circumstances impact on ideas? What are the comparisons and contrasts between old and new ideologies?

Debatable: Why do people follow radical ideologies?

Now **share and compare** your thoughts and ideas with your partner, or with the whole class.

○ IN THIS CHAPTER, WE WILL ...

■ **Find out** about the ideas of key ideological and intellectual movements in the nineteenth and twentieth centuries.

■ **Explore:**
   ■ the factors that led to new ideologies and intellectual movements
   ■ the ways in which socio-economic changes lead to new ideas.

■ **Take action** by examining which ideas have an impact on us today.

KEY WORDS

authoritarian	ideology	tyranny
authority	repressive	universal suffrage
capitalism	rights	utopia
dictatorship	sanctions	

- Communication skills
- Critical-thinking skills
- Information literacy skills
- Media literacy skills
- Organization skills
- Transfer skills

● We will reflect on this learner profile attribute …

- Knowledgeable – understanding more about the key ideological and intellectual movements of the nineteenth and twentieth centuries.

◆ Assessment opportunities in this chapter:

- **Criterion A:** Knowing and understanding
- **Criterion B:** Investigating
- **Criterion C:** Communicating
- **Criterion D:** Thinking critically

DISCUSS

In pairs, **identify** the ideas expressed in Sources A and B. What types of government are suggested? With which political ideas do you think Proudhon might be associated?

SOURCE A

'To be governed is to be watched over, inspected, spied upon, directed, legislated at, regulated, docketed, indoctrinated, preached at, controlled, assessed, weighed, censored, ordered about. Such is government, such is justice, such is morality.'

Proudhon, P.-J. 1851. General Idea of the Revolution in the Nineteenth Century. *France.*

SOURCE B

Adolf Hitler, in a speech to the Nazi party, Nuremberg, October, 1934

'Our party. What is it? What do we believe? Here is the foundation of our party: First, we shall be the party of truth. Second, we shall be a party without compromise. Third, we shall be a party with total political control over Germany.'

THINK–PAIR–SHARE

Look at the key words. These terms can be used to talk about politics and you will come across them in this chapter.

Think about what these words mean yourself, then share your ideas with your neighbour and finally share your definitions with the rest of the class. You could check your understanding in a dictionary too.

What were some of the intellectual movements and ideologies of the nineteenth and twentieth centuries?

WHAT IS ANARCHISM?

Anarchists believe that there should be stateless societies. Many anarchists argue societies should be self-governed by voluntary institutions. This ideology claims that governments are repressive, sometimes harmful and always unnecessary, and should be abolished. Anarchists oppose authority in society and have often been linked with socialists and communists, who also wanted revolution. Some anarchists want total rights of the individual and others want individuals to be subordinate to the 'collective'.

Anarchists have played important roles in modern history: they were involved in setting up the short-lived Paris Commune in 1871, attempted to set up an anarchist state in the Ukraine during the Russian Civil War (1918–21) and were an important group during the Spanish Civil War (1936–39).

Anarchism has its roots in the early modern era, but anarchist ideology was first clearly set down in modern times after the French Revolution by William Godwin in a book called *Social Justice* in 1793. Godwin argued that as 'reason' spread to the ordinary people, the need for government would die out.

He did not argue for a revolution but saw the decline of governments as a peaceful and evolutionary process. He believed that laws, property and even marriage 'enslaved' people and prevented them from using their own 'powers of reason' to develop mutually beneficial societies.

However, it was a Frenchman who first called himself an 'anarchist': Pierre-Joseph Proudhon. He wrote *What is property?* in 1840, in which he, now famously, claimed 'property is theft'. He believed that organizations would develop on their own without the imposed ideas of an authority. He said that there would result 'spontaneous order' in an anarchist society.

An influential Russian anarchist was Mikhail Bakunin, who had met Proudhon in Paris. Bakunin had been sent to prison in Russia for protesting against tsarism and its imperial oppression and was later sent to Siberia to carry out hard labour. In 1868 he joined the socialist 'International' which was a federation of working-men, trade unions and organizations from Europe and some Latin American and North African nations.

Bakunin promoted socialist-anarchism and was influential in the development of Spanish anarchism. Bakunin clashed with another leading member of the 'International', Karl Marx (we will look at him in more detail later on in this chapter). Marx and the Marxists argued that the state was needed to bring about socialism, whereas Bakunin and the anarchists argued the state should be replaced by self-governing factories and farms which would create a socialist society for themselves.

The argument between Bakunin and Marx came to a head at a Congress meeting at The Hague in 1872. Bakunin was unable to attend the meeting and the Marxists expelled him from the 'International'.

■ **Figure 7.2** Mikhail Bakunin

■ **Figure 7.3** Karl Marx speaking at the 1872 Hague Congress

However, Bakunin's socio-anarchism remained a strong movement and it had many followers across Europe. The Paris Commune that was set up in 1871 followed many of Bakunin's principles, including self-management and decentralization. Proudhon, who had been a key influence on Bakunin, was a key participant in the Commune.

In 1870 Bakunin argued for a revolution of peasants and workers and said that the time was right to:

> '… spread our principles, not with words but with deeds, for this is the most popular, the most potent, and the most irresistible form of propaganda.'

Bakunin was concerned that Marxism would lead to 'authoritarian socialism' and a **dictatorship**, and he was totally against this. Bakunin did not want any privileges in society. He believed that both capitalism and the state, in any form, prevented the working class and peasantry from gaining freedom. Bakunin also believed that religion prevented people from using their own power of reason and therefore also took away their freedom. He said that religion led to the 'enslavement of mankind'.

Nihilists

Another group sometimes associated with the anarchists were the nihilists. They believed that government and society must regularly be destroyed so that they can start anew. They often favoured violence and the use of terrorism. Both nihilists and anarchists were often linked with socialists, as all three groups called for revolution.

ACTIVITY: Anarchism

Read Sources C and D, and review the material you have read on anarchism. In pairs:

- **Discuss** the ideas of the anarchists.
- **Identify** the groups in society that would be attracted to the ideas of the anarchists.
- **Think** of groups that might be worried by the ideas of the anarchists.
- **Reflect** on the problems that an anarchist society might face.

Figure 7.4 The American anarchist Emma Goldman

WHAT IS LIBERALISM?

SOURCE C

Italian anarchist, Errico Malatesta

'By anarchist spirit I mean that deeply human sentiment, which aims at the good of all, freedom and justice for all, solidarity and love among the people; which is not an exclusive characteristic of self-declared anarchists, but inspires all people who have a generous heart and an open mind …'

Malatesta, E. April 1922. Umanita Nova.

SOURCE D

'No real social change has ever been brought about without a revolution … revolution is but thought carried into action.'

'Ask for work. If they don't give you work, ask for bread. If they do not give you work or bread, then take bread.'

Goldman, E. 2006. Anarchism and Other Essays. 3rd edition. USA. Cosimo Classics, p. 25

THINK–PAIR–SHARE

'Every man has a property in his own person. This nobody has a right to, but to himself.'

John Locke, Two Treatises of Government, The Second Treatise, 1690

'Let us therefore animate and encourage each other, and show the whole world, that a Freeman contending for Liberty on his own ground is superior to any slavish mercenary on earth.'

George Washington, July 1776

'We hold these truths to be self-evident, that all men are created equal, and are endowed by their creator with certain unalienable rights, that among these are life, liberty, and the pursuit of happiness.'

Jefferson, T. 1776. The Declaration of Independence. USA.

Read these quotes. What do you think liberalism means?

Liberalism first became a political movement in the seventeenth century. In general, liberals believe in democracy and free and fair elections. They believe in the rights of the individual and the right to own private property.

Many liberal groups were supported by middle-class interests and wanted to pursue legal means to attain political control. However, liberal movements in the late eighteenth century in France and the USA also argued that the violent overthrow of a tyrannical regime may be justified in order to realize their aims for a liberal and democratic society.

Overall, liberalism argues for the following:
- The establishment of governments which are elected by the people through voting
- Universal **suffrage**, i.e. all people above a certain age having the right to vote
- Voters to be able to choose from a number of different political parties
- A government holding power for a limited period of time, usually four or five years, before another election must be held
- A clear balance between the rights of the government and the rights of the individual: everyone has to obey the laws of the land – including the government itself, but freedoms and rights of the individual are upheld, for example, the right to free speech, the right to follow any religion and the right to join trade unions
- An economy based on capitalist principles, private ownership, property and the freedom to be as wealthy as you can be
- 'Free trade' between nations (no tariffs or trade barriers)

When the French Revolution began, the **abolition** of the feudal system was hailed as a 'triumph of liberalism', as the old inherited rights and privileges were outlawed in France. Even when liberal principles seemed to have been overthrown by a new Napoleonic dictatorship, Napoleon kept in place some of the new liberal laws which were enforced in the Code Napoléon.

Radical liberal ideas were not only taking hold in France, but spread across the Western world and were adopted in the American Revolution and by radical liberals such as the British-born Thomas Paine. Paine wrote an influential book called *The Rights of Man* in 1791 and was actively involved in both the French and American Revolutions.

The principals of liberalism were challenged by economic slumps and economic crises. By the end of the nineteenth century, in the industrialised West, people were discontented with poor living standards, awful working conditions and periodic unemployment. The working classes were beginning to organize themselves into trade unions. The role of individuals in working to improve their own position was giving way to the idea of collective action.

WHAT IS MARXISM?

In the mid-nineteenth century, Karl Marx and Friedrich Engels, two German political philosophers, wrote highly influential works outlining their 'world view'. They argued that the development of capitalism, with a middle class that owned the factories and mines (the propertied or bourgeois class) exploiting the labour of the working class (the proletariat) would lead to a class struggle or 'class war' and the working class would ultimately overthrow their 'capitalist' oppressors. There would then follow a 'workers' state', where the people would rule for the benefit of all.

Marx thought there would be a series of revolutions before the 'workers' utopia' would be realized. First, the middle class would overthrow the old aristocracy and take power. Then the workers would overthrow the middle class. The results would be a socialist society.

CIRCLE OF VIEWPOINTS

Marx thought that society would be based on the principle: 'from each according to his ability, to each according to his need'. He also said that 'religion is the opium of the people'.

In pairs, consider each person below and feed back to the class what you think each person would have considered to be the positives and negatives of Marx's ideas:

- A landowner
- A priest
- A peasant
- A factory worker
- A doctor
- A banker

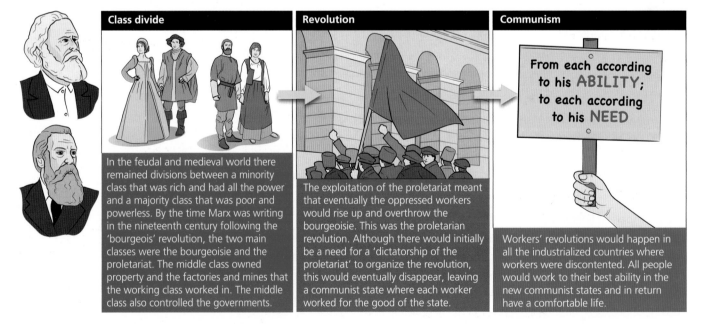

Class divide

In the feudal and medieval world there remained divisions between a minority class that was rich and had all the power and a majority class that was poor and powerless. By the time Marx was writing in the nineteenth century following the 'bourgeois' revolution, the two main classes were the bourgeoisie and the proletariat. The middle class owned property and the factories and mines that the working class worked in. The middle class also controlled the governments.

Revolution

The exploitation of the proletariat meant that eventually the oppressed workers would rise up and overthrow the bourgeoisie. This was the proletarian revolution. Although there would initially be a need for a 'dictatorship of the proletariat' to organize the revolution, this would eventually disappear, leaving a communist state where each worker worked for the good of the state.

Communism

From each according to his ABILITY; to each according to his NEED

Workers' revolutions would happen in all the industrialized countries where workers were discontented. All people would work to their best ability in the new communist states and in return have a comfortable life.

■ **Figure 7.5** The main ideas of Marx and Engels

WHAT IS COMMUNISM?

The final stage in Marx's theory of revolution is communism. The Communist Manifesto, written by Marx and Engels, closes with the famous words:

'Let the ruling classes tremble at a Communist revolution. The proletarians have nothing to lose but their chains. They have a world to win.

'Working men of all countries, unite.'

The first communist revolution happened in Russia where, in fact, there were two revolutions in 1917. The first one in March overthrew the absolutist government of Tsar Nicholas II. This was largely a result of the impact of the First World War on Russia, which had brought appalling food and fuel shortages as well as a high death toll. However, the 'provisional' or temporary government that followed could not bring stability and the Marxist Bolshevik party seized power.

This revolution did not involve the proletariat rising up in the way Marx had planned (see Figure 7.5). Instead, Vladimir Lenin, who went on to establish the USSR in 1924, believed that he could implement revolution by getting an elite group to take power in the name of the workers and soldiers. He held that the communist party would establish socialism and the rule of the party would bring this about for the people.

When Lenin died in 1924, Joseph Stalin emerged as leader of the USSR. He enforced his own brand of Leninist–Marxism: Stalinism.

The next country to become communist was China following a civil war between the nationalists of General Jiang Jieshi and the communists of Mao Zedong. Despite receiving significant aid from the USA, Jiang was defeated by Mao in October 1949 and fled to the island of Taiwan. Mao pronounced the People's **Republic** of China (PRC) and his communist government set out to create a state following Mao's own brand of Marxism – Maoism.

Maoism, unlike Soviet communism, was based on the revolutionary role of the peasantry rather than the industrial workers. China was mainly agricultural and had very few industrial workers, so Maoism was a practical solution to the problem of making Marxism work for a pre-industrialized society.

Stalinism

- The state has all the power.
- Stalin rules as a dictator; individuals have no rights.
- All other political parties are banned.
- The party and society is 'purged' of enemies of the state; terror is used as a means of control.
- Religion is banned.
- There is no private property.
- Wealth is owned and redistributed by the state.
- All land and industry is owned by the state.

ACTIVITY: Communism in action

■ ATL

- ■ Information literacy skills – Access information to be informed and inform others
- ■ Media literacy skills – Communicate information and ideas effectively

What is your goal?

Your goal is to find out more about how communist societies worked in practice.

How will you achieve this?

Research the methods and impact of Stalin's domestic policies from 1929 to 1941 or research the methods and impact of Mao's domestic policies from 1949 to 1966.

You should write a report that is between 700 and 1500 words long. Make sure you correctly and consistently cite your sources and submit a 'works cited' list with your report.

Follow-up discussion

As a follow-up to your report, get into mixed groups that include both those who have researched Stalinism and those who have researched Maoism. Compare and contrast the methods and results of the two regimes.

◆ Assessment opportunities

- ◆ This activity can be assessed using Criterion B: Investigating and Criterion C: Communicating.
- ◆ In the final discussion activity you have practised skills that are assessed using Criterion A: Knowing and understanding.

WHAT IS DEMOCRATIC SOCIALISM?

Democratic socialists follow peaceful and democratic methods to achieve socialism. Like other socialists, they also want a classless society where all share in the ownership of land and industries. Whereas communists want revolution, democratic socialists want to achieve their goals through democracy and aim to follow a slow and evolutionary process towards a socialist society.

A democratic socialist government would move society towards socialism gradually, and this would include solving economic inequalities through a welfare state where the government provides assistance to the poor and unemployed and improves health and housing.

ACTIVITY: Democratic socialism

ATL

■ Information literacy skills – Access information to be informed and inform others

List the key ideas of democratic socialism based on the information given above.

Investigate the current governments and their policies in Scandinavia. With reference to your list, consider the extent to which these governments seem to follow the ideas of democratic socialism.

■ **Figure 7.6** Social Darwinist, Herbert Spencer, who famously coined the expression 'survival of the fittest' in *Principles of Biology* (1864)

WHAT IS SOCIAL DARWINISM?

Social Darwinism was an intellectual movement that developed in the late nineteenth century. This movement is linked with other movements and ideologies such as eugenics, **imperialism**, fascism and Nazism. Social Darwinists applied basic principles from Charles Darwin's theory of evolution and the concept of natural selection and the 'survival of the fittest' to society and politics.

They argued that the wealth and power of the strong and fit should increase while that of the weak should decrease. Most Social Darwinists believed that the state should follow laissez-faire policies and should not intervene to assist the poor. Competition was seen as good and should be encouraged, as this would favour the strong over the weak. They saw this as a natural process and religious Social Darwinists saw it as part of God's plan.

More extreme followers argued that different racial groups had evolved more highly than others, and 'superior' races should be encouraged to dominate other 'inferior' races.

Social Darwinist ideas were used to justify the colonial exploitation of other races by the European powers in the vast empires they built by the end of the nineteenth century (see Chapter 9, page 192). Not all Social Darwinists agreed on which groups were 'strong' and which were 'weak'. Some Social Darwinists also studied the 'genetics' of the poor and working classes and promoted the sterilization of 'degenerate' groups in society. The idea of a superior or 'fittest' gene pool developed, and Social Darwinists wanted to protect the superior races from being undermined by inferior genes.

These ideas meant that Social Darwinists wanted governments to allow the weak to 'die out'. They believed there should be no active support or welfare and that people with disabilities, those with genetic illnesses and those with low IQs should not be encouraged to have children. Some wanted programmes of mass sterilization to protect the evolution of the 'fittest'. They believed aiding these 'degenerate' types of people was interfering with the natural order.

Herbert Spencer was a key figure in the development of Social Darwinist theories. He wrote *The Social Organism* in 1860, in which he compared society to a living organism and argued that just as biological organisms evolve through natural selection so society evolves through natural selection as well.

Charles Darwin's own cousin, Francis Galton, adopted these social interpretations of Darwin's biological theories. Galton developed the genetic element of these ideas further into a theory that became known as eugenics.

Galton argued it was not only physical features that were inherited in families, but also intelligence and aptitudes. Galton wanted society to ensure that the less fit had fewer children and those who were 'fittest' were encouraged to have more children. Galton was concerned that the 'less fit' were having too many children and that this would have a negative impact on the evolution and progress of society. Galton did not want welfare institutions to support the 'inferior' humans. Eugenics was the theory that you could improve the genetic quality of human society by selective breeding and control. Galton suggested that the mentally ill should be sterilized.

The Social Darwinist movement became increasingly popular in the late nineteenth century and its ideas took hold with many writers and thinkers worldwide. Its influences could be seen in political and social movements and in the arts.

Eugenics became an academic discipline and could be studied at reputable universities. There were International Conferences for Eugenicists held in London and New York between 1912 and 1932.

Programmes to sterilize the mentally ill and those with low IQs were implemented around the world – in the USA, Canada, Brazil, Sweden and Japan. There were state policies on birth control, including forced abortions, and policies encouraging those identified as the 'fittest' to increase their reproduction. In certain countries these ideas fostered racial segregation.

Following the Second World War, and after the horrors of the Nazi-perpetrated Holocaust, the genocide of Europe's Jews, the UN outlawed the implementation of 'measures intended to prevent births within [a population group]' as part of the Convention on the Prevention and Punishment of the Crime of Genocide (see Chapter 13 for more discussion of this).

DISCUSS

Consider the implications that developments in genetic engineering and genome technology in the late twentieth and early twenty-first centuries are having on societies. Reflect on the lessons that the modern world could take from the impact of the eugenicists in the 1920s and 1930s.

▼ Links to: Sciences

Think about what you have learnt in Science classes about scientific research in genetic engineering and genome technology. Do you think scientists should pursue 'knowledge and understanding' even when their research might be used by groups to politically and socially divide communities or nations?

■ **Figure 7.7** Benito Mussolini and his blackshirts, the paramilitary wing of the National Fascist party

WHAT IS FASCISM?

Fascism is a movement and ideology that developed after the First World War in Italy. It promotes strong authoritarian government, traditional values with regard to family and the role of women in society, and glorified war and militarism.

Fascists usually support a strong individual leader and believe that violence and war are good for society. Fascists also advocate imperialism as a means of unifying and strengthening the nation. Often, fascists follow a Social Darwinist view that other nations are inferior and that imperial conquest is desirable to foster the growth of 'superior races'. Indeed, they believe it is natural for stronger nations to replace weaker nations.

Fascism can also be understood by what its followers were against: for example, they opposed liberalism and Marxism. Fascists replaced the ideas of socialists, who argued for a war between the different classes, with the idea of conflict between nations and races.

However, fascist ideology has elements of socialism in its ideas, for example, it wants some state control over the economy and is against free-market capitalist principles.

In Italy, Benito Mussolini set up the first fascist government in 1922. He set out to achieve an economy that would end the class divisions between the owners of property, the middle class and the working class in a 'Corporate State' where all would work for the good of the state. Mussolini wanted to achieve economic self-sufficiency, or autarky,

and protect Italian goods from foreign imports by imposing heavy protectionist tariffs.

Although Mussolini adopted expansionist and imperialist ambitions in the 1920s, it was only in the 1930s that he acted upon these. In 1935 he invaded Abyssinia in East Africa and in 1939 he invaded Albania in the Balkans in Europe.

ACTIVITY: Comparing different ideological movements

■ ATL

- Transfer skills – Make connections between subject groups and disciplines

The idea of taking direct action to bring about change was also similar to the ideas of the anarchist Bakunin, who argued that violent actions were necessary for political ends.

Identify the similarities and differences that existed between the anarchists, the communists and the fascists.

◆ Assessment opportunities

- ◆ In this activity you have practised skills that are assessed using Criterion A: Knowing and understanding and Criterion D: Thinking critically.

WHAT IS NATIONAL SOCIALISM?

SOURCE E

'All the people of German blood … must be allowed to live in a Greater Germany … We demand land and colonies to feed our people and to house our surplus population … We demand a strong central government led by a single strong leader, a Führer … The Germans are the 'Master Race'. They must keep themselves pure. Only those of German blood may be citizens. No Jews may be members of the nation. It was the Jews who helped bring about Germany's defeat in the First World War. They must be destroyed.'

Hitler, A. 1925. Mein Kampf.

The German Workers party was set up in 1919 after the end of the First World War and was a small right-wing group with some similarities to the Fascist party in Italy. Adolf Hitler joined the party after being outraged at Germany's defeat in the war. Hitler quickly became leader of the party and changed its name to the National Socialists (Nazis).

National Socialists were not 'socialists' in terms of aiming to redistribute wealth – the term 'socialist' was included to attract support from the working classes. Hitler did promise that his party would give workers a better standard of living and bring an end to mass unemployment and insecurity. The National Socialists despised communism and liberalism and were opposed to capitalism. Nazis opposed ideas of equality and international solidarity, and sought to defend private property and create a German Empire through conquest.

The Nazi party aimed to bring about a 'rebirth' of the German nation. To do this, all classes would be united to work together – *Volksgemeinschaft* – and restore national pride. All other parties would be eliminated. There would be a strong, authoritarian government and all aspects of people's lives would be organized and controlled by the state. The state could use terror and violence to this end. The needs of the individual would be subordinate to the needs of the state. Propaganda would be used by the state to ensure that all classes worked together and were working for the good of the state. There could be no dissent.

ACTIVITY: Hitler's ideology and aims

ATL

- Critical-thinking skills – Evaluate evidence and arguments

Identify some of the key points made by Hitler in his book *Mein Kampf* (see Source E). As leader of the National Socialists (Nazi party), what would his aims be if he became leader of Germany?

Write a short report on 'Hitler's aims' to the Weimar German government in 1925. After **explaining** what Hitler aims to do, based on his book *Mein Kampf*, warn officials of what he would do if he were to come to power. Your report should be a maximum of 500 words.

◆ Assessment opportunities

- ◆ In this activity you have practised skills that are assessed using Criterion A: Knowing and understanding.

A key aim of the Nazis was to achieve greatness through war, and war and militarism were glorified. They also wanted to achieve economic self-sufficiency, or autarky, so that they could be independent from other nations and would not be vulnerable to economic **sanctions**. Their economy had to be geared towards creating a powerful arms industry to enable it to successfully engage in wars of conquest.

The Nazis also promoted Social Darwinist ideas and wanted to develop a large empire in which the German Aryan race could flourish. The first territorial ambition was to create *Lebensraum* or 'living space' in Eastern Europe. The Nazis' views on race were more extreme than those of the Italian fascists. According to the Nazis, humans could be divided into two races – Aryan and non-Aryan. They identified the *Untermenschen* as the inferior races that should be prevented from polluting the Aryan racial gene pool. The typically blond, blue-eyed, tall and strong Aryans were thought to be the master race. Other races such as Slavs in Eastern Europe were destined to be the 'slave races' of the Aryans, and the Jews were seen as a race that were not only 'sub-human' but were dangerous and had to be removed from society. Other groups considered to be 'unfit' by the Nazis were Roma and homosexuals. (Read more about the impact of Nazism in Chapter 13.)

Figure 7.8 National Socialism

When Germany was economically devastated by the **Great Depression**, German politics polarized, and the liberal government failed to manage the crisis. In January 1933, Hitler was made Chancellor of Germany and began to implement his National Socialist policies. He set up a single-party state under his complete control and ruled as a dictator or Führer.

SOURCE F

Figure 7.9 Nazi propaganda poster which reads: 'Support the help organization Mother and Child'

ACTIVITY: Ideologies in practice

1 Review your research and notes from the group discussions on the regimes of Stalin and Mao.

   Now research either the impact of fascist ideology and policies on Italy between 1922 and 1940 or the impact of Nazi ideology and policies on Germany between 1933 and 1939. Consider their economic policies, attitudes towards the arts and culture, treatment of political opposition, policies on the family and the role of the women, and attitudes towards religion.

2 Feed back to a group that has researched a different case study. What were the similarities and differences between each case study? What benefit and disadvantages did their ideologies bring to their people?

   Work in pairs or small groups. Complete a Venn diagram (like Figure 7.10) to show where fascist and National Socialist ideas overlap and where there are differences.

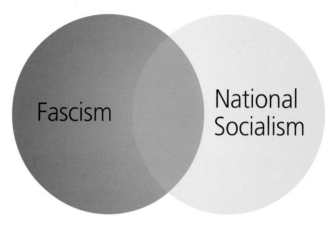

■ **Figure 7.10** Venn diagram

SOURCE G

■ **Figure 7.11** Propaganda poster blaming Jews for the war: 'HE is to blame for the war'

SOURCE H

■ **Figure 7.12** Propaganda poster aimed at the youth: 'The German student fights for the Führer and the people in the National Socialist German Students' League

■ **Figure 7.13** Simone de Beauvoir said: 'Change your life today. Don't gamble on the future, act now, without delay.'

WHAT IS EXISTENTIALISM?

Existentialism is a philosophy that developed through the nineteenth and twentieth centuries. The existentialists argued that philosophy should be focused on the conditions of existence for individuals and their actions, emotions and thoughts. Many believe that the foundation of existentialism was Soren Kierkegaard's work in the 1840s. Kierkegaard believed that the responsibility of an individual was to give their own life meaning and to live their life as passionately and sincerely as possible.

The existentialists that followed Kierkegaard still focused on the individual but had different views on how to achieve a 'fulfilled life'. Some questioned whether there was a God or not, and what the implications of God were on the individual. Many also believed that traditional philosophy was too 'abstract' and not relevant to human experience.

After the Second World War, existentialism became popular, led by notable cultural icons such as philosophers and writers Jean-Paul Sartre and Simone de Beauvoir in France, who wanted to promote the importance of human individuality and freedom after the horrors of mass dehumanized and industrialized slaughter.

WHAT IS HUMANISM?

In the words of American writer, Kurt Vonnegut:

'Being a Humanist means trying to behave decently without expectation of rewards or punishment after you are dead.'

Although the origins of humanism lie further back in history, in the nineteenth century humanists became more clearly defined as promoting the importance of human dignity and the importance of human reason.

Humanists argue against higher authorities, particularly the 'supernatural' and humanism is associated with groups that are against established religion. In the twentieth century, humanists argued for human rights, gender equality, social justice and the separation of religion from government.

WHAT IS FEMINISM?

The suffragist Millicent Garrett Fawcett said in a speech in Birmingham, UK in 1872:

'To promote the improvement of the condition of women is a great and noble cause to devote one's life to. Success in such a cause is a goal worthy of the noblest ambition; failure in such a cause is a better thing than success in any meaner or paltrier object.'

Feminism is a collective term for movements and ideologies that aim to establish and defend equal political, economic, social and cultural rights for women. Feminists believe that women should be treated equally to men, from their right to vote to equal opportunities in education, work and pay.

A French philosopher, Charles Fourier, was probably the first person to use the term 'feminism' in the late 1830s. The term 'feminist' was used in Britain and the USA by the end of the 1890s; however, not all groups that sought rights for women called themselves feminists.

In the West there have been three key stages or waves in the feminist movement. The first wave was the nineteenth- and early twentieth-century 'women's suffrage' movements that sought political reform and the right to vote. The second wave developed in the 1960s and advocated 'women's liberation', which wanted total legal and social equality with men. The third wave began in the 1990s to inspire a new generation to build on what had been achieved by earlier feminist movements. This recent wave argued that equality in many areas had still not been achieved, with lower pay levels for women, few women in senior and management roles, a minority of women in political positions and women sexualized and marginalized socially and culturally.

Feminist activists have achieved, particularly in Western countries, significant changes in their societies. They have fought for and won female suffrage, have gained reproductive rights such as access to contraceptives and abortion, and have the right to own property. They have won important reforms in the workplace that enable women to have maternity leave and fairer salaries. Feminist groups have argued for more protection for women and girls against domestic violence, sexual exploitation and harassment.

Some feminists argue that as women seek gender equality, men must be involved in the movement too. However, some extreme feminists believe men, as the 'oppressor' gender, should not have a voice in their movement.

Women's suffrage

In the liberal democracies, it was women in New Zealand who were first given the right to vote, in 1893, and then South Australia followed in 1895. After a protracted, and at times violent, campaign in Britain by the suffragettes, women over 30 years of age were finally given the vote in Britain after the First World War in 1918.

Suffragettes had demonstrated, petitioned and taken more direct action to promote their cause in Britain, such as chaining themselves to the railings outside Buckingham Palace, and the government responded by sending activists to prison.

■ **Figure 7.14** Emmeline Pankhurst, the leader of the British Women's Social and Political Union, being arrested for protesting for women's suffrage outside Buckingham Palace in London

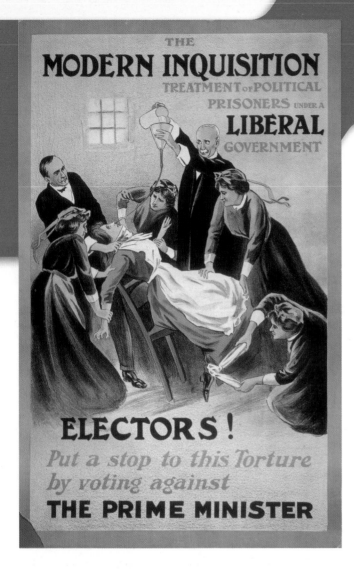

■ **Figure 7.15** A poster highlighting the treatment of prisoner suffragettes who went on hunger strike, 1910

EXTENSION

In Britain before 1914, the women who were fighting for the vote were divided into suffragists and the suffragettes.

Research further the activities used by each group of women in their attempt to secure the vote. Which of their activities do you think a) helped their cause and b) harmed their cause? (You can look at Chapter 11 for more discussion on protest movements.)

While in prison, suffragettes went on hunger strike. The British government responded with force feeding (see the poster in Figure 7.15).

One woman, Emily Davison, threw herself in front of King George's horse Anmer at the world famous horse race – the Epsom Derby – in June 1913. She later died of her injuries and became a martyr to the cause of women's suffrage.

Therefore, before the First World War, there had been direct confrontation between many women in the suffrage movement and the British government. Some historians have suggested that the women's increasingly **militant** and violent acts resulted in politicians refusing to consider new legislation as this would have been 'at gunpoint'. Nevertheless, many Members of Parliament were sympathetic to the cause and there is some evidence that the outbreak of the First World War in fact delayed reform.

During the First World War, the leader of the Women's Social and Political Union, Emmeline Pankhurst, did not advocate passivism and she and her daughter were employed by the government to persuade women to take on work in munitions factories. Due to the mass **mobilization** of men to fight, significant areas of the economy that had been traditionally male domains were now taken on by women.

At the end of the war, women had clearly proven themselves equal and capable and the British government passed the Representation of the People Act in 1918, giving women over 30 the right to vote. This reform was extended in 1928 to give the vote to all women over 21.

In the USA, many of the women's suffrage leaders were also involved in the nineteenth-century movements to abolish slavery – women such as Lucretia Mott, Susan Anthony and Elizabeth Cady Stanton. In 1919, the USA passed the Nineteenth Amendment to the Constitution, which gave women the vote. Many American feminists later became involved in the fight for racial equality – see Chapter 11 and the civil rights movement in the USA.

Figure 7.16 International Women's Day march in New York City, USA

Women's suffrage came later in France: it was not until 1944 that women were given the vote.

In Egypt, an Islamist modernist and founder of Cairo University, Qasim Amin, has been called the 'father' of Arab feminism. Amin wrote a book called *The Liberation of Women*, in which he argued for social reforms for women and linked women's rights to nationalism. However, the key figure in Arab women's rights was Hoda Shaarawi, who set up the Egyptian Feminist Union in 1923. After 1956, President Gamal Abdel Nasser outlawed discrimination based on gender in what he termed 'state feminism'.

Socialists and communists believed in gender equality. The Bolshevik Revolution in Russia in October 1917 brought Marxists to power and the new Bolshevik regime gave women total equality and implemented liberating social and legal reforms with regard to divorce, abortion and state childcare, and women had equal rights in the workplace.

When Mao Zedong's communists won the civil war in China in 1949 Mao also passed reforms to give women equal rights and proclaimed that 'women hold up half the sky'.

In Latin America, Castro's revolution in Cuba in 1959 led to equality reforms, and women saw radical improvements in their education and health care. In Nicaragua, the Sandinista revolutionary regime in the 1980s aimed to bring about more equality but was able to implement only limited change.

EXTENSION

Research feminism in the arts. You should attempt to focus on one of the following areas in the twentieth century: visual arts, music, literature, theatre or cinema. Try to find examples from different regions.

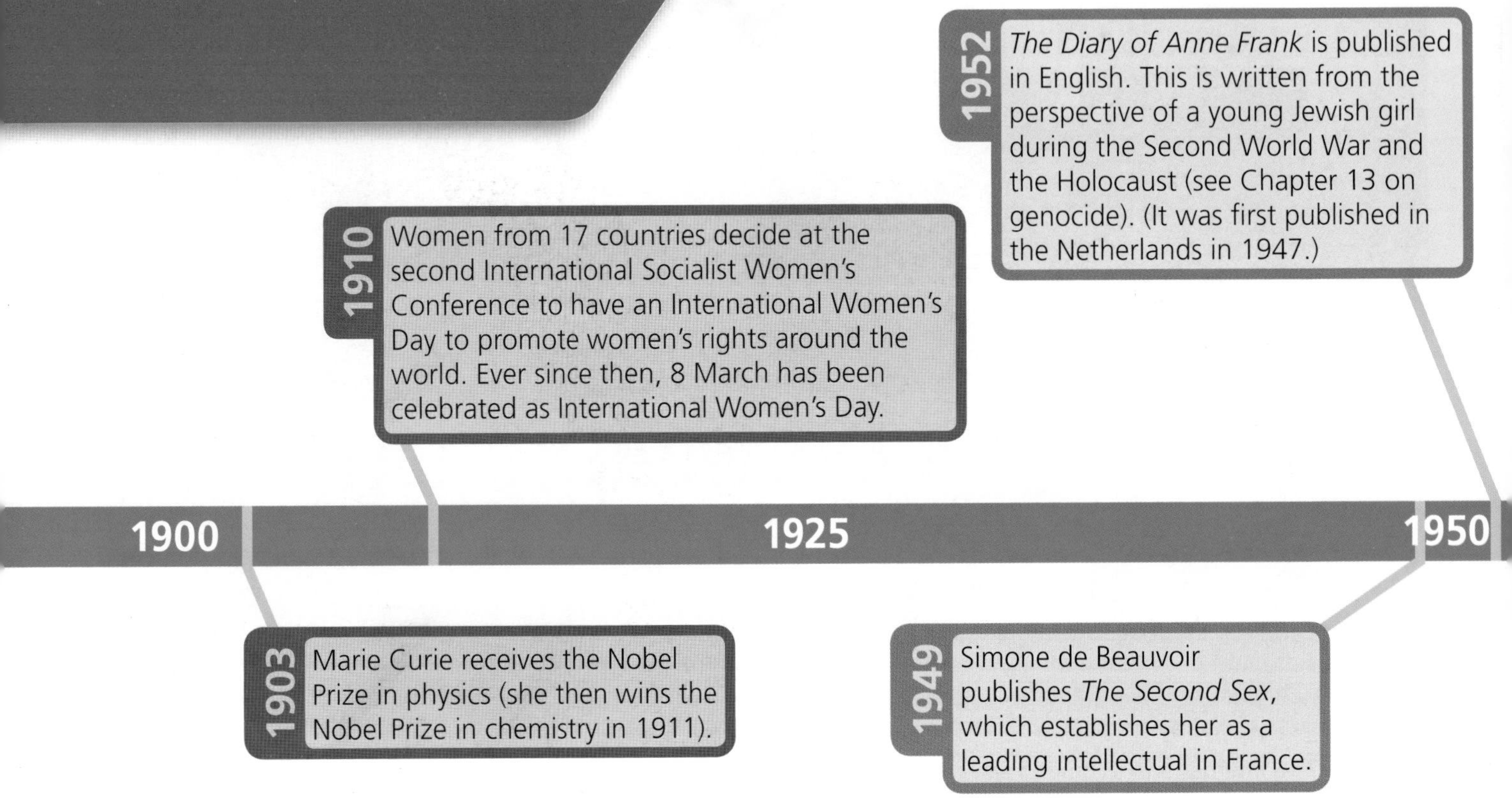

1952 *The Diary of Anne Frank* is published in English. This is written from the perspective of a young Jewish girl during the Second World War and the Holocaust (see Chapter 13 on genocide). (It was first published in the Netherlands in 1947.)

1910 Women from 17 countries decide at the second International Socialist Women's Conference to have an International Women's Day to promote women's rights around the world. Ever since then, 8 March has been celebrated as International Women's Day.

1900 | **1925** | **1950**

1903 Marie Curie receives the Nobel Prize in physics (she then wins the Nobel Prize in chemistry in 1911).

1949 Simone de Beauvoir publishes *The Second Sex*, which establishes her as a leading intellectual in France.

■ **Figure 7.17** Timeline of some significant women and their achievements in the twentieth century

ACTIVITY: Successes of women's rights movements

■ **ATL**

■ Critical-thinking skills – Gather and organize relevant data to formulate an argument

Look at the timeline of some significant women and their achievements in the twentieth century (Figure 7.17). The list comes from a short video made in 2012 for International Women's Day:

www.internationalwomensday.com/about.asp

What does this list suggest about the successes of women's rights movement in the last 100 years?

Refer back to Chapter 2. In small groups, brainstorm in what ways these women could be considered pioneers. Include specific examples and **explanations**. Your group should then feed back its conclusions to the class. Try to make sure each person in your group has a chance to speak.

◆ Assessment opportunities

◆ In this activity you have practised skills that are assessed using Criterion C: Communicating.

1955 Rosa Parks is arrested for not giving up her seat for a white person on a bus in the southern states of the USA (see Chapter 11 on the civil rights movement).

1979 Margaret Thatcher becomes the first British female prime minister.

2004 Ellen Johnson Sirleaf is elected President of Liberia and becomes the first elected female head of state in Africa.

1963 Valentina Tereshkova, a cosmonaut, is the first woman in space.

1996 Madeleine Albright becomes the first female US Secretary of State.

2003 Shirin Ebadi becomes the first Muslim woman to win the Nobel Peace Prize for her efforts to promote democracy and human rights, particularly the rights of women and children.

1975

2000

1981 Sandra Day O'Connor is appointed the first female judge in the US Supreme Court.

1988 Benazir Bhutto is elected the first female prime minister of Pakistan.

2000 The UN Security Council adopts resolution 1325, setting down that all member states and all international organizations must actively protect women and children from violence and armed conflicts.

ACTIVITY: Gender equality in the twenty-first century?

■ ATL

- Communication skills – Use a variety of speaking techniques to communicate with a variety of audiences

◆ Assessment opportunities

- This activity can be assessed using Criterion A: Knowing and understanding, Criterion C: Communicating and Criterion D: Thinking critically.

The class will be split into two groups.

- **Group A will develop the case that feminism and the women's rights movements have achieved gender equality in the twenty-first century.**
- **Group B will argue that there needs to be another wave of feminism and women's rights movements as gender equality has not been achieved.**

Both groups should **investigate** examples from a variety of countries and in different regions where possible.

ACTIVITY: The impact of intellectual and ideological movements on women

ATL

- Critical-thinking skills – Evaluate evidence and arguments; Recognize unstated assumptions and bias

Look at Sources I–M.

1 With reference to their origin and purpose, **analyse the values and limitations of using Sources L and M to study the impact of ideology on women.**
2 **Using** Sources I–M and your own knowledge, assess the impact of intellectual movements and ideologies on the role of women in society.

◆ Assessment opportunities

◆ This activity can be assessed using Criterion A: Knowing and understanding and Criterion D: Thinking critically.

SOURCE I

'During the 1960s a militant feminist trend emerged in the United States. It was encouraged by significant feminist studies, such as The Second Sex (1953) by Simone de Beauvoir and The Feminine Mystique (1963) by Betty Friedan; it was also aided by a general legislative climate favourable to minority rights and antidiscrimination movements. Militant women's groups were formed. The Women's Liberation Movement, which was social rather than political and was manifested in literature and demonstrations by radical feminists, may have raised the awareness of the nation to the prevalence of discriminatory beliefs and attitudes.'

*Women's Rights Movements. 2014. Grolier Multimedia Encyclopaedia.
Grolier Online.*

SOURCE J

Benito Mussolini, Italy, 1927

'The fate of nations is intimately bound up with their powers of reproduction. All nations and all empires first felt decadence gnawing at them when their birth rate fell off.'

SOURCE K

'In order to build a great socialist society it is of the utmost importance to arouse the broad masses of women to join in productive activity. Men and women must receive equal pay for equal work in production. Genuine equality between the sexes can only be realized in the process of the socialist transformation of society as a whole.'

Mao Zedong. 1955. Quoted in 'Women Have Gone to the Labour Front'.

SOURCE L

'Woman's world is her husband, her family, her children and her home. We do not find it right when she presses into the world of men.'

Hitler, A. 1925. Mein Kampf.

SOURCE M

为加速实现农业机械化而奋斗

■ **Figure 7.18** A Chinese poster from 1971: 'Struggle to Increase the Mechanization of Agriculture'

ACTIVITY: The impact of ideological and intellectual movements

■ ATL

- Organization skills – Create plans to prepare for summative assessments; Use appropriate strategies for organizing complex information

Review the material in this chapter and draft an essay plan for the following question: '**Analyse** the ways in which intellectual and ideological movements have changed our identities and have impacted on relationships within communities and between nations.'

or

Take a large piece of paper and attempt to show the different intellectual and ideological movements visually. How could you represent these different ideas in diagrammatic or visual form? Can you show links between the different movements?

Hint

Consider different thematic ways ideologies have had an impact, for example the role of women in society, the distribution of wealth in society, how minority groups are treated, and so on.

◆ Assessment opportunities

- This activity can be assessed using Criterion A: Knowing and understanding, Criterion C: Communicating and Criterion D: Thinking critically.

! Take action

! Find out about different political parties, and social and interest groups in your local community. **Identify** what types of ideas they promote. How do political and social groups attempt to involve young people? Are there any new ideological or intellectual movements developing in the twenty-first century?

Reflection

In this chapter we have studied different intellectual and ideological movements of the nineteenth and twentieth centuries. We have looked at the role of different individuals and organizations within these movements and have considered the impact that they have had on our lives today.

Reflecting on our learning … Use this table to reflect on your own learning in this chapter.						
Questions we asked	Answers we found	Any further questions now?				
Factual						
Conceptual						
Debatable						
Approaches to learning you used in this chapter:	Description – what new skills did you learn?	How well did you master the skills?				
		Novice	Learner	Practitioner	Expert	
Communication skills						
Critical-thinking skills						
Information literacy skills						
Media literacy skills						
Organization skills						
Transfer skills						
Learner profile attribute	Reflect on the importance of being knowledgeable for our learning in this chapter.					
Knowledgeable						

8 Why do nations go to war and why is peacemaking difficult?

○ *Global competition for resources* can be a cause of **conflict** and **peacemaking** is dependent on **global cooperation and justice**.

○ IN THIS CHAPTER, WE WILL …

- ■ **Find out** about why there were two world wars in the twentieth century.
- ■ **Explore**:
  - ■ the nature of total war and its impact
  - ■ the attempts at peacemaking.
- ■ **Take action** by investigating wars that are currently taking place around the world.

CONSIDER THESE QUESTIONS:

Factual: What were the key events that led to the outbreak of the First and Second World Wars? What were the challenges to making a lasting peace?

Conceptual: Why do nations resort to waging war? Why is a lasting peace so difficult to maintain? Why do historians have different perspectives on the causes of war?

Debatable: To what extent can war be prevented and peace be established and maintained?

Now **share** and **compare** your thoughts and ideas with your partner, or with the whole class.

◆ Assessment opportunities in this chapter:

- ◆ **Criterion A:** Knowing and understanding
- ◆ **Criterion B:** Investigating
- ◆ **Criterion C:** Communicating
- ◆ **Criterion D:** Thinking critically

KEY WORDS

alliances	ideologies	peacemaking
arms race	militarism	treaty
diplomacy	peacekeeping	

■ **Figure 8.1** British Vickers machine gun crew wearing gas masks during the First World War

■ **These Approaches to Learning (ATL) skills will be useful …**

■ Collaboration skills

■ Communication skills

■ Critical-thinking skills

■ Information literacy skills

■ Organization skills

■ Transfer skills

● **We will reflect on this learner profile attribute …**

● Thinker – using critical and creative thinking skills to analyse complex problems.

At the end of the nineteenth century, many people believed that war would disappear in the twentieth century as industrialization and technology had made it too destructive. Yet, what had been predicted as the century of peace and diplomacy would become the century of war. Millions died.

The causes of war and the problems of creating a lasting peace are important to study because the turning point events of the last century have shaped our present. Many of the same factors that led to conflict then, remain issues for our societies now. The difficulties in maintaining peace are problems for our global community today.

THINK–PAIR–SHARE

Look at the key words on page 148. What do you think the meanings of these words are? Share your ideas with a partner and see if you agree on their meaning. Then see if you can think of any examples in history or today of where these terms could be applicable.

What key factors led to the outbreak of the First World War?

One of the most brutal, horrific and destructive wars in human history began in Europe in August 1914. It lasted until November 1918. It led to an appalling death toll – around 9 million people died in the fighting, with millions more permanently disabled and disfigured. For example, in France 20 per cent of those aged between 20 and 40 were killed. Millions more died indirectly as a result of famine and disease at the end of the war. A generation had been lost.

What led the 'civilized' Great Powers of Europe to go to war with each other? Why had diplomacy failed to prevent such a catastrophe?

SEE–THINK–WONDER

Look at Source A. In pairs, **discuss** what the images convey about the nature of fighting in the First World War.

SOURCE A

■ **Figure 8.2** Images of the First World War

To understand what Europe was like at the beginning of the twentieth century, you should turn to Chapter 9, pages 199–202. Read through the material on each Great Power. What key sources of tension can you identify?

By 1914, some of these sources of tension had developed further, and there were also new areas of disagreement. The key factors which created tension were as follows.

THE ALLIANCE SYSTEMS

The European powers had formed two rival alliance blocks by 1907: the Triple Alliance of Germany, Italy and Austria–Hungary and the Triple Entente of France, Russia and Britain. These two alliance systems were a significant cause of tension and anxiety. Therefore, the alliance systems were one key causal factor in the build-up of tension between the European states that would ultimately lead to a general war in 1914.

ANGLO–GERMAN RIVALRY

One of the most serious causes of tension in Europe in the lead-up to 1914 was the naval rivalry that existed between Germany and Great Britain. The Second Naval Law passed in Germany in 1900 called for a doubling of the German battleship fleet by 1916, including the building of 41 battleships and 60 cruisers. This significantly threatened Britain's leading naval position. It also meant that Germany could potentially be a major naval power as well as the strongest land power. Britain needed a navy to protect its empire. Germany did not have such an empire, and so why did it need a large navy if not to threaten its neighbours?

Britain responded by increasing its navy and also, in 1906, building a new battleship, the *HMS Dreadnought*. This was a new class of warship which made other battleships **obsolete**. Germany at once started to build its own fleet of dreadnoughts, starting a full-scale naval race. By 1914, however, the intensity of the race had calmed. Britain remained in the lead, with 29 dreadnought-class ships compared to Germany's 17.

■ **Figure 8.3** *HMS Dreadnought*

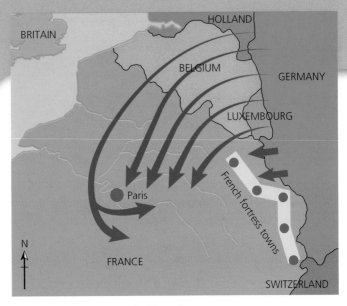

Figure 8.5 The Schlieffen Plan

THE INCREASE IN MILITARY SPENDING

The naval race was part of a wider **arms race** that took place between all the powers of Europe. In the period 1900–14, the main European countries more than doubled their spending on their armies. The introduction of conscription on the continent after 1871 allowed for the creation of huge standing armies and, to support these armies, more destructive weapons were developed.

Attempts to stop the massive arms build-up took place in The Hague in 1899 and in 1907. However, the nations were unable to agree on limiting **armaments** production, though agreements were made on the practice of war.

THE NEED TO PLAN FOR WAR

The growth of armies increased the feeling that war was likely to happen sooner or later. Thus all the European powers developed detailed plans for what to do in the case of being attacked. Mobilization (getting the army ready for war) was key to any successful plan, which meant railways played an important role. Only the railways could transport these vast armies quickly to the battle front. However, this meant detailed timetabling, the success of which depended on rigid implementation. Once a plan was set in motion it could not be altered or stopped without creating chaos.

The common feature of these plans was that they all assumed that war would be a speedy affair. No one had anticipated a war that would last more than a few weeks.

Germany: The Schlieffen Plan

The key problem for Germany was how to fight a war on two fronts – against France and Russia – at the same time. Count von Schlieffen thus came up with a plan that would involve attacking France quickly and then moving all forces to Russia in time to meet the mobilized Russian army on its eastern front.

This plan made several assumptions: that Russia would take six weeks to mobilize its troops, that Germany would need to fight a war with two countries rather than just France or Russia, and that invading France through neutral Belgium would not provoke the British who were a guarantor of Belgian **neutrality**.

% increase

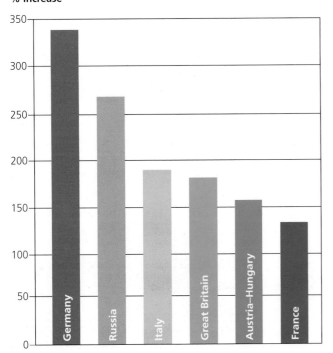

Figure 8.4 Armaments spending 1872–1912

France: Plan 17

France's Plan 17 involved a high-speed mobilization of its forces and a speedy attack to capture Alsace and Lorraine before crossing over the Rhine into Germany.

Austria–Hungary

Austria–Hungary had Plan R and Plan B – both involving attacks on Russia and Serbia.

Russia

Russia had a complex plan to attack Austria–Hungary and Germany – which ultimately relied on overwhelming the German and Austrian armies by sheer weight of numbers.

Timelines

A timeline is a horizontal (or vertical) list of the key events of a certain period of history. It gives a visual representation of when events happened. It has dates chronologically plotted, and to a basic scale. Look at some examples of timelines in this book (Figures 1.6, 7.17, 9.21, 9.22 and 13.7).

A timeline can help you to understand which events took place over a long period of time, and which were short lived. It is also your key tool when you are attempting to build an argument. For example, if you were attempting to answer the question 'To what extent did imperialism cause the First World War?', you would look at your timeline and write down all the events where imperial rivalry was involved. This would be the foundation evidence you could use when arguing that imperialism was to blame.

What were the short-term causes of the First World War?

Figure 8.6 A German cartoon of 1911: 'The mailed fist of Agadir'

The system of alliances backed up by increased military spending and war plans created much tension in Europe in the years after 1900. However, this tension increased dramatically – due first to the actions of Wilhelm II in Morocco and then through events in the Balkans.

THE MOROCCAN CRISES, 1905 AND 1911

Morocco in North Africa was one of the few parts of Africa not controlled by a European power. In 1905 France was getting ready to change this situation and to make Morocco one of its colonies. Britain, now an ally, had agreed to allow France a free hand here, but Germany decided it would oppose the move. This was partly because Wilhelm II did not want France to extend its empire and partly because he wanted the world to see that Germany was an important power in North Africa as well. It was also because he wanted to test the new alliance between France and Britain: would Britain come to the aid of France?

The Kaiser visited the Moroccan port of Tangiers in 1905. He was clearly determined to make an impact, as he rode through the streets of Tangiers on a white horse accompanied by a military band and Moroccan troops. He then made a speech saying that Germany supported independent Morocco. The French were furious; they refused to back down but did agree to the Kaiser's demand for an international conference to discuss the future of Morocco. The conference took place at Algeciras in Spain but was a disaster for Wilhelm. Only Austria–Hungary

supported his views. Britain and Russia supported France. It was decided that France could have special rights in Morocco, even though it could not have Morocco as a colony. More seriously for Wilhelm was the fact that the friendship between France and Britain had been strengthened and in fact they began secret military talks after the conference.

THE AGADIR CONFERENCE, 1911

Five years later, Kaiser Wilhelm interfered again in Morocco. In 1911 Moroccan rebels attacked the town of Fez. The Sultan asked the French for help, who responded by sending a French army to help put down the rebellion. Wilhelm accused the French of invading Morocco and sent a warship, the *Panther*, to the port of Agadir to protect German interests.

Once again, this was an over-reaction by Wilhelm and, indeed, was seen as a warlike action by the other European countries. The British, already annoyed by Germany's naval build-up, was now concerned that Germany was planning to build an Atlantic base which would challenge Britain's navy base at Gibraltar. Thus, Britain supported France again and preparations for war were made.

At the last moment, Germany backed down. France took control of Morocco and Germany accepted land in central Africa as compensation.

THINK–PAIR–SHARE

Look at the cartoon in Figure 8.6. What is the message of this cartoon?

Figure 8.7 Conflicting interests in the Balkans

This crisis had important results:

- It left Germany humiliated and less likely to back down in any future crisis. The Kaiser started to be concerned that Germany was becoming 'encircled' by hostile countries.
- British opinion became more hostile towards Germany. Britain was now convinced that Germany wanted to dominate Europe.
- A secret agreement was reached between France and Britain, by which France would patrol the Mediterranean and the Royal Navy would defend France's Atlantic and North Sea coasts.

PROBLEMS IN THE BALKANS

The Balkans was a very unstable area. Turkey was the ruler of this area at the start of the century but, once a great empire, it was now known as 'the sick man of Europe'. Its declining status meant that its power over the Balkan peoples was weakened. The various national groups in the Balkans were keen to get independence for themselves, but Russia and Austria–Hungary were also interested in taking advantage of Turkey's weakness and asserting power in this area. Figure 8.7 shows a map of the different conflicting interests in this area.

THE BOSNIAN CRISIS, 1908

In 1908 Austria–Hungary took advantage of growing chaos within the Balkans and added Bosnia–Herzegovina to its empire. This created another international crisis following on from the Moroccan Crisis of 1905. Most of the inhabitants of this area were Serbs and disliked Austria; indeed, Serbia had hoped to make Bosnia part of a 'Greater Serbia'. Russia joined Serbia in condemning the move but, when Germany made it clear that it supported Austria–Hungary, Russia had to back down. They were not prepared to risk war over this issue. However, although the crisis itself did not end in open conflict, the consequences had a serious impact on the international situation. Russia, determined not to have to back down again, intensified its rearming programme. It also drew closer to France and Britain. Serbia was also furious and wanted revenge on Austria. Meanwhile, Austria grew in confidence as it believed that Germany would now support it in any future disputes with Serbia and Russia.

THE BALKAN WARS OF 1912 AND 1913

Between 1912 and 1913, there was a series of local wars within the Balkans. A key result of these wars was that Serbia doubled its size. This had serious consequences for the area:

- Serbia was now even more determined to unite all Serbs into a Greater Serbia.
- The growing threat of Serbia made Austria–Hungary even more determined to crush the Serbians.

Figure 8.8 The Balkans in 1908 (*left*) and in 1914 (*right*)

Figure 8.9 The assassination of Franz Ferdinand is announced in the *Los Angeles Times*

THE JULY CRISIS, 1914

Although we have seen that the events of 1900–14 considerably increased tension between the Great Powers, in fact it should not be seen that war was 'inevitable'. By mid-1914, the naval race between Germany and Britain had calmed down and a Royal Navy squadron even paid a goodwill visit to Germany in June of that year. The crises that you have read about had also all been resolved. Thus the events of July 1914 in the Balkans and the actions of the Great Powers during this month can be seen as crucial in bringing about the major European war that started in August.

The assassination at Sarajevo

On 28 June 1914, Archduke Franz Ferdinand, heir to the Austro-Hungarian throne, was visiting the capital of Bosnia, Sarajevo, to inspect army exercises in the area. He was with his wife Sophie and it was their wedding anniversary. He arrived at Sarajevo Station at 9.28a.m. Among the cheering crowds lining the streets was a group of Serbian men who planned to assassinate the Archduke. They belonged to an organization called The Black Hand – which was dedicated to the cause of getting rid of Austrian influence and creating a Greater Serbia.

The assassination attempt failed. One of the Serb terrorists, Cabrinovic, threw a bomb at the car which was carrying the Archduke and his wife. However, it exploded under the car behind, injuring several people. The Archduke's car sped off to the town hall; meanwhile the police pulled Cabrinovic out of the river. He had taken poison but it had not worked.

A fateful error then occurred. After an official visit to the town hall, the Archduke's chauffeur took a wrong turning. One of the terrorists, Gavrilo Princip, now found himself right by the Archduke's car as the chauffeur started to reverse to get onto the correct route. Princip stepped forward and fired his revolver, killing both the Archduke and his wife.

What was the reaction of the Great Powers?

Austria–Hungary

Austria–Hungary was outraged at the assassination and immediately blamed Serbia for the terrorist attack. It seemed like an opportunity to punish Serbia by crushing the country once and for all. However, Austria–Hungary needed to know that it had Germany's support in case Russia should come to the aid of Serbia. At a meeting in Berlin on 5 July, Germany reassured Austria–Hungary that it would support it in whatever action it decided to take; this became known as 'the Blank Cheque'.

Backed up by the promise of Germany's unlimited military support, Austria–Hungary then drew up an ultimatum to present to the Serbian government. This was intended to be so harsh that Serbia would not be able to accept its demands; it was finally presented to Serbia on 23 July – almost one month after the assassination. Serbia agreed to all but the most extreme demands; however, this conciliatory reply was not enough for Austria–Hungary, which declared war on Serbia on 28 July and started a bombardment against Belgrade.

Russia

Russia was now determined to fully support Serbia. On 30 July, the Tsar ordered Russia's mobilization. This accelerated the pace of events and made it much harder to reach a peaceful settlement.

Germany

With Russia mobilizing, Germany could not waste any time. The Schlieffen Plan dictated that France had to be defeated before the German army attacked Russia. Thus, on 31 July, Germany gave the French an ultimatum: unless they promised to remain neutral in the event of a Russo-German war, Germany would declare war. Russia was also given an ultimatum: 12 hours to demobilize.

When the ultimatum to Russia expired, Germany declared war and began to mobilize. On the same day the French rejected their ultimatum and started to mobilize. On 2 August, the Germans presented Belgium with an ultimatum demanding the right to send troops through their country.

Britain

As an ally of Russia and France, it was likely that Britain would get involved in the war. However, the trigger for Britain's involvement was the German invasion of Belgium following Belgium's rejection of Germany's ultimatum. Britain was a signatory of the 1839 Treaty of London, which guaranteed Belgium's neutrality. Although the Kaiser considered this Treaty to be just 'a scrap of paper', it ensured that when the Germans started to invade Belgium on Tuesday 4 August, Britain kept its promise to protect Belgium and declared war on Germany.

In just five weeks, a dispute between two countries in the Balkans had escalated into a European war; eventually nations from all continents would become involved.

ACTIVITY: Causes of the First World War

■ ATL

- Critical-thinking skills – Evaluate evidence and arguments

Look at Sources B–D.

1 **Interpret** the message of the cartoonist in Source B.
2 **Identify** the key points (at least five) made about the causes of the First World War in Sources C and D.
3 From their origin and purpose, **evaluate** the values and limitations of Sources B and D for historians studying the causes of the First World War.
4 **Using** the sources and your own knowledge, **analyse** the causes of the First World War.

◆ Assessment opportunities

- ◆ This activity can be assessed using Criterion A: Knowing and understanding and Criterion D: Thinking critically.

PUNCH, OR THE LONDON CHARIVARI.—October 2, 1912.

BALKAN TROUBLES

THE BOILING POINT.

■ **Figure 8.10** Cartoon published in the British magazine, *Punch*, 2 October 1912

SOURCE C

'… it seems very unlikely that the Russians positively desired a major war. Mobilisation for them meant preparation for a possible war. The Germans, however, interpreted mobilisation as the virtual equivalent to a declaration of war, and Germany's Schlieffen Plan meant that the German army would have to attack and defeat France before moving eastwards to combat Russian forces.'

Pearce, R. and Lowe, J. 2001. Rivalry and Accord: International Relations, 1870–1914. *London, Hodder Education.*

SOURCE D

'All the mobilization plans had been timed to the minute, months or even years before and they would not be changed. [A change] in one direction would ruin them in every other direction. Any attempt, for instance, by the Austrians to mobilise against Serbia would mean that they could not mobilise as well against Russia because two lots of trains would be running against each other. Any alteration in the mobilization plan meant not a delay for 24 hours, but at least six months before the next lot of timetables were ready.'

Taylor, A.J.P. 1979. How Wars Begin. *Hamish Hamilton.*

How was the First World War fought?

FAILURE OF THE WAR PLANS IN THE WEST AND IN THE EAST

Within three weeks, the war plans of each of the western **belligerents** had failed. The Belgians were able to resist Germany and hold the German advance for ten days. The small British 'expeditionary force' was also able to slow the momentum of the Schlieffen Plan in a battle at Mons. The French army which invaded Alsace-Lorraine met a bloody fate at the hands of German machine-gun defences. The German war plan – the Schlieffen Plan – failed to take France rapidly as the Russians attacked Germany far more quickly than anticipated and the German generals had to send forces to the east to fight there. This meant that the force that was to sweep through to Paris was weakened. The Germans were held back at the Battle of the Marne in September 1914 by British and French forces.

To prevent themselves from being pushed back, and to defend their position and men from machine guns and artillery, the Germans 'dug in'. This triggered the construction of trenches across the western front of the war – from Flanders in Belgium to Switzerland. Trench warfare meant **stalemate** – and mass slaughter.

In the east, instead of taking six weeks to get its armies to the front, Russia took only ten days. The Russians split their forces, attacking Germany and Austria. After some initial success for Russia, the Germans replaced their generals in the east with Hindenburg and Ludendorff. The Germans saw that the Russian armies were split in two by the Masurian Lakes and were able to inflict a heavy defeat on them at the Battle of Tannenburg in August 1914. The Russians suffered a further defeat in September at the Battle of the Masurian Lakes. The casualty rate was horrific – over a quarter of a million Russians were killed.

However, the Russians were successful in the south against the Austro-Hungarian forces. The Austro-Hungarian attack on Russia (pursuing 'Plan R') was repelled and their invasion turned into a rapid retreat – they even abandoned their weapons and heavy guns. This was an important victory for Russia as it had taken Galicia and could now attack Germany from the south.

WHY DID A CONFLICT BETWEEN THE EUROPEAN POWERS DEVELOP INTO A WORLD WAR?

At the outbreak of the war the Triple Alliance – or Central Power – **belligerents** were Germany, Austria–Hungary and the Ottoman Empire (Turkey) and the Entente belligerents were France and its empire, Britain and its empire, Russia and Belgium. In 1915 Bulgaria joined the Triple Alliance side, and Italy joined the side of the Entente. In 1916 Romania and Portugal joined the Entente powers, and in 1917 Greece and, most significantly, the USA entered the war for the Entente. The war was also a world war in the sense that it drew in human and material resources from the vast European empires that straddled the globe. Japan was the first independent nation outside of Europe to join the war and it attacked German colonies in the Far East.

ACTIVITY: Research project on the theatres of war

- Communication skills – Structure information in summaries, essays and reports
- Organization skills – Use appropriate strategies for organizing complex information
- Information literacy skills – Access information to be informed and to inform others; Make connections between various sources of information

What is your research project?

You are going to research the impact of technology within one of the following 'theatres' of war:

- War on the land
- War at sea
- War in the air
- War on the home front

You could begin your research on one theatre of war and then refine a research question that is more specific.

Hint

As you research your topic, keep in mind the research question you are attempting to answer.

Make notes on only relevant information that answers the set question.

Possible topics you could research

War on the land

- Which new weapons were developed and how were they used? Consider: heavy artillery, machine guns, tanks, grenades, gas.
- The nature and impact of trench warfare
- The impact of new technology on key battles on the western front
- Campaigns that were less affected by technology, e.g. the Arab Revolt

War at sea

- The impact of technology on key battles at sea
- The U-boat war in the Atlantic; the impact of new technology on fighting U-boats
- Communications and code-breaking

War in the air

- Reconnaissance
- Dog-fights and ground attacks
- Civilian bombing

War on the home front

- Defending civilians on the home front and in war zones
- Propaganda and communications
- Medicine

Your research, and the research by your class, will help you to understand why, after the brutality and slaughter of war, drawing up a peace settlement was going to be very difficult.

How will you organize your project?

This project is divided into five tasks:

Task 1: Group discussions – this brainstorming session should enable you to draft possible questions and help **formulate** your research question.

Task 2: Action plan – **formulate** a plan of how you will conduct your research.

Task 3: Collate and evaluate your research – **evaluate** your research process and results.

> **Hint**
> - Make sure you have details, dates, examples and statistics where possible (remember, they all need citations).
> - Include photos, drawings and diagrams where possible (again, they all need citations).
> - Make sure you not only reference all your sources, but you develop a 'works cited' list or bibliography of all the sources you use.

Task 4: Research document – create a document on the chosen research question related to one of the theatres of war, with all information cited and a full 'works cited' list that uses one recognized convention.

Task 5: Presentation – present your research to the class (10–15 minutes).

Your final document

Your research project should:

- have a cover page with your research question, an image and your name on it
- have information that is organized under subheadings; themes or questions can be used as subheadings
- be submitted with your research action plan
- use language and images that are appropriate for your audience
- reference your information using a recognized system
- be based on a minimum of five different sources
- have a conclusion, based on the evidence presented, that clearly addresses your research question.

◆ Assessment opportunities

- ◆ This activity can be assessed using Criterion B: Investigating and Criterion C: Communicating.

THINK–PAIR–SHARE

Consider the innovators and inventors that you have researched in your project. How were they similar to and different from the innovators and inventors that you studied in Chapter 2?

What brought the First World War to an end?

■ **Figure 8.11** During the infamous Battle of Passchendaele the mud was so deep that men and horses drowned

The USA entered the First World War on the side of the Entente powers on 6 April 1917. The Americans had been provoked to join the war by German U-boat action in the Atlantic when the cruise liner the *Lusitania* was torpedoed and sunk in 1915, killing 128 of its American passengers. This led to an increase in anti-German sentiment in the USA and a rise in support for American intervention. The Germans did agree to restrict their U-boat campaign but, by the beginning of 1917, Germany wanted to bring about a quick end to the war by blockading supplies to Britain and France – and unleashed unrestricted submarine warfare again. The final trigger for the US President Woodrow Wilson was the publication of the 'Zimmerman Telegram', which apparently revealed a plot to bring Mexico into the war by attacking the USA.

The Germans now needed to win the war in the west quickly, before the full weight of American men and resources arrived in France. But, in October 1917, Russia was convulsed by revolution and the communist Bolshevik party seized power. The Bolsheviks had promised in their slogans and manifesto to bring peace and therefore the new government entered into separate negotiations with Germany. The Entente had lost its Russian ally. The Germans had won the war in the east and imposed a severe peace settlement on the new communist regime. They could now focus their forces on the western front. Determined to win the war in the west before the USA fully engaged, the Germans launched a massive **offensive** on 21 March. This 'spring offensive' opened with a bombardment of 6000 heavy guns, combined with mustard gas. The British, overwhelmed, fled their defensive trenches. The German General Ludendorff had broken the stalemate.

The Entente and American combined forces, under the leadership of General Foch, seemed at first unable to resist the German advance. However, Ludendorff had overstretched his forces and sent too many men, and too quickly, forward into France. The Germans had created a 'salient' – meaning that the front line projected outwards so that it could be attacked on three sides. German forces were exposed to allied attack. The German momentum had been lost.

In October 1918 the Italians defeated the Austrians in the Battle of Vittorio Veneto and the Turkish were also defeated. On the home front in Germany there were widespread strikes and riots and talk of revolution. Ludendorff had to accept that Germany could not win on the western front. He asked the German government to request an **armistice** or ceasefire from the USA. The Germans hoped that they would be able to get a negotiated peace settlement from the more moderate American government in line with President Woodrow Wilson's '14 Points' (see page 165).

As the western allies discussed the terms for peace, a last attempt was made to win the war by Germany. The navy was ordered to prepare for battle but the sailors refused and revolution spread from the port town of Kiel across Germany.

Kaiser Wilhelm was smuggled out to Holland and a new Republic was proclaimed. General Foch met two representatives of the new German government in a railway carriage in northern France. The terms for the armistice were harsh – and the Germans were reluctant to sign. But they did sign on 11 November 1918 and the armistice came into effect at 11a.m. the same day.

The First World War was finally over.

What peacemaking agreements were made after the First World War?

THE TREATY OF VERSAILLES

The First World War killed 10 million people. The European powers that had gone to war in 1914 were utterly changed by the war. The political regimes and empires of Russia, Turkey, Germany and Austria–Hungary were no more. Even the victorious powers, Britain and France, were devastated by the conflict. The totality of the war meant that no one in Europe was left untouched by it.

How could the USA, Britain, France and their ally Italy create a lasting peace from this catastrophe?

Following the armistice of 11 November 1918, the leaders and ministers of the victorious powers met to draw up peace treaties to impose on the defeated powers. The President of the USA, Woodrow Wilson; the Prime Minister of France, Georges Clemenceau and the British Prime Minister, David Lloyd George, went to Paris in January 1919. The peacemakers were the leaders of democratic states, and the general public, particularly in Britain and France, wanted Germany to pay for the war and their suffering.

Each defeated belligerent had its own treaty drawn up, including two separate treaties for the newly independent states of Austria and Hungary. The treaty we will focus on here is the treaty signed with Germany: the Treaty of Versailles.

The peacemakers were working under immense pressure. Germany was held under a blockade to ensure that it could not resume fighting while the talks took place, and this meant that the German people continued to suffer from acute food and fuel shortages. The 'Big Three', as they were known – Clemenceau, Lloyd George and Wilson – were expected to demand compensation from Germany for the losses incurred in the war. Indeed, in Britain, Lloyd George had won a recent election on the slogan 'Hang the Kaiser'

Figure 8.12 Celebration following the news of the armistice, November 1918

and, for the French, who had suffered the horrors of the war taking place on their territory, there was a particular appetite for revenge. There was not only the human cost to take into account, but the impact of the war on industry and agriculture – Britain and France were economically exhausted. The Big Three had to agree on terms for a peace settlement – difficult when you have to assess the 'cost' of the lives of hundreds of thousands of soldiers, for example – but it was made more challenging as the peacemakers themselves did not agree on what the terms should be.

France

France believed that Germany was relatively strong at the end of the war. France's economy lay devastated and a generation of young men had been killed. Germany's land and industry had not been as badly affected. The mood in France was for Germany to be permanently weakened. The French wanted a settlement that would mean Germany could never attack France again. The French President Poincaré even

■ **Figure 8.13** Leaders from the USA, Britain, France and Italy meeting to talk about the Treaty of Versailles

suggested that Germany be broken up into smaller states, with the Rhine becoming an independent state. Georges Clemenceau was realistic and knew that the USA and Britain would not accept anything extreme – but he also had to satisfy his French public and so he worked to weaken Germany as much as he could.

The USA

Although Woodrow Wilson also believed Germany should be punished, he was perceived internationally as a man who wanted to build a more peaceful world after the 'war to end all wars' was over. When the USA entered the war Wilson announced, in January 1918, his '14 Points' as a basis for drawing up a fair and lasting peace settlement.

Overall, Wilson's view was that the treaty with Germany should not be too harsh as this would not be good for a lasting peace. Germany would recover later on and may then be intent on revenge. Wilson's intention was to strengthen **democracy** in the defeated nations and then the people themselves would prevent their leaders from engaging in another horrific conflict.

Wilson's key plan for maintaining peace in the post-war world was based on a new organization, the League of Nations. This would be an international body that would be the mechanism for cooperation between nations. Any dispute between states would be taken to the League before a war developed. The international community would then act as an arbiter and put forward resolutions to inter-state disagreements.

As well as fostering democracy, Wilson believed in the principle of self-determination, which is the belief that nations should rule themselves rather than be ruled over by another nation. He believed that the peoples of eastern Europe should have their own nation states – rather than being part of the empires of Austria–Hungary and Russia.

Britain and France viewed some of Wilson's vision for the future as being a little too idealistic – and some thought that he did not really understand the complexity of the situation in eastern and central Europe. It would be difficult to give self-determination to the people of eastern and central Europe as they were scattered across many nations.

Britain

It has often been said that at the peace talks Britain's position was somewhere in the middle ground between that of the USA and that of France. Lloyd George agreed that Germany should be punished and – like Clemenceau – had his public at home pressuring him to 'make Germany pay'. Certainly, Lloyd George wanted Germany to lose its navy and colonies, as they were seen as a threat to the British Empire. However, he also agreed with Wilson's view that Germany should not be dealt with too harshly, as this might provoke a war of revenge in the future. The war had cost the British economy dearly and, as Germany had been Britain's second largest trading partner, Lloyd George needed the German economy to recover and resume trading to safeguard employment at home.

Italy

Vittorio Emanuele Orlando, the prime minister of Italy, represented Italy at the Peace Conference in Versailles. Although Italy had suffered huge casualties on the Isonzo front, fighting Austria–Hungary, its role in the negotiations was more minor than that of the Big Three. Italians wanted to get the territories that had been promised to them in the Treaty of London in 1915 when they had joined the Entente powers in the war. They wanted something for all the suffering and slaughter they had endured. This included land from Austria, some of Germany's former colonies and **reparations**. Italy was in favour of a weakened Germany and preventing a new 'super' German state being formed if it joined with Austria on Italy's border.

All the victorious powers wanted to establish the 'guilt' of Germany and her allies for starting the war. This was the premise from which they could extract terms such as reparations.

Not only was there pressure to come to an agreement quickly to relieve the starving German people, but there was also pressure on the peacemakers in terms of their fear of the spread of communism. Russia had experienced a year of upheaval and revolution in 1917, culminating in the seizure of power by the Bolshevik party. As we have seen, this led to Russia signing a separate peace treaty with Germany and exiting the First World War. The Bolsheviks established the first communist state in the world and the western democracies were very worried that their revolution would spread – particularly in Germany. The peacemakers had to draw up a treaty to stabilize the situation in post-war Germany and to support its new democracy.

ACTIVITY: The fear of communism

ATL

- Transfer skills – Inquire in different contexts to gain a different perspective

Think about the ideologies that you read about in Chapter 7 and specifically about the ideas of Karl Marx and the communists (page 133). **Discuss** why these ideas would frighten the leaders of the western capitalist democracies.

Draft a brief discussion for a radio broadcast to be given to either the US, British, French or German public in the 1920s explaining the 'danger posed by communism'.

◆ Assessment opportunities

- ◆ In this activity you have practised skills that are assessed using Criterion D: Thinking critically.

ACTIVITY: The problems of peacemaking – the Versailles Conference

■ **ATL**

■ Collaboration skills – Practise empathy

What is your goal in this task?

You will be making your own peace treaty to deal with the post-war problems.

How will you achieve this?

Get into groups of five.

Each member takes on one of the following roles:

- Georges Clemenceau – France
- Woodrow Wilson – USA
- Lloyd George – Britain
- Vittorio Emanuele Orlando – Italy
- Count Brockdorff-Rantzau – Germany

> **Hint**
>
> The student representing Germany should be aware that although Germany wants to negotiate terms, the other leaders can decide whether or not to let the German representative join the discussion.

Read more about your role on the following pages. Then, as a group, consider the following issues and decide on your stance:

1. War guilt
   - Germany to blame?
   - Other power to blame?
   - No power to blame?
2. Reparations – payment for war damage
   - Germany should not pay?
   - Germany pay limited amount?
   - Germany pay large amount?
3. Limitation of German armed forces
   - No limitations on armed forces?
   - No armed forces allowed at all?
   - Limited army/limited armaments only?
   - Equal armed forces with France?
4. Germany's colonies
   - Germany should keep colonies?
   - Germany can retain some colonies?
   - All colonies should be removed?

5. Union between the new state of Austria and Germany (two German-speaking nations)
   - The two states should be forbidden to unite?
   - If their people want it, the two states should be allowed to join together?
   - Forbid it for 15 years – then let Austria decide?
6. The important trading German trading port – Danzig
   - It should remain German?
   - The new Polish state should have it?
   - It should be under international control via the League of Nations?
7. West Prussia and Posen
   - Give to Poland, so new state has access to the sea?
   - Remain German? (Most who live there are German speaking.)
   - Put territories under control of League of Nations?
8. The Sudetenland – formerly part of Austria–Hungary's empire
   - New state of Czechoslovakia should have it, as it offers the defensive advantage of a mountain range?
   - Give to Germany? (Many German speakers there)
   - Sudetenland to govern itself?
9. Alsace-Lorraine
   - Remain German?
   - Give to France? (Mainly French-speaking)
   - Put territory under control of League of Nations?
10. Saar – coal-mining area
    - Germany to keep the area?
    - Give it to France?
    - Put territory under control of League of Nations?
11. The Rhineland – border between France and Germany
    - France should take it for security?
    - Germany should keep it?
    - Germany keeps it but it becomes a demilitarized zone?
    - Make it an independent state?

You have 30 minutes to **discuss** the issues listed. You must come to a decision on each issue – even if you don't all agree – by the end of the time period.

Reflect on your final treaty?

Which delegate was most happy with it? Who was least happy with the final terms?

France

You will be playing the role of Georges Clemenceau and should consider the following:

- The war on the western front mainly took place in your country.
- Your country lost one-and-a-half million men.

'America is very far from Germany, but France is very near and I have preoccupations which do not affect President Wilson as they do a man who has seen the Germans for four years in his country: There are wrongs to be righted.'

■ **Figure 8.14** Georges Clemenceau, January 1919

The USA

You will be playing the role of Woodrow Wilson and should consider the following:

- You understand that the USA suffered less than the Europeans in the war.
- You understand that the other victorious powers want compensation and that France needs to feel secure. However, you believe that punishing Germany too harshly would sow the seeds of future conflict.
- You want to pursue and implement your '14 Points' as the basis for a lasting settlement.
- You want Poland and a new state of Czechoslovakia to be strong neighbouring states on the border of Germany.

'It must be a peace without victory … Only a peace between equals can last.'

■ **Figure 8.15** Woodrow Wilson, January 1917

- You also want to set up the League of Nations as the key organization to safeguard the peace.
- You do support some 'payment' from Germany – but want limited reparations.

Britain

You will be playing the role of Lloyd George and should consider the following:

- You want to make a fair settlement with Germany.
- You understand some of the French objectives. Your public at home is also keen to 'make Germany pay!'
- However, you also agree with many of Wilson's 14 Points.
- You aim to seriously limit the German navy; you support an independent Poland as a 'buffer state' to German expansion.
- Like France, you want reparations, and you also hope to take over some of Germany's former colonies.
- You agree with the principle of self-determination – in certain cases.

'… our terms may be severe … but at the same time they can be … just [so] that the country on which they are imposed will feel in its heart that it has no right to complain. But injustice … displayed in the hour of triumph will never be forgotten or forgiven.'

■ **Figure 8.16** Lloyd George, March 1919

- Your economy has been devastated with 75 000 properties and 23 000 factories destroyed. France needs considerable compensation for the losses and suffering.
- Germany must never be able to attack France again. You want to punish Germany – and, yes, there is an appetite for revenge. Specifically, you are interested in: the crushing of all Germany's land armed forces, the return of Alsace-Lorraine, heavy reparations, an independent Poland to act as a buffer state to Germany, the formation of a new state in the Balkans (Yugoslavia), preventing Italy from gaining the Tyrol and the Dalmatian Coast, gaining some former German colonies, the division of Austria–Hungary into two separate states, the occupation of the Rhineland for at least 50 years, control of the coal-rich Saar territory and ensuring that Germany has no air force.

Italy

You will be playing the role of Vittorio Emanuele Orlando and should consider the following:

- You realize that you are not seen as being as 'important' as the Big Three at the conference and this is frustrating.
- You want to put forward your claims to the Tyrol and to the Dalmatian Coast.
- You also, as a Mediterranean power, are keen to limit Germany's navy – ensure that they are not permitted any submarines.
- You support Polish independence as a buffer state to Germany, and want a small and independent Austria on your own border. Germany and Austria should be forbidden to join together.
- You want to gain some of Germany's former colonies and you want reparations from the Central Powers.

■ **Figure 8.17** Vittorio Emanuele Orlando

Germany

You will be playing the role of Count Brockdorff-Rantzau and should consider the following:

- You had anticipated being able to 'negotiate' the terms of the peace settlement.
- You wanted the USA to have more influence – and to offer you a treaty based on the 14 Points. You claim that the 14 Points were a key reason that Germany called for an armistice as it meant that there would be no need for an 'unconditional' surrender with the American peace plan on the table.
- You do not believe the war was Germany's fault. You fear a severe punishment – particularly from the French. The democratic politicians in Germany are worried that a harsh treaty would damage the reputation of the new government there. BUT – the reality is that you will have to accept *whatever* terms the Big Three impose.
- You do not want an independent Poland, nor an independent Czechoslovakia – either of which would mean the loss of some German territory.
- You want your military left intact.

■ **Figure 8.18** Count Brockdorff-Rantzau

8 Why do nations go to war and why is peacemaking difficult?

169

What were the terms of the Treaty of Versailles?

As the talks continued at Versailles, it became clear that the very different aims and perspectives of the Big Three meant that not all would be happy with the final terms of the treaty with Germany. (You probably found the same in your class activity.)

The French resented the more conciliatory approach of the USA – Clemenceau declaring:

> 'Mr Wilson bores me with his Fourteen Points; why, God Almighty has only Ten!'

They disagreed over what to do with the Rhineland and the Saar. Wilson had to give up on many of his ideas. The French and British in return gave in with regard to self-determination in the east of Europe – although as imperial powers they had reservations about this 'principle' being taken too far. Lloyd George also was worried about Point 2 of the 14 Points, which allowed all nations access to the seas.

But the British and French also clashed over the severity of a settlement, as the British wanted an economically recovered Germany, whereas the French felt that they were much more threatened by this.

In the end, when the final Treaty of Versailles was drafted, none of the Big Three was satisfied with it. All had been forced to compromise to get the treaty finished.

■ **Figure 8.19** German cartoon published in June 1919. The men in suits are Woodrow Wilson, Georges Clemenceau and Lloyd George

Table 8.1 The terms of the Treaty of Versailles

War guilt	Germany and her allies had to accept responsibility for the war.
Reparations	A final sum was not agreed until 1921 when it was set at £6600 million. This was an enormous figure.
Territory (1)	In the east, West Prussia and Posen were given to Poland. This gave Poland a corridor of territory through Germany and access to the sea. East Prussia was now cut off from the rest of Germany.
	The port of Danzig was run by the League of Nations as a free city.
	Poland was also given upper Silesia.
	There was a vote or 'plebiscite' in Schleswig, and the north went to Denmark. In the west, the Saarland would be run by the League until a vote could be held after 15 years.
	The Rhineland became a demilitarized zone and Alsace-Lorraine was given to France.
	The territory that Germany had taken from Russia when it won the war in the east in 1917 was set up as new nation states.
	Union between Germany and Austria was forbidden.
Territory (2)	Former German colonies became mandates, which meant that they were officially under the control of the League of Nations but were administered by the British and French.
Military	German armed forces were heavily restricted. The army was to be limited to 100 000 men. Conscription was banned. Germany was not allowed armoured vehicles. The navy could only have six battleships to protect shipping and trade. It was not allowed submarines. The country was not allowed an air force. The border with France, the Rhineland, became a demilitarized zone.
Diktat	The Germans were not invited to join the talks and had not been able to negotiate any of the final terms. Therefore, they viewed the treaty as a 'Diktat' or a peace that had been dictated and imposed on them.
League of Nations	Germany was not allowed to join the new League of Nations until it had proved itself a 'peace-loving nation'.

ACTIVITY: Impact of the Treaty of Versailles

1 What is the message of Source E?
2 What does it suggest about the German perspective of the Treaty of Versailles in 1919?
3 Consider: To what extent did the Treaty of Versailles set up conditions for a lasting peace?
4 Make a copy of the table below and fill it with bullet-point notes on the terms of the Treaty of Versailles.

ATL

- Critical-thinking skills – Evaluate evidence and arguments

Assessment opportunities

- In this activity you have practised skills that are assessed using Criterion D: Thinking critically.

	Terms	Positives for peace in Europe	Problems for peace in Europe
War guilt			
Armed forces			
Reparations			
Territories and colonies			
League of Nations			

What was the impact of the Treaty of Versailles?

Germany had lost 10 per cent of its land, 12.5 per cent of its population, 16 per cent of it coalfields and almost 50 per cent of its iron and steel industry. It had also lost all of its colonies. Its army was severely limited and it had a tiny navy. It had had to accept war guilt and a huge reparations bill. The reaction in Germany was outrage towards the 'vengeful' peacemakers – in particular the French.

The war guilt clause was particularly hated as the German public believed that responsibility for the war was shared between the European powers. The fact that Germany was forced to accept 'war guilt' meant that the victors were able to justify making Germany pay the cost of the war in reparations. The German economy lay in devastation after the war – and with all the territorial and human losses imposed by the treaty, the Germans feared reparations would destroy them.

The military clauses were also an issue. First, 100 000 armed men as permitted in the treaty was barely sufficient to keep the peace on the streets at home. Germans felt that their country had been disarmed to the extent that they were now defenceless. Wilson's 14 Points had called for general disarmament but the victors had not disarmed – and France was in fact rearming. The loss of so much territory was not just an economic blow, it was also damaging to German pride – their people were now under the rule of foreign powers. Most Germans had hoped for a fair peace settlement based on Wilson's 14 Points – but the Treaty of Versailles was seen as vengeful and crippling.

SOURCE F

Article 231 of the Treaty of Versailles (known as the 'war guilt clause')

'The Allied and Associated Governments affirm and Germany accepts the responsibility of Germany and her allies for causing all the loss and damage to which the Allied and Associated Governments and their nationals have been subjected as a consequence of the war imposed upon them by the aggression of Germany and her allies.'

SOURCE G

A German newspaper on the day the Treaty of Versailles was signed in 1919

'Today in the Hall of Mirrors the disgraceful Treaty is being signed. Do not forget it! The German people will, with unceasing labour, press forward to re-conquer the place among nations to which it is entitled … Germany has lost important territory. This is fatal for our economy. Britain and France have increased their empires by taking control of the German colonies … this is against the ideas set down in Wilson's 14 points!'

Deutsche Zeitung *[German News]*.

SOURCE H

A British historian, William Carr

'Severe as the Treaty seemed to many Germans, it should be remembered that Germany might easily have fared much worse. If Clemenceau had had his way … the Rhineland would have become an independent state, the Saar would have been annexed [joined] to France and Danzig would have become part of Poland … The German economy remained strong, and had the potential to recover quickly from the War.'

Carr, W. 1972. A History of Germany.

SOURCE I

The value of the German Mark in relation to the British pound

Jan 1914	£1 =	20 marks
Jan 1922	£1 =	760 marks
Nov 1922	£1 =	50 000 marks
Nov 1923	£1 =	16 000 000 000 marks

Figure 8.20 British cartoon published in January 1921. The man holding the whip is French, and the man holding the spade is British. The horse represents Germany. 'Unlimited indemnity' refers to reparations

ACTIVITY: The impact of the Treaty of Versailles

1 According to Sources F–J, what are three negative points and two positive points about the terms of the Treaty of Versailles?

2 Outline the purpose, values and limitations for Sources G and H with reference to the origins stated in the table.

Source	Origin	Purpose	Values	Limitations
G	From *Deutsche Zeitung* (German News) on the day the Treaty of Versailles was signed in 1919			
H	Written by a British historian, W. Carr, in his book *A History of Germany* in 1972			

3 'The terms of the Treaty of Versailles were too harsh on Germany.' To what extent do you agree with this claim? Answer with reference to Sources F–J and also with reference to your own knowledge of the treaty.

 ATL

■ Critical-thinking skills – Evaluate evidence and arguments; Recognize unstated assumptions and bias

◆ **Assessment opportunities**

◆ In this activity you have practised skills that are assessed using Criterion A: Knowing and understanding and Criterion D: Thinking critically.

What were the key events that led to the Second World War?

THE WEAKNESSES OF THE LEAGUE OF NATIONS

As you will see in Chapter 9, the League of Nations had many weaknesses. It was never the body envisioned by President Woodrow Wilson and was inadequate for preventing conflict and ensuring 'collective security'. Some historians consider the failure of the League of Nations to be a key cause of the Second World War.

> ## DISCUSS
>
> Read pages 204–205 and **discuss** how the limitations of the League meant that it would not be able to prevent another major conflict.

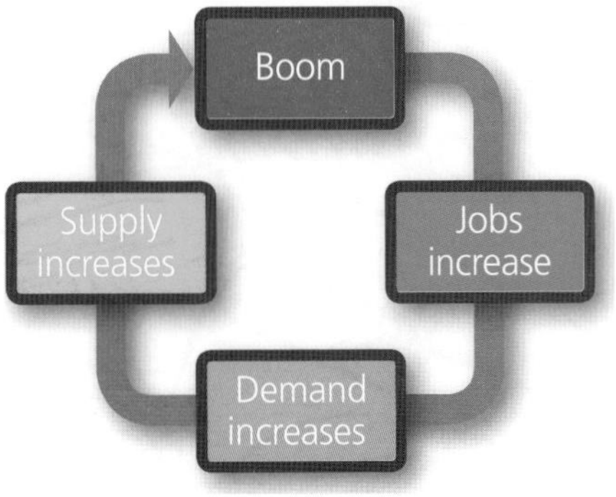

THE GREAT DEPRESSION

After the First World War the European economies were seriously damaged and the USA emerged as the dominant global economic power. Its economy enjoyed an economic 'boom' in the 1920s as industry grew, there was ready employment and the stock market in Wall Street went only one way – up and up. People believed that they could get rich quick and there was for the first time widespread speculation on the market; ordinary Americans could borrow a few dollars to invest in shares, to be rewarded a few months later with a profit. This was all fine as long as the markets continued to do well.

American banks and investors had put a lot of money into post-war Weimar Germany – helping it to recover from the war and to pay reparations.

> ## ▼ Links to: Economics
>
> Think about the factors which caused the boom and bust cycles of other key financial markets over the years, e.g. the Asian financial crisis and the global financial crisis.

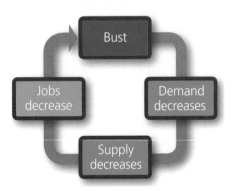

■ **Figure 8.21** Boom cycle of the early and mid-1920s

■ **Figure 8.22** Bust cycle from 1929 onwards

> ## ACTIVITY: Boom and bust cycles
>
> ### ■ ATL
>
> ■ Communication skills – Paraphrase accurately and concisely
>
> **Explain** to a partner the above economic processes. **Discuss** why a boom cycle might foster good international relations. Now **discuss** why a bust cycle might foster a more hostile international environment.

However, by 1929 this upward spiral of growth and prosperity began to slow down. The mass productivity of American industry had begun to saturate the markets; there was a similar picture in American agriculture and the stock market was overheated. Whereas stocks had *always* risen month on month, big investors could see the economic indicators were bad and began to sell their shares – which meant for the first time that decade the price of shares fell. Then it was the turn of the middle and small investors to panic and try to sell their shares for whatever they could get. Ultimately, in October 1929, Wall Street crashed. Thousands of American companies went bankrupt and shareholders were ruined. This had a knock-on effect and American banks collapsed. The most powerful economy in the world descended into the most severe economic slump in its history.

The Great Depression spread quickly around the world as many other nations' economies were dependent on, or at least linked to, the American economy. International trade slumped. Factories closed down and millions of people lost their jobs. As unemployment grew, the domestic market for goods fell further. Many nations were now caught in a vicious downward spiral: falling demand led to more job losses which in turn led to lower demand for goods.

The Great Depression threatened international cooperation and peace. As governments struggled to cope, they introduced protective tariffs on imports to try to foster a recovery in their own industries and increase demand for goods produced at home by making foreign goods more expensive. This was called protectionism. But the more countries acted to protect their own citizens, the more they moved away from the principles of cooperation embodied in the League of Nations.

The Depression also caused great social problems as mass unemployment and poverty grew. Many people blamed the weakness of their government for their suffering and more extreme political parties gathered support. In Germany, where significant loans from the USA were called in as the economic crisis deepened, there were 6 million unemployed by the end of 1932. Japan had been dependent economically on its exports, particularly on the export of the luxury fabric, silk. Its main market for silk had been the USA. Fifty per cent of Japan's factories closed and its peasants starved. Radical political parties seemed to offer salvation where liberal democracies had failed.

It may also be seen that Germany and Japan, and to some extent Italy, were increasingly jealous of the British and French overseas empires during the Depression. This was because the British and French could offset some of the effects of the global slump by increasing trade with their empires.

You have already seen that the weaknesses of the League of Nations meant that it would struggle to challenge powerful nations that did not want to adhere to the principles of international cooperation and peace. The League's one key tool to enforce its resolutions was economic sanctions. But after the Great Depression took hold globally, member states were even more reluctant to impose sanctions that might damage further their already devastated economies.

EXPANSIONIST IDEOLOGIES IN EUROPE – 'HITLER'S WAR'

The key challenge to peace in the 1930s came from the aggressor and expansionist states – Hitler's Germany and Mussolini's Italy in Europe and the increasingly militarist government of Japan in Asia.

In Europe, Hitler had come to power in 1933 and he had clear foreign policy ambitions that could only be achieved through force. Hitler was leader of the national socialist Nazi party. Its ideology was a brand of fascism, with elements of Social Darwinism (see Chapter 7). The Nazis' aims included the revision of the Treaty of Versailles, rearming Germany, unifying all Germans – including *Anschluss* (union) with Austria and gaining 'living space' (*Lebensraum*) in the east. The Nazis wanted to create *Lebensraum* for the development of the 'Aryan race' and other races would be subjugated as slaves to this master race.

Hitler ultimately wanted to destroy the communist USSR and gain power over continental Europe. He also despised the liberal nature of the American government and foresaw a war with the USA after his initial objectives had been achieved. Hitler began to put his aims into practice as soon as he was in power. He secretly told his military commanders that he would begin rearmament.

■ **Figure 8.23** Hitler driving past, saluting SA members (*see page 298*)

ACTIVITY: How did fascism and Nazism encourage war?

■ ATL

■ Transfer skills – Inquire in different contexts to gain a different perspective

Think about the ideologies that you read about in Chapter 7 and specifically about the ideas of the fascists and the Nazis. **Discuss** why these ideas would foster an expansionist foreign policy and make war more likely.

In 1935 Hitler announced publicly in a huge rally his rearmament plans and reintroduced conscription. He also for the first time admitted the construction of a German air force. All this was in direct breach of the military terms of the Treaty of Versailles (see page 171). In response, the British – rather than standing firm with France and challenging the German rearmament programme – signed a naval agreement with Germany. This basically meant that Britain accepted German plans to rearm but hoped to limit the threat to its own navy by entering into an agreement to allow Germany to build a navy 35 per cent the size of Britain's.

In March 1936 Hitler marched a German army into the Rhineland. This was set down as a demilitarized zone, as it was the border territory with France. Hitler claimed that this was to protect Germany from the new agreement for mutual assistance signed between France and the USSR. However, it was another breach of the treaty and Hitler had used force. France hesitated – Hitler only had 30 000 troops at this point and he had instructed his forces to withdraw if there was resistance – but France would not act alone and Britain refused to act. Hitler claimed that he just wanted peace and the British argued that the Germans had simply occupied their own 'backyard'. The use of force had been successful and France's security was compromised.

NEW ALLIANCES

In November 1937, Hitler made alliances with both Italy and Japan. These agreements would develop into the Axis Pact, which envisaged a New World Order that would revolve around the axis of Berlin, Rome and Tokyo.

In the same year, despite being a member of the Non-Intervention Committee, Hitler sent military assistance to General Franco in the Spanish Civil War. The Germans used the civil war to test out their new arms, their new aircraft and their new tanks and to give their troops invaluable training and experience in a real-life battlefield. Hitler and Commander Göring practised the formations and combined forces of air power and armoured divisions and tanks that would later become the blitzkrieg tactics in the Second World War. The German Condor Legion also tested the impact of bombing civilians from the air – infamously in the

■ **Figure 8.24** Hitler with the Italian leader, Mussolini

case of the Basque town of Guernica. It was in Spain that the Germans grew closer still to Benito Mussolini's Italy. Mussolini had also sent forces to aid Franco, so Germany and Italy fought on the same side against the Soviet-backed Republican forces.

In 1938, Hitler took personal command of the armed forces. Militarily, and with his new alliance with Mussolini, he believed Germany was now strong enough to begin to bring Germans – who since the end of the First World War had been under the control of foreign powers – into the German 'Third Reich'. In March 1938, Hitler sent his army into Austria and declared *Anschluss* – unification of Germany and Austria. He argued that his forces had gone in to restore order in Austria. The Austrian leader Schuschnigg had asked for help from Britain and France but they had refused. Hitler replaced Schuschnigg with an Austrian Nazi and claimed that a subsequent vote on whether to join Germany, taken by the Austrian people, had returned an overwhelming 99.75 per cent in favour. *Anschluss* had been forbidden in the Treaty of Versailles and Hitler had again revised the terms forcibly and without resistance from the western democracies.

What were the short-term causes of the Second World War?

Just a few months later, in September 1938, Hitler announced that he was prepared to invade the Sudetenland to 'protect the German population' there – some 3 million people – from persecution by the Czechoslovak government. As the Austrian Nazis had done earlier that year, the Sudeten Nazi party incited unrest and held mass rallies, demanding that the territory become part of Germany.

This time it seemed that there might be war. France had made agreements to defend Czechoslovakia and prepared for war, and the Czechs had also been promised support from the USSR. However, Britain under the leadership of its new prime minister, Neville Chamberlain, wanted to avoid conflict. Chamberlain believed that a compromise could be found. Hitler agreed to meet to discuss terms.

THE MUNICH AGREEMENT

In a series of meetings between 15 and 29 September, the British, French, Italians and Germans met to discuss the crisis over the Sudetenland. Initially, Chamberlain persuaded the Czechoslovaks to give up parts of the Sudetenland and presented this to Hitler. At first it seemed that Hitler would agree, but when he saw how keen the democracies were to avoid a war he refused anything less than the whole of the Sudetenland. In the end, Chamberlain agreed to Hitler's demands – as long as it meant no further expansion and a guarantee that the rest of Czechoslovakia was safe. All parties signed the Munich Agreement. Chamberlain was sure that he had prevented a European war. However, Czechoslovakian security and territory had been sacrificed and their president, Beneš, was not allowed to negotiate terms. He said afterwards that he hoped that his people's sacrifice would secure the peace – but that he feared it would not. The agreement also impacted on the foreign policy of Joseph Stalin's USSR.

Stalin had hoped to form a 'Popular Front' with the western democracies, against the fascist states. By proving themselves unwilling to take a stand against the fascist dictatorships, and by allowing Hitler to expand his frontier to the east, the western democracies gave Stalin reason to believe that his policy would not work. It seemed to him that the democracies were weak and were more afraid of the threat posed by Soviet communism than Italian and German fascism. It seemed they were intent on encouraging Hitler to expand eastwards towards a confrontation with the USSR. In October, in line with the Munich Agreement, Hitler marched his troops into the Sudetenland.

■ **Figure 8.25** Map showing the Sudetenland

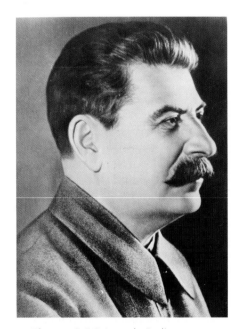

■ **Figure 8.26** Joseph Stalin

Up until this point Hitler had been challenging the terms of the Treaty of Versailles, and Britain had argued that his demands should be satisfied, due to the relative harshness of the peace treaty. Chamberlain hoped that Hitler would be satisfied after his concessions over the Sudetenland.

However, in March 1939, Hitler went beyond mere revision of the treaty. For the first time he invaded a sovereign state with no claim to be 'saving Germans'. Hitler sent troops over his new border to seize and occupy the rest of Czechoslovakia. He tore up the terms of the Munich Agreement. Britain could no longer argue for appeasement on the grounds of revision of the Treaty of Versailles – Hitler clearly was intent on aggressive expansionism. Although they did nothing to save the Czechoslovaks, Britain and France knew that Poland would be Hitler's next target and promised to defend Poland if it were attacked by Germany.

THE NAZI–SOVIET PACT

Hitler did intend to attack Poland. But with the guarantees given by Britain and France to Poland he could face a two-front war. The USSR would feel very threatened by a German invasion of a territory on its border. Hitler, the sworn enemy of communism who had given speeches setting down his plan to destroy the USSR, set out to make a deal with Stalin. In August 1939, Hitler pulled off one of the most significant diplomatic coups of the twentieth century: his foreign minister, Ribbentrop, signed a pact with Stalin's foreign minister, Molotov. In the Nazi–Soviet Pact, as it was known, Germany and the USSR agreed not to attack each other. They also secretly agreed to divide Poland between them.

Hitler had his deal and was ready to move. In the late summer of 1939, he demanded the return of the port of Danzig and the territory given to Poland in the Treaty of Versailles. He asserted that it was wrong to divide Germany in two via the Polish 'corridor', and claimed that Germans living in Poland were being badly treated. Knowing that the British and French had agreed to defend Poland, Hitler invaded on 1 September. This time the response was different. Britain sent Germany an ultimatum to withdraw from Poland within 24 hours or there would be war. German forces continued their invasion. Britain and France declared war on Germany on 3 September.

ACTIVITY: The Nazi–Soviet Pact

■ ATL

■ Critical-thinking skills – Draw reasonable conclusions and generalizations

1 In pairs, reflect on why the Nazi–Soviet Pact was such an unlikely agreement. Why would these dictators, with opposing ideologies, have engaged in a 'pact' in August 1939? What might this mean for the prospects for peace in Europe?

2 What is the message of the cartoonist in Source K?

◆ Assessment opportunities

◆ In this activity you have practised skills that are assessed using Criterion D: Thinking critically.

SOURCE K

Figure 8.27 'Someone is taking someone for a walk', cartoon published in a British newspaper, October 1939

8 Why do nations go to war and why is peacemaking difficult?

179

THE POLICY OF APPEASEMENT

Despite the many reasons for appeasement, there were problems with this policy. Indeed, some historians put the blame for the Second World War on appeasement as it strengthened Hitler, encouraged and rewarded him for aggressive actions and meant that when the crisis developed over Poland in September 1939 Hitler may have believed that Britain and France would not go to war. After all, they had had agreements with Czechoslovakia, a democratic state with state-of-the-art military defences and the support of the USSR, whereas Poland was not a democracy, was too far away to effectively assist militarily and Britain and France no longer had the support of the USSR.

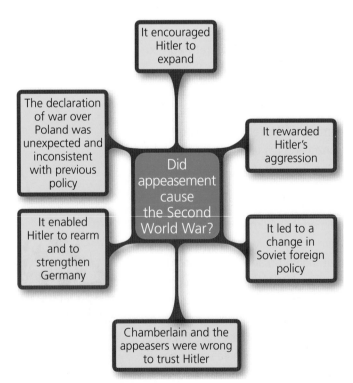

■ **Figure 8.28** Why appease Hitler's Germany?

■ **Figure 8.29** Did appeasement cause the Second World War?

■ **Figure 8.30** Japanese ground troops in the Second World War

EXPANSIONIST IDEOLOGIES IN ASIA – 'JAPAN'S WAR'

In Chapter 1 we looked at how Japan rapidly industrialized in the second half of the nineteenth century, having been forcibly opened up to outside trade by the Americans. As a result of revolutionary reforms, Japan was able, by 1900, to compete with the west.

Japan demonstrated the effectiveness of its military modernization when it defeated Russia in a war in 1905. This was the first time in modern history that an Asian nation had defeated a European power. This war gave Japan control over Korea; it had begun to build an empire. Japan became a major trading nation and fought in the First World War on the side of the Entente Alliance. Although it had a liberal democracy, the military had always remained an influential force in politics.

An issue for Japan's economy was that it was dependent on imports of raw materials and food and was too reliant on the export of certain materials – especially silk. The economic crisis hit Japan particularly badly in the early 1930s, as its economic prosperity was, like that of Germany at the time, closely tied to that of the American economy. When Wall Street crashed and the global depression took hold (see pages 174–75) Japan's economy spiralled downwards into a deep slump. As you have read earlier in this chapter, the US market for silk collapsed. The market for Japan's other manufactured goods also fell as international trade declined. Fifty per cent of factories closed down and the peasants starved. The Japanese people were in a desperate state and the government seemed unable to help. This undermined the newly established democracy in Japan, as the general public looked for more radical political solutions to end their suffering. Again, there are similarities with the situation in Germany in the early 1930s.

In 1930 some army officers demanded the overthrow of the democratic government in a military coup. The army also wanted to conquer Manchuria and in 1931, the military stationed in Manchuria devised a plot to do this. They claimed Manchuria had coal and iron, which was needed for Japanese industries. Its people would provide a market for Japanese goods, and it was thought that the territory would provide 'living space' for Japan's surplus population. Despite the League of Nations finding against Japan and condemning its actions, its army in Manchuria continued the conquest.

By 1932 the army had control over Manchuria and renamed it Manchukuo. The army had acted without the agreement of Japan's government in Tokyo. The takeover was popular with the people in Japan and this seriously undermined the credibility of the country's liberal democratic government. As the military seized more control domestically, Japan's foreign policy became more expansionist. Its army had grown from 250000 men in 1930 to 950000 in 1937.

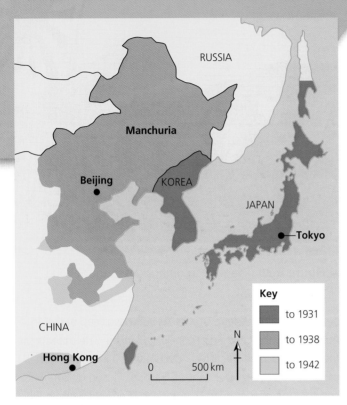

RUSSIA

Manchuria

Beijing

KOREA

JAPAN

Tokyo

CHINA

Hong Kong

Key

to 1931

to 1938

to 1942

N

0   500 km

■ **Figure 8.31** Japanese expansion in China up to 1942

THINK–PAIR–SHARE

In pairs, **discuss** why you think historians have different perspectives on the causes of war.

The USA had important economic interests in East Asia, as did the Europeans. With the rise of Hitler and his ally – fascist Italy – the French and the British could not divert their attention to the actions of another aggressor state – Japan. The USA had major trading links with China but its main trading partner in the Far East was Japan. The USA condemned Japan's actions in Manchuria but did nothing else. However, its concern increased in 1936 when Japan joined in a pact with Germany. With its newly strengthened army, Japan launched a full-scale invasion of China in 1937.

The Americans decided to try to contain Japan's expansion into China by limiting the supply of materials to it. US President Franklin D. Roosevelt was unable to take direct military action in Asia due to the restrictions of the Neutrality Acts, which prevented the USA from getting involved in other countries' conflicts.

Japan struggled to defeat China from 1937, and despite taking key cities along the coast, including Shanghai and Nanjing, the Chinese refused to surrender. The Chinese Nationalist government believed that Japan would eventually have to negotiate, as China was simply too big for Japan to occupy. Japan was now engaged in a protracted and expensive war.

In 1941, Japan invaded Indo-China in an attempt to gain more resources. Roosevelt responded by banning all trade, including oil supplies to Japan. This was significant as Japan was dependent on American oil – 80 per cent came from the USA. Japan would not be able to continue the war in China when its oil ran out. At the same time the USA stated that it was to increase the size of its navy.

Japan decided it had to act to prevent the USA entering the war in Asia. On 7 December 1941, Japan launched a massive attack on the US naval base at Pearl Harbor, Hawaii. The following day, Roosevelt called the attack 'dastardly' and declared war on Japan.

Shortly afterwards, Hitler declared war on the USA. The world was at war.

ACTIVITY: The causes of the Second World War

■ ATL

- ■ Communication skills – Use appropriate forms of writing for different purposes and audiences

What is your goal?

Your goal is to write a biased or one-sided newspaper report as a journalist explaining why war broke out in Europe in September 1939 or in Asia in December 1941. Take the perspective *either* that 'Hitler caused the war' *or* that 'the policy of appeasement caused the war' if you are writing about Europe; or, if you are writing about Asia, *either* that it was 'Japan's war' *or* that 'the USA provoked Japanese aggression'.

You will be given one of these themes to write up a one-sided persuasive argument that **explains** how your theme caused the outbreak of the Second World War. This should be between 700 and 1500 words long.

How will you achieve this?

Your finished product must include the following and be laid out like a newspaper report:

- An appropriate name for your paper
- A banner headline
- A front-page biased report on the causes of the Second World War in Europe
- All the key events from the 1930s leading to the outbreak of war
- Visual images to support your version of events, e.g. cartoons, photographs, etc.

◆ Assessment opportunities

- ◆ This activity can be assessed using Criterion A: Knowing and understanding and Criteria C: Communicating.

ROAD TO WAR IN ASIA

Japan's war		America's war	
1920s	Economic boom/liberal democratic government/ controls Korea and some territories in China	**1920**	Race laws limit emigration to the USA from Japan
1929	Wall Street crash – severe economic crisis due to dependence on silk trade; increase in Japanese nationalism	**1929**	Wall Street crash – investment to Japan ends; the USA stops buying silk, which it has encouraged Japan to supply
1930	Military gaining more power in government; USA blamed for Japan's economic problems	**1931**	The USA condemns but does not act when Japan invades Manchuria
1931	Japanese army invades Manchuria (China); Japan leaves League of Nations	**1936**	The USA criticizes Japan's decision to join Axis power alliance
1932	Army in control of government; rapid increase in Japan's armed forces	**1937**	The USA still trading war supplies with Japan after Japanese invasion of China's mainland – including 80% of oil supplies
1936	Japan joins Axis power alliance; army aims to build empire in Asia	**1939**	The USA imposes trade sanctions when Japan ignores US warnings to end war in China; the USA begins to focus on development of its own navy
1937	Japan invades mainland China; still depends on war materials – 80% of oil supplies – from the USA	**1941**	All supplies to Japan are blocked – including oil; Japan responds by bombing Pearl Harbor
1939	Japan ignores US warnings to end war in China; the USA imposes some trade sanctions		
1941	Japan invades Indo-China; the USA blocks all trade; Japan sends diplomats to negotiate in the USA to cover plot –Japan bombs Pearl Harbor (December)		

(Timeline markers: 1920, 1930, 1940)

■ **Figure 8.32** Timeline of Japan's war and America's war

ACTIVITY: The role of Japan in causing the Second World War

ATL

- Critical-thinking skills – Gather and organize relevant information to formulate an argument; Consider ideas from multiple perspectives

1 From their origin and purpose, what are the values and limitations of Sources L and N for historians studying the causes of the Second World War?

2 'Japanese aggression and expansionism led to war with the USA in December 1941.' Using Sources L–P and your own knowledge, to what extent do you agree with this statement?

   You can use the approaches to essay planning outlined earlier in this chapter, and in previous chapters.

◆ Assessment opportunities

- ◆ This activity can be assessed using Criterion A: Knowing and understanding and Criterion D: Thinking critically.

These sources relate to the causes of the war in the Pacific.

SOURCE L

'Some of our people like to believe that wars in Europe and Asia are no concern of ours. But it is a matter of most vital concern to us that European and Asiatic war-makers should not gain control of the oceans which lead to this hemisphere. If Great Britain goes down, the Axis Powers will control the continents of Europe, Asia, Africa, Australasia and the high seas. All of us would be living at the point of a gun.'

President of the USA, Franklin D. Roosevelt. 1940. Radio broadcast. USA.

SOURCE M

'In October the new Prime Minister, General Tojo, put Japanese demands to the United States for a free hand in Asia. It was agreed in secret that, should the Americans refuse, which was likely, war would be declared on 8th December. The oil situation for Japan was now critical.'

Overy, R.J. (historian). 2008. The Origins of the Second World War. UK. Routledge.

THINK–PAIR–SHARE

In pairs, **discuss** why you think nations resort to waging war.

SOURCE N

1 'Our Empire is determined to follow a policy that will result in the establishment of the Greater East Asia Co-prosperity sphere and will thereby contribute to world peace, no matter what changes may occur in the world situation.

2 'Our Empire will continue its efforts to effect a settlement of the China Incident, and will seek to establish a solid basis for the security and preservation of the nation. This will involve taking steps to advance south, and … will involve a settlement of the North …

3 'Our Empire is determined to remove all obstacles in order to achieve the above mentioned objectives.'

Agenda: 'Outline of National Policies in view of the changing situation.' Japanese Imperial. Conference. 2 July 1941.

SOURCE O

Joseph Grew, US ambassador to Japan, gives an assessment in 1939 of how the Japanese would respond to sanctions

'… The Japanese are so constituted and are now in such a mood and temper that sanctions, far from intimidating, would almost certainly bring retaliation, which in turn, would lead to counter-retaliation. Japan would not stop to weigh ultimate consequences …'

SOURCE P

■ **Figure 8.33** Five Chinese prisoners of war with their Japanese captors, China 1937

ACTIVITY: Research project – War in Europe and war in the Pacific

ATL

- Information literacy skills – Access information to be informed and inform others; Present information in a variety of formats and platforms
- Organization skills – Use appropriate strategies for organizing complex information
- Communication skills – Structure information in summaries, essays and reports

You will research a theatre of war from either the war in Europe or the war is Asia.

This project is divided into five tasks:

Task 1: Individual research planning – this brainstorming session should enable you to draft possible questions and help **formulate** your research question.

Task 2: Action plan – **formulate** a plan of how you will conduct your research.

Task 3: Evaluate your research process and results.

Task 4: Research document – create a document on the chosen research question related to a theme/topic in the war in Europe or in the war in Asia, with all information cited and a full 'works cited' list that uses one recognized convention.

Task 5: Presentation – present your research to the class (10–15 minutes). You will present on your specific topic and region while your class makes notes on your presentation. Your role is to present the significance of your research in understanding the course and outcome of the Second World War.

Possible topics for the war in Europe

- **War in the air:** blitzkrieg and the fall of Western Europe; Battle of Britain; bombing campaigns on Germany; D-Day
- **War on the land:** the war in the Mediterranean/Balkans; Operation Barbarossa – war in the east; turning point battles (1942 – Stalingrad and El Alamein; 1943 – Kursk); resistance movements
- **War at sea:** battle for the Atlantic
- **Home front:** Britain; Germany; USSR

Possible topics for the war in Asia

- **War on the land:** Japan's initial conquests in Asia; island-hopping
- **War at sea:** turning point battles: 1942 – Midway
- **War in the air:** air campaigns; total defeat: Hiroshima and Nagasaki
- **Home front:** Japan and the USA

> **Hint**
>
> Remember to focus your presentation on answering the research question you have formulated. You need to be able to communicate your knowledge and understanding clearly for your class to make meaningful notes. You should practice your presentation before you deliver it to the class - try not to be too brief, but also try not to go over the 15 minutes set for the task.

◆ Assessment opportunities

- ◆ This activity can be assessed using Criterion A: Knowing and understanding, Criterion B: Investigating and Criterion C: Communicating.

What peacemaking agreements were made after the Second World War?

THE TREATY OF SAN FRANCISCO

Japan was totally defeated militarily in August 1945 and surrendered unconditionally. The Americans occupied Japan until a treaty was finally signed in 1952. The USA had total control over Japan until this was signed, and so was not limited by the conditions of an armistice or a treaty that had been signed quickly at the end of the war. The Americans were the sole occupiers of Japan and so did not have to compromise with any other power. General Douglas MacArthur led SCAP (Supreme Commander for the Allied Powers – the control commission), and had unlimited power.

■ **Table 8.2** The terms of the Treaty of San Francisco

Occupation	US forces would occupy Japan until a new government and constitution was implemented.
Territorial	Japan lost all the territory it had conquered during the Second World War. It also lost its control over Korea and Taiwan. The Bonin Islands and the Ryukyu Islands, including Okinawa, could be under American influence. China was given back all Japanese assets in Manchuria and inner Mongolia worth around US$18 758 600 000 in 1945.
Military	The USA demilitarized Japan. The entire Japanese military was disbanded and its weapons were destroyed. All armaments factories were closed down. The new constitution (see Political below) gave up the right to go to war and the development of armed forces was forbidden.
Reparations	All assets owned by the Japanese government, companies and private citizens. China, Korea and Taiwan were to receive billions of dollars of reparations. Occupied territories, for example, Indo-China, received reparations. Allied prisoners of war were to receive compensation too. The total reparation bill was finally agreed at 1.03 trillion Yen.
Political	Japan's post-war constitution was written by the USA. This Constitution (1947) changed the political system in Japan completely. The American imposed a liberal democratic system on Japan. Women were given equal voting rights.
War crimes	The USA held war crimes trials between 1946 and 1948 and seven key political leaders were executed. A further 18 leaders were sent to prison. Two military leaders were executed and 18 others went to prison. The Emperor was not put on trial.

The Treaty of San Francisco created a lasting peace, unlike the Treaty of Versailles with Germany at the end of the First World War. Japan became a close ally of the USA in the Pacific and it adhered to Article 9 of its new constitution, outlawing war as a means of settling disputes with another nation.

SOURCE Q

Extracts from the Treaty of San Francisco, September, 1951

Chapter I: Peace – Article 1

a   The state of war between Japan and each of the Allied Powers is terminated as from the date on which the present Treaty comes into force …

b   The Allied Powers recognize the full sovereignty of the Japanese people over Japan and its territorial waters …

Chapter III: Security – Article 5

a   Japan accepts the obligations set forth in the Charter of the United Nations, and in particular the obligations … to settle its international disputes by peaceful means in such a manner that international peace and security, and justice, are not endangered …

SOURCE R

'The resulting treaty was signed at San Francisco in September 1951 by most of the countries which had fought in the Pacific War. Russia refused to accept it, as did India and mainland China. But since these three played no direct part in governing Japan the military occupation came to an end when the treaty was ratified in April 1952. This did not mean a withdrawal of the occupation forces, however, since Japan, having little choice in the matter, had also signed a defence agreement by which she undertook to continue providing bases for American troops, ships and aircraft, thereby committing herself to an American alliance …'

Beasley, W.G. (historian). 1982. The Modern History of Japan. *Charles E. Tuttle.*

ACTIVITY: Comparing the Treaty of Versailles and the Treaty of San Francisco

ATL

- Transfer skills – Inquire in different contexts to gain a different perspective
- Critical-thinking skills – Consider ideas from multiple perspectives

Task 1

In small groups, compare and contrast the terms of the Treaty of Versailles (see page 171) and those of the Treaty of San Francisco (see page 186).

a   **What are the similarities and differences between the terms of the two treaties?**

b   **Do the terms of San Francisco explain why it kept the peace longer than Versailles?**

c   **To what extent do you agree that the 'context' in which the treaties were drawn up was more important than the treaty itself in keeping the peace?**

Task 2: Debatable question

To what extent can war be prevented and peace be established and maintained?

This will be a class role play. The class should be divided into two groups – one group arguing that peace can be maintained and the other arguing that it cannot. Allow 30 minutes for preparation and then 30 minutes for the class to debate the question.

Alternatively, you could decide to adopt your own position and to debate the question in an open forum.

You could take on the role of different historical figures with specific viewpoints.

◆ Assessment opportunities

◆ In this activity you have practised skills that are assessed using Criterion A: Knowing and understanding, Criterion C: Communicating and Criterion D: Thinking critically.

What other types of wars have taken place in the twentieth century?

This chapter has focused on the two most devastating wars of the twentieth century, the First World War and Second World War. However, there were many other wars fought in this period.

■ **Figure 8.34** Vietnamese units using guerilla tactics against the Americans during the Vietnam War

■ **Figure 8.35** Burning oil wells following the defeat of Iraq in the Gulf War, Kuwait 1991

■ **Figure 8.36** Woman clutching a loaf of bread at the end of the Spanish Civil War, 1936

The two World Wars are known as 'total' wars because they involved a total mobilization of the human, economic and military resources of each country involved. Other wars of the twentieth century have been termed 'limited' because, for at least one of the combatants, this was not the case. Examples of the limited wars include the Korean War of 1950–53 and the Vietnam War of 1965–73, the Gulf War of 1990 and the Falklands War of 1982.

The century also saw devastating civil wars. A civil war involves two sides *within* a country fighting. The Spanish Civil War of 1930–36 is one example. The war in the former Yugoslavia in the 1990s is another.

The two World Wars were fought with big armies using huge amounts of military hardware. The tactics and weaponry used were similar in all armies, though there was always competition to move ahead in terms of superior weapons or new tactics. However, after 1945, the use of guerrilla tactics became increasingly popular with armies fighting against a superior power, for example in the fight for decolonization against an imperial power such as Britain, or in the fight for independence against one of the superpowers. Guerrilla tactics were used for instance by the Vietnamese against the USA, by the Afghans against the USSR and by the Mau Mau against the British in Kenya.

ACTIVITY: War research

ATL

- Information literacy skills – Access information to be informed and inform others
- Collaboration skills – Listen actively to other perspectives and ideas

The class is divided into four large groups. Each group is given a region to investigate.

Depending on the size of your group, choose one or two wars in your region to research. Identify the main causes of the war, the ways in which it was fought and how peace was finally established. Prepare a report that is between 5 and 10 minutes long and includes images and interviews to present to the class.

Here are some examples for you to consider:

- **Group 1 Africa and the Middle East: Nigerian Civil War (1967–70) or the Iran–Iraq War (1980–88)**
- **Group 2 Americas: Falklands/Malvinas War (1982) or Mexican Revolution (1910–20)**
- **Group 3 Asia and Oceania: the Chinese Civil War (1927–49) or Indo-Pakistan Wars (1947–49 or 1965 or 1971)**
- **Group 4 Europe: Spanish Civil War (1936–39) or the Balkan Wars (1990s)**

Reflection

In mixed regional groups, reflect on the following:

- **What were the common causes of wars cross-regionally in the twentieth century?**
- **What were the similarities and differences in the way wars were fought?**
- **Which wars ended with peace treaties?**
- **Reflect on the following and write a report of around 700 words:**
  Are there lessons that can be drawn from your presentation for conflict prevention and peacemaking in the twenty-first century?

◆ Assessment opportunities

- ◆ The reflection report can be assessed using Criterion A: Knowledge and understanding and Criterion D: Thinking critically.

！ Take action

！ Research the wars which are taking place at this moment. Create a display to show current conflicts and their impact.

Reflection

In this chapter, we have examined the causes of the two world wars, and also looked at the way in which these wars were fought. We have also studied the peacemaking process at the end of each war, comparing the Treaty of Versailles with the Treaty of San Francisco. As part of this investigation, we have also considered the problems of creating and maintaining a lasting peace.

Reflecting on our learning ... Use this table to reflect on your own learning in this chapter.					
Questions we asked	**Answers we found**	**Any further questions now?**			
Factual					
Conceptual					
Debatable					
Approaches to learning you used in this chapter:	**Description – what new skills did you learn?**	**How well did you master the skills?**			
		Novice	Learner	Practitioner	Expert
Collaboration skills					
Communication skills					
Critical-thinking skills					
Information literacy skills					
Organization skills					
Transfer skills					
Learner profile attribute	*Reflect on the importance of being a thinker for our learning in this chapter.*				
Thinker					

9 Why do nations build empires and form supra-national alliances and organizations?

Unequal *inter-state relationships*, empires, are created for economic and ideological reasons. Nations develop *systems* of *interdependence* to protect their interests.

■ **Figure 9.1** The signing of the UN Charter in 1945

CONSIDER THESE QUESTIONS:

Factual: What key factors led to the rapid expansion of empire building in the nineteenth century? What factors led to the development of supra-national alliances and organizations? What factors and events led to the development of superpowers?

Conceptual: What role do economic self-interest and ideology play in the development of empires? Why do nations form alliances? In what ways can nations dominate other nations?

Debatable: How far do you agree that imperialism brings benefits to the colonized? To what extent are supra-national alliances and organizations forces for peace and stability in the world?

Now **share and compare** your thoughts and ideas with your partner, or with the whole class.

IN THIS CHAPTER, WE WILL …

■ **Find out:**
  ■ why there was an expansion of empires in the nineteenth century
  ■ why the superpowers emerged after the Second World War
  ■ why nations formed supra-national alliances and organizations.

■ **Explore:**
  ■ the impact of empire building, superpower confrontation, alliance systems and the supra-national organizations of the League of Nations and the United Nations (UN)
  ■ the impact of empires, superpowers, supra-national alliances and organizations on international relations.

■ **Take action** by finding out more about the work of the UN today.

ACTIVITY: The growth of empires

Look at the maps in Sources A and B and answer the following questions:

1 **Which European powers had empires in 1800?**
2 **In which areas of the world had European control increased by 1914?**
3 **Which countries controlled the most land by 1914?**

■ These Approaches to Learning (ATL) skills will be useful …

- Collaboration skills
- Communication skills
- Creative-thinking skills
- Critical-thinking skills
- Information literacy skills
- Media literacy skills
- Organization skills
- Transfer skills

● We will reflect on this learner profile attribute …

- Knowledgeable – engaging with issues and ideas that have local and global significance.

◆ Assessment opportunities in this chapter:

- ◆ **Criterion A:** Knowing and understanding
- ◆ **Criterion B:** Investigating
- ◆ **Criterion C:** Communicating
- ◆ **Criterion D:** Thinking critically

KEY WORDS

alliances	imperialism
capitalism	liberal democracy
communism	missionary
empire	

SOURCE A

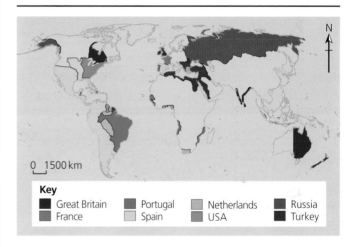

Key

■ Great Britain	■ Portugal	■ Netherlands	■ Russia
■ France	■ Spain	■ USA	■ Turkey

■ **Figure 9.2** Empires in 1800

SOURCE B

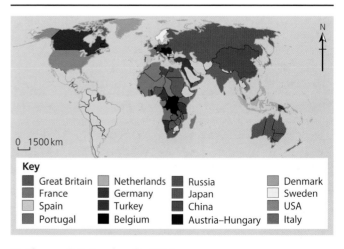

Key

■ Great Britain	■ Netherlands	■ Russia	■ Denmark
■ France	■ Germany	■ Japan	■ Sweden
■ Spain	■ Turkey	■ China	■ USA
■ Portugal	■ Belgium	■ Austria–Hungary	■ Italy

■ **Figure 9.3** Empires in 1914

Why was there a rapid expansion of empire building in the nineteenth century?

In the nineteenth century, the terms imperialism and imperialist were not seen as negative terms. Many Europeans believed that the building of a great empire was something to feel proud and patriotic about.

By the end of that century, Britain and France had vast overseas empires. The Belgian King Leopold had an African colony that was 80 times bigger than Belgium itself. Italy and Germany (new countries founded in 1871) rapidly developed overseas empires at the end of the century. Austria–Hungary had a large land-based empire in Europe, and so did Russia – its empire reaching into Asia.

By 1900 the European empires controlled 85 per cent of the globe.

Some colonies were taken over directly by the colonial power and ruled over as their own territory. Other colonies were more indirectly controlled by the Europeans, for example, some were forced to sign agreements over trading rights.

TECHNOLOGICAL ADVANCES

Technology was a key motive for Europeans to build empires, as the Industrial Revolution had led to an ever-growing demand for raw materials to feed the new factories and industries. In turn, when home markets were saturated by mass-produced goods, new markets for the products were sought.

Technology made the building of empires *possible*. Without the advantages that new technology gave the Europeans, they would not have been capable of so rapidly expanding their overseas empires in the nineteenth century. A few hundred Europeans armed with guns – fast-firing rifles and, later, machine guns – could overwhelm thousands of indigenous peoples in Africa armed with only spears and shields. The courage of the Zulus was no match for British troops armed with machine guns. In China, the government gave in to British demands after their wooden sailing junks were destroyed by steam-driven ironclad ships (see Chapter 3).

Technology facilitated the expansion of empires. Travel to distant lands was made easier as steam ships were faster, more comfortable, safer and more reliable than sail ships. In addition, medicine had advanced and doctors were more able to treat people suffering from tropical diseases. The new technology of refrigeration in the 1880s meant that it was possible to export perishable products around the world – for example, meat could be brought from New Zealand for sale in Europe. The building of railways in colonies meant that materials could be quickly transported across the empire and opened up new territories for farming.

EXPLORERS AND MISSIONARIES

Both explorers and missionaries 'discovered' new territories and identified the potential resources in other lands. Some missionaries were explorers – like Dr Livingstone, who kept detailed records of places that had never been mapped before.

■ **Figure 9.4** A steam-powered sailing ship

Some explorers were just seeking adventures, whereas others were looking for opportunities to make themselves very wealthy. Many took armed men with them, and their governments often had to support them when conflicts developed. A private army of Cecil Rhodes, a British millionaire, conquered a huge area of Africa – what today is Zimbabwe – and called it Rhodesia.

The churches of Europe (and the USA) were important in the growth of empire. Missionaries believed that they were 'saving souls' and that they were doing what was right for the people they encountered. Often the missionaries undermined the local power structures and traditional beliefs of the societies they entered.

When missionaries ran into difficulties, their governments often took action to support them – for example, in 1897, after two German missionaries had been murdered, the German government protested to the Chinese government and then seized the port of Kiaochow (Jiaozhou).

Figure 9.5 Dr Livingstone

ⓘ
Lenin's view of imperialism

The British economist, J.A. Hobson, and the Russian communist, Vladimir Lenin, both believed that imperialism was caused by the capitalists in the European countries. The capitalists always wanted to expand their markets, increase their output, and spend less on materials and labour to maximize profits. Lenin believed that the capitalists stripped the wealth from the colonies for themselves. He also believed that they used this wealth to prevent revolutions at home.

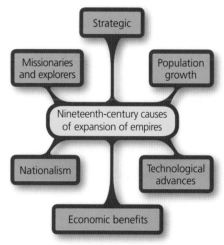

■ **Figure 9.6** Why did empires expand in the nineteenth century?

ECONOMIC REASONS

Raw materials, new markets and cheap labour were three key economic motives for building and expanding an empire.

The territories of an empire would contribute raw materials and food products – many of which were not available in the 'mother' country, for example, bananas from Ghana; cocoa, palm oil, tea from China; rubber from the Congo and diamonds from South Africa.

They would provide markets for manufactured goods and there would be no 'tariffs' or import taxes to pay. India was a huge market for British goods; it purchased 40 per cent of Britain's cotton goods. The Europeans also wanted to develop the vast market potential of China.

POPULATION GROWTH

During the nineteenth century, Europe's population increased rapidly – from 200 million to about 600 million. This was faster than anywhere else in the world. In 1914, one in three people in the world were European. In 1800 it had been one in five. This growth led to acute land shortages in the countryside and overcrowding in the cities. Thus many people looked to emigrate in search of a better standard of living. Sometimes people had to emigrate to survive due to famines; for example, in Ireland in the 1840s, approximately 1 million people starved to death – and 1 million emigrated. By the 1890s, around 1 million Europeans were emigrating every year. Many went to North America, others went to Africa, Australasia and the Far East.

NATIONALISM AND NATIONAL RIVALRIES

To the European general public, an empire was something to take great pride in. It was sign of your nation's importance and greatness. It demonstrated your superiority. The public supported their governments both in expanding empire and fighting for it.

Many European leaders wanted colonies to compete with rival European powers. Therefore, some territories were colonized even when there was no economic reason to have them. In fact some territories were an economic drain on the imperial powers, as occupying forces had to be funded to prevent other powers taking them. One example is the British in the Sudan. Their main concern was to keep other Europeans out!

STRATEGIC REASONS

Britain had a much larger navy than the other Europeans but its army was small. Therefore India was an important colony for the British for military reasons, as they recruited Indian soldiers under British officers. Having a reliable supply of coal to fuel a navy was also important – fighting wars overseas required a reliable coaling station to keep steam-powered ships at sea. Individual trading ships also needed to be able to take on fuel and food at stations en route to lands far from Europe. For example, in 1884 a steamship that left Britain to travel to Hong Kong would take on coal at Gibraltar, Malta, Aden, Bombay, Trincomalee and Singapore.

▼ Links to: Individuals and societies; Economics

Think about the role of governments and other economic agents in pursuing their own self-interests. How might these affect government foreign policy? Is the global economy dominated by certain key industrialized states? To what extent should global companies or the governments of wealthy nations attempt to address poverty and inequality?

What were the different perspectives on empire building?

Cecil Rhodes

'I am content that we [the British] are the first race in the world and that the more of the world we inhabit the better it is for the human race.'

'I contend that every acre added to our territory provides for the birth of the English race, who otherwise would not be brought into existence.'

'I believe it to be my duty to God, Queen and my country to paint the whole map of Africa red, red from the Cape to Cairo. That is my creed, my dream and my mission.'

■ **Figure 9.7** Cecil Rhodes

Edward Wakefield

Edward Wakefield was a British politician. Wakefield argued that Britain has a rapidly growing population – there were about 23 million people living in Britain and Ireland in 1831 when he founded his Colonization Society – and that some of these people should be encouraged to emigrate overseas. He wanted active colonization that would involve all classes in society and not just the poor and convicts.

New colonies in Canada, Australia and New Zealand should be developed that would be '… extensions of an old society … emigration from Britain would not be confined to paupers.'

Wakefield wanted '… a balanced and representative society', which included men and women from every class.

He wanted to encourage British emigration to the colonies by offering land at a fair price – and that the funds raised from this could be used to pay the fares of people that could not afford to travel and provide for the welfare of colonists once they were there.

Wakefield's ideas were influential on the colonization of Australia and New Zealand.

J.A. Hobson

Hobson argued that:

'… the new imperialism has been bad business for the nation, but has been good business for certain classes and certain trades … armaments, costly wars that caused injury to the nation, have served well the present business interests of certain industries and professions.'

Vladimir Lenin (Russian communist revolutionary)

Lenin believed that capitalism inevitably led to imperialism, and this in turn would lead to world conflict. He argued that the whole world would eventually be carved up by the imperialists, and they would then fight among themselves in an attempt to expand their empires into those of their rivals. This would lead to a world war, which Lenin defined as an 'imperial war'.

'When the colonies of the European powers in Africa, for instance, comprised only one-tenth of that territory, colonial policy was able to develop … by the 'free grabbing' of territories, so to speak. But when nine-tenths of Africa had been seized, when the world had been divided up, there was inevitably ushered in a period of colonial monopoly and, consequently, a period of intense struggle for the division and re-division of the world.'

'If commerce brings wealth to our shores, it is the spirit of literature and philanthropy that teaches us how to employ it for the noblest purposes. It is this that has made Britain go forth among the nations, strong in her native light, to dispense blessings to all around her.'

■ **Figure 9.8** Sir Thomas Raffles

Sir Thomas Raffles

Sir Thomas Stamford Raffles worked for the East India Company and was appalled to discover that the company was about to give up its base in Malacca and move all operations to Penang. He urged the company to expand trade at Malacca, to take the rich island of Java from the Dutch and to found a new base at Singapore. He said everyone would benefit if Britain was serious about colonizing the Far East.

THINK–PAIR–SHARE

In pairs, **discuss** the following question based on what we have considered in this chapter thus far: 'What role do economic self-interest and ideology play in the development of empires?' Then share your thoughts with another pair.

Rudyard Kipling

A poem by Kipling suggests his opinion of British imperialism:

> Take up the White Man's Burden
> And reap his old reward
> The blame of those ye better
> The hate of those ye guard

ACTIVITY: Perspectives on imperialism

■ ATL

■ Critical-thinking skills – Recognize unstated assumptions and bias

1 Examine the different viewpoints from the nineteenth century about imperialism. In pairs, **discuss** these and answer the following questions in note form:
   a Which people supported imperialism?
   b **List** the arguments that they put forward in favour of imperialism.
   c How might the indigenous people in the colonies view these opinions?
   d Which people did not support imperialism?
   e **List** the arguments that they put forward against imperialism.

2 Now consider the following statements. In pairs, decide whose viewpoint is represented by each statement.
   a Sooner or later imperialism will lead to world war.
   b It is the White Man's burden to civilize the primitive parts of the world.
   c It is a good idea for overcrowded populations to make new lives for themselves overseas. Ways should be found to help them do this.
   d Everybody would benefit from the British imperial expansion in the Far East.
   e The British have a duty to gain control over as much of Africa as possible – it is best for Britain and best for the rest of the world too.
   f Imperialism really only benefits certain groups – notably those involved in war industries.

◆ Assessment opportunities

◆ In this activity you have practised skills that are assessed using Criterion D: Thinking critically.

SOURCE C

PUNCH, OR THE LONDON CHARIVARI—November 28, 1906.

IN THE RUBBER COILS.

Scene—*The Congo "Free" State.*

Figure 9.9 British cartoon from *Punch* magazine, published in 1906 showing the impact of King Leopold's rule in the Belgian Congo

SOURCE D

John Smithfield owned a successful merchant shipping company in Liverpool. He had become very wealthy from the expansion of the British Empire

'… Imperialism is good for business for all! I contend that we have civilized the territories under the British flag, and brought the benefits of our civilization to the natives.'

Smithfield, J. August 1836. Letter to The Times [British newspaper].

SOURCE E

This source was written by an Indian historian, in a history textbook

'… Imperialism was not profitable for India. The British stripped away India's raw materials and prevented her from industrializing and modernizing… The British were arrogant and racist… '

1989. The British in India. *India.*

ACTIVITY: Source analysis

Look at Sources C–E.

1. What is the message of the cartoonist in Source C?
2. **Identify** the points made about the impact of imperialism in Sources D and E.
3. State the origin and interpret the purpose of each source and then **analyse** the values and limitations of Sources D and E from their origins and purpose.

■ ATL

- ■ Critical-thinking skills – Evaluate evidence and arguments; Recognize unstated assumptions and bias

◆ Assessment opportunities

- ◆ The written responses to this activity can be assessed using Criterion D: Thinking critically.

After the Second World War, most of the European empires were dismantled, sometimes relatively peacefully but sometimes with a lot of violence and bloodshed.

DISCUSS

Do the former colonial powers still owe their colonies a 'debt' in the twenty-first century for the exploitation of these nations in the nineteenth and early twentieth centuries? **Discuss** this question as a class.

ACTIVITY: Assessing the role of economic factors in imperial expansion

ATL

- Communication skills – Structure information in summaries, essays and reports; Organize and depict information logically

Answer the following essay question: 'Using the sources and your knowledge, assess to what extent economic factors led to the expansion of empires.' Write in full paragraphs. You will have 45 minutes.

Use the guidance below, and apply the essay plan structure.

- **Briefly plan your essay.**
- **Include an introduction that sets down your main arguments – relevant to addressing the specific questions.**
- **Use the sources and refer to them explicitly to analyse the causes of imperialism.**
- **You need to attempt to include examples from your own knowledge.**
- **Refer to the question at the beginning of each paragraph.**
- **Write in paragraphs.**
- **Write a short conclusion that answers the questions. This should be in line with the evidence you have presented from the sources and our own knowledge.**

Therefore, if you have more evidence to support the idea that economic factors led to the expansion of empire this should be stated in your conclusion. However, if you have more evidence for a different factor, for example nationalism, then you would conclude that this was the main causal factor.

How to approach planning your essay

You need to sort the sources into those that seem to 'support' the question and those that seem to be 'against' the assertion in the question. For example, if you were asked 'To what extent are individuals responsible for causing wars?', you would group the sources that agreed and the sources that disagreed with the question. You need to then add relevant details, events, your own knowledge etc. to your plan. For example:

- **Agree – Sources X, Y + examples from own knowledge**
- **Disagree – Source Z + examples from own knowledge**

Assessment opportunities

- This activity can be assessed using Criterion A: Knowing and understanding and Criterion C: Communicating.

Essay frame

Introduction

Set down your lines of argument, for example *Economic factors were a key reason for empires to expand; however, other factors should also be taken into account.*

Argument 1

For example: *Economic factors were a key reason for the expansion of empires* …. Use examples from the European expansion of empire in the nineteenth century … plus sources and your own knowledge.

Counter arguments

For example: *However* … [linking sentence to counter argument] *population growth also was an important motive* … plus sources and your own knowledge.

What other counter arguments can you think of? You should state these here.

Conclusion

Based on the weight of evidence in your essay, and the strength of your arguments, answer the question: Were economic reasons the most important factor in the expansion of European empires in the nineteenth century?

Why did alliance systems develop before the First World War and what was their impact?

In 1914, the year in which the First World War started, the six most powerful nations of Europe were divided into two opposing alliances – the Triple Entente and the Triple Alliance.

In order to understand why the Great Powers ended up in a war in 1914, it is important to understand the strengths, weaknesses, fears and concerns of each of these countries.

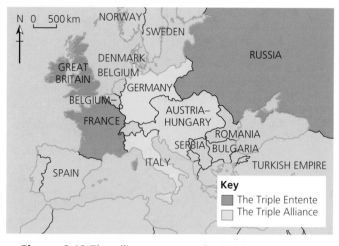

■ **Figure 9.10** The alliance systems in 1914

THE TRIPLE ALLIANCE (ALSO KNOWN AS THE CENTRAL POWERS)

Germany

Germany had been a country only since 1871. Before this, there was no such country – only a collection of small states, each with its own ruler. Chancellor Otto von Bismarck, the Prussian statesman, had united these states after defeating both Austria and France in wars. Following the Franco-Prussian War in 1870, in which France was defeated by Germany, Bismarck was able to create a new and powerful empire.

CIRCLE OF VIEWPOINTS

■ ATL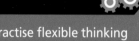

■ Creative-thinking skills – Practise flexible thinking – develop multiple opposing, contradictory and complementary arguments

In groups, **discuss** the effects of imperialism on the colonies. Did many colonized people benefit from imperialism? How did imperialism damage the societies that were colonized? Each member of your group should chooses a character from the following list:
- **Indian government official working for the British**
- **French settler in Algeria**
- **Congolese miner working for King Leopold of Belgium**
- **The British colonist Sir Cecil Rhodes**
- **Indian farmer instructed by the British to grow cotton or opium instead of food crops**
- **Merchant from the Ivory Coast**

- **British missionary in South Africa**
- **Tribal leader in Kenya**

Write a short speech regarding your views on the impact of imperialism. You are writing in 1900. You should write up to a maximum of 400 words and address the ideas of imperialism benefiting or damaging your society. What questions might you have?

Use these opening sentences:
- 'From the viewpoint of … I think …
- 'A question I have from this view point is …'

◆ Assessment opportunities

◆ This activity can be assessed using Criterion A: Knowing and understanding and Criterion C: Communicating.

Figure 9.11 Wilhelm II

Austria–Hungary

Figure 9.12 Nationalities in Austria–Hungary

Between 1870 and 1914, Germany's industrial strength grew rapidly and by 1914 it was in a position to rival the economic strength of Britain. Up until 1890, Bismarck continued to have a strong influence on German foreign policy. He made sure that Germany did not get involved in any more wars and he ensured that France – now sworn to revenge its defeat and treatment at the end of the Franco-Prussian War – was kept isolated. However, this all changed when a new Kaiser – Wilhelm II – took power in 1890. He dismissed Bismarck and embarked on a much more aggressive foreign policy.

Wilhelm II was determined to make Germany a world power. He loved the army and enjoyed dressing up in military uniform. He was jealous of Britain with its empire and believed that Germany should also have 'a place in the sun' with colonies overseas. This also meant building up the German navy, which soon rivalled Britain's navy.

Wilhelm hoped that this emphasis on making Germany a great power would detract from domestic problems; workers were starting to join trade unions and join strikes in an attempt to force the government to improve their conditions. The Socialist party was growing in strength and this threatened the autocratic power of the Kaiser as the socialists wanted more power for Germany's parliament (Reichstag).

As can be seen from the map (Figure 9.12), Austria–Hungary consisted of many different nationalities, each with its own language and customs. The ruler of this multinational empire was the ageing Emperor Franz Joseph. He was a hard-working emperor who had faced much personal tragedy, his son having committed suicide and his wife having been stabbed to death by an assassin. His heir was his nephew, Franz Ferdinand, who had caused a scandal by marrying a countess called Sophie Chotek – considered to be beneath him.

Unlike Wilhelm II of Germany, Franz Joseph had no desire to acquire colonies. He knew that all his energies had to be devoted to holding his empire together. Many of the different national groups wanted independence, for instance the Serbs in the south of the empire, who wanted to be joined to the neighbouring state of Serbia, and the Czech people in the north, who wanted to rule themselves.

Outside of its borders, Austria–Hungary also faced problems: the newly independent Serbia was a threat as it encouraged the nationalism of the Serbs within the empire. The Serbs were also supported by Russia, thus putting Austria–Hungary and Russia on a potential collision course.

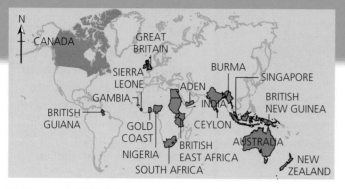

■ **Figure 9.13** Britain's extensive empire

Italy

Like Germany, Italy was a recently formed country; the unification of several smaller states in the Italian peninsular had finally been completed in 1871. By 1914, it felt settled enough to look for opportunities to expand its power and saw it could do this by gaining colonies. It hoped to increase its influence also by joining Germany and Austria–Hungary in its Dual Alliance – thus making it the Triple Alliance. However, Italy remained the weaker partner of the alliance as it was not a strong industrial or military power.

THE TRIPLE ENTENTE

Britain

Britain at this time was the world's greatest power. The Industrial Revolution had started in Britain and, by 1914, Britain was the richest and most powerful nation on earth. Its empire covered a third of the earth's surface and the British navy was the lifeline for Britain, allowing it to dominate world trade between the different colonies and Europe.

Unlike the monarch in the other large powers of Europe, however, the British king, George V, had little individual power. Britain was a constitutional monarchy, meaning that political decisions were made in Parliament and by his government of ministers.

In the nineteenth century, Britain had avoided getting involved in European politics and had maintained a policy of 'splendid isolation'. It felt it did not need to get involved in alliances and wanted to concentrate on its empire. However, by 1914, it was becoming concerned about Germany's growing economic strength and its desires to obtain a navy and to gain colonies. Thus, Britain signed an alliance with France in 1904 and with Russia in 1907.

France

Although twice the size of Britain, France was weaker economically. It had also lost two valuable, industrial provinces to Germany after the Franco-Prussian War – Alsace and Lorraine. It was, however, the second largest empire in the world with extensive colonies in Africa and also in Indo-China.

The growing strength of Germany since 1870, however, was a worry to France, which feared another attack. It thus spent money building up its army and it also set up an alliance with Russia. Its foreign policy in Europe was dominated by the two aims of protecting itself from Germany and trying to get back Alsace and Lorraine.

Unlike the other powers of Europe, France was a republic, meaning that its rulers were elected. In 1914, the president was Raymond Poincaré.

■ **Figure 9.14** 'The Alsatian Bogeyman' (1913). Germany annexes Alsace-Lorraine in 1871 following French defeat in the Franco-Prussian War. The cartoon, which was drawn by Olaf Gulbransson and published in *Simplicissimus* in November 1913, features small, powerless Alsatian citizens and a larger-than-life Prussian officer, who scoops up frightened villagers

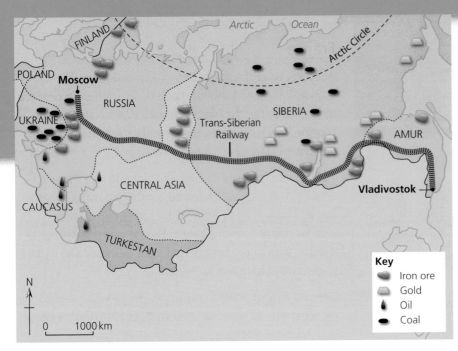

Figure 9.15 The Russian Empire in 1914

Key
- Iron ore
- Gold
- Oil
- Coal

N

0 1000 km

THINK–PAIR–SHARE

In pairs, or groups, **discuss** and consider the following questions:

1 **How might the alliances prevent an argument between two countries escalating into a general European war?**
2 **How might the alliances help to increase tension or even help to widen local conflicts into wider conflicts?**

Russia

Russia was the largest country of all of the six powers, but in 1914 it was also the most backwards in terms of economic development. Despite a huge population and vast resources, industry was late in developing and the size of its empire and weak transport links made progress difficult. Vast amounts of land were too cold for farming and much of the coastline was frozen for six months of the year, which limited the use of the navy. The empire was also made up of many different nationalities, which made it difficult to govern. Russia's military weakness was highlighted when it was defeated by Japan in 1905; its concern not to be humiliated again led to the development of a much larger army by 1914.

The Russian Empire was ruled by Tsar Nicholas II, who attempted to gain total power over his people despite growing unrest and demands for more political freedom. He survived a revolution in 1905, after which he was forced to allow a Duma (parliament), but this failed to result in any fundamental changes. Demands for political change were fuelled by the appalling conditions for workers in the towns and the primitive agricultural conditions which meant life was extremely hard.

Russia shared France's and Britain's concerns regarding Germany's strength. It was also a rival to Austria–Hungary as it hoped to expand into the Balkans – an area that Austria–Hungary was also interested in. For this reason, and also because they were fellow Slavs, the Russians supported Serbia against Austria–Hungary.

Figure 9.16 Comparison of the strengths of the Great Powers in 1914

		Britain	France	Russia	Germany	Austria–Hungary	Italy
Population (millions)		46	40	167	65	50	35
Steel production (millions of tons)		7.9	4	4	17	2.6	3.9
Merchant ships (millions of tons)		20	2	0.75	5	3	1.75
Foreign trade (£ million per year)		1	0.4	0.2	1	0.2	n/a
Number of soldiers available (in thousands), excluding reserve forces		248	1800	3409	2200	1338	750
Warships (including under construction)		122	46	26	85	24	36
Submarines		64	73	29	23	6	12

ACTIVITY: Country profiles of the Great Powers of Europe

■ ATL

- ■ Communication skills – Structure information in summaries, essays and reports

In groups, pick one of the countries of the Great Powers of Europe before the outbreak of the First World War.

In your groups, read through the information on your country and **discuss** the key characteristics. Also refer to Figure 9.16 showing a comparison of the resources of each country.

You should then each make bullet-point notes. These notes should include information on the following:
- Type of government
- Size of population
- Colonial territories
- Size of army and navy
- Industrial output – e.g. coal and steel
- Key strengths and key weaknesses/problems
- Sources of tension with other countries

You have 30 minutes.

Feedback to class

- Listen carefully to the notes from other groups.
- You need to make notes on each of the other Great Powers.
- When they have finished giving feedback, you can ask questions.

Concluding task

Make notes on the following questions discussed in class:

1 Which European power was the strongest and why?
2 Which European powers had problems with nationalism?
3 Which ruling regimes / political systems seem weak?
4 What tensions existed between the different countries?
5 Overall, which alliance system seems to be the strongest? Give reasons for your answer.

◆ Assessment opportunities

- ◆ In this activity you have practised skills that are assessed using Criterion A: Knowing and understanding and Criterion C: Communicating.

ACTIVITY: The role of alliances

■ ATL

- ■ Critical-thinking skills – Evaluate evidence and arguments

Why do nations join supra-national alliances? Consider these reasons: for self-defence and security; to prevent inter-state conflict and war; to promote self-interest and economic or territorial gain; ideology.

Examine whether the alliance systems were a key cause of the First World War. (Refer to Chapter 8 for a discussion of the other causes of the war.) **Justify** your answer.

ACTIVITY: Source work

■ ATL

- ■ Critical-thinking skills – Evaluate evidence and arguments

In pairs, read Source F and **identify** the ways in which Stephen Lee claims the Triple Entente and Triple Alliance helped cause a general war in August 1914.

SOURCE F

'There were … two ways in which the alliances did affect international relations and contribute to the growth of tension in Europe in the decade before 1914. First they provided the links across which crises could spread from peripheral areas like North Africa and the Balkans to the major powers themselves. Normally, the dangers were seen and the connections cut. … But as the sequence of events after Sarajevo (the assassination of the heir to the Austro-Hungarian throne) showed only too clearly, the means existed whereby a local conflict could be transformed into a continental war. Second, the alliances had a direct bearing on the arms race and the development of military schedules.'

Lee, S.J. 1988. Aspects of European History 1879–1980. UK. Routledge.

Why are supra-national organizations formed and what is their impact?

THE LEAGUE OF NATIONS

The first international supra-national cross-regional organization to facilitate international cooperation was promoted during the First World War by the US President Woodrow Wilson.

After the devastation of the First World War, countries were willing to pursue this idea in the hope that it would prevent another catastrophic conflict. The League of Nations was set up in 1920. At its peak there were 60 member states. Its purpose was to avoid war through discussion, negotiation and diplomacy. Wilson also hoped that it would be possible through the League to move towards universal disarmament.

The League offered its member states 'collective security', in other words, nations would stand together to protect each other. If a country attacked a member state, the League collectively could impose sanctions – stop trading with the aggressor state. If these economic sanctions failed to deter the aggressor, the League could ask its member states to send in soldiers to resist the attack.

The League also undertook humanitarian work to improve the health and living standards of people throughout the world. It had special commissions to work against slavery, to share medicines and to help refugees. The special commission on disarmament was set up in 1926 to prepare for the 1932–34 World Disarmament Conference.

The Court of International Justice was set up in 1921 at The Hague and included 15 judges from across the world. Countries could bring disputes to the court and the judges would decide who was in the right, and how the dispute could be resolved.

The League also paid for the International Labour Organization (ILO) (see Figure 9.17), which tried to improve wages and conditions for workers in different countries.

Secretariat
This body carried out the decisions taken by the council

The Council
This was the key committee as it took the major decisions

General Assembly
All member states had one vote in the assembly. It met once a year.

International Labour Organization
Each member sent two government ministers, one employer and one worker. It discussed and got countries to improve working conditions

Court of International Justice
15 judges met at The Hague in the Netherlands. They settled international disputes from disagreements over borders to fishing rights

■ **Figure 9.17** The structure of the League of Nations

This did have some notable successes, improving working conditions, encouraging better health and sanitation practices, giving economic assistance to countries that were in difficulty and supporting refugees. It raised money to help Austria, whose economy was facing collapse after the First World War.

However, the key function of the League was to maintain peace and prevent war. It did have some successes in preventing conflict in the 1920s but it also had many limitations, which meant that it was less effective as an international peacekeeping body:

- Although the League was an American idea, the USA did not join it.
- The USSR and Germany were not initially allowed to be members.
- The most powerful body was 'The Council' – initially this was made up of the permanent members Britain, France, Italy and Japan. This made it seem too European rather than genuinely a 'world' organization. (Japan was the only non-European member.)
- It could also be seen as an 'imperialists' club' or 'victors' club', as all Council members were imperial powers and all had been on the winning side in the First World War.
- It did not have its own standing League army.
- It took a long time for decisions to be made and action taken.
- It relied on economic sanctions to get states to comply with its decisions.

How did the League respond to the challenge of the aggressor states?

The weaknesses of the League itself were exposed when, in the 1930s, new aggressor states challenged peace. The failure of the League to successfully challenge the actions of these states ultimately destroyed its credibility.

Japan

In Japan the liberal democracy was increasingly challenged by its own military. The Japanese army invaded Manchuria in China in 1931. It claimed that the Chinese had blown up a section of the railway at Mukden where the Japanese had stationed troops to protect it. The Japanese army used this as an excuse to expand and occupy Manchuria to gain resources and living space for Japan.

As a member state, China appealed to the League for help. It took the League almost a year to report that Japan was to blame and that the occupation should end. The League imposed limited economic sanctions. The Japanese ignored the League and, in protest, left the League in 1933. The League had been powerless to stop the occupation and Japan, through the use of force, had been successful.

Unchecked, the Japanese launched a full-scale war against China in 1937 and again China appealed to the League for help. But the League's leading European powers, worried about the impact of the Great Depression on their own countries, did not want sanctions that could also damage their own economies.

Italy

Italy, led by the dictator Benito Mussolini, was a member of the League's Council. Mussolini wanted to expand the Italian empire and saw that aggression would go unopposed by the League. Italy attacked Abyssinia in 1935. Abyssinia had limited weapons and resources and the Italian assault was ferocious, using aircraft and poison-gas attacks.

Abyssinia was a member of the League, and its leader, Emperor Haile Selassie, appealed to it for help. The brutality of the attack meant there was much international sympathy for Abyssinia, but the other European states would not take strong action. In October 1935 the League imposed economic sanctions on Italy – but these did not restrict the supply of key war materials such as oil, steel or copper. The League's weak response meant that Italy was able to secure the conquest of Abyssinia in 1936.

Mussolini then took Italy out of the League. The League's reputation was in ruins. It was completely incapable of dealing with the aggressor states.

Germany

These lessons were not lost on the dictator of Germany, Adolf Hitler. He saw his opportunity to begin to rearm in 1935, to send troops into the Rhineland in 1936 and to intervene in the Spanish Civil War in the same year. He could breach the Treaty of Versailles with relative impunity, as Britain and France had shown themselves as weak leaders of the international community through the League. How could this weak organization that had failed to uphold some of the peace treaty settlements in the 1920s hope to uphold the Treaty of Versailles with Nazi Germany?

Figure 9.18 Why did the League of Nations fail?

ACTIVITY: Why did the League of Nations fail to prevent conflict?

What is your goal?

You will examine the weaknesses of the League of Nations. Each group will take on a different weakness and present a case that their 'weakness' was the most significant reason for the League of Nations' failure to prevent conflict.

How will you achieve this?

The class will be split into three groups. You will be assigned a number – Group 1, 2 or 3. Your number corresponds to one of the key weaknesses in the League of Nations (listed in the table below) that may have led to its failure to maintain peace before 1939.

In your groups, you must review the material in this chapter about the League of Nations. Collate supporting evidence to create a clear case for your 'weakness' as the most significant problem for the League of Nations.

Group 1	Structure, membership and self-interest of member states
Group 2	Impact of Great Depression
Group 3	Rise of the aggressor states

Your notes should include:
- **an explanation of your weakness, e.g. which member states did not join?**
- **examples of when this led to the League failing to maintain peace**
- **dates and details.**

You have 30 minutes to complete your notes.

How will you present your findings?

Write an individual speech that should last between one and two minutes. Your speech will argue that your weakness was the key reason that the League of Nations failed to keep the peace. Do not include material that is relevant to the other arguments.

Your speech should:
- **include examples, dates and details**
- **use persuasive language.**

You do not have to memorize your speech, but you should practise reading it out loud.

◆ Assessment opportunities

◆ This assessment could be peer assessed using Criterion A: Knowing and understanding and Criterion C: Communicating.

THE UNITED NATIONS

As we have seen, the catastrophe of the First World War (1914–18) led to the setting up of an international organization to foster peace and cooperation and to prevent another general war – the League of Nations. However, the League of Nations failed to keep the peace and the Second World War that followed was the most horrific in human history. More than 50 million people were killed in the Second World War.

The victorious powers agreed that a new and improved organization should be set up to enable the international community to settle disputes before another conflict developed. The new organization would learn lessons from the weaknesses of its predecessor, the League. The world would be invited to join – and this time, the most powerful countries joined the organization. Indeed, the two new superpowers, the USA and the USSR, became members of the key UN body – the Security Council.

How was the UN created?

Prime Minister Winston Churchill and President Roosevelt had signed the Atlantic Charter in 1941, when both men had stated their aims for the post-war world. They were both conscious that the League of Nations had been a failure and were keen to ensure that any new organization had the support of *all* nations.

The Atlantic Charter re-affirmed the idea of self-determination and also indicated that a new world peace organization would be set up after the end of the war. The Atlantic Charter was confirmed by the signing of the United Nations Declaration in January 1942, and at meetings in 1943 in Teheran and Moscow it was decided to set up a 'general organization' before the end of hostilities.

The conference which drew up the structure of the UN was held in August 1944 at Dumbarton Oaks, near Washington DC. Diplomats from Great Britain, the USA, the USSR and China decided that there would be a General Assembly and a Security Council. The latter would have permanent representatives and others who would serve for a specific term. There were disagreements about how voting would take place but these were resolved at the Yalta Conference in early 1945. The United Nations would be set up to be the mechanism for peacemaking and peacekeeping in the post-war world.

At Yalta it was agreed that the Big Four – Britain, the USA, the USSR and China – would be permitted a veto in the Security Council. The veto meant that one of these four could block a Security Council decision simply by voting 'No'.

On 25 April 1945, delegates from around the world met in San Francisco in the USA to draft a charter for the new organization. There were representatives from 50 nations and it took two months for the details to be agreed.

Finally, on 25 June 1945, the delegates formally signed the new UN Charter.

■ **Figure 9.19** A UN peacekeeper

SOURCE G

US President Harry Truman's speech to the opening session of the San Francisco conference, 12 April 1945

'At no time in history has there been a more important conference or a more necessary meeting than this one …

'You members of this conference are to be architects of the better world. In your hands rests our future …

'We, who have lived through the torture and the strategy of two world conflicts, must realize the magnitude of the problems before us. We do not need far-sighted vision to understand the trend in recent history … With ever-increasing brutality and destruction, modern warfare, if unchecked, would ultimately crush civilization. We still have a choice between the alternatives – the continuation of international chaos or the establishment of a world organization for the enforcement of peace …'

DISCUSS

Look at Source G. What key points are made by President Truman about why the UN was set up?

The UN Charter consisted of 111 articles that detailed the purposes of the UN and explained how it would work. It set up six organs to carry out specific functions: there was a General Assembly, a Security Council, an Economic and Social Council, a Trusteeship Council, an International Court of Justice and a Secretariat.

You can read through the UN Charter here:

www.un.org/en/documents/charter/

The Security Council was to consist of 11 members of the UN. There were initially five permanent members of the Security Council: China, France, the USSR, the UK and the USA. The General Assembly would elect another six states to be non-permanent members. In order for the UN to act quickly in a crisis the Security Council was given by the member states the responsibility of maintaining international peace and security. Each member of this Council had one vote. Decisions would be passed if there was agreement from seven members. It had the right to investigate any dispute or situation that might lead to international friction or tension. It had the power to impose partial or full economic sanctions, cut off rail, sea, air, postal, telegraphic, radio and other means of communication and it could also cut diplomatic relations with a country. Importantly, however, the UN Security Council also had the power, if other measures had not worked, to use armed force. Indeed, it could use sea, land or air forces to strike a country that refused to comply with its decisions. The UN had its own 'blue beret' troops to keep the peace if necessary. The permanent members each had the power of veto, which meant that they could block a resolution put forward by the other powers.

The General Assembly consisted of all the members of the UN. It would discuss general principles on international peace and security and could make recommendations to promote international cooperation and promoted health and education and the realization of human rights and freedoms for all. Each member state had one vote. Decisions could only be passed if there was a two-thirds majority supporting it. The General Assembly would meet once a year.

The Economic and Social Council was set up to promote higher standards of living, full employment, and conditions for economic and social progress. It was also to find solutions for international economic, social and health problems and promote cultural and educational cooperation. It set out to promote universal respect for human rights and fundamental freedoms for all without distinction as to race, sex, language or religion. It had specialized agencies, which had international responsibilities for economic, social, cultural, educational, health and related fields. The Economic and Social Council consisted of 27 members, who were elected by the General Assembly. The Council could make reports on international economic, social, cultural, educational and health matters and could make recommendations to the UN for action. Each member of this council had one vote.

The International Court of Justice was set up as the principal judicial organ of the UN. All members of the UN were involved in the court. Each member of the UN agreed to comply with the decision of the court in any case that it ruled on. The court consisted of 15 members, each chosen from a different country.

The Trusteeship Council was responsible for territories whose peoples had not yet attained self-government and was to look after the interests of the inhabitants. The territories it looked after were called Trust Territories. This council aimed to promote the political, economic, social and educational advancement of the inhabitants of the Trust Territories and develop the territories towards self-government or independence.

The Secretariat was chaired by the Secretary-General, who was the chief administrative officer for the UN. The Secretary-General would be appointed by the General Assembly and had staff to assist in running the organization.

Who has most influence in the UN?

At its inception, and for the first decade and a half, the UN was dominated by the USA and its powerful Western allies. However, after the Second World War, the independence movements grew stronger and challenged their imperial rulers. There were over 80 colonial territories across the globe, including over a third of the world's population, and these were ruled by just seven European powers.

Weakened by the war and facing international criticism of imperialism, the Europeans were not able to meet the increasingly organized and widespread decolonization movements. The UN declared that it would foster and manage the transition from colonial rule to independence.

In order to do this the UN set up the International Trusteeship System. The UN Charter stated that the countries that had 'trusteeship' over colonial territories had to protect its people and prepare them for independence. The Trusteeship Council met yearly to check that this role was being properly carried out by the 'trustees'. In 1960 the UN set out the Declaration of Independence, which formally denounced imperialism as a denial of human rights and an obstacle to world peace. From 1960, many former colonies became independent. The balance of power in the UN General Assembly shifted as each new country became a member state with one vote.

■ **Figure 9.20** The UN offices in New York

This meant that from the late 1960s the Western allies were no longer the majority voice in the UN, with the new African and Asian states joining the organization. The new states could form their own blocs to vote on UN activities and resolutions.

Bloc voting became a feature of UN activities. There was the US-backed Western bloc, the USSR-led communist bloc, the developing nations bloc that included states from Africa, Asia and Latin America, a non-aligned bloc that attempted to be independent from the influence of the superpowers and the Islamic Conference of Islamic states in the Middle East and Asia. In addition to these blocs there were also regional groupings for certain issues where votes would be grouped into an African bloc, a Latin American bloc, a Western European bloc and an Arab bloc.

By the 1980s, many states in the UN argued that there should be the same principle for each component of the UN, in other words all states should be treated equally and have one vote in each UN body, including the Security Council. The USA argued against this, stating in 1985:

> *'Voting rights [in the UN should be] proportionate to the contribution of each member state to the budget of the United Nations and its specialized agencies.'*

The UN's specialized agencies

1 **Food and Agriculture Organization of the United Nations (FAO):** Achieving food security for all, to make sure people have regular access to enough high-quality food

2 **International Atomic Energy Agency (IAEA):** Promotes the peaceful use of atomic energy

3 **International Civil Aviation Organization (ICAO):** Promotes safety in aviation

4 **International Development Association (IDA):** Fosters economic development in developing nations by providing loans with low repayment terms

5 **International Fund for Agricultural Development (IFAD):** Gives loans to developing nations to improve farming methods

6 **International Labour Organization (ILO):** Works to improve working and living conditions, wages and the rights of workers

7 **International Monetary Fund (IMF):** Promotes monetary cooperation between states. Can loan money to nations with balance of payments issues and to stabilize a currency

8 **International Maritime Organization (IMO):** Promotes safe and secure shipping and the prevention of pollution by ships

9 **International Telecommunication Union (ITU):** Monitors international radio frequencies and improves the world telephone and telegraph networks

10 **UN Educational, Scientific and Cultural Organization (UNESCO):** Fosters cooperation between nations through education, culture and science

11 **UN Industrial Development Organization (UNIDO):** Works to develop industry in developing nations

12 **Universal Postal Union (UPU):** Works to ensure that the world's citizens have access to affordable postal services

13 **World Bank Group:** Provides loans and technical assistance to developing countries to reduce poverty and advance sustainable economic growth

14 **World Health Organization (WHO):** Provides leadership in health matters, shapes medical research and promotes and monitors standards, and monitors world health situations

15 **World Intellectual Property Organization (WIPO):** Works to protect copyright, patents and inventors from illegal copying of their work

16 **World Meteorological Organization (WMO):** Encourages nations to work together on forecasting weather events and monitors weather through its weather stations around the world

17 **World Tourism Organization (WTO):** Serves as a global forum for tourism policy issues

Food and Agriculture Organization of the United Nations

International Atomic Energy Agency

The World Bank's Fund for the Poorest WORLD BANK GROUP

Investing in rural people

INTERNATIONAL MARITIME ORGANIZATION

United Nations Educational, Scientific and Cultural Organization

UNITED NATIONS INDUSTRIAL DEVELOPMENT ORGANIZATION

UNIVERSAL POSTAL UNION

WORLD BANK GROUP

World Health Organization

WMO

UNWTO

www.un.org/en/sections/about-un/funds-programmes-specialized-agencies-and-others/index.html

How successful were the UN's specialized agencies?

The UN has a number of specialized agencies and organizations that carry out its non-political work.

These specialized agencies had some great successes in the post-war period. The WHO began a campaign to wipe out smallpox as a disease in 1967 and could report that by 1984 it had been totally successful as no cases were reported around the world.

The ILO was developed to set up an extensive list of rules that all member states had to comply with, which improved working and living conditions internationally. However, not all agencies could work without disagreement in the UN. As you have read, from the 1980s the membership of the UN had changed significantly as new post-colonial states joined the organization. For example, the USA withdrew from the ILO in 1977 in protest at the agency's inability to effect positive change to human rights in the Soviet bloc, and there was disagreement over the role of UNESCO as new African and Asian states promoted different ideas and programmes to the initiatives from the Western states.

Most of UNESCO's funding came from the West and, due to disputes over how the money would be spent, the USA withdrew from the agency in 1985. This seriously undermined its ability to fund projects as the USA had paid 25 per cent of its budget.

To what extent has the UN been a success in peacekeeping around the world?

The UN's key function was to keep the peace. However, in the first 50 years of its existence there were over 50 conflicts around the world. Millions of people have died and, in some of these wars, leading members of the Security Council were directly involved in the causes and in the fighting itself. To what extent, therefore, has the UN failed in its role as peacekeeper?

▼ Links to: Geography; Economics

Think about the role played by UN organizations and associations in promoting international aid and exchange. Also consider the role the UN attempts to play in preventing abject poverty and inequality. What initiatives and solutions has it developed?

ACTIVITY: How successful is the UN?

■ ATL

- ■ Critical-thinking skills – Draw reasonable conclusions and generalizations

Look at Figures 9.21 and 9.22 on the following pages. Make notes of where and when the UN appears to have been successful and where it seems to have failed.

In small groups, **discuss** whether there appears to be a pattern of when and why the UN succeeds or fails in preventing war.

Write up a short report on your conclusions of approximately 300 words. You should **explain** your conclusions using examples to support your opinion.

◆ Assessment opportunities

- ◆ In this activity you have practised skills that are assessed using Criterion D: Thinking critically.

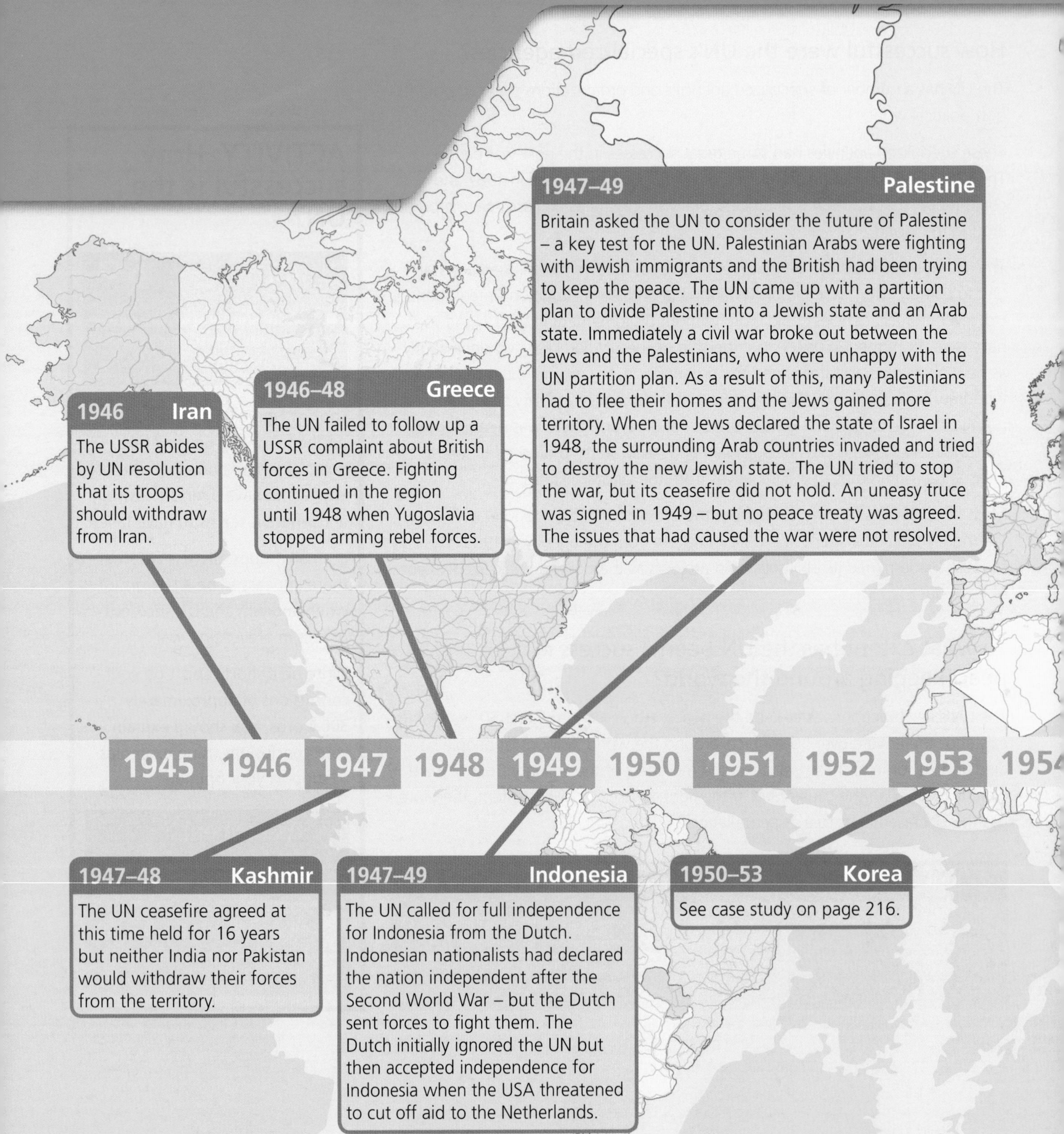

1947–49 · Palestine

Britain asked the UN to consider the future of Palestine – a key test for the UN. Palestinian Arabs were fighting with Jewish immigrants and the British had been trying to keep the peace. The UN came up with a partition plan to divide Palestine into a Jewish state and an Arab state. Immediately a civil war broke out between the Jews and the Palestinians, who were unhappy with the UN partition plan. As a result of this, many Palestinians had to flee their homes and the Jews gained more territory. When the Jews declared the state of Israel in 1948, the surrounding Arab countries invaded and tried to destroy the new Jewish state. The UN tried to stop the war, but its ceasefire did not hold. An uneasy truce was signed in 1949 – but no peace treaty was agreed. The issues that had caused the war were not resolved.

1946–48 · Greece

The UN failed to follow up a USSR complaint about British forces in Greece. Fighting continued in the region until 1948 when Yugoslavia stopped arming rebel forces.

1946 · Iran

The USSR abides by UN resolution that its troops should withdraw from Iran.

1945 1946 1947 1948 1949 1950 1951 1952 1953 1954

1947–48 · Kashmir

The UN ceasefire agreed at this time held for 16 years but neither India nor Pakistan would withdraw their forces from the territory.

1947–49 · Indonesia

The UN called for full independence for Indonesia from the Dutch. Indonesian nationalists had declared the nation independent after the Second World War – but the Dutch sent forces to fight them. The Dutch initially ignored the UN but then accepted independence for Indonesia when the USA threatened to cut off aid to the Netherlands.

1950–53 · Korea

See case study on page 216.

Figure 9.21 Timeline of UN peacekeeping missions, 1945–63

History for the IB MYP 4&5: *by Concept*

1956 — Suez

The Israelis broke the ceasefire of 1949 – with British and French backing – by invading Egypt in 1956. The UN, unaware of the involvement of others in the invasion, met to discuss the crisis and to call for Israeli forces to withdraw. The British and French had wanted to regain control of the important Suez Canal which had been nationalized by Egypt's leader, Nasser, and had plotted to send forces in to 'protect' the canal during the fighting. Therefore, Britain and France vetoed the resolution against Israel. The Security Council used the 'Uniting for Peace' process and passed the matter to the General Assembly (GA). The GA called for a ceasefire and the withdrawal of Israeli forces and set up an international army to supervise on the ground. The British and French continued with their plan, ignoring the UN resolutions. The USA was furious that it had not been consulted and threatened to cut oil supplies through the Suez Canal. Britain and France were dependent on these supplies and had no choice but to withdraw. The 'blue beret' UN forces patrolled the ceasefire line for the next ten years.

1962 — Indonesia

The Indonesians disputed the Dutch claim to the island of West Irian. The UN resolved that it was Indonesian and oversaw the transfer of the territory to Indonesia within seven months.

1962 — Yemen

In 1962 a civil war broke out in Yemen between the Republicans backed by Egypt and the Royalists backed by Saudi Arabia. The Royalists appealed to the UN. However, Egypt and Saudi Arabia came to an agreement outside of the UN to withdraw forces. A UN observation mission reported that forces had been withdrawn.

1960 — Congo

See case study on page 217.

1955 1956 1957 1958 1959 1960 1961 1962 1963 1964

1956 — Hungary

Soviet troops invaded Hungary to put down anti-Soviet protests there. The UN set up an investigation and called for Soviet forces to withdraw. The USSR ignored the UN and vetoed action.

1958 — Lebanon

Internal rebellion broke out in 1958 and the Lebanese government claimed to the UN that the crisis was fostered by Syria and that the Syrians were arming the rebels. The UN set up an observation group to ensure no arms came across the border from Syria. It reported back to the UN that no arms were coming over the border and the Lebanese accepted the findings.

1963 — Cyprus

Cyprus became independent from Britain in 1960, and within three years a civil war had broken out between the Greek and Turkish communities. The UN sent a peace-keeping force to keep the sides apart and remained in Cyprus for ten years. It did not prevent hostilities breaking out again in 1974.

1964–73 Vietnam

Vietnam was 'temporarily' divided along the 17th parallel at the end of the Second World War. Vietnam had attempted to claim independence from the French in 1945 under their leader Ho Chi Minh. However, the French resisted this and went to war to prevent the 'communists' taking over. The French were defeated in 1954. The division in the country was similar to that in Korea in that the North developed into a communist state and the South into a pro-Western state. It was agreed in multi-party talks after the French had withdrawn, including the USA and the USSR, that there would be free elections to unify an independent Vietnam. However, the free elections did not take place and the USA supported a 'two state' solution to prevent the South falling to the communists from the North. In 1964 the North Vietnamese attacked an American patrol off the Gulf of Tonkin. The US president, Lyndon Johnson, declared this to be an act of war. The Americans engaged in a war with the communist Vietnamese until 1973. They had taken action without UN backing. The USSR condemned the USA in the Security Council for their illegal aggression.

1966–80 Zimbabwe

The white minority set up a government after independence from Britain in 1966 to prevent the black majority from gaining power. The UN condemned their actions and imposed sanctions. These sanctions failed as the white apartheid government in South Africa refused to comply with them. A guerrilla war broke out in 1973 against the white government in Zimbabwe. Eventually, the 'Patriotic Front' forces won in 1980.

1971 Kashmir

Hostilities broke out again in Kashmir and the UN again ordered both sides back to the ceasefire line of 1947. The UN sent observers to supervise withdrawal and remained on the ceasefire line.

1975 East Timor

Indonesia sent troops to occupy the Portuguese colony of East Timor. UN resolutions ordered the withdrawal of its troops but Indonesia ignored the calls.

1964 1965 **1966** 1967 **1968** 1969 **1970** 1971 **1972** 1973 **1974** 1975 197

1965–66 Dominican Republic

The President of the Dominican Republic was overthrown, leading to a civil war. The USA sent troops to prevent a communist takeover. The UN sent a representative to observe, who remained until 1966. The USA oversaw a combined force sent by the Organization of American States.

1967 Kashmir

Hostilities broke out again in 1967 (see 1947 for details). The UN ordered both sides back to the 1947 ceasefire line and sent observers. Both sides agreed to talks and to withdraw to the ceasefire line under UN supervision.

1967 Six-Day War

See case study on pages 216–17.

1974 Cyprus

Greek separatists tried to unify with Greece, and the Turkish army joined the Turkish Cypriots in resisting and seizing northern Cyprus. The UN enforced a ceasefire and its forces in Cyprus held positions along the divide between north and south.

■ **Figure 9.22** Timeline of UN peacekeeping missions, 1964–89

1973 — Yom Kippur War

The new Egyptian president, Anwar Sadat, declared that peace talks had failed and that the Arab states must settle their issues with Israel militarily. In October 1973, the Arab states invaded Israel. The UN passed Resolution 338, which called for a ceasefire and to open talks based on Resolution 242. UN-led peace talks failed to bring an end to the conflict. The USA took over brokering peace and Secretary of State Henry Kissinger 'shuttled' between the two sides, ultimately drawing up a Disengagement Agreement in January 1974. A new UN force was sent to the border between Israel and Egypt and another to the border with Syria. In 1978 President Carter of the USA had both sides meet in America at Camp David. The UN had become more hostile towards Israel's position while the USA was mediating. It accused Israel of racism and ordered it to allow Palestinians to return to their homes. The following year the UN demanded Israel hand over territory it had occupied to the Palestine Liberation Organization (PLO) and was highly critical of Israel's 'settlement' of the occupied land.

1982 Malvinas/Falklands

Argentine forces invaded the British colony of the Falkland Islands (Malvinas). The islands are just off the Argentine coast and Argentina had called for the UN to find in favour of their claim to the territories after the Second World War. The UN condemned the use of military force and a resolution was passed calling for a withdrawal of Argentine forces. Argentina ignored the resolution and Britain and Argentina went to war.

1982–85 — Lebanon

Members of the PLO had settled in Lebanon and sent raids from there into Israel. Israel responded with air raids on their bases. In 1975 a civil war broke out between Christians and Muslims in Lebanon. Israel supported the Christians and invaded in 1978. The UN attempted to stop the war developing further by passing Resolution 425 to call for Israel to withdraw and sent troops to the Lebanon. The Israelis withdrew after giving a 10km strip of territory on their border to a pro-Israeli Christian leader. This meant they could cross back whenever they wanted. The Israelis invaded again in 1982 and forced the PLO out of the capital Beirut. A UN-backed multinational force stayed on in Lebanon to try to prevent continued fighting between Christians and Muslims. They failed and the civil war continued until 1985.

977 **1978** 1979 **1980** 1981 **1982** 1983 **1984** 1985 **1986** 1987 **1988** 1989

1979–89 — Afghanistan

The USSR sent in troops to support a pro-Soviet government in Afghanistan against Mujahideen fighters. The Security Council and the General Assembly passed resolutions calling for the withdrawal of Soviet forces. The USSR vetoed the resolutions and kept its troops in. The Soviet–Afghan war lasted until 1989.

1980–88 — Iran–Iraq

A territorial dispute led to an Iraqi invasion of Iran in 1980. The UN passed a resolution for a ceasefire but both sides ignored it. Iran was defeated in an eight-year war and the UN went in to supervise the ceasefire.

1989 — Namibia

Namibia was a UN Trust Territory and was initially governed by South Africa but when South Africa sent troops in to annex the territory the UN removed its trusteeship. South Africa ignored the UN and kept troops in Namibia. It attempted to extend its policies of apartheid there from 1964. The UN tried to pressure South Africa into leaving Namibia and supported Namibian armed resistance. The UN finally persuaded South Africa to agree to UN supervised elections in 1988, which would lead to Namibia's independence. However, UN supervisors could not stop South African troops fighting Namibian forces, which delayed its independence until 1990.

ACTIVITY: Comparing UN actions

1 Consider at least three case studies of countries where the UN has got involved with an event. Try to choose different regions around the world, referring to the world map of interventions on pages 212–15. In groups, research the events and **identify** similarities and differences between the reasons for UN intervention and the impact of the intervention on events. **Discuss** whether the UN was successful in maintaining peace and the possible reasons for its successful or unsuccessful interventions.

2 Now read the more detailed information on the three case studies below. In pairs, **discuss** what conclusions can be drawn regarding why the UN failed to prevent these conflicts.

■ ATL

■ Collaboration skills – Listen actively to other perspectives and ideas

◆ Assessment opportunities

◆ In this activity you have practised skills that are assessed using Criterion C: Communicating and Criterion D: Thinking critically.

Case study: Korea, 1950–53

■ **Figure 9.23** Korea and the 38th parallel

Korea had been left temporarily divided at the end of the Second World War along the 38th parallel. The 38th parallel is a circle of latitude in the northern hemisphere, used as the pre-Korean War boundary between North Korea and South Korea. The North had been occupied by the USSR and the South by the USA. Both sides had agreed to withdraw their forces and allow free elections to decide the future government of a united Korea. However, two separate governments developed: a pro-Soviet communist government in the North and a pro-American government in the South.

On 25 June 1950, the North Koreans invaded the South in an attempt to unify the country under their regime. The UN had to act. The Security Council had to have a majority of seven 'yes' votes in order to act, and this had to include *all* permanent members. Any one of the permanent members could veto a decision. The USSR would clearly vote 'no' to any action against its ally, the North Koreans.

However, the USSR was boycotting the UN Security Council as the member states had refused to recognize the newly established communist government in China under Mao Zedong.

When the Security Council met, the USA was able to push through a resolution condemning the North Koreans for breaking the peace and demanding a withdrawal of their forces. The North Koreans ignored this and continued their offensive into the South. The UN then resolved, again without the USSR, to send troops to Korea. The war brought horrific losses to both sides in Korea and involved a much longer and harder war for the USA under the UN flag than it had anticipated. In the end, a ceasefire was signed in 1953. Korea was again divided at the 38th parallel. The UN gained some credit for its swift response, but also was quickly undermined. The USSR returned to the Security Council and vetoed further decisions in Korea. To get around this, the USA put forward a resolution 'Uniting for Peace' which would put the decisions to the General Assembly when agreement could not be found in the Security Council. The USSR did not agree that this move was legal. The UN had shown itself to be dominated by the USA, at least for the time being.

Case study: Arab–Israeli War, 1967

During the Suez Crisis (see Figure 9.21), UN troops were stationed in the Sinai desert, thus providing a buffer between Egypt and Israel.

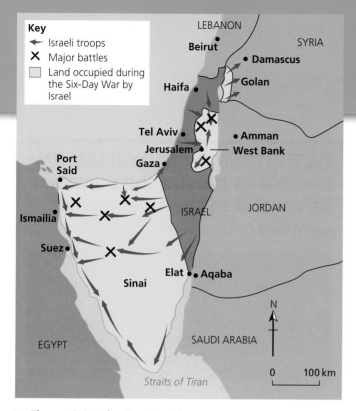

Figure 9.24 The Six-Day War

President Nasser (the second president of Egypt) requested that UN peacekeepers leave in 1967. Nasser then announced that he would blockade the Straits of Tiran, which were essential to Israeli shipping.

The Israelis took these moves as signs that the Arab states were preparing for a war. Israel attacked Egypt and its Arab supporters and were able to defeat the armies of the Arab states in just six days. The war has become known as the 'Six-Day War'. The UN ordered a ceasefire and drew up Resolution 242 to restore peace to the region.

The Arab states, except Syria, and Israel signed the resolution. However, neither side kept to the agreement. The Arab states were only interested in the withdrawal of Israeli forces and Israel refused to comply until the Arabs had met the other points on the resolution.

Resolution 242

This resolution set down:

1 the withdrawal of all Israeli forces from occupied Arab land
2 the right of states in the area to peace
3 secure boundaries between each state
4 free navigation of international waters
5 a solution to the Palestinian refugee issue.

Case study: Congo, 1960

The Congo became independent from Belgium in 1960. There were still 100 000 Belgians in the Congo and many had positions of influence. Soon after independence, there was a mutiny in the army in the capital, Léopoldville, against the white officers. The mutiny developed into widespread attacks against Europeans in the Congo. The new government was undermined by the mutiny and it also terrified the Belgians, who sent paratroopers to protect their community. The Belgian troops were 'illegally' in the Congo as they had not been invited in by the new government. The mineral-rich province of Katanga declared itself an independent state. The prime minister of Congo, Patrice Lumumba, appealed to the UN as chaos spread in his country. The UN created a UN army to restore the peace and sent 10 000 troops.

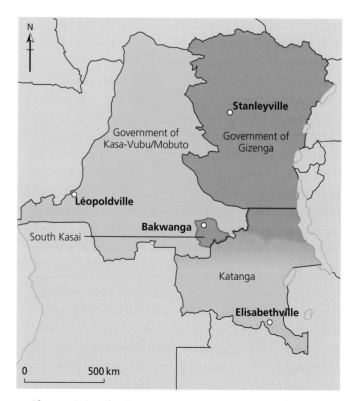

Figure 9.25 The Congo Crisis, 1961, showing the division of the country

The UN force was tasked with restoring order to prevent other countries interfering, to assist building the economy and to restore political stability. But it could only take military action in 'self-defence' and it could not help one side more than the other. Lumumba claimed that the UN force was helping Katanga as it would not attack the separatist state to force it to rejoin Congo.

Lumumba then asked the USSR for help and received arms to attack Katanga. This attack failed and Lumumba was dismissed. Lumumba then set up a rival government in Stanleyville, before he was murdered in January 1961. The Congo divided into four separate groups: Lumumba's supporters in Stanleyville, a military government in Léopoldville, the Katangan government in Elisabethville and another government in Kasai province. The Stanleyville and Kasai groups had arms from the USSR. Katanga was backed by the Belgians. The UN authorized its troops to use force to prevent a civil war. An agreement was reached by three of the four groups and a **coalition** government was formed in August 1961 under Cyrille Adoula.

With UN help, Adoula focused on crushing the breakaway Katanga province. It was not until January 1963 that the Congo was finally united. The UN had achieved some of its key aims: it had removed the Belgian influence from the Congo, it had stopped the USSR from getting directly involved in the civil war and it had unified the Congo. UN organizations had been involved in supporting the economy and health care during the conflict and had prevented famines and epidemics.

ACTIVITY: How far will the UN be able to pursue the aims in its charter in the twenty-first century?

ATL

- Critical-thinking skills – Evaluate evidence and arguments
- Communication skills – Use a variety of speaking techniques to communicate with a variety of audiences

The key problems that the UN faced by the end of the twentieth century remain key issues for the organization today – the state of the world's economy, poverty, the inequality between the wealthy north and the poor south and developing nations' foreign debt. The UN itself has funding problems and huge debts and it has faced criticism that its agencies are 'politicized' and acting to influence the political nature of countries it is supposed to support.

Research news articles from the last few years on the UN. Use these articles and the information in this chapter to set up a class debate:

'The UN has no future as a peacekeeping and peacemaking supra-national organization.'

Divide into two teams. One side will argue for the motion and one will argue against the motion

You should follow a formal debating style.

Use the search terms **formal debating style** to find out how you should conduct your debate.

However, this had been costly for the UN. A sum of $400 million dollars was spent on the Congo at this time – and the USSR, France and Belgium disagreed with the UN action and refused to help fund it. This almost led the UN to bankruptcy and the mission had to be called off early. The UN was also criticized for 'shedding blood in the name of peace' and for not preventing the murder of Lumumba.

ACTIVITY: Evaluating the effectiveness of supra-national organizations in maintaining peace

1 Outline the origin, purpose, values and limitations for Sources J and K (page 220) in a table. Use the table on page 9 as a guide. You should not spend more than 30 minutes on this.

2 **Using** Sources H–L and your own knowledge, **analyse** how effective supra-national organizations have been in maintaining peace. You should not spend more than 1 hour on this.

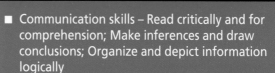

■ **ATL**

■ Communication skills – Read critically and for comprehension; Make inferences and draw conclusions; Organize and depict information logically

◆ Assessment opportunities

◆ This activity can be assessed using Criterion A: Knowing and understanding, Criterion C: Communicating and Criterion D: Thinking critically.

SOURCE H

'The Russians, remembering their difficulties in the League of Nations, which culminated in their expulsion, were worried that they would find themselves isolated in a new international organisation controlled by the United States and the United Kingdom through their Allies, clients, dominions and 'Good Neighbours.' The Russians accepted an American compromise, whereby the Great Powers retained a veto in the Security Council, and the Western leaders agreed to support the admission of two or three constituent Soviet Republics.'

Yergin, D. 1978. The Shattered Peace. *Houghton Mifflin.*

SOURCE I

'Many writers point to the immense growth of links between nations. They see a line of continuing development … from the League of Nations to the UN today. Parallel with these go a growth in other organisations which lock states into communities greater than themselves. Each involves some loss of sovereignty, some willingness to act with others. Eventually, the idealists believe, a 'supranational' power, one above individual states, will emerge. This development may be spurred on by factors like nuclear weaponry, or the information revolution. The resulting supranational authority may be a reconstructed United Nations, or perhaps a UN properly used by its members. Ultimately, the latter will be forced to surrender their sovereignty to the vital need to keep the peace and regulate our use of the planet.'

Gibbons, S.R. 1992. International Co-operation. *UK. Longman Group.*

THE FLOWER.

Figure 9.26 Cartoon by David Low

Appeared in The Star, *a British Newspaper, 11 November 1919*

SOURCE K

Speech by Maxim Litvinov, Soviet Foreign Affairs Minister, to the League of Nations at Geneva, 1934

'[the aggressor states] are now still weaker than a possible bloc of peace-loving states, but the policy of non-resistance to evil and bartering with aggressors, which the opponents of sanctions propose to us, can have no other result than further strengthening and increasing the forces of aggression ... And the moment might really arrive when their power has grown to such an extent that the League of Nations ... will be in no condition to cope with them ... the programme envisioned in the Covenant of the League must be carried out against the aggressor ...'

Quoted in Matel, G. 1999. The Origins of the Second World War Reconsidered. *Routledge.*

SOURCE L

'The lack of a permanent UN army ... means that it is difficult to prevail upon powerful states to accept its decisions if they choose to put self-interest first. If persuasion of world opinion fails, the UN has to rely on member nations to provide troops to enable it to enforce decisions ... UN involvement in Somalia (1992–5) and Bosnia (1992–5) showed the impossibility of the UN being able to stop a war when the warring parties were not ready to stop fighting.'

Lowe, N. 2005. Mastering Modern World History. *UK. Palgrave.*

Why did the USA and the USSR become superpowers after the Second World War?

The term **superpower** is specifically used to describe the USA and the USSR after 1945. They were considered superpowers as they dominated international relations and created bi-polar divisions around the world. Indeed, they were not just great powers in the traditional sense but also had economic, political and military superiority over most other countries.

Each superpower used its strengths to create 'spheres of influence'. Unlike nineteenth-century European empires, the superpowers did not directly run the nations in their spheres of influence but could exert economic, political and military pressure on states to adhere to their policies.

There were several reasons for the emergence of the superpowers:

MILITARY REASONS

The USA and the USSR had created powerful armed forces to defeat Nazi Germany and Japan in the Second World War. The USA emerged in 1945 with the biggest air force in the world and had nuclear weapons. The USSR had the largest land-force power in the world and lacked any strong military neighbours. The old military powers of Britain, France and Germany were no longer strong military nations.

ECONOMIC REASONS

The USA's economy had been strengthened by the Second World War; for example, its agricultural output had increased by 30 per cent and its industrial output by 60 per cent during the war. The USSR's economy was badly damaged and so too were those of the other European economies. Agricultural land was left to waste, while industry, the transport links and housing had been bombed and destroyed. The USA could out-produce all other countries put together. It wanted to promote free trade and to secure markets and resources for its economy. It wanted to avoid another devastating global economic slump like the Great Depression in the 1930s. The USA had the economic strength to prevent instability in Europe and could help pay for Western Europe's post-war reconstruction. The USSR was able to influence the economies of Eastern Europe, as these states were not able to be economically independent at the end of the war.

IDEOLOGICAL REASONS

For the USA and much of the West, the Second World War had been a victory for their ideology – liberal capitalist democracy – and they believed the political system of the USA was the right path for other nations. For the USSR, the outcome of the war had been a victory for communism over fascism and it believed its system was the right one for the post-war world. Both ideologies had gained credibility during the war for defeating fascism. The USSR's extraordinary human costs – 27 million Soviet soldiers and citizens died in the war – strengthened its claim to have influence over how Europe was to be reconstructed. Communism could fill the political vacuum in the East and American-style liberal democracy the political instability in the West.

The USSR and the USA had conflicting ideologies (see Table 9.1).

■ **Table 9.1** Ideologies of the USSR and the USA

	Communism	Capitalism
Political	A one-party state. Only the communist party is allowed. Individual rights, such as freedom of speech, are not as important as the success of the state.	Multi-party state. Voters choose their government in free elections. Rights of the individual are important.
Economic	All industry, banking, communications, businesses and agriculture are owned by the state. There is no private property. People work for the good of society not for individual profit. The state distributes wealth – 'according to need'.	All industry, agriculture, business and communications are privately owned. Private property is encouraged and people work for individual profit. There is limited redistribution of wealth by the state.

Why did the superpowers develop spheres of influence?

The USSR believed that the capitalist West wanted to destroy communism and the West believed that communism wanted to destroy capitalism. The communists followed a Marxist doctrine that promoted the workers of the world rising up to liberate themselves from capitalist exploitation. The West feared that communists would damage their trade and capital and could potentially threaten the whole political and economic system in the West. The West also accused the communists of ignoring basic human rights and oppressing their people.

During the Second World War, the USSR and the USA had joined together in an alliance to fight the fascist dictatorships in Europe and the militarist government in Japan. At the end of the war, this alliance broke down and developed into a protracted Cold War; this meant the hostility between the superpowers led to confrontations and competition but stopped short of an all-out war.

Both superpowers developed spheres of influence. Initially these were created in Europe. However, by the 1950s, superpower competition had globalized. The Soviets created a sort of 'empire' in Eastern Europe between 1945 and 1949. They began by keeping the Red Army in occupation after the war, and then slowly removing political opposition until they could place reliable pro-Soviet governments in each country. Through the use of intimidation and force, the USSR had created communist governments in Poland, Hungary, Romania, Bulgaria, Albania, Czechoslovakia and East Germany by 1949. The former British prime minister Winston Churchill had given a warning to the world about what was happening in Soviet-dominated Eastern Europe in a speech given in the USA in February 1946 – he claimed that an 'Iron Curtain' had descended across Europe.

■ **Figure 9.27** Churchill delivering his famous Iron Curtain speech, 1946

ACTIVITY: Churchill's Iron Curtain speech

■ ATL

■ Critical-thinking skills – Evaluate evidence and arguments

Watch this video clip:

http://youtu.be/S2PUIQpAEAQ

In pairs, **discuss** the key points made by Churchill in this speech. How do you think the USSR might have reacted to this speech?

Why did the superpower confrontation go global?

Although the origins of the superpower confrontation grew out of developments in Europe, by 1950 the Cold War had globalized. This was due to a number of factors. First, the USSR had developed its own nuclear weapon by September 1949, and this alarmed the USA, which could not match the USSR in conventional forces at this time. In addition, China's civil war was won by Mao Zedong's Chinese communist party. This meant that the most populous nation on earth had become a Soviet ally. The USA was devastated by the loss of 'their China' and feared the opening of a second front in the Cold War – what was termed the 'bamboo curtain'. When North Korea invaded South Korea in June 1950, the USA believed it had to act to stop the spread of communism (see page 216) in Asia.

The superpowers would engage in confrontations around the globe until the fall of communism in 1989–91. Their ideologies and self-interest would draw them into conflicts in Asia, Africa and the Americas as each superpower attempted to contain the influence of the other or to extend their spheres of influence in other regions.

ⓘ Perspectives

Some historians, such as Arthur Schlesinger, argued that the superpower confrontation was caused by Soviet ideology and that the USSR had created a 'satellite' empire in Eastern Europe with the use of its military force. Other historians, such as William Appleman Williams, suggested that the 'spheres of influence' had been created primarily by the pursuit of 'dollar imperialism' by the USA. It could also be argued that the superpowers had acted 'defensively' in the creation of spheres of influence and both sides had acted out of fear of the other rather than aggression or expansionism.

ACTIVITY: The superpowers – protecting and expanding their spheres of influence

■ ATL

- Information literacy skills – Access information to be informed and inform others
- Communication skills – Organize and depict information logically; Make inferences and draw conclusions

What is your goal?

To prepare a report to the United Nations on superpower involvement in a particular conflict

How will you achieve this?

Investigate one of the following events:
- **Cuban Missile Crisis, 1962**
- **Vietnam War, 1964–73**
- **Angolan Civil War, 1975–89**
- **Soviet–Afghan War, 1979–89**

Then prepare a speech that includes:
- **the specific involvement of the superpowers**
- **an assessment of whether the war/crisis led to a superpower protecting or expanding their sphere of influence**
- **an analysis of the impact of the war/crisis on the region affected**
- **an analysis of the impact of the involvement on relations between the superpowers.**

You must prepare sufficient cited information and explanations to speak for five to ten minutes.

You will present your speech to the United Nations (the rest of the class).

> Hint
>
> Remember to document your sources correctly as you research one of the crises/conflicts. You will need to submit a full works cited list with your speech to the United Nations.

◆ Assessment opportunities

- ◆ This activity can be assessed using Criterion B: Investigating and Criterion C: Communicating.

CHINA

A final comment on the superpowers should include a consideration of the role played by the People's Republic of China (PRC). Mao Zedong won a civil war in China in 1949. At first the USA believed that Mao was a 'puppet' of the USSR but within a decade relations between the two communist states had soured. By the 1960s China had its own atomic weapons and was following its 'own path' to communism. Hostility between the USSR and the PRC meant that there was a border war between the two countries in 1969. China emerged as a third superpower and this added some fluidity into what had been a bi-polar global confrontation between the USA and USSR.

According to historian Jonathan Pollack, in his book *China and the Global Strategic Balance* (1984):

> 'China has often defied the demands of both superpowers. At other times it has behaved differently from what others expect. Despite its seeming vulnerability, China has not yielded to either Moscow or Washington. China has assumed a unique international position as a participator in many of the central political and military conflicts in the post war era. Indeed China must be judged as a candidate superpower in its own right. China represents a force too important to be regarded as an ally of either Moscow or Washington or simply as an intermediate power.'

ACTIVITY: Comparing nineteenth- and twentieth-century empires

■ ATL

■ Transfer skills – Inquire in different contexts to gain a different perspective

Go back to pages 192–94 and review the reasons for the expansion of empire in the nineteenth century.

In pairs, consider the similarities and differences between the European empires at the end of the nineteenth century and the superpower spheres of influence at the end of the twentieth century. Complete a table like this:

Motive for gaining influence or control	Similarities	Differences
Economic		
Ideology		
Strategic		
Technology		

◆ Assessment opportunities

◆ In this activity you have practised skills that are assessed using Criterion A: Knowing and understanding and Criterion D: Thinking critically.

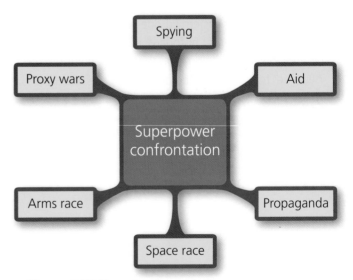

■ **Figure 9.28** The ways in which the superpowers developed their spheres of influence and confronted each other

Why did alliance systems develop after the Second World War?

Two significant military alliances developed after the end of the Second World War. The North Atlantic Treaty Organization (NATO) was set up in 1949 and an opposing alliance bloc, the Warsaw Pact, was formed in 1955. These alliances divided Europe into two armed camps.

NATO

NATO was formed after a confrontation between the superpowers over Berlin in Germany. The city had been temporarily divided by Allied agreement in 1945 into different sectors that mirrored the division into sectors of Germany itself. As no agreement could be found between the USA and USSR regarding the political and economic future of an unoccupied and united Germany, the superpowers divided Germany into two separate states – a 'westernized' West Germany and a 'sovietized' East Germany. However, the rationale for the West to be in Berlin had been that Germany would eventually be united and the West therefore needed a presence in its 'capital' city even though this was in the heart of the Soviet East Germany. The Soviets attempted to force the USA out of Berlin by blockading all access routes, rail and road, from West Germany into Berlin. The USA then embarked on a huge airlift to transport supplies to millions of West Berliners from the air. In the end, the USSR gave in and lifted the blockade.

During the Berlin Crisis of 1948–49, there had been a real fear that this could trigger a third world war. The USA decided that it needed a strong military presence in Europe to deter any further 'expansion' of Soviet influence. The US policy was to 'contain' communism in the east. On 4 April 1949, the North Atlantic Treaty was signed in Washington. Originally, NATO had 12 member states: Britain, France, Belgium, Holland, Luxembourg, Portugal, Denmark, Ireland, Italy, Norway, Canada and the USA. Greece and Turkey joined NATO three years later and West Germany joined in 1955.

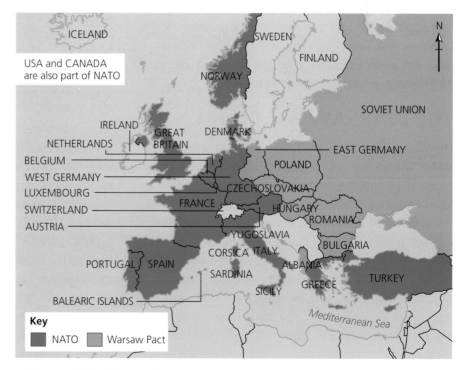

■ **Figure 9.29** Alliances in Europe

By far the strongest member of NATO was the USA. Member states agreed that an attack on any one of them would be viewed as an attack on all NATO members. The member states also had to put their defence forces under a joint NATO command, which would co-ordinate the defence of the West. This alliance meant that the USA had a permanent and direct role in Europe and for the first time had agreed to go to war in defence of another nation. Up until the end of the Cold War, after 1989, the USA stationed 350 000 troops in European bases. This fundamental shift in US foreign policy was due to the perceived threat posed by the USSR. NATO was to protect the US sphere of influence in Western Europe from Soviet aggression. NATO's European members had wanted the alliance and military commitment from the USA. The USA could back up NATO with their air power and nuclear weapons systems. The Americans later formed an alliance with pro-Western Asian states – the Southeast Asia Treaty Organization (SEATO) – in February 1955. This alliance similarly committed member states to the joint defence of a state that was attacked.

THE WARSAW PACT

The Warsaw Pact alliance was formed a few years after NATO. The Berlin Blockade also had a significant impact on the USSR and its satellite states in Eastern Europe. Stalin's attempt to push the West out of Berlin had failed. The wartime agreement that Germany would be united was not going to happen. Therefore, both sides created their 'own' German state. The USA blamed the Soviets for the breakdown by not allowing free elections in the East, whereas the USSR blamed the USA for creating a separate economy in West Germany. The Soviet response to NATO was delayed, as the USSR attempted to persuade the West

to disband their military alliance. The greatest fear for the USSR was a rearmed Germany. When West Germany was admitted to NATO in 1955, the Soviet fear became a reality.

In response, on 14 May 1955, the Warsaw Pact was signed. All the communist countries in Eastern Europe signed the treaty, which formed a military alliance, although it was officially called the 'Treaty of Friendship, Cooperation and Mutual Assistance'. Warsaw Pact nations agreed to come to each other's defence if a member state was attacked by the West. Communist China also joined the alliance. The strongest military power in the alliance was again the superpower – the USSR. The USSR had the largest conventional ground force in the world and, from September 1949, it also had nuclear weapons. Soviet tanks, aircraft and guns were used throughout the Warsaw Pact countries. The military command of the Warsaw Pact was directed by Moscow. Unlike NATO, with most of its forces made up of professionals, most of the Warsaw Pact forces were made up of male and female conscripts. This may have undermined its capability compared to NATO. However, the strength of each alliance bloc was never tested, as NATO and the Warsaw Pact never went to war against each other.

WHAT WAS THE IMPACT OF THE SUPERPOWER ALLIANCE SYSTEMS?

Tension remained high throughout the Cold War between the two alliance blocs – each fearing an attack from the other side. NATO believed that the USSR's conventional forces were technologically inferior by the 1980s and this could mean, in the event of a conflict, the USSR would resort to the use of nuclear weapons. Analysts in Britain believed that if a conventional war broke out in Europe in the 1980s it would take less than a week for it to develop into a nuclear war. In 1984, a report by the Royal Swedish Academy of Sciences estimated that if the Warsaw Pact launched a 'limited' nuclear attack on NATO bases in Germany around 10 million West Germans would be killed.

The two alliance blocks subsequently engaged in a nuclear arms race, which by the 1960s could destroy the world. Today, over 80 per cent of the world's nuclear weapons are held by the USA and the Russian Federation. Trillions of dollars were spent on weapons that would become obsolete within a decade and have to be disposed of at a great cost to the environment. Initially, the USA provided the nuclear capability for NATO but Britain and France later developed their own nuclear weapons. There was some discontent at putting forces effectively under US command and the French withdrew its forces from NATO's command in 1959 – but remained a member of the alliance. NATO based a large land and air force in West Germany to respond to any Soviet aggression from Eastern Europe. The military build-up by both alliance blocs could be seen in the deployment of US Cruise and Pershing II missiles to Western Europe. The Soviets responded with deployments of SS-20 missiles in Eastern Europe.

After the communist regimes in Eastern Europe and then the USSR itself collapsed between 1989 and 1991, the Warsaw Pact was disbanded in July 1991, whereas NATO actually increased in size after the end of the Cold War.

ACTIVITY: Source evaluation

ATL

- Critical-thinking skills – Evaluate evidence and arguments

1 **What key points does Einstein make in Source N about the arms race that developed between the superpowers?**
2 **Look at Source M. Why might supra-national alliances foster militarism?**

◆ Assessment opportunities

- ◆ In this activity you have practised skills that are assessed using Criterion D: Thinking critically.

SOURCE M

The superpower military arms race in Europe

1983	NATO	Warsaw Pact
Ground troops	2 000 000	1 700 000
Divisions	90	85
Tanks	21 000	25 500
Submarines	182	190
Anti-submarines	385	183
Capital ships	314	206
Other naval craft	821	607
Fighter planes	4 338	8 512
Anti-aircraft/ surface-to-air missiles	6 869	6 737

SOURCE N

Extract from a speech by physicist and philosopher Albert Einstein in 1950

'The armament race between the USA and the USSR, originally supposed to be a preventative measure, assumes hysterical character. On both sides, the means to mass destruction are perfected with feverish haste, behind respective walls of secrecy. The H-bomb appears on the public horizon as a probably attainable goal … If successful, radio-active poisoning of the atmosphere and hence annihilation of any life on earth has been brought within the range of technical possibilities. The ghost-like character of this development lies in its apparently compulsory trend. Every step appears as the unavoidable consequence of the preceding one. In the end, there beckons more and more clearly general annihilation.'

THINK–PAIR–SHARE

Why do you think nations form alliances? Make a list of reasons and support your ideas with evidence from this chapter. Then share your ideas with a partner. Finally, **discuss** this question as a class.

The alliances that developed after 1945, led by the superpowers, did not lead to a third world war. Why was this? Compare and contrast the alliance systems in Europe before the First World War with the post-1945 alliances.

ACTIVITY: Concluding questions

ATL

- Critical-thinking skills – Make connections between various sources of information

Draw together the notes, sources and information in this chapter and from your own research activities to answer the following questions:

1 **Do you agree that imperialism can bring benefits to the colonized?**
2 **Evaluate the extent to which supra-national alliances and organizations are forces for peace and stability in the world.**

You should write a detailed summary of the key evidence and themes for each question. Address the command term, e.g. 'Evaluate', which means you must include evidence that suggests the strengths and then the limitations of supra-national organizations as forces of peace and stability in the world. You should write between 700 and 900 words for each question.

◆ Assessment opportunities

- In this activity you have practised skills that are assessed using Criterion A: Knowing and understanding and Criterion D: Thinking critically.

▼ Links to: Sciences

Discuss whether scientists should be involved in advising governments and international organizations. Should they determine how their discoveries and inventions are used?

You could also consider the impact of scientific knowledge and progress, for example development of knowledge and understanding of atoms and atomic structure, which then led to the development of the first atomic weapons of mass destruction.

How does scientific progress impact on the power and influence of nation states and, more widely, in terms of global stability, international relations and peace?

ACTIVITY: Do supra-national alliances make the world a safer place?

ATL

- Information literacy skills – Access information to be informed and to inform others
- Media literacy skills – Seek a range of perspectives from multiple and varied sources

Using the knowledge you have gained from this chapter to guide you, find a range of sources that address the following statements:

- **Supra-national alliances make the world a safer place.**
- **Supra-national alliances make the world a more dangerous place.**

◆ Assessment opportunities

- This activity can be assessed using Criterion B: Investigating.

! Take action

- ! Does your school participate in the Model United Nations (MUN)? The MUN is an excellent way to deepen your understanding of how the UN works and the role played by world leaders in maintaining peace and global security. You could set up a Model United Nations group in your school if there is not one to join. You can find out more about MUN, which has participating schools in every region, online.

- ! Alternatively, go to **www.un.org/en/aboutun/structure/**. Look through the subsidiary bodies, programmes and funds and find out more about an area that interests you, for example the United Nations Children's Fund (UNICEF) or the Committee on the Peaceful Uses of Outer Space (COPUOS).

- ! Share the information you find with your class and suggest ways in which you, your class and/or your school could get involved in raising the profile of the UN's aims and support its work.

Reflection

In this chapter, we have studied the reasons nations create empires and the role played by economic interests and ideology in their development. We have found out about different supra-national alliances and why they are formed as systems to protect national interests. We have also inquired into the work and actions of supra-national organizations and compared and contrasted the strengths and weaknesses of these organizations.

Reflecting on our learning…					
Use this table to reflect on your own learning in this chapter.					
Questions we asked	Answers we found	Any further questions now?			
Factual					
Conceptual					
Debatable					
Approaches to learning you used in this chapter:	Description – what new skills did you learn?	How well did you master the skills?			
		Novice	Learner	Practitioner	Expert
Collaboration skills					
Communication skills					
Creative-thinking skills					
Critical-thinking skills					
Information literacy skills					
Media literacy skills					
Organization skills					
Transfer skills					
Learner profile attribute	Reflect on the importance of being knowledgeable for our learning in this chapter.				
Knowledgeable					

10 Why have nationalist movements been successful?

○ In certain *environments* a sense of national *identity* within and between *communities* fosters successful independence movements.

CONSIDER THESE QUESTIONS:

Factual: What were the factors that led to the development of nationalist movements in India and in Kenya? What factors allowed these movements to achieve their aims?

Conceptual: How does a sense of national independence develop?

Debatable: Was nationalism the key reason for decolonization or were economic factors more important? Is nationalism a force for good in the world?

Now **share and compare** your thoughts and ideas with your partner, or with the whole class.

KEY WORDS

boycott	nationalism
independence	terrorism

○ IN THIS CHAPTER, WE WILL ...

■ **Find out** about:
  ■ the forces for independence that developed in India and Kenya
  ■ the actions and strategies used by individuals and groups in their attempts to get independence.
■ **Explore** the impact of these actions.
■ **Take action** by looking at forces of nationalism that exist today.

● We will reflect on this learner profile attribute ...

● Inquirer – developing skills for inquiry and research.

◆ Assessment opportunities in this chapter:

◆ **Criterion A:** Knowing and understanding
◆ **Criterion B:** Investigating
◆ **Criterion C:** Communicating
◆ **Criterion D:** Thinking critically

■ These Approaches to Learning (ATL) skills will be useful ...

■ Critical-thinking skills
■ Communication skills

THINK–PAIR–SHARE

Consider what Gandhi is trying to say in each of these quotes about nationalism. Can you give examples from history or from events today that would provide evidence to support these views?

Below are quotes from Mohandas Gandhi, who was the man most responsible for leading the Indian nationalist challenge to the British after the First World War. He came to be known as 'Mahatma', meaning 'great soul'.

'No people exists that would not think itself happier under its own bad government than it might really be under the good government of an alien [foreign] power.'

'If every component part of the nation claims the right of self-determination for itself, there is no one nation and there is no independence.'

'It is impossible for one to be internationalist without being a nationalist. Internationalism is possible only when nationalism becomes a fact, i.e., when peoples belonging to different countries have organized themselves and are able to act as one man. It is not nationalism that is evil, it is the narrowness, selfishness, exclusiveness which is the bane of modern nations which is evil. Each wants to profit at the expense of, and rise on the ruin of, the other.'

■ **Figure 10.1** Mohandas 'Mahatma' Gandhi

Nationalist movements in the British Empire

THINK–PAIR–SHARE

The basis of nationalism is the concept of national identity, which can be defined as:

*'a person's **identity** and sense of belonging to one state or to one nation, a feeling one shares with a group of people, regardless of one's citizenship status'*

en.wikipedia.org/wiki/National_identity

Consider how far you consider yourself to have a strong sense of national identity. Then share your thoughts with a partner. Finally, as a class, consider how important national identity is to you as a group. Do some nationalities have a stronger national identity than others? If so, why do you think that is?

As you have read in Chapter 9, Britain had gained a large empire by the start of the twentieth century. In many colonies, the nature of British rule encouraged the growth of nationalist movements that sought to challenge Britain and take over countries for themselves. The First and Second World Wars helped to hasten the decline of British power and this encouraged these nationalist movements further.

This chapter will examine the role of two nationalist movements in two countries seeking to gain independence from Britain. India was the first colony to gain independence from Britain, and the role of national identity, the nationalist movement and strong nationalist leaders was key to its decolonization by 1947. In Kenya, the nationalist movement took a very different form, and the repercussions of the violence that took place as a result are still being felt today.

■ **Figure 10.2** An artist's impression of the Amritsar 1919 Massacre

What factors led to India gaining independence in 1947?

India was the 'Jewel in the Crown' for the British Empire due to the important economic and strategic benefits that it brought Britain. It was ruled by the British Viceroy, and Indians had little say in how their country was governed. However, at the end of the nineteenth century, two organizations were created that were to play an important part in the struggle for self-rule. In 1885, the Indian National Congress was created. This organization, led by educated and influential Hindus, campaigned for increased participation in the government of their country. In 1906, the Muslim League was created to safeguard Muslim interests.

In 1909, with growing pressure for reform, the Viceroy, Lord Minto, and the Secretary of State for India, Lord Morley, introduced changes which allowed more Indians to be involved in government. They hoped that this would prevent more violent resistance to British rule. During the First World War, the Secretary of State for India in 1917, Edwin Montague, promised further involvement of Indians in the government. Indeed there was hope by many that the help that Indians had given to Britain during the war would be rewarded by increased independence. However, two events after the war dashed this hope:

1 The Rowlatt Act

During the First World War, the rights of citizens such as freedom of speech and the right to hold protest meetings were temporarily suspended in India. Indians accepted this during wartime; however, in 1919, the British passed the Rowlatt Act, which allowed them to keep the same situation in peacetime. Congress immediately led a campaign against the measures put in place by the Rowlatt Act.

2 The Amritsar Massacre

In the north-western city of Amritsar the protests turned violent and General Dyer, the army commander, ordered a ban on public meetings. However, on Sunday 13 April, a large, unarmed crowd gathered in an area known as the Jallianwala Bagh. General Dyer marched his soldiers to the meeting, which was peaceful and made up of men, women and children. Despite this, Dyer lined up his men on a bank overlooking the area and ordered them to fire. This account by Churchill, who was then Secretary for War and thus in charge of the army, explains what happened next:

> 'When fire had been opened upon the crowd to disperse it, it tried to run away. Pinned up in a narrow place with hardly any exits, and packed together so that one bullet would drive through three or four bodies, the people ran madly this way and the other. When the fire was directed upon the centre, they ran to the sides. The fire was then directed to the sides. Many threw themselves down on the ground, then the fire was directed down on the ground. This was continued for eight to ten minutes, and it stopped only when the ammunition had reached the point of exhaustion. Finally, after 379 persons had been killed and when most certainly 1200 or more had been wounded, the troops, at whom not even a stone had been thrown, swung round and marched away.'

Following the massacre, Dyer set up a series of punishments for the Indians. These included the 'Crawling Order'. This involved Indians wishing to use a particular street, being forced to crawl on their hands and knees as a mark of respect to the British.

At the official inquiry into the massacre, Dyer stated that:

> 'My idea … was to make a wide impression throughout the Punjab. It was a merciful act, though a horrible act, and they ought to be thankful to me for doing it.'

GANDHI AND NON-COOPERATION

The Amritsar Massacre was a turning point for one Indian, Mahatma Gandhi. He declared the British Government as evil, saying:

> 'The British government today represents Satanism. When a British government takes up arms against its unarmed subjects then it has forfeited the right to govern.'

Ghandi had already shown his attitude to prejudice and oppression when, before the First World War, he had worked as a barrister in South Africa. Here he used non-violent protest against the South African regime.

For Gandhi, self-rule meant two things:

1 Self-government for India
2 Self-control for each individual

He believed that the second of these would help achieve the first. He believed that individuals should learn to control their passions and live simple lives; this would help them to develop 'soul-force' or *satyagraha*. He believed that the British would be defeated by satyagraha rather than by violence and so he advocated a campaign of non-cooperation.

■ **Figure 10.3** Gandhi and his spinning wheel or charkha; Gandhi would often spin in public to promote his campaign of non-cooperation

■ **Figure 10.4** Gandhi and his followers on the salt march, 1930

Non-cooperation took many forms:

- Many Indians renounced titles and honours.
- Lawyers refused to work for the British.
- Students boycotted schools and universities established by the British.
- People refused to buy British cloth; Gandhi encouraged men (as opposed to just women, who were the traditional spinners) to make their own cloth at home and wear clothing made from this homespun cloth. This cloth was called khaddar or khadi which means 'rough'.
- People refused to pay taxes.

In spite of Gandhi's wishes, violence broke out in several places. Gandhi was appalled. He went on a five-day fast and

called off the campaign. However, Gandhi was arrested and charged with sedition (encouraging other people to disobey the law). He was sentenced to six years in prison, though he was released after 22 months.

On his release, Gandhi worked hard in the Indian National Congress to get the different groups to work together – in particular Hindus and Muslims. This unity would make it harder for the British to resist Indians' demands. In Congress, which was led by the President, Jawaharlal Nehru, Gandhi brought about a vote to declare immediate self-rule for India, regardless of British actions. Congress passed the motion and Nehru unfurled the Indian tricolour flag for the first time.

Gandhi started a campaign of non-violent, yet active, civil disobedience. He marched with thousands of followers 400 kilometres to the coast, where he picked up salt on the seashore. This challenged the hugely unpopular British law that taxed salt and forbade Indians to avoid this tax by making their own salt.

Although the British did not initially see this action as a threat, its symbolism, which so clearly showed India's dependence on Britain, captured the imagination of millions and received massive publicity.

Gandhi, along with 100 000 other Indians, was arrested and put in jail.

WHAT WAS THE RESPONSE OF THE BRITISH TO CIVIL DISOBEDIENCE?

The civil disobedience campaign had a significant impact; many people in both Britain and India began to realize that Britain could not hold India by force. There was also concern about Britain's use of force in retaliation for non-violent protest, which harmed Britain's international image. As a result, Gandhi was released from prison and invited to attend a series of meetings with the Viceroy. He was then invited to attend a conference in 1931 in London (see the information box 'Gandhi in Britain').

In 1935, the British Parliament passed the Government of India Act. This handed over the government of the 11 provinces of British India to Indian ministers, subject only to the veto of the British provincial governors. However, it did not include any plans for independence.

The first elections to be held after this Act resulted in a victory for the Hindu Congress Party. The Muslim League, representing a quarter of India's population, failed disastrously and its leader, Mohammed Ali Jinnah, who had previously favoured working with the Congress Party, resolved to build up the Muslim League into an organization capable of challenging it.

ACTIVITY: Reviewing the impact of civil disobedience

■ ATL

- Critical-thinking skills – Gather and organize relevant information to formulate an argument

- What is the difference between non-cooperation and civil disobedience?
- Which do you think was a more effective tactic to use against the British?
- Which actions of a) the British and b) Indians helped to increase a sense of national identity in India?
- Which factor undermined a united nationalist movement?

Hint

When you write up your response to these questions, remember to include details, dates and examples as this will be assessed using Criterion A.

◆ Assessment opportunities

- This activity can be assessed using Criterion A: Knowing and understanding.

ⓘ Gandhi in Britain

Gandhi became very popular with the British working classes of London when he refused to stay in an expensive hotel but instead stayed in a social-services community hall in a poor London neighbourhood. While in London, Gandhi also travelled to the north of England, to Lancashire, to meet cotton mill workers. Although many of them had lost their jobs due to his campaign to boycott British cotton, they still gave him a warm welcome.

■ **Figure 10.5** A warm welcome in Lancashire, England, 1931

ACTIVITY: What did the British think of Gandhi?

■ **ATL**

- Critical-thinking skills – Recognize unstated assumptions and bias; Gather and organize relevant information to formulate an argument

Watch Gandhi's arrival in Britain on Pathé news:

http://youtu.be/P6njRwz_dMw

What is the attitude of the news commentator to his visit?

Imagine that you are a British reporter writing an account of Gandhi's visit for a British newspaper. You should write between 700 and 900 words.

You may want to refer back to the Pathé news report for ideas. Also include an account of what is going on in India. You are writing from a British perspective here, so you may have a rather one-sided view on what Gandhi is doing in India and what this means for the British Empire.

Hint

Refer back to Chapter 9 and British ideas about imperialism for some extra ideas for this activity.

◆ **Assessment opportunities**

- In this activity you have practised skills that are assessed using Criterion C: Communicating and Criterion D: Thinking critically.

WHAT WAS THE IMPACT OF THE SECOND WORLD WAR ON THE NATIONALIST MOVEMENT IN INDIA?

As a result of Gandhi's actions, Indian nationalism was well advanced and organized by the time of the Second World War. India was also becoming increasingly free of British control, with its own tariff system against British goods and a well-developed civil service.

However, when Britain declared war on Germany, the Viceroy of India, without consultation with Indians, also declared that India was at war. The leaders of the Indian National Congress were outraged at this arrogant treatment of India. They decided to cooperate with Britain, but only on certain terms; in return for their support, they wanted Britain to promise that India could become independent after the war. They also demanded that Indians should be included immediately in the Viceroy's government. Both of these demands were rejected; thus all seven Congress ministers in the provinces resigned and their areas were run instead by British governors for the rest of the war.

In 1941, the Japanese entered the war on the side of Germany and by 1942 were threatening India. Winston Churchill, the prime minster of Britain, decided he needed to take action to keep India loyal at this crucial time. He thus asked Sir Stafford Cripps to lead a mission to India and to offer it independence as a self-governing dominion after the war in return for cooperation in the war.

However, negotiations with Congress broke down. At this point, Gandhi called for another civil disobedience campaign. He announced that the time had come for Britain to 'quit India'. On 8 August 1942, Congress passed

Figure 10.6 A British propaganda poster during the Second World War

THINK–PAIR–SHARE

Discuss what message the poster in Figure 10.6 was trying to give to Indians.

the 'quit India' motion, which demanded that the British leave India immediately.

The British arrested Gandhi, and the Congress Party was banned. Demonstrations and violent protest followed in all the major cities. This included the blowing up of railway lines, attacks on police stations, and sabotage on telegraph lines. However, the Indian army and Indian police stayed loyal and the British army was able to hold off the Japanese from attacking India.

HOW DID THE OUTCOME OF THE SECOND WORLD WAR AFFECT THE FIGHT FOR INDEPENDENCE?

The Second World War had a damaging effect on relations between the British and the Indians; in order to fight the war effectively, economic controls were introduced and labour was conscripted. In addition, political rights were repressed. However, the Japanese victories over the British had shown that the British were no longer invincible. In addition, many Indians had gained senior jobs in the army and civil service during the war, which gave them experience and self-confidence in running their own affairs. Thus, when Gandhi and the other nationalist leaders were released in 1944–45, they could continue to agitate for independence in circumstances which were becoming more favourable to their demands.

In Britain, the Labour party won the election. The leaders of this political party supported the idea of Indian independence and Clement Attlee, the new prime minster, wanted India to become independent as soon as possible so he could concentrate on rebuilding Britain. In addition, Britain was nearly bankrupt and so not in a strong position to maintain the resources necessary to put down any future Indian rebellions. In fact the Second World War had shown that India no longer provided Britain with substantial economic advantages. At the time of the First World War, Britain had received millions of pounds from Indian taxpayers and India had been an important market for British cloth. By the time of the Second World War, India was providing 86 per cent of its own cloth and Indian taxes were now being spent on projects in India. In fact, India had become a financial liability as, by 1945, Britain was £1.3 billion in debt to India.

In addition, Britain needed financial support from the USA in order to stave off bankruptcy and the USA did not support the idea of an empire. Indeed, in 1941, Britain and America had signed the Atlantic Charter, in which they described 'their hopes for a better future of the world' and their intention to 'respect the right of all peoples to choose the form of government under which they will live.'

These forces helped push forward plans for India's independence.

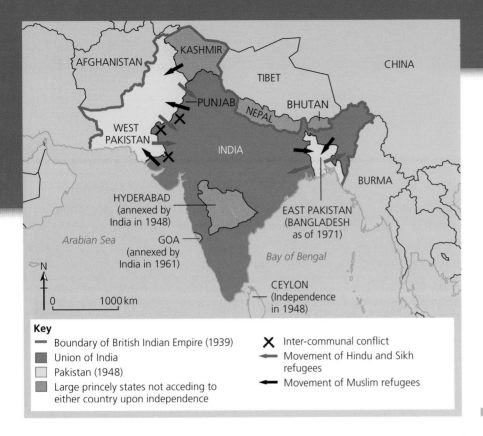

■ **Figure 10.7** The partition of India

WHAT WAS THE SITUATION OF JINNAH AND THE MUSLIM LEAGUE?

'The great irony in India was not that nationalism was ineffective in bringing about independence but that the conflicting national groups delayed independence.'

Alfred, J. 2004. British and Imperial policy 1846–1914. *Heinemann, p.171.*

As you read on page 236, Jinnah decided to build up a separate Muslim League to challenge Congress, which he believed favoured Hindus. In 1940, Jinnah claimed that India had never been one nation and he demanded the creation of a separate Muslim state when India became independent, claiming that 'Muslims are a nation according to any definition of a nation, and they must have their homelands, their territory and their State'. This new state was to be called Pakistan.

This went against the position of Congress leaders, who believed that they represented all Indian people. However, the British were pleased to be able to weaken Congress, which they believed was anti-British, by supporting Jinnah. Cripps, for example, as part of his plans in 1941 to offer India the chance to become a self-governing dominion after the war, had proposed that any province which did not want to join the new dominion of India should be allowed to become a separate dominion in its own right, thus giving British backing for a separate Muslim state.

> **THINK–PAIR–SHARE**
>
> Consider the following questions and then **discuss** as a class:
>
> What role does religion play in fostering a national identity? How did religion a) strengthen the independence movement, b) undermine it in India?

In the new elections, Congress gained a massive victory, but in Muslim areas, the League won overwhelmingly. Attlee sent a 'Cabinet mission' to negotiate the terms of independence with Congress and Jinnah. When the negotiations fell through, Jinnah launched a day of 'Direct Action', which was to be a silent day of protest against both the British and Congress. However, in Calcutta, peaceful protest turned violent. As many as 4000 people were killed and some 100 000 lost their homes.

The violence in India convinced the British that they must hand over power quickly. In 1947, a new Viceroy, Lord Mountbatten, was sent to India to arrange this. By the summer of 1947, Congress was beginning to accept the idea of giving Jinnah some of what he wanted and Mountbatten soon decided that there was no alternative but to partition India into two countries – India and Pakistan (see Figure 10.7).

WHAT WAS THE RESULT OF PARTITION?

British rule ended on 15 August 1947. However, even after partition, 40 million Muslims remained in India and 8 million Hindus remained in the new Pakistan. There were also millions of Sikhs in the Punjab, who felt that they belonged to neither country. Almost immediately, violence broke out. Millions of people attempted to move to their new homes but came under attack as they did so:

'Day after day, columns of migrants, sometimes 50 miles long, trudged along the roads of India, Muslims in one direction, Sikhs and Hindus in the other. They were attacked in the dust, humidity and blazing heat of the Punjab in August, thousands were killed each day. Trains carrying migrants were stopped and the passengers slaughtered. Sikhs and Hindus killed Muslims. Muslims killed Sikhs and Hindus. Official estimates say 250,000 were killed, but other independent observers put the figure at nearly 1 million people. The killings continued through September and October and began to peter out only in November 1947. Only then were the new governments able to restore some sort of order, and to begin to build their new separate states.'

Cloake, J.A. 1994. Britain in the Modern World. OUP.

ACTIVITY: Celebrating Gandhi

■ ATL

- ■ Communication skills – Use appropriate forms of writing to communicate with a range of audiences

What is your goal?

Write an obituary for Gandhi as it would have been written in 1948 in an Indian newspaper. An obituary is an as sessment of a person's life after he or she has died.

How will you achieve this?

Before you start writing, research an obituary that has been written for a famous person so that you can see the style and tone to use.

You could include points on:
- **Gandhi's views on non-violent protest**
- **his actions against the British government**
- **his impact on the nationalist movement in India**
- **his visit to Britain.**

You should write between 700 and 900 words. Remember to consider your audience.

◆ Assessment opportunities

- ◆ In this activity you have practised skills that are assessed using Criterion A: Knowing and understanding and Criterion D: Thinking critically.

WHY WAS GANDHI ASSASSINATED?

Gandhi continued to preach tolerance and to try to work against the cycle of violence which horrified him. He undertook a fast to death to try to shame those who had taken part in the violence, saying, 'Death for me would be a glorious deliverance rather than that I should be a helpless witness of the destruction of India, Hinduism, Sikhism and Islam.' However, in the post-independence atmosphere, there were many who opposed this stance, believing that Gandhi's insistence on non-violence and non-retaliation prevented them from defending themselves against attack. On 30 January 1948, a militant Hindu shot Gandhi three times in the chest.

ACTIVITY: Was nationalism just anti-colonialism?

■ **ATL**

■ Critical-thinking skills – Evaluate evidence and arguments

Gary Thorn, in his book *End of Empires* (2001), writes, 'sometimes nationalism was really no more than anti-colonialism. It united people temporarily against a common enemy. Once that enemy was expelled, it dissolved into numerous smaller identities, ethnic, tribal or religious.'

- **Discuss** what point Thorn is making.
- How can this be applied to India?
- To what extent did Indians have a shared national identity in 1948?

◆ Assessment opportunities

◆ In this activity you have practised skills that are assessed using Criterion A: Knowledge and understanding and Criterion D: Thinking critically.

SOURCE A

'The First World War was a significant turning point in that it strengthened the determination of Indian nationalists to press Britain for independence at a time of economic crisis in Britain in the interwar years. The key players in Indian nationalism, Gandhi and Jinnah, had displayed an irresistible determination. Indian nationalism was a truly mass movement and one that was driven by religious and ethnic commitment. Had Britain decided that India was an asset, it is highly unlikely that it could have resisted the tremendous force of nationalism there. The Indian experience was one in which nationalism really did override all other factors that contributed in other parts of the British Empire to the granting of independence.'

Alfred, J. 2004. British and Imperial policy 1846–1914. *Heinemann, p.172.*

SOURCE B

Gandhi, 1930

'I hold the British rule to be a curse. It has impoverished millions by a system of exploitation and by ruinously expensive military and civil administration. It has reduced us politically to serfdom. Nothing but organised non-violence can check the organised violence of the British government.'

Adaptation

SOURCE C

'Both war and depression fuelled the rise of nationalism in India. One and a half million Indians had fought in the war and far more paid increased taxes. But nationalists felt that Britain lacked gratitude.'

Thorn, G. 2006. End of Empires: European Decolonisation 1919–1980. *Hodder Education.*

SOURCE D

'Gandhi's policy [of civil disobedience] was highly successful. He was often imprisoned, and so were thousands of his supporters and he was not always able to prevent violence. But the Congress Party became stronger and stronger as more and more Indians came to feel that they were members of a proud nation and had a right to run their own country.'

Scott, J. 1989. The World Since 1914. *Heinemann.*

ACTIVITY: Assessing the overall impact of Gandhi on nationalism

■ ATL

■ Critical-thinking skills – Evaluate evidence and arguments; Gather and organize relevant information to formulate an argument

Read Sources A–D.

1 **Identify** the factor(s) that each source identifies as encouraging nationalism in India.
2 Using these sources and the information in this chapter, write an essay which answers the following question: 'How important was Gandhi's leadership in bringing about Indian independence in 1947?'

Hint

Before you write up your essay, you should organize the source material into themes. You should refer directly to the sources as you use their content in your essay, for example, as Source C says ... Remember to bring in ideas and examples from your own knowledge. You should review this chapter for dates, details and events to use as evidence in your essay.

◆ Assessment opportunities

◆ This activity can be assessed using Criterion A: Knowing and understanding, Criterion C Communicating and Criterion D: Thinking critically.

Why did a nationalist movement develop in Kenya?

In 1952, a State of Emergency was declared in Kenya. Over the eight years which followed, Kenya became one of the most brutal battlegrounds of the end of empire. It has also been seen as one of the darkest moments of British colonial history, and the impact is still being felt today, with many Kenyans bringing legal cases against the British government for the atrocities that took place in this period.

WHY DID RESENTMENT DEVELOP AGAINST THE BRITISH?

From the end of the nineteenth century, large numbers of white settlers from Britain moved to Kenya. They took over land in the fertile Aberdare Mountains in what became known as the White Highlands. This had a disastrous impact on the large Kikuyu tribe, who had farmed these highlands and who were no longer allowed to own land in this area, but instead were crowded into tribal reserves. The white

ⓘ
Some of the laws that affected Kenyans

- Black people were not allowed to own land in the fertile White Highlands; those in the White Highlands were there as squatters, which meant that they could farm and keep crops on small pieces of land owned by the whites in return for working unpaid on the white farmers' plantations.
- Africans had to pay taxes, but to get the money to do so, they had to work for the white settlers.
- All Africans had to carry a pass when they left their reserves.

settlers were also given preference in all spheres of politics, administration and society, and Africans were prevented from getting involved in politics.

Unlike India, there was no clear nationalist movement in Kenya in the years after the First World War, and no sign that Britain was considering giving any extra powers to Kenyans. The economic situation of black squatters worsened during the Second World War, and although a new British governor took office in 1944 and promised to increase the proportion of black people in the Kenyan government, his changes were not planned to take effect for nearly ten years.

In 1944, the Kenyan African Union (KAU) was founded, which finally gave a voice to African nationalism; it accused the whites of land theft and demanded the restoration of the White Highlands into their hands. It was led by Jomo Kenyatta, who was a member of the Kikuyu tribe. However, the KAU was banned in 1950.

WHAT ACTIONS DID THE MAU MAU TAKE?

By 1949, the discontent of the Kikuyu emerged in the form of an organization that became known as Mau Mau. This organization led attacks on White farms and the settlers, as well as arranging the murder and mutilation of Africans they suspected of being collaborators. Cattle were also maimed. Those who fought had to take an oath as part of an initiation ceremony, which further deepened the fears of the Whites. By this oath the Mau Mau committed themselves to overthrow White rule.

The British responded to this violence by declaring a State of Emergency. Mass arrests of Kikuyu tribesmen were carried out and the suspects were held in special detention camps. The forests were also cleared to prevent Kikuyu hiding there. This led to atrocities also on the part of the British; conditions in the camps and brutality by some guards led to the death of 20000 suspects. At the Hola camp, ten men were beaten to death by drunken guards. Kenyatta was also imprisoned, even though he was never found to be directly linked to the Mau Mau.

■ **Figure 10.8** Cartoon by Illingworth, 22 February 1954

SOURCE F

■ **Figure 10.9** Cartoon by Illingworth, 22 October 1952

ACTIVITY: British propaganda against the Mau Mau

■ **ATL**

- Critical-thinking skills – Evaluate evidence and arguments; Recognize unstated assumptions and bias

1 **What is the message of each of the British cartoons in Sources E and F with regard to the Mau Mau rebellion?**
2 **Analyse these cartoons in terms of origin and purpose, in order to assess their value and limitations for understanding the Mau Mau rebellion.**
3 **Watch the following Pathé news extract about the Mau Mau rebellion:**

http://youtu.be/Ob7M632C1lQ

What does this tell you about the difficulties faced by the British in fighting the Mau Mau?

◆ **Assessment opportunities**

◆ In this activity you have practised skills that are assessed using Criterion D: Thinking critically.

■ **Figure 10.10** Kenyatta on Independence Day, 13 December 1963, holding the official document of Kenyan independence

WHAT WERE THE RESULTS OF THE MAU MAU REBELLION?

Mau Mau terrorism had largely been defeated by 1956. White settlers hoped that they would be able to go back to their old ways of life before the 'emergency'. However, the world situation had changed and it was clear that this could not happen and that the calls for Kenyan independence could no longer be ignored.

Measures were taken by the British to establish a new constitution that offered voting rights to native Kenyans and equal representation for them on the new Legislative Council by 1957. The British also legalized political parties in Kenya. Then, in 1960 at the Lancaster House Conference, it was accepted that Africans should have a majority in the legislative. Finally, in 1962, at a second Lancaster House Conference, it was agreed that Kenya would have independence from December 1963. Kenyatta became Prime Minister and then President of Kenya.

HOW IMPORTANT WAS THE MAU MAU REBELLION IN GETTING BRITAIN TO GIVE INDEPENDENCE TO KENYA?

THINK–PAIR–SHARE

Consider each of the factors below and decide how important each one was in putting pressure on Britain to give independence to Kenya. Think about this on your own first. Then share your ideas with your partner. Finally, **summarize** your ideas to the rest of the class.

How do your conclusions compare with the reasons for why India gained independence?

- **Dealing with the Mau Mau had cost Britain a lot of money. It was estimated that the capture of just one of the thousands of Mau Mau terrorists cost about £10 000. Ultimately defeating the Mau Mau cost the British £60 million at a time when the British economy was relatively weak.**
- **The USA was against the idea of imperialism. Britain had borrowed large amounts of money from the USA and could not ignore its views, especially as it depended on US support in Europe for the new Cold War that was developing (see page 223).**
- **In 1960, the British prime minister, Harold MacMillan, addressed the South African parliament and made a speech which became known as the 'wind of change' speech. This basically said that Britain supported the idea that Africans should gain independence:**

  'In the twentieth century, and especially since the end of the war, we have seen the awakening of national consciousness in people who have for centuries lived in dependence on some other power …. The wind of change is blowing through this continent, and, whether we like it or not, this growth of national consciousness is a political fact. We must accept it as a fact, and our national policies must take account of it.'

- **By 1960, all European countries (with the exception of Portugal) were leaving their colonies.**
- **In east Africa, the process of decolonization was already underway; in 1961, Tanganyika (Tanzania) gained independence from Britain, as did Uganda in 1963.**
- **An economic review of Britain showed that, by the 1960s, Britain was no longer economically benefiting from its empire; British investments in non-colonial markets were more profitable than in colonial ones.**
- **After the Mau Mau had been suppressed, new political leaders emerged in Kenya, such as Oginga Odinga and Tom Mboya. These men were not just focused on the Kikuyu tribe, but were able to create a new inter-tribal movement which allowed talks with the British about independence to go ahead.**

ACTIVITY: Reasons for success

ATL

- Critical-thinking skills – Evaluate evidence and arguments
- Organization skills – Use appropriate strategies for organizing complex information

In pairs, compare and contrast the reasons for the success of the Indian and Mau Mau nationalist movements in gaining independence.

Draw a diagram, for example a Venn diagram, to show the similarities and differences.

Share your results with the class. Reflect on whether there are more similarities or differences in the reasons for their success.

What conclusions can be drawn regarding the role of leadership, a strong national identify or other key factors?

ACTIVITY: Nationalist movements in other colonial countries

■ ATL

- ■ Information literacy skills – Access information to be informed and inform others

In pairs, research more about nationalist movements in other colonial states. You could investigate Zimbabwe, Ghana, Portugal and Angola.

Consider the following:

- **What factors led to a nationalist movement?**
- **What methods were used by nationalists to gain independence?**
- **What was the reaction of the colonial power?**
- **What factors finally led to the country getting independence?**

◆ Assessment opportunities

- ◆ This activity can be assessed using Criterion B: Investigating and Criterion C: Communicating.

EXTENSION

Explore further … Research news articles on the court cases brought against the British by Kenyans in recent years. What has new evidence now revealed concerning British actions against Kenyans during the fight against the Mau Mau?

What actions have Kenyans taken against the British government?

Do you think that governments today should apologize and compensate for actions of previous governments?

■ **Figure 10.11** Veterans of Kenya's independence struggle seeking compensation from the British government in 2013

Take action

! Research nationalist movements that exist today – their goals and the methods they are using to achieve their goals.

! Create a wall display; include recent news articles.

! What conclusions can you draw about these movements? Do you think that nationalism is a force for good in the world?

■ **Figure 10.12** Supporters of Scottish independence, 2014

Reflection

In this chapter, we have examined the reasons for the growth of nationalist movements in India and Kenya. We have also looked at the form that these nationalist movements took and the role that they played in bringing about independence in both countries.

Reflecting on our learning ... Use this table to reflect on your own learning in this chapter.		
Questions we asked	Answers we found	Any further questions now?
Factual		
Conceptual		
Debatable		

Approaches to learning you used in this chapter:	Description – what new skills did you learn?	How well did you master the skills?			
		Novice	Learner	Practitioner	Expert
Critical-thinking skills					
Communication skills					
Learner profile attribute	*Reflect on the importance of being an inquirer for our learning in this chapter.*				
Inquirer					

How have civil rights and social protest groups brought about change?

Civil rights and social protest moments have led to significant changes in the fairness and equality of societies.

CONSIDER THESE QUESTIONS:

Factual: Which individuals, actions and events have led to the development of civil rights and social protest groups? What have been the successes and failures of these civil rights and social protest groups?

Conceptual: What is the difference between prejudice, segregation and discrimination? How effective is non-violent protest? How can protest bring about change?

Debatable: To what extent do you agree with this statement: 'Civil rights and social protest groups are irrelevant in the twenty-first century'?

Now **share and compare** your thoughts and ideas with your partner, or with the whole class.

■ **Figure 11.1** Police dogs attacking a civil rights campaigner in Birmingham, Alabama, USA, 1963

IN THIS CHAPTER, WE WILL …

- **Find out** why there was a need for protest movements in America and South Africa.
- **Explore:**
  - the methods used by these protest movements
  - the impact of these protest movements.
- **Take action** by finding out where people are still campaigning for civil rights today.

◆ **Assessment opportunities in this chapter:**

- ◆ **Criterion A:** Knowing and understanding
- ◆ **Criterion B:** Investigating
- ◆ **Criterion C:** Communicating
- ◆ **Criterion D:** Thinking critically

■ **These Approaches to Learning (ATL) skills will be useful …**

- ■ Collaboration skills
- ■ Critical-thinking skills
- ■ Information literacy skills

KEY WORDS

discrimination	racism
integration	segregation
lynching	supremacist
prejudice	

■ **Figure 11.2** Billie Holiday

● **We will reflect on this learner profile attribute …**

- ● Communicator – expressing your ideas in a variety of ways.

WHAT MAKES YOU SAY THAT?

Read the lyrics on the left from a song sung by Billie Holiday and written by Abel Meeropol. You can also listen to it here:

www.bbc.co.uk/news/entertainment-arts-25034438

In pairs, discuss the lyrics of the song. What do you think the song is about? How effective is the imagery?

Southern trees bear strange fruit,
Blood on the leaves and blood at the root,
Black bodies swinging in the southern breeze,
Strange fruit hanging from the poplar trees.

Pastoral scene of the gallant south,
The bulging eyes and the twisted mouth,
Scent of magnolias, sweet and fresh,
Then the sudden smell of burning flesh.

Here is fruit for the crows to pluck,
For the rain to gather, for the wind to suck,
For the sun to rot, for the trees to drop,
Here is a strange and bitter crop.

This chapter will examine the way in which ordinary people have fought to achieve civil rights by looking at the civil rights movement in the USA and the fight against apartheid in South Africa. As you work through the chapter, consider the similarities and differences between the two protest movements, both in terms of the nature of the protest and the reasons for success. We will come back to this theme at the end of the chapter.

How has protest led to change in America?

CIVIL RIGHTS IN AMERICA

The USA emerged from the Second World War as a superpower – the most prosperous and powerful country in the world. It had proved itself victorious over fascism and stood for freedom and democracy in its fight against Japan and Hitler, yet there was still much inequality in the country with regard to both wealth and rights. One group in society which suffered social, economic and political discrimination was that of black Americans.

Despite the Second World War bringing about some advances in civil rights, for example in the military, discrimination throughout the whole of America and segregation in the southern states remained key features of life for black Americans.

SOURCE A

'Our foreign policy is designed to make the United States an enormous positive influence for peace and prosperity throughout the world … But our domestic civil rights shortcomings are a serious obstacle. The United States is not so strong, the final triumph of the democratic ideal is not so inevitable that we can ignore what the world thinks of us or our record.'

Report of the President's Committee on Civil rights: 'To Secure These Rights'. 1947.

DISCUSS

Look at Source A. What point is President Harry S. Truman making regarding America's position in the world after the Second World War?

WHAT WAS THE SITUATION IN THE SOUTHERN STATES OF THE USA?

■ **Figure 11.3** Segregation signs enforcing the Jim Crow laws

How did segregation operate?

Life in the southern states was determined by a series of laws called the Jim Crow laws. These laws forced black people to live in separate areas and to use separate facilities for everything from restrooms to clinics to schools. Although, in theory, the US Constitution gave everyone equal rights, the fact that states could pass their own laws meant that they could pass these discriminatory laws.

Their case for doing this and thus ignoring the Constitution was made stronger when the Supreme Court in 1896, in the case Plessy vs Ferguson, ruled that individual states could impose segregation as long as the segregated facilities, such as schools and hospitals, were 'separate but equal'. However, this was rarely the case; in most cases the facilities for Blacks were vastly inferior.

Voting rights

Although voting rights should have been protected by the Constitution, Blacks were prevented from voting through various means. Literacy tests, difficult reading tests and tests which included such questions as 'Name all the Vice Presidents and Supreme Court Justices throughout America's history' were some of the measures put in place to make it impossible for Blacks to register to vote.

All of this was backed up by the threat of violence. Anyone who went against the Jim Crow laws risked losing their jobs or their homes or even their lives. The legal system was dominated by Whites and supported such intimidation.

ⓘ
Jim Crow laws

Jim Crow laws were named after a white entertainer, Thomas Dartmouth Rice (1808–60), who performed a popular song and dance act that was supposed to be based on a slave, who he called Jim Crow.

You can read some of the Jim Crow laws here:

www.nps.gov/malu/forteachers/jim_crow_laws.htm

WHAT WAS THE SITUATION IN THE NORTHERN STATES OF THE USA?

Although Jim Crow laws and segregation did not exist in the northern states, there was still much prejudice and discrimination against black Americans. Black workers generally only earned half of the wages of white workers and often lived in the worst areas. Increased migration of black Americans from the South to the northern industrial cities after the war increased racial tension.

Key
- Segregated by law
- Optional
- Segregation prohibited
- No specific legislation

■ **Figure 11.4** Map showing segregation in education by 1954

WHAT ATTEMPTS WERE MADE TO IMPROVE THE SITUATION FOR BLACK AMERICANS BEFORE THE 1950S?

Two important organizations were established before the 1950s with the aim of improving equality for black Americans. The NAACP (The National Association for the Advancement of Colored People) had been set up in 1909 by a group of leading black intellectuals. Its aim was 'to ensure the political, educational, social and economic equality of right of all persons and to eliminate racial hatred and racial discrimination' and it did much to raise awareness of issues. It used legal means to achieve equality.

A new organization was established in 1942. CORE (the Congress of Racial Equality) was inspired by the non-violent tactics of Mahatma Gandhi in India and so encouraged tactics such as 'sit-ins' in restaurants.

Both the NAACP and CORE did much to raise awareness of discrimination issues in both black and white communities, and membership of both organizations grew after the Second World War. However, there had only been limited gains in civil rights by the end of the 1940s.

Improving the rights of Blacks remained slow, difficult and dangerous. President Truman's attempt to guarantee greater civil rights for Blacks was turned down by Congress because Southern Democrats voted against it. Meanwhile, individuals who tried to take action on their own faced both threats and actual violence.

However, two ways which proved effective in challenging discrimination in the 1950s and 1960s were:
- legal action
- community action, in the form of direct action.

LEGAL ACTION

Brown vs Topeka Board of Education, 1954

In September 1952, the NAACP brought a court case against the Board of Education in Topeka, Kansas. This involved Oliver Brown suing the city school board for preventing his eight-year-old daughter, who was black, from attending a white school. Instead his daughter was forced to travel much further in order to go to a black school.

Marshall Thurgood, a black lawyer, represented the NAACP in putting the case against segregation and he won. Chief Justice Warren of the Supreme Court concluded the following:

> 'Separating white and coloured children in schools has a detrimental effect upon coloured children. The impact is greater when it has the sanction of law; for the separating of the races is usually interpreted as denoting the inferiority of the Negro group … We conclude that in the field of public education the doctrine of "separate but equal" has no place. Separate educational facilities are inherently unequal.'

He also ordered that the southern states should set up integrated schools 'with a deliberate speed'. Some areas began to desegregate and, by 1957, more than 300 000 black children were attending schools that had previously been segregated.

However, implementing the decision was often deliberately delayed, with southern states claiming states' rights – that each state should be able to decide such issues for themselves. Tom Brady, a judge in the southern state of Mississippi, recalled the struggles of the civil war in his justification of opposition to the Supreme Court ruling:

> '… when a law transgresses the moral and ethical sanctions and standards of the mores [customs], invariably strife, bloodshed and revolution follow in the wake of its attempted enforcement. The loveliest and purest of God's creatures the nearest thing to an angelic being that treads this terrestrial ball is a well-bred, cultured southern white woman or her blue-eyed, golden-haired little girl … We say to the Supreme Court and to the northern world, "You shall not make us drink from this cup" … We have, through our forefathers, died before for our sacred principles. We can, if necessary, die again.'

Such views were supported by the increasing activities of the Ku Klux Klan and White Citizens' Councils. Violence against Blacks increased; the most famous case of this time was the death of 14-year-old Emmett Till in 1955, who was brutally murdered while staying with relatives in Mississippi. Those believed to be his murderers were acquitted by an all-white jury.

ⓘ The Ku Klux Klan

The Ku Klux Klan played a role in the intimidation of Blacks. This was a white supremacist group that aimed to maintain white supremacy over black people and immigrants. Dressed in white sheets and white hoods and carrying American flags, they carried out violence and intimidation through whipping, branding, kidnapping and lynching.

Central High School, Little Rock, 1957

The first test of the Supreme Court ruling and of the government's commitment to see that it was enforced came in 1957, when Little Rock high school in Arkansas decided to allow nine black students to attend. However, the nine students who attempted to enrol on 3 September were turned away by the governor, Orval Faubus. He ordered State National Guardsmen to block their entry.

Faced with this defiance, Eisenhower was forced to order federal troops to the town to protect the students. Press and television coverage of this event across the world was an embarrassment to America, which prided itself on being a country of freedom and equality.

ACTIVITY: *Eyes on the Prize*

■ ATL

- Information literacy skills – Access information to be informed and inform others

To find out more about the events at Little Rock, watch the video *Eyes on the Prize (Part 2)*:

www.youtube.com/watch?v=CSRSUp-nTZM

What form did white opposition to the students take? What is your reaction to this? What points does Eisenhower make in his speech? What factors in the Little Rock case helped raise the profile of the civil rights movement?

◆ Assessment opportunities

◆ In this activity you have practised skills that are assessed using Criterion A: Knowing and understanding and Criterion D: Thinking critically.

■ **Figure 11.5** Central High School in Little Rock, Arkansas, 1957

11 How have civil rights and social protest groups brought about change?

257

DIRECT ACTION

The Montgomery Bus Boycott

On 1 December 1955, Rosa Parks, a black woman travelling on a bus in Montgomery, Alabama, refused to give up her seat to a white male and stand at the back of the bus as was required by law. She was arrested and fined $10.

Parks was an NAACP activist and it was clear to the NAACP that Rosa Parks's case could be used to highlight the unfairness of discrimination. On the day of her trial, members of the NAACP organized a 24-hour bus boycott. This was so successful that it was decided to continue this protest.

The Montgomery Improvement Association was set up (MIA) and the bus boycott continued. Since 75 per cent of the bus company's business was made up of black passengers, the boycott was very damaging. The black people of Montgomery either walked or shared lifts through car pools to get to work, with the slogan 'People, don't ride the bus today. Don't ride it, for freedom'.

A young Baptist preacher called Martin Luther King was chosen to lead the protest. He was a brilliant and moving speaker who believed in non-violent political protest. The Montgomery Bus Boycott put him in the national spotlight:

> 'The great glory of American democracy is the right to protest for right. There will be no crosses burned at any bus stops in Montgomery. There will be no white persons pulled out of their homes and taken out on some distant road and murdered. There will be nobody among us who will stand up and defy the constitution of the Nation.'

The boycott lasted for 381 days. Finally, following much national publicity, the Supreme Court ruled that segregation on buses was unconstitutional; this also implied that all segregation of public services was illegal.

Throughout the boycott, the leaders were intimidated and arrested, and churches and homes were set on fire. However, the end result was a great victory for the non-violence of the civil rights movement. Martin Luther King emerged as a key leader of the civil rights movement. He went on to form the Southern Christian Leadership Conference (SCLC), which trained civil rights activists in non-violent tactics.

■ **Figure 11.6** Rosa Parks sitting on a bus after the successful campaign against bus segregation

ACTIVITY: The impact of the Montgomery Bus Boycott

In pairs, inquire further into the Montgomery Bus Boycott and the role of Martin Luther King. Consider the following:

- **Identify** factors that led to the success of the Montgomery Bus Boycott.
- **Evaluate** how effective Martin Luther King was in leading this protest.
- **Describe** the main results of the Montgomery Bus Boycott for the civil rights movement in the USA.
- **Identify** other examples in history you can think of that have used non-violent protest.

WHAT MAKES YOU SAY THAT?

What's going on in the photo in Figure 11.7 and what does it show about the tactics of the students during the sit-in campaigns?

What makes you say that?

What impact would such tactics have when shown on television and in photos in newspapers?

Sit-ins

During the late 1950s and 1960s, there were several other examples of direct action. In 1960, four black students asked to be served at a Whites-only counter in Woolworths in Greensboro. The next day, 23 more students did the same. The following day there were 66 students – both black and white. Within 18 months, 70 000 had taken part in similar sit-ins and 3000 had been arrested. These demonstrations were supported by a new student organization known as the Student Nonviolent Coordinating Committee (SNCC). By the end of 1960, lunch counters had been desegregated in 126 cities.

■ **Figure 11.7** A sit-in at the Greensboro Woolworth's store lunch counter, 1963

11 How have civil rights and social protest groups brought about change?

259

The Freedom Riders

In December 1960, the Supreme Court ordered the desegregation of all bus station facilities. To test whether integration was taking place, CORE activists in 1961 started riding interstate buses in the South in mixed racial groups. They were known as the Freedom Riders. They faced some of the worst violence of the civil rights campaign; riders were stoned, or beaten with baseball bats, and buses were fire-bombed. The police looked the other way.

Over the summer, more than 400 freedom riders were arrested – many more were beaten up. Nightly television pictures angered many. It forced the Interstate Commerce Commission and the Justice Department under Attorney General Robert Kennedy to enforce desegregation on interstate transportation.

■ **Figure 11.8** The Freedom Riders' bus following an attack at Anniston, Alabama, 1961

DISCUSS

Watch this video on Bull Connor's actions:

http://youtu.be/j9kT1yO4MGg

Why did Bull Connor turn out to be a help to the civil rights movement?

MARCHES

Birmingham

The Freedom Riders had shown how white violence against civil rights protesters displayed in the media could help achieve increased support for the civil rights movement. In April 1963, Martin Luther King decided to take on Birmingham, Alabama, which he called 'the most segregated city in the United States'.

Birmingham's Chief Commissioner of Public Safety, Bull Connor, provided the kind of reaction that King was hoping for: in full flare of the media he used electric cattle prods, powerful water hoses and vicious dogs to attack the peaceful marchers. A thousand marchers, including hundreds of children and Martin Luther King himself, were arrested.

Martin Luther King replied to critics who accused him of stirring up violence deliberately:

> 'Instead of submitting to surreptitious cruelty in thousands of dark jail cells and on countless shadowed streets, we are forcing our oppressor to commit his brutality openly – in the light of day – with the rest of the world looking on.

> 'To condemn peaceful protesters on the grounds that they provide violence is like condemning a robbed man because his possession of money caused the robbery.'

The scenes in Birmingham were shown on national television and caused anger at home and condemnation abroad. The government was forced to act; President John F. Kennedy pressured Governor Wallace to get all prisoners released and the Supreme Court declared that Birmingham's segregation laws were unconstitutional.

■ **Figure 11.9** Civil rights protestors being attacked with water hoses in Birmingham Alabama, 1963

Washington

The most high profile event of this period of civil rights activism was the March to Washington organized by Martin Luther King. About 250000 demonstrators attended and King gave his famous 'I have a dream' speech. The march was a great publicity success and put further pressure on President Kennedy to push through his civil rights bill, which he had introduced earlier in the year.

■ **Figure 11.10** Martin Luther King delivering his 'I have a dream' speech

History for the IB MYP 4&5: *by Concept*

THE CIVIL RIGHTS ACT 1964

Despite President Kennedy's commitment to the Civil Rights Bill, there was much opposition to the bill from Republican senators. Violence continued against Blacks and then the whole movement faced a blow when, in November 1963, Kennedy was assassinated. However, President Johnson, Kennedy's successor, was able to push through the bill, partly as a result of his political skills and also because there was a wave of sympathy for Kennedy's ideas following his assassination. The Civil Rights Act banned discrimination in education, housing and work.

CORE, SNCC and NAACP now worked together to organize the Freedom Summer. The aim of this was to get black voters to register to vote. This was an issue in the southern states where Blacks were prevented from voting by various measures (see page 253).

Selma

To bring more attention to the issue of voting rights, King organized another high profile march through Selma, Alabama. Here, only 383 Blacks out of 15000 had been able to register to vote and the attitude of the sheriff, Jim Clark, to racial equality was similar to that of Bull Connor in Birmingham.

King realized that brutal treatment of the marchers would again be televised and would again work in favour of the movement. On 7 March, on what became known as Bloody Sunday, the marchers were indeed subjected to clubs and tear gas. As a result of this, President Johnson agreed to introduce a voting act. The march went ahead peacefully in the end, with King leading 25000 people from Selma to Montgomery.

THE VOTING RIGHTS ACT

The Voting Rights Act which was passed in 1965 ended literacy tests and ensured that federal agents could intervene if they felt discrimination was taking place. The number of black voters registered increased dramatically, along with the number of elected black representatives.

WHY DID SOME BLACK AMERICANS CRITICIZE NON-VIOLENT PROTEST?

Not all black Americans supported the civil rights movement and its non-violent approach to achieving civil rights. In the mid-1960s violent riots took place in many cities; large areas of cities such as Newark and Detroit were looted and burnt. In 1967, 83 people were shot dead – most of the casualties were black Americans. A government report that investigated the riots concluded that 'White racism' was chiefly responsible for the explosion of rage.

Many believed that progress in achieving civil rights was too slow, that non-violence as a tactic had failed and that violence against Whites was therefore an acceptable tactic. Some groups, such as the Nation of Islam, also believed that Blacks should work for complete separation from Whites. They argued that discrimination would not stop with the end of segregation.

THINK–PAIR–SHARE

In pairs, look at some of the quotes from Malcolm X on page 265. What do these tell you about the difference in views between Malcolm X and Martin Luther King?

ACTIVITY: What factors were important to the progress made in civil rights?

■ ATL

■ Critical-thinking skills – Evaluate evidence and arguments

1 a What was the contribution of each of the following towards achieving civil rights?
- Legal battles
- Marches
- Direct action
- Actions of individuals
- Actions of the government

b Which factor do you consider to have been the most important in helping the movement to make progress?

2 **Evaluate** the progress that had been made in achieving civil rights by the end of 1965.

Hint
You should consider what had been achieved as well as what had not been achieved.

◆ Assessment opportunities

◆ In this activity you have practised skills that are assessed using Criterion D: Thinking critically.

THE NATION OF ISLAM AND MALCOLM X

A key figure in the Nation of Islam was Malcolm X. The Nation of Islam openly supported separatism and many of its members rejected their slave surnames and substituted them with an X. Malcolm X was a brilliant speaker and organizer and helped to raise the profile of the Nation of Islam and increase its membership.

However, in 1964, following a visit to Mecca, Malcolm X began to change his views. He believed that Whites could play a role in helping Blacks fight for equality. As a result, the Nation of Islam split, with Malcolm X leading a breakaway group. He was assassinated in 1968 by three black Muslims.

'If we don't get to cast the ballot, then we're going to have to cast a bullet.'

'The government of America is responsible for the oppression and exploitation of black people in this country.'

'I am for violence if non-violence means we continue postponing a solution to the American black man's problems. If we must use violence to get the black man his human rights in this country then I am for violence.'

'The white man has taught the black people in this country to hate themselves as inferior; to hate each other; to be divided against each other. The brainwashed black man can never learn to stand on his own two feet until he is on his own.'

'We want freedom by any means necessary. We want justice by any means necessary. We want equality by any means necessary.'

■ **Figure 11.11** Malcolm X

WHAT WAS MEANT BY BLACK POWER?

The term 'black power' was first used by Stokely Carmichael. He was leader of the SNCC, which became more radical following his election as chairman. The Nation of Islam, as well as CORE and the Black Panthers, all supported the idea of increasing the power of black people in American life. This meant black people taking responsibility for their own lives and rejecting white help (SNCC and CORE both expelled white members in 1966). It also involved promoting pride in African heritage, dress and appearance.

The Black Panthers went even further and were the most violent of these groups. Set up in 1966 by Huey Newton and Bobby Seale, the Black Panthers promoted revolutionary means to achieve their aims of equality. They gained much publicity as they wore striking uniforms of black berets, sunglasses and black leather jackets and were trained to use weapons. By the end of 1968, they had 5000 members, but clashes with the police and internal divisions led to a decline of support and, by 1982, they had disbanded.

ℹ️ **1968 Olympics**

The Black Power salute of Tommie Smith and John Carlos at the 1968 Olympics created a political furore in the USA. They were accused of damaging the Olympic spirit by involving sport in politics. However, it succeeded in raising international awareness of the Black Power movement.

■ **Figure 11.12** Black Power salute of Tommie Smith and John Carlos at the 1968 Olympics

The Black Power movement had declined in influence by the end of the 1960s. However, Martin Luther King continued to campaign on a range of issues, including living conditions, job opportunities and wages. He continued with his ideas of non-violence and working with all races – poor white Americans and Hispanics as well as Blacks.

He also opposed the war in Vietnam, focusing on the fact that many more black than white people ended up fighting and dying for the cause of stopping communism while their own fight for equality was not yet over in America itself. He also pointed out the huge sums of money being spent in Vietnam when there was so much poverty in the USA.

Martin Luther King gained many enemies and these increased with his attack on the Vietnam War. He was assassinated in Memphis, Tennessee in 1968 by a white gunman, which resulted in riots breaking out across America.

ACTIVITY: The impact of non-violent protest

ATL

- Critical-thinking skills – Evaluate evidence and arguments, Gather and organize relevant information to formulate an argument

'The use of non-violent protest had only limited success in improving the position of African Americans in US society in the 1960s.' To what extent do you agree with this claim?

Write an essay, with reference to Sources B–F and your own knowledge, and **discuss** the impact of the civil rights movement. You could use this essay frame. You have 1 hour to complete this task.

◆ Assessment opportunities

- ◆ This activity can be assessed using Criterion A: Knowing and understanding, Criterion C: Communicating and Criterion D: Thinking critically.

SOURCE B

From a speech by Malcolm X

'… I don't go along with any kind of nonviolence unless everybody's going to be nonviolent. If they make the Ku Klux Klan nonviolent, I'll be nonviolent, if they make the White Citizens' Council nonviolent, I'll be nonviolent. But as long as you've got somebody else not being nonviolent, I don't want anybody coming to me talking any nonviolent talk …

'You get freedom by letting your enemy know that you'll do anything to get your freedom then you'll get it. It's the only way you'll get it … fight then, and you'll get your freedom.'

http://web.mit.edu/21h.102/www/Primary%20source%20collections/ Civil%20Rights/MalcolmX.htm

SOURCE C

'One of the problems of historians is judging the success of the civil rights movement. It undoubtedly led to legislation and public policies, enforced by the federal government, which radically changed the access and opportunities that black Americans had to education, employment voting rights and housing. … But the legacy of racial hatred and the attitude that black Americans were inferior citizens was much harder to end.'

de Pennington, J. 2005. Modern America. Hodder Murray, p. 246.

Essay frame

Plan

First, organize the sources into those that say that the non-violent approach to civil rights protest gained successes, and those that suggest that it did not. Then add details and examples from your own knowledge to support both sides of the argument.

Introduction

You need to provide some context for your argument, so start by giving examples of non-violent protest that took place in the 1960s. Then set out your argument: do you agree that progress was made, or do you believe that overall non-violent protest only had limited effect?

First section

Explain the positive changes caused by non-violent protest. Do not forget to have a clear opening sentence that links to the question and sets out your argument, e.g. *Non-violent protest led to several successes in civil rights in the 1960s. First, …* Refer to the sources that support this view.

Second section

Now explain problems with non-violent protest and why it was opposed. Do not forget to use linking words, e.g. *However, …* Again, refer to the sources which support this view.

Conclusion

Come back to your key argument, which should fit with the evidence that you have provided.

SOURCE D

Table showing the percentage of black people registered to vote in the southern states of America

	1960	1966
Texas	35%	80%
Arkansas	37%	54%
Louisiana	30%	42%
Tennessee	52%	72%
Mississippi	5%	28%
Alabama	15%	49%
Virginia	24%	44%
North Carolina	31%	46%
South Carolina	16%	45%
Georgia	29%	43%
Florida	35%	62%

DISCUSS

In small groups, review the women's rights movements from Chapter 7. Explore the methods used to gain political, economic and social equality compared to those of the US civil rights movement. What were the most effective methods?

SOURCE E

Table showing US family incomes in the 1960s

	Black	White
1964	$5,921	$10,903
1965	$6,072	$11,333
1966	$6,850	$11,890
1967	$7,201	$12,162
1968	$7,603	$12,688

Bureau of the Census

SOURCE F

'King's commitment to non-violent direct action allowed influential white people, such as Kennedy and Johnson, to support the Civil Rights Movement without damaging their own political positions. His dignified behaviour and stirring speeches attracted international attention – he won the Nobel Peace prize in 1964 – and this also put more pressure on the Federal Government to end discrimination against black people. King worked hard to bring about important new laws; the 1964 Civil Rights Act and the 1965 Voting Rights Act. This laid the basis for yet more progress after his death.'

DeMarco, N. 1994. The USA: A Divided Nation. Longman, p. 123.

11 How have civil rights and social protest groups brought about change?

267

How did protest lead to change in South Africa?

CIVIL RIGHTS IN SOUTH AFRICA

'Who will deny that thirty years of my life have been spent knocking in vain, patiently, moderately and modestly at a closed and barred door? What have been the fruits of moderation? The past thirty years have seen the greatest number of laws restricting our rights and progress, until today we have reached a stage where we have almost no rights at all.'

Cheif Lutuli, President of the ANC, 1952–67

Nelson Mandela was sent to prison in 1964 at a time when South Africa was ruled by a small white minority via a system that was known as apartheid. Mandela was accused of being a terrorist for attempting to overthrow this system. Yet, in 1990, he walked free from prison and four years later became president of South Africa. This momentous change in South Africa was caused by a combination of domestic social protest and international pressure on the South African government.

What was the apartheid system?

South Africa had been part of the British Empire. When it became independent in 1910, the white South Africans were allowed to vote but Africans and Indians had no voting rights at all. The white South Africans were also known as Afrikaners; they were descended from Europeans who had come from the Netherlands in the seventeenth century.

In 1948, the Afrikaner Nationalist Party won South Africa's whites-only election on a promise that it would bring in a policy of apartheid, which means 'separateness'. This was done by a series of laws (see the information box, above).

Some apartheid laws

The Prohibition of Mixed Marriages Act 1949
This made it illegal for people of different races to marry.

The Population Registration Act 1950 In order to separate the races, the government had to be clear on the race of each individual. This law therefore put each South African into a different racial group. With children of mixed marriages, however, this was almost impossible.

The Group Areas Act 1950 This gave the government the power to declare areas for 'whites only'. Black people were made to leave urban areas where they lived and were moved to places chosen by the government.

The Suppression of Communism Act 1950
This banned communism and any other political group 'which aimed to bring about political … change or the promotion of disturbances and disorder'.

The Native Laws Amendment Act 1952
This controlled the movement of Blacks in and out of towns and cities.

The Abolition of Passes Act 1952 This was a much hated law. Contrary to its name, this forced all black men living in 'white' areas to carry a pass or reference book containing information about the holder, including

■ Figure 11.13 Nelson Mandela with his wife, Winnie Mandela, on his release from prison in 1990

address, employment, fingerprints and racial group. Without a pass, working in a white area was illegal. This gave the government a powerful way of controlling where Blacks lived and worked. Renewing a pass often involved waiting in queues for days outside government offices.

The Separate Amenities Act 1953 This was similar to the Jim Crow laws in the southern states of America. It designated all public services and public spaces – post offices, trains, buses, parks, beaches – as either 'Europeans only' or 'Non-Europeans only'. As in America, the non-European facilities were usually of a far lower standard.

The Bantu Education Act 1953 This was designed to keep black children inferior to white children. Black schools had to provide different courses from white ones and each in their ethnic language, not in English. Pupils were educated just enough to work in factories and urban areas. They were encouraged to think of the homelands as where they belonged.

The Separate Representation of Voters Act 1956 This ended the right of the Cape Coloureds (mixed race people living in the Cape area of South Africa) to vote with the Whites in elections.

The Bantu Self-government Act 1959 This set up 'homelands' – areas where Blacks would have political rights, thus justifying their exclusion from mainstream politics. The homelands (Bantustans) separated people not only along racial lines, but also into various tribal groupings. The land set aside for the homelands was only 13 per cent of the total land of South Africa, whereas the Blacks made up 70 per cent of the population.

THINK–PAIR–SHARE

In pairs, **discuss** and consider the following question:

Which of the apartheid laws were aimed at:

- dividing up the different races
- controlling the movement of Blacks
- keeping Blacks in a position where they would not be able to challenge the Whites?

Figure 11.14 An apartheid notice on a beach near Cape Town, 1976

11 How have civil rights and social protest groups brought about change?

269

How was the apartheid system maintained?

These laws were enforced by the police and the army, who carried out harsh measures against anyone who opposed them. Banning orders could stop a person from writing, attending meetings or leaving a particular area without permission. Any meeting that, in the eyes of the Minister of Justice, could 'seriously endanger public peace' could be banned, newspapers were censored, and people could be held without trial for up to 90 days. The Suppression of Communism Act also meant that any protest could be seen as 'communist-inspired'.

The system was also underpinned by the white education system, which taught that God had created separate nations and that children should be educated within their own nations, separately from other nations.

■ **Figure 11.15** Leaders of the FSAW holding the petition. The leader was a black woman, Lillian Ngoyi (*second from left*) and the secretary was a white social worker, Helen Joseph (*second from right*)

HOW SUCCESSFUL WAS NON-VIOLENT PROTEST IN OPPOSING THE APARTHEID REGIME?

In 1912, the South African Native National Congress was formed; this became the African National Congress (ANC) in 1923. Initially, the ANC aimed to keep on good terms with the Whites and did not believe in breaking or disobeying the law. However, after 1948, new leaders of the ANC such as Nelson Mandela and Oliver Tambo moved towards the tactics that had been used by Gandhi (see Chapter 10) with non-violent protests.

The Defiance Campaign

In 1952, Mandela led the Defiance Campaign. This campaign saw ANC supporters refusing to follow the apartheid laws. They sat in 'Whites-only' compartments in trains and used 'Whites-only' facilities. This resulted in the arrest of over 2000 supporters, but also an increase in the membership of the ANC, from 7000 to 100000. In addition, the international community took notice; in 1952, the UN General Assembly passed its first resolution condemning apartheid.

Bus boycotts

Between 1957 and 1959, there were a number of bus boycotts. In order to protest at the rising cost of living, thousands of Blacks walked 48 kilometres a day to work and back.

Protests against passes

When, in 1956, the government said that black women would also have to carry passes, the Federation of South African Women (FSAW) organized a large demonstration. On 27 October 1955, 2000 women protested in Pretoria. By 9 August, 20000 women had joined the protests and they presented a petition to the prime minister.

ACTIVITY: Women in the resistance against apartheid

ATL

- Information literacy skills – Access information to be informed and inform others

Research the role of women in the resistance against apartheid. Organizations and individuals that you could look at include: the Black Sash Organization, the FASW (see Protests against passes), and the actions of Winnie Mandela, Helen Suzman and Ruth First.

For the individual or organization that you choose, consider what actions they took against apartheid and what impact their actions had.

You should write between 700 and 1500 words and correctly cite your sources. Present your research to the class.

◆ **Assessment opportunities**

- ◆ This activity can be assessed using Criterion B: Investigating and Criterion C: Communicating.

DISCUSS

In pairs, read through the Freedom Charter (right). Which apartheid laws would have to be abolished if points 4, 5, 6 and 8 were carried out? What was the reaction of the Nationalist Party likely to be to this charter?

Summary of the Freedom Charter

1. THE PEOPLE SHALL GOVERN!
   Every man and woman shall have the right to vote for and stand as a candidate for all bodies which make laws …
2. ALL NATIONAL GROUPS SHALL HAVE EQUAL RIGHTS!
   All apartheid laws shall be set aside.
3. ALL PEOPLE SHALL SHARE IN THE NATION'S WEALTH!
   The national wealth of our country, the heritage of all South Africans, shall be restored to the people; the mineral wealth beneath the soil, the banks and monopoly industries shall be transferred to the ownership of the people …
4. THE LAND SHALL BE SHARED AMONG THOSE WHO WORK IT!
   Restriction of land ownership on a racial basis shall be ended, and all land re-divided among those who work it …
5. ALL SHALL BE EQUAL BEFORE THE LAW!
   No one shall be imprisoned, deported or restricted without fair trial.
6. ALL SHALL ENJOY HUMAN RIGHTS!
   The law shall guarantee to all the right to speak, to organize, to meet together, to publish, to preach, to worship, and to educate their children. … Pass laws, permits and all other laws restricting these freedoms shall be abolished.
7. THERE SHALL BE WORK AND SECURITY!
   All who work shall be free to form trade unions. … Men and women of all races shall receive equal pay for equal work … sick leave for all workers and maternity leave on full pay for all working mothers …
8. THE DOORS OF LEARNING AND CULTURE SHALL BE OPENED!
   Education shall be free, compulsory, universal and equal for all children. …
9. THERE SHALL BE HOUSES, SECURITY AND COMFORT!
   Rent and prices shall be lowered, food plentiful, and no one shall go hungry; free medical care … shall be provided … slums demolished … the aged, orphans, the disabled and sick cared for by the state …
10. LET THERE BE PEACE AND FRIENDSHIP!
    Let all who love their peace and their country now say, as we say here: THESE FREEDOMS WE SHALL FIGHT FOR, SIDE BY SIDE, THROUGHOUT OUR LIVES UNTIL WE HAVE WON OUR LIBERTY.

The Freedom Charter

In 1955, the ANC called a nationwide meeting to bring together all groups that were calling for change. Nearly 3000 people attended the meeting, which was held at Kliptown near Johannesburg. Here they drew up the Freedom Charter. This was a clear revolutionary manifesto setting out the guiding objectives of the movement and demanding a non-racial, democratic government with equality for all.

Visit this website to read the Freedom Charter in full:

www.anc.org.za/show.php?id=72

The Treason Trial

The government soon responded to these actions. A total of 156 people, including most of the leaders of the ANC and of the Indian community, were arrested and charged with high treason in 1956. However, it was difficult to prove the case against the accused and they were all released. It took five years for the trial to finish.

WHY DID BLACK SOUTH-AFRICANS START USING VIOLENCE TO ACHIEVE THEIR AIMS?

In 1959, the ANC began a campaign against the Pass laws. The ANC announced single-day anti-Pass marches. At the same time, the newly formed PAC or Pan-African Congress called for a more forceful protest, which involved refusing to carry passes, marching on police stations and demanding to be arrested. At Sharpeville, this protest ended in a horrific bloodbath when police opened fire; 69 were killed and many more wounded. Many had been shot in the back.

At the same time, there were clashes between police and protesters in Cape Town. At Langa township, the police ordered demonstrators to leave and then baton-charged them. The demonstrators threw stones; the police responded with bullets, killing two and wounding 49.

There was worldwide condemnation of apartheid as a result of these shootings. The UN called for sanctions against South Africa and anti-apartheid groups were set up in many countries. The reaction of the South African government, however, was to ban the PAC and the ANC and to arrest thousands of people.

For the black leaders of protest, these events confirmed that peaceful protest was no longer an option. Nelson Mandela used the African saying, 'Sebatana ha se bokwe ka diatla' (the attacks of the wild beast cannot be fought off with only bare hands) as a reason for why the ANC now had to use violence. He went underground to form 'Umkhonto we Sizwe' (The Spear of the People), also known as MK. However, the violence carried out by Umkhonto we Sizwe was planned to avoid killing innocent people. It focused at first on the tactic of sabotage, and key targets such as electricity pylons were blown up.

Mandela travelled all over South Africa, organizing the sabotage attacks. He also trained as a guerrilla fighter in Ethiopia and visited Britain and other African states looking for advice and support. Meanwhile, Oliver Tambo went abroad to establish the ANC in exile and to persuade foreign governments to put pressure on the South African government to end apartheid.

In 1962, Mandela was finally caught in a police trap between Johannesburg and Durban. His link with MK was not known and so he was charged with 'leaving the country without permission' and given a five-year prison sentence.

However, the secret headquarters of MK was raided in 1963; as a result the police arrested nine leading members of MK and also discovered many papers outlining MK plans and linking Mandela to the organization.

The Rivonia Trial

The Rivonia Trial lasted from December 1963 to June 1964. Due to the intense international interest, the defendants, including Mandela and Walter Sisulu, did not get the death penalty, but were given life imprisonment. The South African government was able to destroy MK and the ANC inside South Africa, but the trial gave the accused the opportunity to tell the world about apartheid.

You can hear another part of Mandela's speech at the Rivonia Trial here:

http://youtu.be/g5OJ2O5MdKI

'The ideological creed of the ANC is, and always has been, the creed of African Nationalism. It is not the concept of African Nationalism expressed in the cry, "Drive the White man into the sea". The African Nationalism for which the ANC stands is the concept of freedom and fulfilment for the African people in their own land. The most important political document ever adopted by the ANC is the "Freedom Charter". It is by no means a blueprint for a socialist state. It calls for redistribution, but not **nationalization**, of land; it provides for nationalization of mines, banks, and monopoly industry, because big monopolies are owned by one race only, and without such nationalization racial domination would be perpetuated despite the spread of political power. …

'The ANC has never at any period of its history advocated a revolutionary change in the economic structure of the country, nor has it, to the best of my recollection, ever condemned capitalist society.

'Africans want to be paid a living wage. Africans want to perform work which they are capable of doing, and not work which the Government declares them to be capable of. Africans want to be allowed to live where they obtain work, and not be endorsed out of an area because they were not born there. Africans want to be allowed to own land in places where they work, and not to be obliged to live in rented houses which they can never call their own. Africans want to be part of the general population, and not confined to living in their own ghettoes. African men want to have their wives and children to live with them where they work, and not be forced into an unnatural existence in men's hostels. African women want to be with their menfolk and not be left permanently widowed in the Reserves. Africans want to be allowed out after eleven o'clock at night and not to be confined to their rooms like little children. Africans want to be allowed to travel in their own country and to seek work where they want to and not where the Labour Bureau tells them to. Africans want a just share in the whole of South Africa; they want security and a stake in society.

'Above all, we want equal political rights, because without them our disabilities will be permanent. I know this sounds revolutionary to the whites in this country, because the majority of voters will be Africans. This makes the white man fear democracy.

'But this fear cannot be allowed to stand in the way of the only solution which will guarantee racial harmony and freedom for all. It is not true that the enfranchisement of all will result in racial domination. Political division, based on colour, is entirely artificial and, when it disappears, so will the domination of one colour group by another. The ANC has spent half a century fighting against racialism. When it triumphs it will not change that policy.

'This then is what the ANC is fighting. Their struggle is a truly national one. It is a struggle of the African people, inspired by their own suffering and their own experience. It is a struggle for the right to live.

'During my lifetime I have dedicated myself to this struggle of the African people. I have fought against white domination, and I have fought against black domination. I have cherished the ideal of a democratic and free society in which all persons live together in harmony and with equal opportunities. It is an ideal which I hope to live for and to achieve. But if needs be, it is an ideal for which I am prepared to die.'

■ **Figure 11.16** Extracts from Mandela's speech at the Rivonia Trial

ACTIVITY: The Rivonia Trial

■ ATL

■ Critical thinking skills – Evaluate evidence and arguments

1 In pairs, **analyse** Mandela's speech. What attitude does Mandela have towards:
   ● **communism**
   ● **white people?**

Summarize in your own words what Mandela believed he was fighting for.

2 **Discuss** the message of the cartoon in Figure 11.17 (page 274).
   Write your own caption for this cartoon.

◆ Assessment opportunities

◆ This activity can be assessed using Criterion D: Thinking critically.

'THERE! I THINK THAT'LL HOLD HIM'

■ **Figure 11.17** Cartoon by the British cartoonist Illingworth on the result of the Rivonia Trial

OTHER FORMS OF RESISTANCE TO APARTHEID

Although Nelson Mandela was in prison, resistance and protest against apartheid continued both inside and outside of the country.

Steve Biko and Black Consciousness

The Black Consciousness movement grew in popularity during the later 1960s. Influenced by the Black Power movement in America (see page 265), the key idea of this movement was that Blacks should gain confidence in their ability to change things for themselves, end their dependence on Whites and win their own freedom. In 1969, a number of black university students broke away from the National Union of South African Students, which was white dominated, and set up the South African Students Organization (SASO). Steve Biko was its first president.

In SASO articles headed 'I write what I like', he argued that black people had lost confidence in themselves as a result of living in a white-dominated society. He wanted black South Africans to take pride in being black, to learn about the black African heroes of the past and to refuse to accept white superiority. He set up Black Community Programmes, in which Blacks helped each other without white assistance (similar to the work of the Black Panthers in the USA).

In 1977, Biko was arrested. He was dead within 26 days, having been kept naked in a cell, and was so badly beaten up that he went into a coma. The government followed this up by banning 17 organizations and two newspapers. However, Biko had attained international standing and his murder added to the growing opposition to the South African government.

■ **Figure 11.18** Steve Biko

The Soweto uprising and student protest

Biko's ideas also inspired many young South Africans. In 1976, the school pupils of Soweto started an uprising against government education policies, which said that half of the school curriculum had to be taught in Afrikaans – the language of the hated white government. The demonstration ended in a riot and the death of two students.

As news of the deaths spread to other parts of South Africa so did the riots. Students boycotted classes and burned schools. The police continued to use force against the protesters so that by the end of the year 1000 protesters had died.

The government blamed the riots on communists and the ANC. However, the riots were shown on television around the world, turning international opinion even more against white South Africa.

Gandhi and South Africa

You read about the importance of Gandhi in helping to end British rule in India in Chapter 10. But, before this, he lived and worked for 21 years in South Africa as a lawyer. As an Indian, he faced discrimination in the country, and therefore became a spokesman and advocate for Indian rights in South Africa. This is also where he started his idea of non-violent resistance.

ACTIVITY: Macmillan's 'wind of change' speech

■ **ATL**

■ Information literacy skills – Access information to be informed and inform others

In pairs, inquire further into the circumstances of Macmillan's 'wind of change' speech (see extract from the speech on page 247).

● What was the reaction of the South African parliamentarians who were listening to the speech?
● How did the South African Prime Minster respond? Why do you think this was?
● Why do you think this speech was considered a turning point for both Britain and for South Africa?

◆ Assessment opportunities

◆ This activity can be assessed using Criterion B: Investigating and Criterion C: Communicating.

11 How have civil rights and social protest groups brought about change?

275

ACTIVITY: Analysing the Soweto riots

1 Study Sources G–K on the Soweto riots. With reference to origin and purpose, assess how useful Sources G, H and K are for working out the causes of the Soweto riots.

2 Prepare a television documentary on the Soweto riots.

How will you achieve this?

Work in groups. You may want to research the events further. You will need to include the following:

● **Background to the riots – why did they happen?**

● Interviews with eyewitnesses
● Interviews with the South African Government
● Comment on international reaction
● Analysis of the consequences of the riots.

Who is your audience?

Prepare this for a documentary for a non-South African audience, for example a European or American television channel, so you do not have to worry about censorship.

SOURCE G

■ **Figure 11.19** Protest against the use of Afrikaans in schools, Soweto, June 1976

From a novel based on eyewitness reports

'The police, addressing us first in Afrikaans and then in broken Zulu, tried to order us to disperse. But we had grievances which could no longer wait. We surged forward, aiming to sweep them out of our path if they would not give way. By now our frenzied numbers had swelled and swelled. We shouted "Amandla" [Power], "Inkululeko ngoku" [Freedom in our lifetime] and "One Azania, One Nation" as we marched on, our clenched fists held high [Azania – the name the Black Consciousness movement preferred to South Africa].'

Mbulelo Mzamane. 1982. Children of Soweto.

SOURCE I

Figure 11.20 Mbuyisa Makhubo carrying Hector Pieterson accompanied by Hector's sister Antoinette, June 1976

SOURCE J

From an article in a South African newspaper (The New Nation *had as its aim to 'reflect the daily struggles and aspirations of the oppressed majority'; it was banned in 1988.)*

'The story of the boy who picked up and carried Hector is part of a wider tragedy – the flight of young people into exile. The boy's mother tells us that her son, Mbuyisa Makhubo, was in his grandmother's house when he heard the first shots. He ran out of the house and as he approached the crowd, Hector fell at his feet. Mbuyisa was on the run from that day onward. He left the country two months later. His mother received letters from Botswana and Nigeria. The last letter arrived in 1978. She has not heard from him since, and assumes that he died in exile.'

June 1986. New Nation.

SOURCE K

Conclusions of Mr Justice Cillie, who headed the South African government's Commission of Inquiry into the riots

'Because of this intimidation [from Communist agitators who frightened people into rioting] … it cannot be said that the riots were an expression of the Black man's wish or that, by rioting, he was raising his voice against oppression and for a more democratic situation in the Republic of South Africa.'

DISCUSS

From what you have read in this chapter about the USA and South Africa, can you draw any conclusions as to whether violence or non-violence is more effective in achieving aims? How important is direct action?

Refer back to Chapter 6. What other forms of social protest can you identify from this chapter?

HOW DID APARTHEID END?

Ongoing protest, combined with other factors, eventually brought an end to apartheid. Some of these other factors are shown below.

In 1989, a new government in South Africa, led by F.W. de Klerk, realized the need to introduce major changes. Thus de Klerk unbanned the ANC and PAC and released Mandela and other political prisoners from prison.

In 1963, the new Organization of African Unity made the abolition of apartheid one of its main aims.

Throughout the 1960s, newly independent black nations in Africa began to join the United Nations. Consequently the UN became increasingly critical of South Africa's apartheid policy. The loss of friendly white states on its borders, as these states became independent, also impacted on support for South Africa.

Anti-apartheid groups were set up all over the world. When the South African rugby team arrived in Britain in 1970, the anti-apartheid movement set up a 'Stop the tour' campaign, which disrupted games and prevented any other South African sports teams playing in Britain.

In April 1994, the first fully democratic elections were held in South Africa. The ANC gained 62.5% of the vote and Nelson Mandela became the new President of South Africa.

Boycotts against South African goods were organized and demonstrations were held outside South African embassies and companies that traded with South Africa.

Because the apartheid regime in South Africa was so anti-communist, it was always supported by Western governments as part of the wider Cold War struggle. However, once the Cold War ended, there was no need for the West to support South Africa in this way.

Church leaders regularly spoke out against apartheid. Archbishop Desmond Tutu became General Secretary of Churches in 1978. He used his position to criticise apartheid and encourage black South Africans to use non-violent methods to resist apartheid.

The collapse of the communist governments of Eastern Europe also removed the fear of a 'communist onslaught' in southern Africa.

Change of government

Independence of African states

The international anti-apartheid movement

The end of the Cold War

Factors which contributed to the end of apartheid

Archbishop Desmond Tutu and black church leaders

Economic crisis

Trade unions

Growing unrest in black townships

The increasing violence in South Africa meant that by the end of the 1980s many businesses were pulling out of South Africa. The country seemed on the verge of civil war. International sanctions were also having a disastrous effect.

During the 1980s, black workers were allowed to join trade unions. Mass strikes were organized to force change. In 1982, over 365 000 working days were lost as the result of strikes.

In the late 1980s there were a series of uprisings in black townships, which the government found hard to put down despite declaring a state of emergency in the country.

■ **Figure 11.21** Factors which contributed to the end of apartheid

DISCUSS

Refer back to the statement in the debatable question at the start of this chapter: 'Civil rights and social protest groups are irrelevant in the twenty-first century'. Has your study of this chapter and your own research changed your views on this?

▼ Links to: Language A; Literature A

In small groups, **explore** novels, plays and poems that portray or advocate civil rights. Try to find examples from different regions. **Discuss** these in your group.

What are the similarities and differences between the themes, characters and narratives in the literature you find? Are there any examples from the work you cover in Language A? Has your study of civil rights case studies in History given you a richer understanding of this literature?

ACTIVITY: What is South Africa like today?

■ ATL

- Information literacy skills – Make connections between various sources of information

Refer back to Mandela's dream for a multiracial South Africa as set out in his speech at his Rivonia Trial (see page 273). Research South Africa today, its style of government and the rights and wealth of different sections of society. How far have his ideals been realized?

◆ Assessment opportunities

- In this activity you have practised skills that are assessed using Criterion B: Investigating, Criterion C: Communicating and Criterion D: Thinking critically.

! Take action

! Find examples of where people are fighting for rights today. Find a news article to share with the rest of your class. **Discuss** the methods of protest being used and whether they have had any success.

Reflection

In this chapter we have examined the reasons for civil rights protest in America and in South Africa. We have also looked at the nature of this protest and the impact that it had in bringing about change.

Reflecting on our learning … Use this table to reflect on your own learning in this chapter.						
Questions we asked	Answers we found	Any further questions now?				
Factual						
Conceptual						
Debatable						
Approaches to learning you used in this chapter:	Description – what new skills did you learn?	How well did you master the skills?				
			Novice	Learner	Practitioner	Expert
Collaboration skills						
Critical-thinking skills						
Information literacy skills						
Learner profile attribute	*Reflect on the importance of being a communicator for our learning in this chapter.*					
Communicator						

12 Can individuals make a difference in shaping the world?

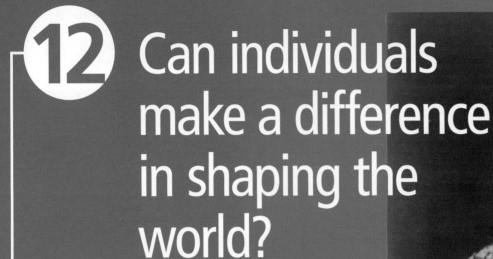

○ Individuals can play a **key role** in the **development of their nation states** and in the **nature and development** of **global interactions**.

■ **Figure 12.1** Significant individuals (*bottom, clockwise*): Nelson Mandela, Marie Curie, Karl Marx, Mao Zedong

CONSIDER THESE QUESTIONS:

Factual: What significant individuals have you studied? How have these individuals been a force for a) socio-economic change, b) political/ideological change, c) health and welfare of their society, d) conflict within their society and e) interstate conflict?

Conceptual: How far are individuals more important in historical processes than impersonal factors?

Debatable: To what extent are 'world-changing' events shaped by significant individuals?

Now **share and compare** your thoughts and ideas with your partner, or with the whole class.

○ IN THIS CHAPTER, WE WILL ...

■ **Find out:**
   ■ about some of the significant individuals who have had an important and long-lasting impact on societies
   ■ about the factors that make an individual significant.
■ **Explore** different views on the role of individuals in shaping history.
■ **Take action** by considering the impact of key individuals shaping our world today.

A significant individual is not simply someone who is famous but someone who has had an impact on society. Who do you consider to be significant individuals in history and in the world today? Make a list of significant individuals for the following categories:

- Politicians and leaders
- Explorers and pioneers
- Campaigners
- Scientists and inventors
- Artists and cultural figures

What do you think makes a person a significant individual?

DISCUSS

What criteria would you use to decide whether a historical figure was a significant individual? Look at the list below and examine how far you agree with these factors. Would you add more factors?

ⓘ

What factors make an individual significant in history?

- Their ideas and/or actions affected many people.
- Their ideas and/or actions had an impact that lasted over time.
- Their ideas and/or actions are relevant to how we understand the world today.

■ These Approaches to Learning (ATL) skills will be useful …

- Collaboration skills
- Communication skills
- Critical-thinking skills
- Information literacy skills
- Organization skills
- Transfer skills

● We will reflect on this learner profile attribute …

- Reflective – reflecting on the individuals that you have covered throughout this two-year programme.

◆ Assessment opportunities in this chapter:

- ◆ **Criterion A:** Knowledge and understanding
- ◆ **Criterion B:** Investigating
- ◆ **Criterion C:** Communicating
- ◆ **Criterion D:** Thinking critically

What is the 'intentionalist' idea of history?

Historians do not agree on what the key driving forces of history might be. Historians who believe that significant individuals are the key factor in history are often known as 'intentionalist'. They argue that the personalities and intentions of key individuals are the main factor in shaping history. This approach has also been called the 'Great men' view of history. As you work through this chapter, and using the material you have studied throughout your two-year history programme, consider the extent to which you agree with the intentionalist viewpoint.

ACTIVITY: Significant individuals

■ **ATL**

- Information literacy skills – Access information to be informed and inform others

Who do you consider to be a 'significant individual' in history? Try to think of someone who has not been covered in this history course. Research further into your chosen individual and bear in mind the factors that might make them 'significant' (see page 281). Present an image of your significant individual for the cover of *Time* magazine with an editorial on 'The significance of X in history'. This should be between 700 and 1500 words long. Correctly cite your sources.

◆ Assessment opportunities

- ◆ This activity can be assessed using Criterion B: Investigating and Criterion C: Communicating.

THINK–PAIR–SHARE

Look at Figure 12.2. You can look back through Chapters 1–11 to review each person. In pairs, **evaluate** to what extent these key historical figures meet the criteria for being significant individuals. Then **discuss** your ideas with the rest of the class.

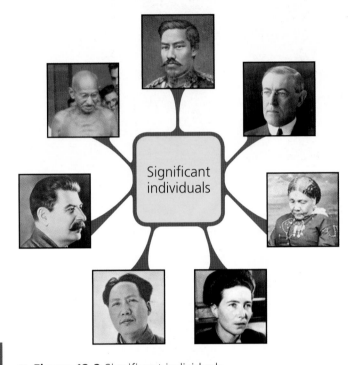

■ **Figure 12.2** Significant individuals

SOURCE A

■ **Figure 12.3** Ford car, c.1923

ACTIVITY: The impact of individuals in medicine and industry

ATL

- Transfer skills – Inquire in different contexts to gain a different perspective

With reference to Chapters 4 and 5, look at Sources A and B and answer the questions using your knowledge from those chapters.

1 **Who were the significant individuals responsible for the innovations in Sources A and B?**
2 **Describe** the impact of their innovations on society.

◆ Assessment opportunities

◆ In this activity you have practised skills that are assessed using Criterion A: Knowing and understanding.

SOURCE B

John Collins Warren, a surgeon in Massachusetts, USA, 1846

'The patient was arranged for the operation in a sitting posture, and everything was made ready … The patient was then made to inhale fluid from a tube with a glass globe. After four or five minutes he appeared to be asleep, and was thought by Dr Morton to be in a condition for the operation. I made an incision between two or three inches long in the direction of the tumour, and to my great surprise without any starting, crying or other indication of pain.'

ACTIVITY: The impact of individuals on trade

ATL

- Information literacy skills – Access information to be informed and inform others

Work in two groups, A and B, and refer to Chapter 3,

Group A: **investigate** the role of pioneers and entrepreneurs in the development and growth of global trade in the nineteenth century.

Group B: **investigate** the role of significant individuals in the abolition of the slave trade and the development of alternative trades with the African continent. Attempt to include examples from different regions.

Collate the research from each person in your group into one short report (maximum 900 words) entitled: The impact of individuals on trade. Each group reads the report of the other group. Discuss the extent to which you agree with the idea that individuals are important to the development of fair trading practices.

◆ Assessment opportunities

◆ In this activity you have practised skills that are assessed using Criterion B: Investigating and Criterion C: Communicating.

ACTIVITY: Individuals and innovation

ATL

- Organization skills – Use appropriate strategies for organizing complex information
- Reflection skills – Consider content (What did I learn about today? What don't I yet understand? What questions do I have now?)

With reference to Chapters 1 and 2, **explore** the role of significant individuals in the development of the Industrial Revolution. How important was their role? Would the revolution still have happened without people with new ideas and inventions?

Consider the roles that innovators and pioneers have played. Draw a mind map or spider diagram that **identifies** the roles played by significant individuals as inventors, **entrepreneurs**, developers, pioneers and innovators in the nineteenth century.

◆ Assessment opportunities

◆ In this activity you have practised skills that are assessed using Criterion A: Knowing and understanding and Criterion C: Communicating.

■ **Figure 12.4** Dada artist Marcel Janco said: 'We had lost confidence in our culture. Everything had to be demolished. We would begin again.'

ACTIVITY: The impact of individuals on intellectual and ideological movements

■ ATL

- Organization skills – Use appropriate strategies for organizing complex information

With reference to Chapter 7, create an annotated timeline of significant individuals in leading and inspiring intellectual and ideological movements in the nineteenth and twentieth centuries. In your annotations, add notes on whether your significant individual/movement created conflict or cooperation in society and between societies.

Share your timelines with a partner.

Now consider the following questions in pairs:

'How did new intellectual movements and ideologies foster a) conflict and b) cooperation?'

◆ Assessment opportunities

- ◆ In this activity you have practised skills that are assessed using Criterion A: Knowing and understanding.

ACTIVITY: The impact of individuals in art and culture

■ ATL

- Collaboration skills – Listen actively to other perspectives and ideas

With reference to Chapter 6, and in small groups, **discuss** the significant individuals involved in artistic and cultural movements of the nineteenth and twentieth centuries. What factors made them important? How similar were these individuals?

◆ Assessment opportunities

- ◆ In this activity you have practised skills that are assessed using Criterion D: Thinking critically.

ACTIVITY: The impact of individuals on the development of conflict and on peacemaking

■ **ATL**

■ Critical-thinking skills – Draw reasonable conclusions and generalizations

With reference to Chapter 8, and in pairs, read the names of the significant individuals involved in war and peace shown in Figure 12.5. What arguments could be made about some of these individuals as a) peacemakers and b) key figures causing conflict?

Watch the following clip and make notes on Woodrow Wilson's vision for a world without interstate conflict:

http://youtu.be/r0ldr18Rnho

Compare and contrast the role of significant individuals in a) causing war and b) making peace.

◆ **Assessment opportunities**

◆ In this activity you have practised skills that are assessed using Criterion D: Thinking critically.

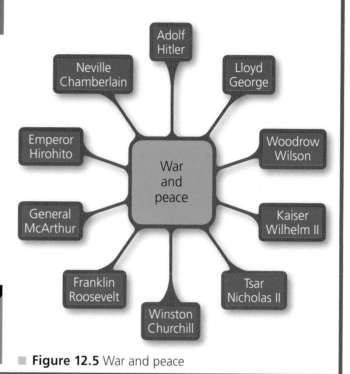

■ **Figure 12.5** War and peace

ACTIVITY: The impact of individuals on empires and alliances

■ **ATL**

■ Collaboration skills – Listen actively to other perspectives and ideas

After reviewing Chapter 9, **identify** where a significant individual's ideas and actions have led to the creation of an alliance system, the development of an empire or the establishment of a supra-national organization.

Also consider the impersonal factors, i.e. those factors that are not specifically driven by an individual such as economic growth or economic crises, nationalism, intellectual movements and social factors.

In small groups, complete a copy of the following table:

	Role of significant individuals	Role of impersonal factors
Empires		
Supra-national alliances		
Supra-national organizations		

◆ **Assessment opportunities**

◆ In this activity you have practised skills that are assessed using Criterion A: Knowing and understanding and Criterion D: Thinking critically.

SOURCE C

From a statement by the African National Congress of South Africa, Johannesburg, South Africa, October 1994, on the leadership of Julius Nyerere in Tanzania

'Julius Nyerere was an outstanding leader, a brilliant philosopher and a people's hero – a champion for the entire African continent. He shall always be remembered as one of Africa's greatest and most respected sons and the father of the Tanzanian nation.

'Throughout his long life he enjoyed the respect and popularity that extended far beyond the borders of Tanzania. His wise counsel was sought from around the globe, even after he resigned from the presidency in 1985. A legacy in his own lifetime; he served as a symbol of inspiration for all African nations in their liberation struggles to free themselves from the shackles of oppression and colonialism.'

SOURCE D

Extract from a book by Martin Luther King, USA, 1959

'We are often too loud and too boisterous, and spend too much on drink. Even the most poverty-stricken among us can purchase a ten-cent bar of soap; even the most uneducated among us can have high morals. By improving our standards, we will go a long way towards breaking down the arguments of those who are in favour of segregation.

'The other part of our programme must be non-violent resistance to all forms of racial injustice, even when this means going to jail; and bold action to end the demoralisation caused by the legacy of slavery and segregation, inferior schools, slums and second-class citizenship. A new frontal assault on the poverty, disease and ignorance of a people too long ignored by America's conscience will make victory more certain.'

ACTIVITY: The impact of individuals on political and social change

■ ATL

- Transfer skills – Inquire in different contexts to gain a different perspective

With reference to Chapters 10 and 11, read Sources C and D.

1   **Highlight where Source C supports the criteria you have defined for a significant individual.**
2   **Make notes on what these sources suggest about the qualities and characteristics of effective leadership.**

◆ Assessment opportunities

- ◆ In this activity you have practised skills that are assessed using Criterion D: Thinking critically.

ACTIVITY: Assessing the overall impact of individuals

■ ATL

- Organization skills – Use appropriate strategies for organizing complex information

Write an essay, answering this question: 'To what extent are "world-changing" events shaped by significant individuals?'

As always, draft a detailed plan and use your own knowledge to support your points.

> Hint
>
> You should choose two or three specific world-changing events on which to focus your discussion.

◆ Assessment opportunities

- ◆ This activity can be assessed using Criterion A: Knowing and understanding, Criterion C: Communicating and Criterion D: Thinking critically.

Other views on different key factors driving historical change

We have considered the 'intentionalist' idea of history being made by significant individuals. However, there are historians who disagree with this view.

- **Marxist** historians believe that history is shaped by economic factors.
- **Structuralist** historians argue that history is driven by political and military structures.
- The **Annales** perspective is that geography is the key factor in historical change, for example, climate and access to resources.
- In addition, there are some historians, known as **Accidentalists**, who suggest that accidents are the main driving force of historical change.

ACTIVITY: Historical change debate

- ■ ATL

- ■ Communication skills – Use a variety of speaking techniques to communicate with a variety of audiences

The class will be divided into four groups:
a) Structuralists, b) Marxists, c) Annales and d) Accidentalists.

Each group should work on creating a case for their perspective on historical change from the material in Chapters 1–11. Each group should then present their findings in a live conference forum of university students.

◆ Assessment opportunities

- ◆ In this activity you have practised skills that are assessed using Criterion A: Knowing and understanding, Criterion C: Communicating and Criterion D: Thinking critically

Reflection

In this chapter we have reflected on the content of this book, identifying where individuals have played a key role in bringing about change.

Reflecting on our learning … Use this table to reflect on your own learning in this chapter.						
Questions we asked	Answers we found	Any further questions now?				
Factual						
Conceptual						
Debatable						
Approaches to learning you used in this chapter:	Description – what new skills did you learn?	How well did you master the skills?				
		Novice	Learner	Practitioner	Expert	
Collaboration skills						
Communication skills						
Critical-thinking skills						
Information literacy skills						
Organization skills						
Transfer skills						
Learner profile attribute	*Reflect on the importance of being reflective for our learning in this chapter.*					
Reflective						

13 What are the consequences of inaction?

○ *Inaction by individuals* can be a *significant factor* in the *development of inequality and discrimination in society*.

CONSIDER THESE QUESTIONS:

Factual: What is genocide? What factors led to the perpetuation of genocide in Nazi Germany? What other examples of genocide are there from the twentieth century?

Conceptual: How might cooperation prevent discrimination?

Debatable: Who was to blame for genocide? How can genocide be prevented in the future?

Now **share and compare** your thoughts and ideas with your partner, or with the whole class.

○ IN THIS CHAPTER, WE WILL ...

■ **Find out:**
   ■ how the connections between individuals, minority groups and their communities can break down and lead to violence and conflict
   ■ about the role of individuals and communities in perpetrating acts of genocide and possible reasons for why this happens.
■ **Explore** the role of the international community in historical genocides.
■ **Take action** by looking at ways in which the international community can prevent genocide and crimes against humanity in the twenty-first century.

■ These Approaches to Learning (ATL) skills will be useful ...

■ Critical-thinking skills
■ Information literacy skills
■ Media literacy skills
■ Organization skills

● We will reflect on this learner profile attribute ...

● Thinker – using critical-thinking skills to analyse and take responsible action on complex problems; exercising initiative in making reasoned, ethical decisions.

'For evil to flourish, it only requires good men to do nothing.'
– Simon Wiesenthal

'If the pictures of tens of thousands of human bodies being gnawed on by dogs do not wake us out of our apathy, I do not know what will.' – Under-Secretary-General of the United Nations, Kofi Annan, in The East Africa, 18 March 1996

■ **Figure 13.1** The Rwandan genocide, 1994

◆ Assessment opportunities in this chapter:

- ◆ **Criterion A:** Knowing and understanding
- ◆ **Criterion B:** Investigating
- ◆ **Criterion C:** Communicating
- ◆ **Criterion D:** Thinking critically

KEY WORDS

collaborator	perpetrate
ethical	violate
ethnic	

THINK–PAIR–SHARE

Read the poem (right). What are your thoughts? In pairs, **discuss** the meaning of the poem and how it makes you feel.

First they came for the communists, and I did not speak out –
    because I was not a communist.

Then they came for the socialists, and I did not speak out –
    because I was not a socialist.

Then they came for the trade unionists, and I did not speak out –
    because I was not a trade unionist;

Then they came for the Jews, and I did not speak out –
    because I was not a Jew.

    Then they came for me – and there was no one left to speak out for me.

Attributed to Pastor Martin Niemoller, Germany, 1940s.

Why has genocide taken place in history?

WHAT DOES GENOCIDE MEAN?

Winston Churchill, the British prime minister during the Second World War, referred to Nazi atrocities as 'a crime without a name'. It was not until 1944 that Raphael Lemkin, a Polish Jewish émigré who taught at Yale and Duke universities, coined the term genocide – from the Greek *genos* meaning race/tribe and *cide*, killing. His broad definition was revised after debate in the UN over how it should be defined by the international community.

ⓘ UN definition of genocide

On 9 December 1948, the UN adopted the Genocide Convention, defining genocide as follows:

Genocide means any of the following acts committed with the intent to destroy, in whole or in part, a national, ethnical, racial or religious group (more recently political and social groups have been added) such as:

a Killing members of the group

b Causing serious bodily harm or mental harm to members of the group

c Deliberately inflicting on the group conditions of life calculated to bring about its physical destruction in whole or in part

d Imposing measures intended to prevent births within the group

e Forcibly transferring children of the group to another group

ACTIVITY: Why should we learn about genocide?

■ ATL

■ Critical-thinking skills – Consider ideas from multiple perspectives

Examine Sources A–C and then answer the questions in pairs or in groups.

1 **Identify** the reasons given by Ben Whitaker in Source A as to why research on genocide should be part of a school curriculum.
2 What point is being made by the principal in his letter (Source B)?
3 Do you agree with these writers?
4 What other justifications could be given for studying genocide at school?
5 What point is being made by the cartoon (Source C)?
6 What do Sources A–C identify as the reasons for studying genocide at school?

◆ Assessment opportunities

◆ In this activity you have practised skills that are assessed using Criterion D: Thinking critically.

SOURCE A

'The results of research [on the causes of genocide] could help form one part of a wide educational programme throughout the world against such aberrations, starting at an early age in schools. Without a strong basis of international public support, even the most perfectly re-drafted [UN] Convention [on Genocide] will be of little value … public awareness should be developed internationally to reinforce the individual's responsibility, based on the knowledge that it is illegal to obey a superior order or law that violates human rights.'

Whitaker, B. 1985. Revised and updated report on the question of the Prevention and Punishment of the Crime of Genocide, p. 62 (E/CN.4/ Sub.2/1985/6, 2 July 1985)

A letter sent by the principal of an American high school to all teachers on the first day of term

Dear Teacher,

I am a survivor of a concentration camp. My eyes saw what no man should witness:
- Gas chambers built by learned engineers.
- Children poisoned by educated doctors.
- Infants killed by trained nurses.
- Women and babies shot and burned by high school and college graduates.

So I am suspicious of education.

My request is: Help your students become human.

Your efforts must never produce learned monsters, skilled psychopaths, educated Eichmanns. Reading, writing and arithmetic are important only if they serve to make our children more human.

SOURCE C

■ **Figure 13.2** Cartoon commentating on the situation in Darfur in 2005, *Holocaust and Darfur*, Steve Greenberg

13 What are the consequences of inaction?

What factors led to the Holocaust?

'The language to describe the Holocaust does not exist. The more I study, the less I understand.'

These are the words of Nobel Peace Prize winner and Holocaust survivor, Elie Wiesel. *Holocaust* is a word of Greek origin meaning 'sacrifice by fire'. The Holocaust was the systematic, state-sponsored persecution and murder of approximately 6 million Jews by the Nazi regime and its collaborators.

In order to understand the Holocaust and why it happened, it is necessary to start by looking at Hitler's views on how society should be organized and run.

The Nazis believed in a hierarchy of races. At the top of this hierarchy was the Aryan race or master race. Germans were of Aryan descent and the ideal Aryan was shown as blond, blue-eyed, tall, strong and healthy.

A key idea of Nazi policy was the idea of *Volksgemeinschaft*. This was the creation of a society containing healthy, pure Aryans all working together for the good of the state. Such Aryans were not to be contaminated by the 'subhumans' or *Untermenschen* such as black people, Slavs or Jews. In fact, anyone who did not fit into this idea of a *Volksgemeinschaft* was to be excluded.

■ **Figure 13.3** Propaganda poster showing the Nazi idea of *Volksgemeinschaft*. It reads: 'The NSDAP secures the people's community. Fellow people, if you need help and advice, turn to your local group'

DISCUSS

What can you learn from the Nazi propaganda poster in Figure 13.3 about Nazi views regarding the ideal German family?

Groups who were identified as needing to be eliminated from the *Volksgemeinschaft* included:

- **Asocials:** These included people who did not want to work, such as beggars, criminals and alcoholics. They were rounded up in 1933 and sent to concentration camps.
- **Homosexuals:** Homosexuals were also considered to be asocial. They were brutally persecuted as they were seen not only to go against the laws of nature but also to be a threat to Nazi goals of increasing the population. Up to 15 000 homosexuals were arrested and sent to concentration camps. Some were also castrated or subjected to medical experiments.
- **The mentally ill and physically disabled:** These people were also regarded as a burden on the community. Sterilization was made compulsory for the hereditary ill. This later changed to actual 'mercy killing'. First children and then adults were subject to euthanasia.

DISCUSS

What is the message of the poster in Figure 13.4 regarding the disabled?

Evaluate the purpose, values and limitations of the poster from its origin and purpose.

Figure 13.4 This Nazi propaganda poster reads: '60 000 Reichsmark is the cost of this person with a hereditary illness over his lifetime. Fellow German, that's your money as well! Read 'Neues Volk', the monthly magazine of the NSDAP Office of Racial Policy'

IDEOLOGICAL OPPONENTS TO NAZISM

Socialists and communists were rounded up and put into camps. Religious groups such as Jehovah's Witnesses were also arrested and sent to camps.

Non-Aryans

Non-Aryans included Roma, Jews and black people. Many black Germans were compulsorily sterilized. Roma were despised both for their race and their different lifestyles and there was already much prejudice against them in Germany. They were put into concentration camps where around 500 000 were killed. However, it was the Jews who faced systematic discrimination and persecution from 1933. Why was this?

Hatred of Jews or **anti-Semitism** was not new in Germany; Jews had faced discrimination and had been persecuted for many centuries throughout Europe. Hitler had a hatred of Jews from his time of living in Vienna, where he had resented their wealth and influence. He used the Jews as the 'scapegoat' or group to blame for all Germany's problems since 1919 – from Germany's defeat in the war to the hyperinflation of 1923, to the Great Depression of 1929. Hitler's determination to create a pure, Aryan race meant that he believed that Jews had to be eliminated from German society and he used his power from 1933 to try to ensure that this became a reality.

WHAT WERE THE ANTI-JEWISH POLICIES CARRIED OUT BY THE NAZIS AFTER 1933?

Treatment of the Jews in Germany

Hitler's hatred of the Jews and his determination to eliminate them from German society meant that a series of anti-Jewish laws were passed between 1933 and 1939. At the same time, a relentless campaign of propaganda was launched by Goebbels, the propaganda minister, which had the aim of convincing German people of the inferiority of Jewish people and thereby persuading them that anti-Jewish laws were both acceptable and necessary. Influencing the minds of German children was central to this campaign, and school lessons and textbooks put across anti-Semitic views.

■ **Figure 13.5** An illustration from an anti-Semitic children's textbook, 1938

DISCUSS

Identify the message of each of the examples of Nazi propaganda in Figures 13.5 and 13.6.

What effect do you think this kind of propaganda would have had on German children and German adults?

THINK–PAIR–SHARE

Think about the ideologies you studied in Chapter 7. In pairs, **discuss** which ideologies may foster discrimination and hostility towards minority groups within societies. Share your discussion with the class. Are there any conclusions drawn about the role of certain ideologies in creating tensions and conflict within communities?

■ **Figure 13.6** Nazi propaganda poster; the caption reads 'The Eternal Jew'

1933

- Hitler ordered a boycott of shops owned by Jews. The SA (see box on page 298) painted 'Jude' on shop windows.
- A law excluded Jews from government jobs.
- Jewish books were burnt.
- Anti-Jewish propaganda started.

1934

- Anti-Jewish propaganda increased.
- Local councils banned Jews from public spaces such as parks, playing fields and swimming pools.

| 1930 | 1931 | 1932 | 1933 | 1934 | |

■ **Figure 13.8** 'Jude' (Jew) was painted on shop windows

1936
- Because of the Olympic Games in Berlin, anti-Jewish propaganda was reduced to give a good impression to the international community.
- At the same time, however, Jewish professionals such as dentists, accountants and teachers had their activities banned or restricted.

1937
- Hitler publicly attacked Jews.
- More Jewish businesses were taken over.

1939
- The Reich office for emigration was established under Himmler in order to carry out forced emigration.
- Following the outbreak of war, German Jews were placed under curfew and radios were confiscated.
- Jews had to hand over any jewellery, gold or silver to the police.

5   **1936**   **1937**   **1938**   **1939**   **1940**

1935
- Jews were banned from joining the army.
- Jews were banned from restaurants.
- At the Nuremberg Rally, Hitler announced:
  - the Reich Law on Citizenship – this meant that only those of German blood could be German citizens. Thus, Jews lost their citizenship, and the right to vote and to hold office
  - the Law for the Protection of German Blood and German People – this forbade mixed marriages or sex between Aryans and Jews.

1938
There was a series of anti-Jewish decrees:
- Jewish doctors, dentists and lawyers were prohibited from having Aryans as their clients/patients.
- Jewish children were excluded from German schools and universities.
- Jews had to add Sarah or Israel to their names to show they were Jewish.
- Identity cards had to be stamped with a 'J'.
- In November, Kristallnacht took place (see box on page 298).
- Following Kristallnacht, another decree excluded Jews from German economic life and Jews were excluded from schools and universities.

Kristallnacht

Kristallnacht was triggered by the assassination of a German official in the German Embassy in Paris. The assassination was carried out by a young Polish Jew called Herschel Grynszpan, who was furious at the treatment of his parents who had been deported to Poland.

Goebbels used the outrage that followed the assassination as an excuse to carry out a series of attacks on Jews on 9–10 November 1938. This became known as Kristallnacht (the Night of Broken Glass) because of the number of windows that were smashed. Thousands of Jewish businesses were attacked and synagogues burnt. Ninety-one Jews were murdered and 20 000 were sent to camps. Jews were forced to pay 1 billion Reichsmarks for the damage.

The *Sturmabteilung* and *Schutzstaffel*

The *Sturmabteilung* (SA) were also known as the Brown Shirts. These men played a key role in helping Hitler get to power by providing protection for Nazi rallies and assemblies. They led attacks against political opponents of the Nazi party, such as the communists, and the Jews.

The *Schutzstaffel* (SS) were an elite group led by Heinrich Himmler, who acted as Hitler's bodyguard and later played a key role in carrying out the genocide of Jews in the concentration camps. It was the SS who made up the *Einsatzgruppen*, who carried out the killings of Jews during the invasion of Poland and the Soviet Union.

DISCUSS

Review the different measures taken against the Jews in Germany. Which of these:
- affected children
- had an impact on the economic life of Jews
- stopped Jews from being full citizens of Germany
- had a serious impact on how they lived their lives?

EXTENSION

Visit this weblink:

http://genocidewatch.org/genocide/tenstagesofgenocide.html

Can you identify the ten stages of genocide from the events in the timeline on pages 296–97?

HOW DID THE OUTBREAK OF THE SECOND WORLD WAR AFFECT THE JEWS?

The outbreak of the Second World War changed the situation with regard to the Jews. The Nazis no longer had to worry about international opinion with regard to their actions. The invasion of Poland, then Western Europe and finally Russia substantially increased the number of Jews under their control. It was no longer possible to get Jews to emigrate.

As a result of this new situation, the Nazis had to develop more extreme methods to deal with their ultimate goal of getting rid of Jews from the German Empire.

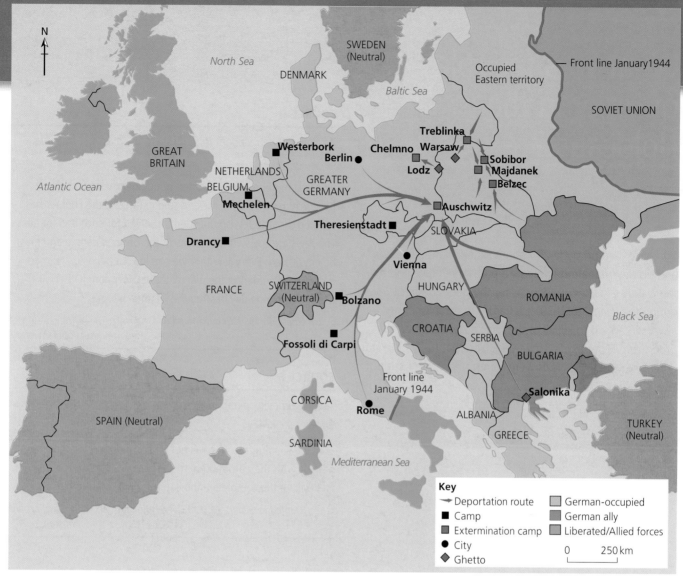

Figure 13.9 Major deportations to extermination camps, 1942–44

Ghettos

The first method of dealing with the increased numbers of Jews was to round them up and put them into **ghettos**. These were walled-off areas of a town, such as Warsaw, where Jews were forced to live. Jews from Germany and occupied countries were sent to the ghettos and conditions were appalling. There was overcrowding and very little food. Thousands died from disease and starvation.

Einsatzgruppen

These were *Schutzstaffel* (SS) death squads, set up to assist in the killing of Jews in the newly occupied territories in Poland and the Soviet Union. They followed the German army, systematically rounding up and killing Jews. It is estimated that 2 million Jews were killed in this way.

The Final Solution

Neither ghettos nor using the *Einsatzgruppen* were satisfactory in dealing with the large numbers of Jews under Nazi control. In January 1942, Nazi leaders met at a conference in Wannsee to work out the details of a more efficient solution. This became known as the Final Solution, as it would involve killing all Jews under German control in death camps. All Jews were to be transported by rail to five 'extermination camps' to be built in remote areas of Poland and equipped with gas chambers.

About 4.5 million Jews were killed in the death camps, by starvation and hard labour, and by being gassed. The total number of Jews killed in Europe was 6 million.

What was the role of Hitler in the Holocaust?

You have read on page 294 about Hitler's hatred of Jews and his determination to create a pure Aryan race and how this clearly laid the foundations for the persecution of Jews during the years 1933–39. It is harder to establish if he always intended to kill all of the Jews as no direct written order from Hitler exists. However, given that the whole state and all high-ranking Nazis were committed to carrying out Hitler's orders, it is very likely that it was his wishes that they were fulfilling in carrying out the mass killings.

SOURCE D

Auschwitz Commandant Rudolf Hoess, in an extract from his autobiography

'In the summer of 1941, I cannot remember the exact date … [Heinrich] Himmler saw me and said in effect: "the Fuehrer has ordered that the Jewish question be solved for once and for all … The Jews are the sworn enemies of the German people and must be eradicated. Every Jew that we can lay our hands on is to be destroyed now during the war, without exception. [Otherwise] … the Jews will one day destroy the German people." '

> Hoess, R. 1959. Commandant of Auschwitz: The Autobiography of Rudolf Hoess. *Popular Library.*

SOURCE E

Adolph Hitler speaking to a crowd at the Sports Palace in Berlin, 30 January 1942

'And we say that the war will not end as the Jews imagine it will, namely with the uprooting of the Aryans, but the result of this war will be the complete annihilation of the Jews.'

> Quoted in Gilbert, M. 1985. The Holocaust. *NY. Holt, Rinehart and Winston, p. 285.*

ACTIVITY: Source evaluation

■ ATL

- Critical-thinking skills – Recognize unstated assumptions and bias

In a table like the one below, outline the purpose, values and limitations of Sources D and E with reference to the origin, for providing evidence that Hitler gave orders for the mass extermination of the Jews.

◆ Assessment opportunities

- This activity can be assessed using Criterion D: Thinking critically.

Source	Origin [given]	Purpose	Value	Limitation
D	Auschwitz Commandant Rudolf Hoess, in an extract from his autobiography *Commandant of Auschwitz: The Autobiography of Rudolf Hoess*, 1959			
E	Adolph Hitler speaking to a crowd at the Sports Palace in Berlin, 30 January 1942			

What was the role of the Nazi state in causing the Holocaust?

It could also be argued that the nature of the Nazi state contributed to the Holocaust. Its totalitarian nature – where obedience was expected and violence was a key part of keeping control – ensured that orders were carried out. In addition, the relentless anti-Semitic propaganda – in posters, films, speeches, schools – created people ready and willing to carry out the orders.

Historians have also pointed out that the way in which high-ranking Nazis competed for Hitler's approval encouraged them to adopt more radical measures. It was also easy for one act of brutality to lead to another. For example, the use of euthanasia against disabled people could lead onto using similar methods of killing for other groups of people.

Nazi leaders and their actions

The actions of some Nazi leaders in particular stand out as being significant for their role in the Holocaust:

- **Joseph Goebbels** was in charge of Nazi propaganda. He used posters, films (documentaries and movies) and newspapers to spread anti-Semitic propaganda. He was also behind Kristallnacht.
- **Hermann Göring** was head of the Gestapo and one of Hitler's closest advisers. In 1941, he gave the order for leading Nazis to develop the 'Final Solution' to the 'Jewish problem'.
- **Heinrich Himmler** ran the SS and was put in charge of carrying out the Final Solution.
- **Reinhard Heydrich** assisted Himmler. He organized the ghettos and *Einsatzgruppen*. He led the planning of the death camps and gas chambers.

SOURCE F

Rudolf Hoess's 1946 Nuremberg testimony

'It was something already taken for granted that the Jews were to blame for everything … It was not just newspapers like the Stürmer, but it was everything we ever heard. Even our military and ideological training took for granted that we had to protect Germany from the Jews … We were all so trained to obey orders without even thinking that the thought of disobeying an order would simply never have occurred to anybody and somebody else would have done just as well if I hadn't.'

SOURCE G

Policeman testifying in 1961 at a war crimes trial

'I believed the propaganda that all Jews were criminals and subhumans and that they were the cause of Germany's decline after the First World War. The thought that one should disobey or evade the order to participate in the extermination of the Jews did not therefore enter my mind at all.'

SOURCE H

Leading article by Julius Streicher from a Nazi newspaper

'The continued work of the 'Stürmer' will help to ensure that every German down to the last man will, with heart and hand, join the ranks of those whose aim is to crush the head of the serpent Pan-Juda beneath their heels. He who helps to bring this about helps to eliminate the devil. And this devil is the Jew.'

Der Stürmer. *No. 39. September 1936.*

ACTIVITY: The role of the Nazi state

■ ATL

- Critical-thinking skills – Recognize unstated assumptions and bias

In what ways do Sources F and G support each other regarding the impact of the Nazi state on the views and actions of Germans?

According to Sources F, G and H, what caused anti-Semitism to grow in Nazi Germany?

◆ Assessment opportunities

◆ The last activity can be assessed using Criterion A: Knowing and understanding and Criterion D: Thinking critically.

What was the role of ordinary German people in causing the Holocaust?

Many people were involved in the process by which so many Jews ended up being killed. There were train drivers, guards who ran camps, clerks who recorded names and so on – in both Germany and in the countries that the Nazis occupied.

Historians have argued about how far the German people, in particular, knew what was going on and how far they willingly participated, but it does seem that the killing was too widespread for it to have been a secret.

SOURCE I

Alfons Heck, member of the Hitler Youth in 1938, interviewed for a television programme in 1989

'Until Kristallnacht, many Germans believed Hitler was not engaged in mass murder. [The treatment of the Jews] seemed to be a minor form of harassment of a disliked minority, but after Kristallnacht no German could any longer be under any illusion, I believe it was the day that we lost our innocence. But it would be fair to point out that I myself never met even the most fanatic Nazi who wanted the extermination of the Jews. Certainly we wanted the Jews out of Germany, but we did not want them killed.'

SOURCE J

'… German anti-Semitic beliefs about Jews were the central causal agent of the Holocaust … The conclusion of this book is that anti-Semitism moved many thousands of "ordinary" Germans – and would have moved millions more, had they been appropriately positioned – to slaughter Jews. Not economic hardship, not the coercive means of a totalitarian state, not the social psychological, not invariable psychological propensities, but ideas about Jews that were pervasive in Germany, and had been for decades, induced ordinary Germans to kill unarmed, defenseless Jewish men, women and children by the thousands, systematically and without pity …'

Goldhagen, B. 1997. Hitler's Willing Executioners: Ordinary Germans and the Holocaust. *Vintage.*

SOURCE K

'If one term above all sums up the behavioural response of the German people to the persecution of the Jews, it is: passivity [indifference]. The passivity was consonant [consistent] with a number of differing … attitudes towards the Jews. Most obviously, it corresponded to latent [hidden] anti-Semitism, and, arguably, to a mentality of "moral indifference". It also mirrored apathy … and a willingness to accept uncritically the state's right to take radical action against its "enemies". Above all … passivity … was a reflection of a prevailing lack of interest in the Jewish Question … At the time that Jews were being murdered in their millions, the vast majority of Germans had plenty of other things on their mind.'

Kershaw, I. 'German Popular Opinion during the Final Solution' in Cohen, A. (ed). 1988. Comprehending the Holocaust. *SHP, p. 154.*

ACTIVITY: Comparing primary and secondary sources on the role of ordinary Germans

■ ATL

- Critical-thinking skills – Recognize unstated assumptions and bias; Evaluate evidence and arguments

1 With reference to the origin and purpose, analyse the values and limitations of Source I for assessing the views of ordinary Germans about the Holocaust.
2 What are the similarities and the differences between the views in Source J and Source K concerning the role of German people in the Holocaust?

◆ Assessment opportunities

◆ This activity can be assessed using Criterion D: Thinking critically.

What was the role of the Second World War in causing the Holocaust?

As you have read on page 298, the Second World War was key for starting the systematic killing of the Jews. War also brutalized people and made them more able to carry out horrific acts. Many historians therefore argue that without the Second World War, the Holocaust would not have happened.

SOURCE L

From the speech of SS Heinrich Himmler, speaking to SS Major-Generals, Poznan, 4 October 1943

'One basic principal must be the absolute rule for the SS man: we must be honest, decent, loyal, and comradely to members of our own blood and to nobody else. What happens to a Russian, to a Czech, does not interest me in the slightest … Whether nations live in prosperity or starve to death interests me only in so far as we need them as slaves for our culture; otherwise, it is of no interest to me. Whether 10,000 Russian females fall down from exhaustion while digging an anti-tank ditch interests me only in so far as the anti-tank ditch for Germany is finished. We shall never be rough and heartless when it is not necessary, that is clear. We Germans, who are the only people in the world who have a decent attitude towards animals, will also assume a decent attitude towards these human animals. But it is a crime against our own blood to worry about them and give them ideals, thus causing our sons and grandsons to have a more difficult time with them. When someone comes to me and says, "I cannot dig the anti-tank ditch with women and children, it is inhuman, for it will kill them", then I would have to say, "you are a murderer of your own blood because if the anti-tank ditch is not dug, German soldiers will die, and they are the sons of German mothers. They are our own blood." '

'Nazi Conspiracy and Aggression'. Washington, US Govt. Print. Off. 1946. Vol. IV, p. 559.

SOURCE M

Engineer Fritz Sander testifying on 7 March 1946

'I decided to design and build a crematorium with a higher capacity. I completed this project of a new crematorium in November 1942 – a crematorium for mass incineration, and I submitted this project to a State Patent Commission in Berlin.

'This "Krema" was to be built on the conveyor belt principle. That is to say, the corpses must be brought to the incineration furnaces without interruption.

'Q. Although you knew about the mass liquidation of innocent human beings in crematoriums, you devoted yourself to designing and creating higher capacity incineration furnaces for crematoriums – and on your own initiative.

'A. I was a German engineer and key member of the Topf works and I saw it as my duty to apply my specialist knowledge in this way to help Germany win the war, just as an aircraft construction engineer builds airplanes in wartime, which are also connected with the destruction of human beings.'

Quoted from the interrogation transcripts by Prof. Gerald Fleming from the University of Surrey, in an article in the New York Times, *18 July 1993.*

ACTIVITY: Interpreting information from sources

■ **ATL**

- Critical-thinking skills – Recognize unstated assumptions and bias

What do Sources L and M show about the impact of war on the attitudes of Germans towards the killing of Jews?

◆ **Assessment opportunities**

- In this activity you have practised skills that are assessed using Criterion D: Thinking critically.

ACTIVITY: Why do communities perpetrate genocide?

ATL

- Critical-thinking skills – Gather and organize relevant information to formulate an argument; Recognize unstated assumptions and bias

Complete a copy of the table below on the factors that led to the Holocaust. Use the information and sources in this chapter as evidence. You could access other books or online sources to add further evidence to the table.

Factor	Evidence from source	Value and limitation from origin (O) and purpose (P)
Leader(s)		
Nature of state		
Attitude of the community/ inaction		
War		
Other		

From the evidence above, what are your conclusions regarding the most important factors that caused the Holocaust?

Hint

When writing your conclusion, remember to use your evidence grid and evaluations to support your points.

◆ Assessment opportunities

- ◆ This activity can be assessed using Criterion A: Knowing and understanding and Criterion D: Thinking critically.

DISCUSS

In pairs or small groups, feed back your findings to the class.

1. **Which factors seem to be the most important in causing the Holocaust?**
2. **Select two sources that offer different perspectives and present the values and limitations of each source from its origins and purpose.**

THINK–PAIR–SHARE

Think about your study of trade and exploitation in Chapter 3, and your study of imperialism in Chapter 9. In pairs, identify how poverty, economic exploitation and colonialism may foster tension within communities. Share your ideas with the class. When you begin your research project think about the extent to which these factors are relevant to your case study.

EXTENSION

1. 'Ordinary people participate in mass murder when they have been brutalized by war.'
   To what extent do you agree with this claim? Answer with reference to Sources B–M and the knowledge and understanding you have gained about the Holocaust in this chapter.

2. Watch the following video about the Holocaust and genocide:

   http://vimeo.com/69539894

   What conclusions does the film draw as to which factors contributed to the Holocaust?

ACTIVITY: Individual research project – A case study in the causes of an instance of twentieth-century genocide

Conduct an individual research project analysing the causes of an instance of genocide in the twentieth century.

In this investigation, you are required to:

- **formulate** a clear and focused research
- **develop and follow a detailed action plan** (see page 40 for an example)
- **reference all your evidence correctly using one standard method**
- **use a wide range of relevant terminology appropriately**
- **evaluate** your investigation and your results.

Your research project must be between 700 and 1500 words long.

▼ Links to: English literature

What literature can you find on the Holocaust or about the genocide you have chosen to research?

Below is a list of possible case studies to choose from. You do not have to choose from this list; however, you must make sure that you can easily access materials on any case study that you choose.

- **Armenia (1915–18)**
- **Cambodia (1975–79)**
- **Guatemala (1980–83)**
- **Bosnia–Herzegovina (1992–95)**
- **Rwanda (1994)**

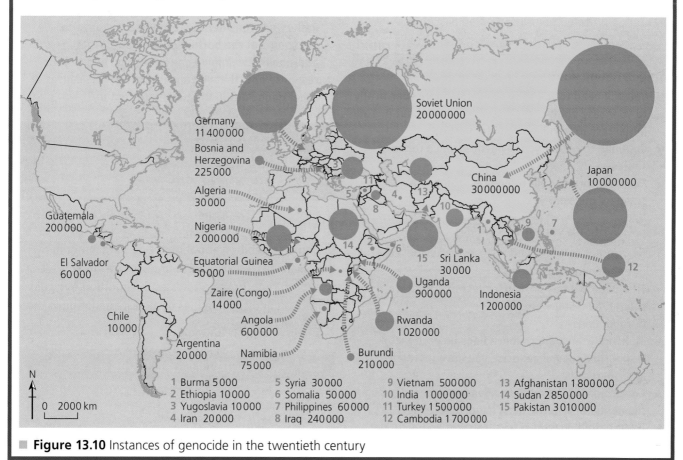

■ **Figure 13.10** Instances of genocide in the twentieth century

Step 1: Select your case study

- **Formulate** an initial research question, e.g. *Was civil war the key factor in causing genocide in X?* Write up an action plan of how you will research your question.
- Make sure you know which method of referencing you will use. Review how to correctly cite your sources using the standard method chosen.

Step 2: Gather your evidence

- Reference your evidence as you gather it.
- Keep a record of your references so you can develop your 'works cited' list.
- You could use a table like the one below. This table identifies some of the factors that you could **investigate** in your case study. However, not all of these factors may be relevant. Alternatively, you may find other factors that are relevant in your study.

Factor	Evidence of contribution
Leader(s)	
Nature of state	
Attitude of the community/inaction	
Economic problems	
War	
Other	

Step 3: Refine your research question

- You will need to focus your question more specifically to your case study as you discover more about it. Your initial research will help you to do this.
- Continue to gather your evidence from a range of sources.
- Keep a record of your references, using one standard method.

Step 4: Write up your project

Use your notes carefully and reference all evidence. Include the following:

- **Title page:** Name / Research question / Total word count (700–1500 words)
- **Introduction**
- **Main body:** including subheadings on each factor responsible for the genocide you have researched and references
- **Conclusion:** based on the evidence presented, which theme/factor was the most important cause
- **'Works cited' list:** must be consistent and accurate, using one standard method

Step 5: Evaluate your research process and results

Task A

1 Divide into groups. Make sure that the group consists of different genocide case studies. Take it in turns to give a brief summary of your research findings to the rest of the group. Make sure that you explain the key causes of the genocide you studied.

2 When other group members are presenting their summary, you should make notes on the key causes of the other case studies.

3 Finally, you and your group must attempt to draw some conclusions about the causes of genocide in the twentieth century. Discuss with your group whether there are causal factors common to *all* the genocides studied. Be ready to feed back to the class on the conceptual unit question: *Why do individuals and communities perpetrate genocide?*

4 **Reflection:** Consider the responses you gave to question 2 at the bottom of page 304. What additional *own knowledge* would you add to your response now that you have examined the causes of other genocides in the twentieth century?

Task B

Design an exhibition about genocide for a museum that examines the key causes of genocide in the twentieth century and addresses the question: Why did individuals and communities perpetrate genocide in the twentieth century?

Take action

! Can the international community prevent genocide in the future?

■ **Figure 13.11** Kofi Annan, UN Secretary-General

! In 2004, UN Secretary-General Kofi Annan stated in a speech:

'There can be no more important issue, and no more binding obligation, than the prevention of genocide.'

! He proposed developing a Genocide Prevention Committee to monitor potential crises, provide early warnings and make recommendations for action.

! In groups, based on the class presentations and discussions, outline a proposal to help prevent genocide in the twenty-first century.

! You could use supporting evidence and ideas from this PowerPoint presentation:

http://genocidewatch.org/genocide/ tenstagesofgenocide.html

(Scroll down to the bottom of the page to download the presentation.)

Reflection

In this chapter we have studied the reasons for the Holocaust. We have researched other examples of genocide and attempted to find causal factors across regions for twentieth-century genocide.

Reflecting on our learning …
Use this table to reflect on your own learning in this chapter.

Questions we asked	Answers we found	Any further questions now?			
Factual					
Conceptual					
Debatable					

Approaches to learning you used in this chapter:	Description – what new skills did you learn?	How well did you master the skills?			
		Novice	Learner	Practitioner	Expert
Critical-thinking skills					
Information literacy skills					
Media literacy skills					
Organization skills					

Learner profile attribute	*Reflect on the importance of being a thinker for our learning in this chapter.*				
Thinker					

Glossary

abolish/abolition To bring to an end or to do away with something (e.g. the slave trade)

acts Laws passed by the British Parliament

alliance An agreement when two or more countries support each other

amputate To cut off a part of the body such as an arm or leg

anti-Semitism Hostility towards Jews

antiseptic A chemical that prevents infection by killing germs

armaments Weaponry

arms race A race between two or more countries to build more or better weapons than the other

armistice An agreement to stop fighting

assassination When someone is murdered for a political reason

bacteria Micro-organisms that cause disease

ballot Vote

belligerent A nation involved in a war or conflict

blockade Cutting of all access to a place or country; preventing supplies getting into that country

boycott To refuse to do business with

campaigner Someone who campaigns (takes part in organized activities) to achieve a certain cause

censorship Controlling what is produced and suppressing anything that is considered to be harmful to the state

chartists A group that demanded changes to the voting system in Britain

civil service An organization that is part of the government and carries out the administrative tasks of running the country

coalition Alliance between political parties in a country

colonialism The practice by which a powerful country controls less powerful countries and uses its resources in order to increase its own wealth and power

colony An area of land somewhere in the world ruled by another country

conscription A law that forces all men to join the armed forces

democracy A system of running a country in which people vote for the party that they want to run the country

demilitarized No military allowed

dictatorship A form of government where all power rests with an individual or one political party

empire A collection of colonies all ruled by one country

entrepreneurs Businessmen and women who take risks in ideas and with money in order to make themselves richer

epidemic When a disease spreads rapidly and affects lots of people

exploitation Treating someone unfairly or taking advantage of them

export When goods are sent to other countries in trade

free trade Allowing countries to trade freely without tariffs or trade barriers

front line The foremost position of an army – nearest to the enemy

ghetto An enclosed part of a city where Jews had to live

Great Depression When many economies in the world declined as a result of the Wall Street Crash in America in 1929

home front During a war, this is the section which concerns the civilians

imperialism When a country follows the policy of getting an empire

laissez-faire A policy of non-interference by the government; leaving things alone

legislation Laws

literacy Ability to read and write

merchant Someone who is a trader – buying and selling goods

middle class People of middle income – between the upper and working classes, e.g. lawyers, doctors, teachers

militant Aggressive or violent in support of a cause

militarism Policy based on the force of the army

missionary A member of a religious mission who aims to spread religion to other people

mobilization Getting troops ready to start fighting

munitions Military (army) equipment

nationalization Where a government controls and owns industries and other businesses

neutrality When a state is not involved in a military alliance

obsolete Not working or in operation any more

offensive A military attack

plantation A huge farm that grows sugar, tobacco, cotton

provenance Information about the origins of a source, e.g. the author, date and place of publication

public health When there are organized measures – usually carried out by the state – to prevent disease and improve the health of the population

radical A person who wants extreme changes; these could be political, economic and/or social

rebellion When people revolt/rise up in protest at something

reparations Compensation paid by a defeated nation for the damage caused during a war

republic A country in which power is held by people who have been elected

sanctions Actions taken against a state by another state or states to try to make it do something

segregation Keeping apart (e.g. racial segregation is keeping races apart)

self-determination The idea that a nation should be able to rule itself

stalemate When neither side can make any progress in a war

suffrage The right to vote

superpower A country which has strong economic, military and political power and global influence

tariffs Taxes put on goods that come into a country

trade union A group of people who work together to try to improve their pay and conditions in a workplace

working class Poorer people who work for a living such as miners, servants, factory workers

Acknowledgements

The Publishers would like to thank the following for their advice and support in the development of this project: Robert Harrison, Head of Middle Years Programme Development, IBO; the *MYP by Concept* series editor, Paul Morris; David Burton and Paul Grace, Renaissance College, Hong Kong for reviewing the manuscript.

The Publishers would like to thank the following for permission to reproduce copyright material. Every effort has been made to trace or contact all copyright holders, but if any have been inadvertently overlooked the Publishers will be pleased to make the necessary arrangements at the first opportunity.

Photo credits

p.2 © North Wind Picture Archives/Alamy; **p.3** *l* © Timewatch Images/Alamy; **p.3** *r* © The LIFE Picture Collection/Getty Images; **p.5** © Print Collector/ Getty Images; **p.7** © Science Museum, London; Science & Society Picture Library; **p.10** © ARPL/Topham; **p.11** © Wellcome Library, London/http:// creativecommons.org/licenses/by/4.0/; **p.19** Library of Congress Prints & photographs/LC-USZC4-10373&LC-USZC4-103734; **p.20** © World History Archive/Alamy; **p.22** © liszt collection/Alamy; **p.23** © akg-images/De Agostini Picture Lib.; **p.28** © Hulton Archive/Getty Images; **p.30** © Wellcome Library, London/http://creativecommons.org/licenses/by/4.0/; **p.31** © Photos.com/Getty/Thinkstock; **p.33** © Everett Collection Historical/Alamy; **p.35** *tl* © North Wind Picture Archives/Alamy; **p.35** *tr* © Library of Congress Prints & Photographs/LC-USZ62-17372; **p.35** *b* © Gilcrease Museum, Tulsa OK; **p.37** *t* © Library of Congress Prints & Photographs/LC-USZC2-5742; **p.37** *b* © Mondadori via Getty Images; **p.39** © Photo Researchers/Mary Evans Picture Library; **p.42** © PRISMA ARCHIVO/Alamy; **p.43** *t* © INTERFOTO/Alamy; **p.43** *b* © INTERFOTO/Alamy; **p.44** © Delphotostock – Fotolia; **p.50** © The Art Archive/Alamy; **p.51** © Universal History Archive/Getty Images; **p.54** © Commissioner Lin Zexu (Wade-Giles: Lin Tse-hsu; 1785–1850) overseeing the destruction of opium at Canton (Guangzhou) in 1839/Pictures from History/Bridgeman Images; **p.55** © Niday Picture Library/Alamy; **p.59** © Lordprice Collection/Alamy; **p.60** © Library of Congress/LC-USZC4-3917; **p.61** *t* © World History Archive/Alamy; **p.61** *b* © North Wind Picture Archives/Alamy; **p.63** *l* © Pictorial Press Ltd/Alamy; **p.63** *r* public domain/http://commons.wikimedia.org/wiki/File:Scourged_back_by_McPherson_%26_Oliver,_1863.jpg; **p.67** © TOBIN JONES/AFP/Getty Images; **p.68** © Lordprice Collection/Alamy; **p.70** © Everett Collection Historical/Alamy; **p.72** © The Granger Collection, NYC/ TopFoto; **p.74** © Mary Evans Picture Library/Alamy; **p.75** *tl* © Mary Evans Picture Library/Alamy; **p.75** *tr* © Chronicle/Alamy; **p.75** *b* © Heritage Image Partnership Ltd/Alamy; **p.80** © Old Visuals/Alamy; **p.81** *t* © ONTHEBIKE.PL/Alamy; **p.81** *b* © Universal Images Group Limited/Alamy; **p.83** © PARIS PIERCE/Alamy; **p.85** © Tony Lilley/Alamy; **p.86** *t* © The Art Archive/Alamy; **p.86** *b* © World History Archive/Alamy; **p.87** © INTERFOTO/Alamy; **p.88** © Classic Image/Alamy; **p.89** © World History Archive/Alamy; **p.91** *t* © Martin Shields/Alamy; **p.91** *b* http://atlantic-cable.com// Maps/1901EasternTelegraph.jpg; **p.92** © Wellcome Images/Copyrighted work available under Creative Commons Attribution only licence CC BY 4.0 http://creativecommons.org/licenses/by/4.0/; **p.93** © Amoret Tanner/Alamy; **p.95** *t* © Wellcome Library, London. Wellcome Images/http:// creativecommons.org/licenses/by/4.0/; **p.95** *b* © Wellcome Library, London. http://creativecommons.org/licenses/by/4.0/; **p.96** © Chronicle/Alamy; **p.97** *r* © Everett Collection Historical/Alamy; **p.101** *l* © Library of Congress Prints and Photographs/LC-DIG-ggbain-17409; **p.101** *r* © Royal College of Surgeons of England; **p.103** © World History Archive/Alamy; **p.104** © Science Museum/Science & Society Picture Library; **p.106** *t* ©Wellcome Library, London/ Copyrighted work available under Creative Commons Attribution only licence CC BY 4.0 http://creativecommons.org/licenses/by/4.0/; **p.106** *b* © Wellcome Library, London.http://creativecommons.org/licenses/by/4.0/; **p.107** Chemical Heritage Foundation/http://commons.wikimedia.org/wiki/ File:Penicillin_poster_5.40.tif; **p.110** © ITAR-TASS Photo Agency/Alamy; **p.111** *t* © FineArt/Alamy; **p.111** *b* © World History Archive/Alamy; **p.112** *t* © The Widower, 1875–76 (oil on canvas), Fildes, Sir Samuel Luke (1844–1927)/Art Gallery of New South Wales, Sydney, Australia/Bridgeman Images; **p.112** *b* © FineArt/Alamy; **p.113** *t* © World History Archive/Alamy; **p.113** *b* © The Artchives/Alamy; **p.114** © Library of Congress Prints and Photographs/ LC-DIG-nclc-01151; **p.116** ©Estate of George Grosz, Princeton, N.J./DACS, 2015/Photo: akg-images/picture-alliance; **p.117** © ADAGP, Paris and DACS, London 2015/The Spirit of Our Time, 1919 (mixed media), Hausmann, Raoul (1886–1971)/Musee National d'Art Moderne, Centre Pompidou, Paris, France/Bridgeman Images; **p.118** © Stapleton Collection/Corbis; **p.120** *t* © Dimon – Fotolia; **p.120** *b* © DACS 2015, Sergei Gerasimov 'A Collective-Farm Festival' (A Kolkhoz Celebration) 1937; photo © World History Archive/Alamy; **p.121** © Heritage Image Partnership Ltd/Alamy; **p.124** *t* © The Image Works/TopFoto; **p.124** *b* © Pictorial Press Ltd/Alamy; **p.126** © Everett Collection Historical/Alamy; **p.127** *tl* © Everett Collection Historical/Alamy; **p.127** *tr* © Corbis; **p.127** *br* © Keystone-France/Gamma-Keystone via Getty Images; **p.128** Public domain/http://commons.wikimedia.org/wiki/File:Bakunin.png; **p.129** © World History Archive/Alamy; **p.130** © Library of Congress Rare Book and Special Collections Division/LC-DIG-ppmsca-02894; **p.134** © SOTK2011/Alamy; **p.136** © Hulton Archive/Getty Images; **p.138** © war posters/Alamy; **p.139** *l* © Eddie Gerald/Alamy; **p.139** *r* © Prisma Bildagentur AG/ Alamy; **p.140** © Pictorial Press Ltd/Alamy; **p.141** © War Archive/Alamy; **p.142** © Museum of London/Heritage-Images/Getty Images; **p.143** © Keystone

Text credits

Index